Indigenous Disability Studi<

This book provides a comprehensive approach to the perspectives, lived experiences, and socio-cultural beliefs of Indigenous scholars regarding disabilities through a distinctions-based approach. Indigenous people demonstrate considerable knowledge in a multitude of capacities in spite of legal, monetary, social, economic, health, and political inequalities that they experience within from administrative authorities whether health, education, or governments.

By including various knowledge systems related to social-cultural, traditional governance, spirituality, educational, and self-representation within a communal understanding, the knowledge brought forth will be a combination of information from within/communal and outwards/infusion by Indigenous teachers, scholars, academics, and professionals who aim to combat the negative effects of disability labels and policies that have regulated Indigenous peoples.

Comprised of five sections:

- The power, wisdom, knowledge, and lived experiences of Elders
- Reframing the narrative – Navigating self-representation
- Learning from within – Including traditional knowledge
- Challenging colonial authority – Infusing regional ideals and concepts
- Interpretations, narratives, and lived experiences of grassroots teachers and social service providers

It will be an asset to those who seek out a deeper understanding of the complexity of Indigenous people and their knowledge, including anyone who deals with predominantly non-Indigenous mindsets and barriers to education.

Courses on disability studies, Indigenous studies, social work, health, education, and development studies will all benefit from this book.

John T. Ward is a Métis and Non-Status Indian from the Algonquin territory of Kitchisibi. His specialization is Indigenous wholistic knowledge, ethics, disabilities, learning disabilities, and dyslexia among Indigenous people in Canada. He also works as a special advisor in disability and Indigenous knowledge in the Government of Canada.

Indigenous Disability Studies

Edited by John T. Ward

Routledge
Taylor & Francis Group

LONDON AND NEW YORK

Designed cover image by Juan Camilo Carrero Vasquez

First published 2025
by Routledge
4 Park Square, Milton Park, Abingdon, Oxon OX14 4RN

and by Routledge
605 Third Avenue, New York, NY 10158

Routledge is an imprint of the Taylor & Francis Group, an informa business

British Library Cataloguing-in-Publication Data
A catalogue record for this book is available from the British Library

Library of Congress Cataloging-in-Publication Data
Names: Ward, John T. (Disability expert), editor.
Title: Indigenous disability studies / edited by John T. Ward.
Description: Abingdon, Oxon; New York, NY: Routledge, 2025. |
Includes bibliographical references and index.
Identifiers: LCCN 2024009885 (print) | LCCN 2024009886 (ebook) |
ISBN 9781032656502 (hardback) | ISBN 9781032643694 (paperback) |
ISBN 9781032656519 (ebook)
Subjects: LCSH: People with disabilities. | Indigenenous peoples.
Classification: LCC HV1569.3.M55 I53 2024 (print) |
LCC HV1569.3.M55 (ebook) | DDC 362.408900973—dc23/eng/20240405
LC record available at https://lccn.loc.gov/2024009885
LC ebook record available at https://lccn.loc.gov/2024009886

ISBN: 978-1-032-65650-2 (hbk)
ISBN: 978-1-032-64369-4 (pbk)
ISBN: 978-1-032-65651-9 (ebk)

DOI: 10.4324/9781032656519

Typeset in Sabon
by codeMantra

I dedicate this book to all the nameless, and voiceless, as well as those unable to rise up because of their trauma, abuse, and hurtful learning experiences that resulted in the suffering of so many. We will not go quietly into the night. We must rise up to reclaim and retake our ways of learning, naming, and teaching of a different way of living. There is no single belief system or teaching approach that must be followed. Indigenous peoples have been on Earth since the beginning of time and have endured many challenges, yet we are still here today, regardless of how any other society, people, or system believes we should act, live, and be. Everyone has a disability. No one is perfect, which is the beauty and uniqueness of being human. It is our differences that make us who we really are. I hope this book will provide some comfort for those who have faced their greatest challenges. This book is for you all my relations and those who will come to be.

What is your (dis)Ability ... beginning

What is your superpower, strength, or talent ...

Contents

Figures

Tables

Contributors

Rodney Adams is a deaf Ngiyampaa man from Australia, living in Darkinjung country on the Central Coast. He is an adjunct lecturer in Auslan and Deaf Studies at the University of Newcastle. His interest is the revitalization of Indigenous Sign Languages. He believes this could have a positive impact on the deaf and hard-of-hearing Aboriginal and Torres Strait Islander people in much the same way as Indigenous Spoken Languages.

Mark Standing Eagle Baez, Ph.D., is a descendant of the Mohawk and Pawnee people and a member of the Tap Pilam Coahuiltecan Nation (Mission Indian) in the United States. He is an assistant professor in the clinical and counseling program at Bemidji State University in Minnesota and has a small private practice (Native L.I.F.E.). He is the President of the Society of Indian Psychologists, where he incorporates cultural methods on mental health among AI/AN and Indigenous populations. For over 20 years, he has developed the "Sweetgrass Method," which focuses on weaving Western approaches and Indigenous methodologies into his practice among tribal communities.

Elder Percy Ballot is from Buckland in the northwest Arctic of Alaska – the Eskimos of the Buckland Tribe called the Iñupiat. He was involved in many areas regarding health, the economy, subsistence, environment, and housing for his tribe, and the town or school board trustee. For 30 years, he was the Tribal President. One of his favorite things to do is create opportunities for kids and culture camps – taking them out to teach them how to prepare and eat what they find – hands-on learning – a great way to experience the Eskimo way of life.

Twinerugaba Barlton is from the Banyankole tribe in Uganda. The tribe is also known as the Ankole people, which is a Bantu ethnic group native to the southwestern part of Uganda. He received training about disabled people during his "Senior SIX vacation" period (one to two years), which is given to all students, before joining University. They are given Community-based Rehabilitation CBR Guidelines – Volumes 1–7 by the World Health Organization for various communities to reach out to families with a disabled person.

I-Yun Cheng is a PhD student at the University of Sydney and comes from Taiwan. She is an English teacher and is pursuing an academic career in disability studies from a Taiwanese perspective.

Elder Tom Dearhouse is Mohawk from Kahnawake in Québec, Canada. He is a social worker at the Kahnawake Shakotiia'takehnhas Community Services and acts as a youth protection caseworker and support counselor. For the last six years, he has worked as a traditional support counselor.

Thomas Dirth is an associate professor of multicultural psychology at Bemidji State University in Minnesota. His scholarly interests are shaped by his experiences as a physically disabled person. They include research in the domains of diversity, intergroup relations, ableism, and a wide range of intersectional disability phenomena elaborated within the disability studies knowledge base. He is an advocate for greater access and inclusion of disabled perspectives (students, faculty, staff) in higher education.

John Gilroy is a Yuin man from Australia and is an associate professor of sociology in Indigenous health, specializing primarily in disability studies. He has worked in disability and aging research. He has led many research projects in urban and rural/remote and done community development with Aboriginal and Torres Strait Islander communities, as well as government and non-government stakeholders for most of his life. John is passionate about Aboriginal-owned and driven research to influence policy.

Pratima Gurung is an academic activist from Nepal member of Padmakanya College and Tribhuvan University focusing on academic research to advocacy. She also contributes as an expert on the Disability National Direction Committee under the Ministry of Women, Children and Senior Citizens, Government of Nepal. Ms. Gurung is a founding member and currently General Secretary of the Indigenous Person with Disabilities Global Network and National Indigenous Disabled Women Association Nepal.

Chief Phil Jane Jr is a member of the Ihanktonwan Dakota and Chickasaw Nations, and a hereditary Chief of the Hinhan Wicasa and Deloria Tiospayes of the Ihanktonwan Dakota. He is a former professor at the Faculty of Education at the University of Lethbridge, where he brought sharing and healing circles to victims of the Indian residential schools, which led to the national investigations of these schools. He established Four Directions University to offer culturally friendly trainings.

Vijaye Lutchmee Davi Jaypal was born in Mauritius as her great-grandparents came from India as indentured laborers to Mauritius. She moved to Canada in 2005, which she now calls as her adoptive land. As she hold a bachelor's degree in occupational health and safety and a master's degree in environmental engineering from Toronto Metropolitan University, she now works for the Government of Canada as a Human Resource Advisor in the Disabilities, Visible Minorities and the Equity, Diversity, and Inclusion Division. She is multilingual in English, French, Hindi, Bhojpuri, and Creole.

Carine Sacerdoce Kananga was originally from Goma in the Democratic Republic of Congo. Her father was of the Mushi tribe and her mother was of the Muhavu tribe. She has a baccalaureate in environmental management and sustainable development. She is a human rights activist, community worker, artist composer, and music therapist. She is also passionate about the humanitarian world. In 2016, she was appointed as the ambassador for girls' rights by the gender office of the MONUSCO (United Nations Mission in Congo) for her involvement in defense rights of girls. She also works at the Canadian Red Cross Canada as an Emergency Responder.

Kui Kasirisir (Hsu, Chun-Tsai) holds a Ph.D. from the University of Brighton. He is a professor in the Department of Social Work at the National Pingtung University of Science and Technology in Taiwan. He has also participated in several Indigenous organizations, such as the Taiwan Association of Indigenous Social Work and the Taiwan Indigenous Professors Association. His areas of interest include Indigenous social work, Indigenous social welfare, health and social care with Indigenous peoples, and Indigenous community development.

Zafar Khan is a faculty member in the Sociology Department, University of Peshawar, Khyber Pakhtunkhwa, Pakistan, with an expertise in Pashtun tribal culture, radicalization, and terrorism. He has conducted research on cultural distortions and their radicalizing effects, cultural violence in Pashtun society, and research under the thematic research grants of the Higher Education Commission of Pakistan (https://orcid.org/0000-0003-2494-4324).

Lavonna Lovern is of mixed heritage and is a member of the Eastern Cherokee Tribe. Her publications and presentations have been primarily focused on Indigenous health, disability, and education. Currently, Lavonna is a Professor in Philosophy and Religious Studies as well as Native American and Indigenous Studies at the Valdosta State University in Georgia where she specializes in knowledge, cultural diversity, and inclusion.

Palle Manisekhar is a disability community advisor. He is an Indigenous student from south India with a B.Ed. from Adikavi Nannaya University. In his spare time, he works with children at the Spurti disability home, a school for disabled children who have physical and mental challenges. He is interested in psychological research, as well as critical and logical thinking.

Kennedy Mapira comes from Chamasowa Village, Malawi. Being an Indigenous Malawian, he belongs to the Lomwe tribe, one of the many Bantu tribes in his country. He received a Malawi School Certificate of Education at Mountain View Secondary School in 2004. He is a pastor, community development advisor, and the founder of Gateway to Heaven Pentecostal ministries, which includes Gateway Christian Orphan School, a charity, where he supports disabled children and orphans spiritually and academically and creates research strategies for how to help those with disabilities and implements how best his community can develop.

Melanie McKay-Cody is an assistant professor at the University of Arizona where she researches in Anthropological study of Indigenous deaf people, Linguistics of North American Indian Sign Language and American Sign Language, and Archeological study of sign petroglyphs and pictographs. Presently, she is a member of Turtle Island Hand Talk and Indigenous Deaf community in United States. Committee member of the American Indian Language Development Institute, and the Linguistic Society of America. Advisory board member of National Center for Deaf Health Research Rochester, NY. Board member of the Society of American Sign Language.

Duke Makori Mogusu is a pastoral Indigenous youth support advisor. He is 21 years old, and his parents died in 2019, leaving him with 6 siblings. Duke is the chairman of the youth in the church, where he also encounters people with disabilities as well as in his workplace. Duke's knowledge, therefore, is primarily from the community around him in Kenya.

Kevin P. Morgan, born Ronald Robert Joynson/Proulx, is a 60s Scoop survivor who has been legally blind since birth and was adopted by an Irish family on the West Coast of Canada. He is of Oji-Cree and French descent, with his ancestral roots found in the Red River in Manitoba and of Chippewa of North Dakota. For over 25 years, Kevin has worked for one of the largest Federal Government organizations in Canada. He has an MA in leadership studies and has held various senior management roles within his home organization, while acting as a special advisor in the areas of Indigenous cultural knowledge, leadership, mentoring, and dialogue/engagement within the contemporary public service context.

Lexi (Giizhigokwe) Nahwegiizhic's traditional name is Giizhigokwe, Little Sky Woman, a two-spirit, Ojibwe woman living with several neurodiverse medical conditions, including ADHD and dyslexia. She comes from Sheguiandah First Nation in Ontario. She is an inspirational leader and keynote speaker frequently called upon for her wisdom in Indigenous teachings and mental health. She strives to empower people to become prouder and more resilient. Her background is in Neuroscience, where she uses her gift for teaching and to serve as a translator between science and business realities.

Elder Peter Nakoochee is from a small island near Moosonee, located in Northern Ontario, but now resides on Fort Albany Indian Reserve. His Indian name is Ministick. He operated the first and only Indigenous-owned general store in Moosonee. He was the Mayor of Moosonee and a regional Indigenous relations officer for the Ontario government. In Moose Factory, he was a Finance Director at Chapa Council, with the Mushkegowuk Council, and he was appointed as the Commissioner for the Ontario Northland Railway Communications by Bob Rae. Peter was also an Indian residential school survivor.

Elder Rodolfo Andres Jauregui Ojeda is a psychologist and part of the Yukpa Community of Cúcuta, Colombia. He works for the city of Cúcuta facilitating dialogue among the Yukpa peoples by providing social services, educational support, and healthcare information in both the Yukpa language and Spanish.

Noah Papatsie was born and raised in Nunavut's Capital, Iqaluit; in 1969, he was born to Josie Papatsie from Baffin Island near Pangnirtung, which is called Tapati, and Malaya Papatsie, his father, was originally from Northern Québec.

Zoila Romualdo Pérez, a Mixe Woman, Ayuujk Jääy, has a Master of Nursing with a focus on Care Administration. She is a professor at the Faculty of Nursing and Obstetrics, Universidad Nacional Autónoma de México. She is a member of the Latin American Council of Social Sciences, Working Group: Critical Studies in Disability, Subgroup "Indigenous-original peoples and disability". Her lines of professional action are Indigenous and native peoples, disability, and community nursing with a focus on primary health care.

Jean-Luc Pierite is from the Tunica-Biloxi Tribe of Louisiana. Currently, he is the International Procurement and Logistics Manager for The Fab Foundation, where currently he serves as the President of the Board of Directors for the North American Indian Center of Boston. He volunteers with his Tribe's Language and Culture Revitalization Program, which is a collaboration with Tulane University in New Orleans.

Angela Patricia Mora Rodriguez is originally from Bogota, Colombia, and is from the Muiscas as well as the Teusacá tribe that brought the knowledge of El Dorado.

She is a linguistic student who speaks multiple languages. She currently works for the Government of Canada as an advisor as well as an English second language teacher. Her desire to connect with people is one of her greatest abilities, which brought her to work at the Slovenia Embassy in Ottawa.

Diane Umuhoza Rudakenga was born to Rwandan parents (both refugees) in Burundi, and her name encapsulates a narrative of colonial influence and Indigenous resilience. As a professional in mental health, neurodiversity, diversity, equity, inclusion, and belonging, her experiences transcend personal boundaries, echoing the voices of many concerning identity and adversity. Her background is in psychoeducation, psychology, and human resources management, which underscores her commitment to a human-centric and holistic approach to well-being.

Maximus Monaheng Sefotho is an associate professor in the Department of Educational Psychology (specialization in Career Guidance and Disability) at the University of Johannesburg. His research and teaching work focus on Career Choice/Construction within the sphere of Contemporary Careers: Protean and Boundaryless as well as hephapreneurship. Sefotho contributed to the area of career development by transitioning differently abled persons from home to work. In search of an Ubuntu Model of Career Development, Prof. Sefotho studies harmonizing Ubuntu with Euro-Western models in addressing equity, social, and justice and avoiding harmful beneficence.

Elder Annie Smith St-Georges is a traditional Algonquin Elder from Kitigan Zibi. As a teacher and social worker, Elder Annie led sharing circles and spoke on accessibility, disability, trauma, and suicide to provide knowledge on the impact of colonial education. Annie has been featured in many documentaries, most notably in "KWEKÀNAMAD" (The Wind is Changing) regarding her son's suicide due to cultural abuse.

Edison Twinemuhwezi/Muwezi Muganga is from the Amukiga tribe in Uganda. He is a disability advisor and works with disabled children. He teaches on social services, living independently within the community, and how families can contribute to success through dialogue. He volunteers in his community as a missionary and is married with three children.

Umar is currently pursuing a PhD at the University of Sydney where he is researching digital disability activism. Born with a physical disability, his research intersects disability and social media. Together with Rumah Disabilitas – a disability-based NGO, since 2021, he actively spreads awareness on disability inclusion through digital campaigns.

Boussad At Yaagun (Djerbid) is a Kabylia who has worked in a multitude of professions including a language teacher and a school principal for most of his life in Algeria. He was involved in the 1962 Algeria independence movement as part of the Kabyle fight for their own freedom to govern. He has worked in agriculture but is most of all known as a principal who includes all students' perspectives regardless of learning differences. He is now retired and lives with his beautiful and young wife Fatma At Ali U Sliman (Chelil) who makes great Kabyle coffee.

Foreword

Hilary N. Weaver

As a social worker and educator, I cover a wide range of issues in my work, but my focus is on working to ensure helping professionals have the skills and insights needed to competently serve different kinds of people, especially, Indigenous clients. I don't have a unique depth of understanding related to disabilities, but instead view this as one of a myriad of important issues relevant to the people social workers serve. As I immersed myself in writing and speaking to help social workers and other professionals become better at serving Indigenous clients, it became clear that there was very little in the professional literature about Indigenous people with disabilities.

I've often seen myself as a bridge between different types of people or different content areas; so when the editor of the *Journal of Social Work in Disability and Rehabilitation* contacted me about developing an Indigenous-focused issue, I was positioned to reach out to Indigenous people, including non-academics and people in tribal territories about getting involved with the project. I felt qualified to be a buffer, telling an academic journal they must be patient while cultural protocols about what can be shared and questions of who owns data collected on tribal lands were negotiated. The project brought Indigenous voices forward speaking about disability issues that would not have entered mainstream academic literature otherwise. I was well positioned to open this door and prepared to hold it open as long as needed for people to step through.

After the publication of this special journal issue in 2015, more requests came and keep coming – requests for webinars, consultations, and articles. There is a tremendous hunger for people to have a better understanding of Indigenous people and disabilities. This is an important topic and one that I address consistently in my work, always with the caveat that I am not an expert, but rather, an Indigenous scholar who brings a traditional understanding of the multifaceted nature of contemporary Indigenous existence, which can include disability.

In 2017, I received a request from an Indigenous PhD student for the introductory article I had written for a special journal issue. He received it with appreciation but asked if there was more I could send him since he had found little published in this area. Over the years, we remained connected, and he authored a chapter on Indigenous learners labeled with disabilities for an edited volume I compiled on Indigenous resilience. Now, having graduated, he has compiled his own edited volume, the one you have in front of you, adding immensely to what has been published on Indigenous people with disabilities. Most notably, this book has been developed in an inclusive, decolonized way.

Perspectives on Indigenous people and people with disabilities

Around the world, Indigenous people persist and resist in contexts where colonial settler societies impose foreign systems, norms, and values. Colonial contexts have stigmatized, pathologized, and marginalized both Indigenous people and people with disabilities. Settler societies attempted to erase us and replace our understandings and ways of thinking that do not frame disability as an individual pathology, while simultaneously viewing Indigeneity as something to be removed or extinguished. Societal attitudes, particularly those in colonial contexts, can be subordinating and disabling, often leading to some of the most debilitating problems.

Both Indigenous people and people with disabilities have been subjected to regulation and government oversight. Those who do not meet the standard of normalcy are inconvenient, to be removed, or to be made invisible. Our perceived lack of value in colonial societies is reflected in our shared history of sterilization and being relegated to places where we are subject to social control such as reservations, boarding schools, and asylums. Institutions have kept Indigenous people and people with disabilities out of sight. We are seen as not really a part of society and need training to know our place. At times, members of colonial societies have developed paternalistic policies based on beliefs that they needed to protect us. We are infantilized, legally restricted, deemed incompetent, and perceived to need guardians.

The attributes that we bring have been medicalized or anthropologized through a colonial lens that denies that we belong or have a place in the world. Through normalizing one way of being that is individualistic, white, male, with a neurotypical able body, we are "othered" and our existence is devalued, excluded, depicted as subhuman, erased, and/or considered disposable. Indigenous people with disabilities often experience a particularly disadvantageous synergy between these stigmatized identities.

Colonial perspectives stand in sharp contrast to Indigenous values that prioritize inclusion, belonging, and everyone contributing. Indigenous conceptualizations of relationship and balance offer a different way of understanding disability. Relational ways of knowing and being emerge from value systems grounded in connection and caring for all our relations. Likewise, we understand there are lessons to be learned and guidance to be received from those seen as outside an idealized norm. Difference is natural and is not inherently hierarchical.

The importance of this book

This volume stands in affirmation of Indigenous values and in defiance of colonial marginalization. Dozens of authors share their insights from around the world, including North and South America, America, Africa, and Asia. Many explore how colonial perceptions and institutions have led to labeling Indigenous people as being defined solely by their disabilities. This deficit perspective is rejected by authors recounting Indigenous understandings, values, and beliefs that refrain from pathologizing differences. In addition to speaking from many different cultural contexts, the authors describe a variety of conditions including physical abilities, psychosocial issues, vision, hearing, and neurodiversity. Throughout the book, readers are reminded of the importance of ethics, empowerment, resistance, healing, and advocacy. The content is organized into five parts: (1) the power, wisdom, knowledge, and lived experiences of Elders; (2) reframing the narrative – navigating self-representation; (3) learning from within – including traditional knowledge; (4) challenging colonial authority – infusing regional ideals and concepts; and (5) interpretations, narratives, and lived experiences of grassroots teachers and social service providers.

The editor of this volume, Dr. John Ward, is the ideal person to convene these authors. He possesses a combination of professional expertise and lived experience that spans the topics of Indigeneity, disability, and traditional knowledge and values, infusing these lenses into this work of scholarship. He understands the crippling impact of colonial systems such as educational institutions designed to undermine Indigenous ways and erase anything beyond these entrenched systems' limited frame of acceptability. In defiance of colonial limitations, Dr. Ward offers readers a wide array of perspectives, conceptualizations, and experiences related to Indigenous people and disabilities.

This edited volume makes great strides toward filling a void in professional literature. No longer will students, practitioners, and academics be at such a loss to find content on Indigenous people with disabilities. The strong voices found within this volume challenge Western ideas of disability and help us find a different way forward. Within these pages are demands for respect and recognition, emphasizing that Indigenous ways of being and doing are no *lesser than* the ways of settler societies that have come to surround us. Rather, Indigenous understandings of difference and balance that characterize what are labeled as disabilities can inform an inclusive vision for the future.

I am thankful that the editor has taken on this important project. He has succeeded in bringing together authors from around the world to share their insights and perspectives. We are all the richer for this endeavor. As is often emphasized in Lakota traditions, *Mitakuye Oyasin*, we are all related.

Acknowledgments

I would like to thank all of the authors who took time out of their busy schedules, putting their lives on the side and opening up to an area that has been the source of trauma on so many levels. Their ability to comprise these chapters has provided a gateway into the unknown, as well as the known realization that there is more to us than what a label has classified us as or how a teacher could have limited our creative side. These different chapters have contributed to an evolving field – Indigenous disability studies as a way to express and better understand ourselves and find new meanings.

This publication, a first of its kind, would not have been created without the support and suggestion of Routledge. When I first approached the Publishing House to contribute my knowledge of Indigenous disabilities, I was advised not to submit an article, but in fact to create a book as an editor, which would bring together the wisdom, lived experiences, and various worldwide Indigenous experience and knowledge systems into one unified book on disability.

I would also like to thank Juan Camilo Carrero Vasquez, who from his steadfast dedication to Indigenous disability knowledge has connected me with Indigenous disability scholars in Colombia. He has also designed the book cover from consultations that I gave. This inspiration has created a visually appealing depiction of this book's contribution as a global leader in the emerging field of Indigenous Disability Studies.

Introduction

John T. Ward

Indigenous Disability is a rather new field within traditional Disability Studies. One area found to be lacking within the existing literature of Indigenous disabilities is the limited insight of Indigenous perspectives by Indigenous contributors. The lack of Indigenous voices related to disability knowledge has been a contentious topic due to the impact of colonialism. Certain areas that most notably come to mind that have been limited if not excluded are the southern territories (Gilroy et al., 2021). For far too long have Indigenous people and their knowledge been excluded from the field of Education and Disability Studies, which has been controlled by non-Indigenous academics and professionals.

There is a need, therefore, a calling to include more Indigenous voices from territories beyond the traditional academic approach of the global west, the United States and among European nations from the global north, as there are incredibly few voices from South America, the Indian subcontinent, South-east Asia and even the African continent. The inability to include Indigenous scholars from beyond Western and Northern countries has resulted in an exclusion from publications. This has resulted in a limited access for Indigenous scholars, teachers, front-line workers and Elders as sources of knowledge to participate in order that we can change how we view disabilities, accommodations, and accessibility.

This ability to include these different areas will bring about a genuine global response with knowledge systems that are far reaching. There are, thus, an impressive number of authors, who have come together because they felt it necessary to share their experience and to collaborate at an international level that can impact and connect with people across great continents – a truly Routledge experience thrives on diversity. Thus, this book focuses on Indigenous disabilities as experienced by Indigenous people, many of whom have a disability or have worked in the field of disability so will give an enlightening new depth of understanding of this developing field.

The need for such a text is real, as it will provide the necessary information that can lead academics, professionals, organizations, associations, undergrads, graduates, and community members to a better and more valuable wealth of knowledge. There are only a handful of world-renowned Indigenous scholars, who contribute to this area of Indigenous disabilities, many of whom I have had the privilege to work alongside and publish with. They have all indicated a need for this area to be developed by including countries that have previously been excluded. Much of the knowledge regarding disabilities lies within communities and with Elders, Knowledge Keepers/Holders, and Grandmothers who are the keepers of their traditional knowledge systems. By including these perspectives, the depth of insight regarding disabilities will be enriched as the book will have reached many diverse Indigenous peoples.

DOI: 10.4324/9781032656519-1

The overall approach of Indigenous people within this context of Indigenous Disability has little to no word or understanding of traditional knowledge and belief systems for disabilities as it is a foreign concept introduced through colonialism. This would explain why Indigenous people view and conceptualize disabilities as well as learning disabilities in a different manner, not through a deficit or negative lens. As Gilroy et al. (2021), revealed there is a substantial amount of research into the area of Indigenous disability, but it is to the point where "(It lacks) the understanding of Indigenous concepts of difference and skills and so fails to offer adjustments to Indigenous cultures and languages" (p. 2084).

This infusion of Indigenous knowledge, belief systems, traditional knowledge, ideas, wisdom, and lived experiences form a global response that will usher in a new age of understanding among the discipline and support the next generation of Indigenous disability writers, speakers, and teachers. So, this emerging field will be spoken of by Indigenous for Indigenous on a crucial Indigenous topic, but the knowledge presented will have positive outcomes for non-Indigenous as they can read, see, and follow in the footsteps of these authors on their journeys, which can impact their own path of rediscovery.

What makes this book unique is that there are only a few unpublished PhDs and articles that briefly touch on understanding disabilities from an Indigenous perspective, which include traditional knowledge. Indigenous people demonstrate considerable knowledge in a multitude of compacities despite legal, monetary, social, economic, health, and political inequalities that they have experienced from administrative and governmental authorities whether in health, education, or other areas. The primary purpose of this compilation of knowledge is, obviously, to highlight and share the traditional knowledge and belief systems from various Indigenous people around the world and their varied perspectives. Including the wisdom and knowledge systems from various Indigenous peoples, makes this book a wealth of information that can help, guide, and provide clarity in the areas of disability, learning disabilities and learning differences in a positive light.

Our diversity and harmonies connect who we are

These stories about how the world's Indigenous peoples view, understand, and explain disabilities are not a mere grouping of peoples, but how their knowledge is alive and can connect us across cultural barriers, different languages, and sociocultural experiences. It is this coming together through unity as (1) Indigenous peoples; (2) disability knowledge; and how this accumulation of Indigeneity and disability spoken, written, and expressed can bring about a change in mindset and recognition that through our differences, we can actually be closer than we might realize. The knowledge presented in this book allows for a diverse representation of disabilities from so many varied Indigenous perspectives from across the world that join us together as we are all children of the earth and are shaped through our experiences, education, sociocultural, family examples, and teaching approaches. Through these diversities and by sharing the world's knowledge on disabilities, pre- and postcolonial contact, harmony can be achieved as we conceptualize how this synergy connects us. As we interweave these various knowledge and belief systems – where we come from – our part of the world, our knowledge and cultural traditions, all this helps us reshape how we view ourselves within the greater disability community and creates who we are and what we are. By grouping these international experiences, we can weave a tapestry of disability knowledge that will grow, thrive, and inspire generations to come.

Therefore, the intent of this book was to include as many Indigenous perspectives as possible, as a comprehensive representation would enable a truly global perspective. Some of these writers are actually first timers so not among the most prominent contributors. Yet, they will all help us understand, assess, and determine how disability, learning disabilities, and learning differences are understood by Indigenous people around the world. It was thus a necessity to have people across the globe to contribute to this endeavor. This book may become a useful guide for Reconciliation-of-Disabilities by involving those who would most likely not be included, many of whom are first-time contributors to sharing personal insight beyond their own communities, their stories, lived experiences, insight, and community knowledge will advance this practically unknown and often exclusive field of Indigenous disabilities by including Indigenous perspectives.

This book that Routledge has provided will become the first of its kind where Indigenous authors can share their own perspectives through struggles in personal, professional, and within colonial spheres of influence (academia and governmental) organizations. This will allow for the approach of Education-as-Reconciliation by connecting Indigenous and non-Indigenous people in their pursuits of disability knowledge and understanding of self. By coming together, we can as all peoples of Mother Earth unite in our common goal of understanding how disabilities are seen, felt, taught, shared, and most importantly represented.

Moving beyond colonial barriers to embrace the knowledge of Indigenous peoples

These articles will be an asset to those who seek out a deeper understanding of the complexity of Indigenous people and their knowledge of disabilities and those who deal with predominantly non-Indigenous mindsets and barriers to education. There is a need to break away from Western perspectives, which is the primary reason why this book is of great significance as it initiates a move away from the previous colonial ways of reporting on disability among Indigenous peoples and communities. As well, the objective of this book is the ultimate reconciliation of those affected by disability labeling and Indian Residential Schools as the chapters will illustrate how we can all adapt to new distinct knowledge systems within a greater repository of Indigenous disability belief systems.

Intersecting of threads that bind us

The notion of intersectionality focuses on how two or more categories (gender, ethnicity, sex, education, colorism, status as in Indigenous or a resident in a country – visitor, citizen or temporary worker, disability, parentism, ageism, etc.) and many more that keep on being added. How these social categories intersect with each other can add to the diversity of the content, depending on the situation and intersections applied can change the outcome of the inquirer (Gjertsen, 2019). Hankivsky (2014) stated "intersectionality [is] to challenge inequities and promote social justice. This practice has also extended to policymakers, human rights activists and community organizers searching for better approaches to tackling complex social issues". The author goes on to explain that "most people don't know about intersectionality and why it is such an innovative framework for research, policy and practice" (p. 1). This process of developing larger and deeper research perimeters meets the needs of our growing and changing world by adding new intersections. Hankivsky (2014) adds to the flavor of the subject as additional lenses to view a topic, situation, or policy as she further reveals this validity,

> Intersectionality promotes an understanding of human beings as shaped by the interaction of different social locations (e.g., 'race'/ethnicity, Indigeneity, gender, class, sexuality, geography, age, disability/ability, migration status, religion). These interactions occur within a context of connected status, and connected systems and structures of power (e.g., laws, policies, state governments and other political and economic unions, religious institutions, media). Through such processes, interdependent forms of privilege and oppression shaped by colonialism, imperialism, racism, homophobia, ableism and patriarchy are created.
>
> (p. 2)

Hancock (2007) explained that intersectionality is "the best chance for an effective diagnosis and ultimately an effective prescription" (p. 73) as these labels of intersections add to the continuously growing diagram. It is these intersections that become the essential part of intersectional analysis (Hankivsky & Cormier, 2019). Intersectionalities provide a diversity of knowledge that would otherwise be unincluded and are not just deemed for research purposes, but can also be seen in our landscape from the topography of the Grand Canyon in each flavorist swirl of a marble cake (Jordan-Zachery, 2007); how a freeway looks when flying overhead or the sand on a beach, if looked upon closely reveals many different colors of pebble.

The text includes threads, which in other words could be called intersectionalities. The term "intersectionality" is used here in particular between the two intersects of Indigeneity and disability. Understanding how these two perspectives intersect will enable a deepening of their necessity. This area of intersectionality is one that is begging to be developed as it interlinks with various other topics, themes, threads, and information to formalize a distinctive nexus of information. Given the topic of Indigenous disabilities is underrepresented by Indigenous authors (Gilroy et al., 2021), there is a need to have these two – Indigenous and disabilities interwoven to render a new perspective, and narrative. These knowledge systems will have intersectionalities within the disciplines of education, social work, psychology, speech-language pathology, pastoral, social services, special education, psychosocial, counselor, and healthcare practitioner. There is, as well, an emergent demand for worldwide acknowledgement and a journey towards how the intersectionality of colonialism and disability impact the daily lives of Indigenous peoples. Recent figures indicate that "there are 476 million Indigenous people around the world and spread across more than 90 countries" (Amnesty International, 2023). However, there is inadequate trustworthy information and data on the predominance of disability among Indigenous peoples and communities on a global level.

These threads or intersectionalities reflect a consistent balance between theoretical/methodological and empirical chapters to balance the intake of Indigenous authors' information with that of traditional knowledge and methodological sources. This collective tapestry will guide and navigate the reader to follow, and interpret, what has been presented so that they can self-represent by looking within to understand how they see themselves whether it is with a disability, a disability or through another knowledge system that allows them to follow their own path towards being, living, or learning about disabilities.

Layout of book

Thus, this compilation of authors was coordinated with the aid of five themes/threads that bind us and serve to make distinct sections that the authors are grouped under. These five threads interweave the authors' contributions together that relate to the common threads of Indigeneity and disability. The threads reveal new perspectives to contribute to the growth of this area. Altogether, it will make disability knowledge more inclusive by including Indigenous voices in an Indigenous topic that has often been kept silent. The stories, wisdom, lived experiences, and belief systems will provide an in-depth overview within the five threads listed below:

- The power, wisdom, knowledge, and lived experiences of Elders
- Reframing the narrative – navigating self-representation
- Learning from within – including traditional knowledge
- Challenging colonial authority – infusing regional ideals and concepts
- Interpretations, narratives, and lived experiences of grassroots teachers and social service providers

Therefore, these threads represent the sections of this book and each author's subject connected to a thread will reflect a new perspective on Indigenous disabilities that has not been revealed prior to this.

Part I The basis of this book on Indigeneity includes the added source of Elders; thereby, making this international collaboration a first of its kind as it intersects Indigeneity and disability from a global perspective. Thus, the themes start by providing *'the power, wisdom, knowledge, and lived experiences of Elders'*. We will launch this great endeavor by beginning with "Indigenous Disability Studies" and Indigenous Elders – 'Indigenous knowledge holders, and their experience and cultural understanding of disabilities'. This approach was chosen because of how Indigenous Elders are perceived, honored, cherished for their place in society, and highly regarded as the keepers of community knowledge. As keepers of knowledge, these six Elders will express over 300 years of knowledge through orality by expounding a global perspective, while connecting intergenerationally through various time periods. The depths of knowledge that these Elders share reveal their struggles, resilience to colonialism, debates, and battling through their ups and downs of life to shape their narratives. These will set the stage for how their perspectives take flight to become the basis of how disabilities and learning disabilities are understood in their respective areas.

Part II will consist of the way Indigenous people must conduct themselves through the process of *'Reframing the narrative – navigating self-representation'*. One of the most significant approaches to conveying Indigenous insight, knowledge, and cultural beliefs is through narratives, which can be passed on orally to a society that basically utilizes written text more and more. Sioui (2012) reveals that "we, as Indigenous peoples, must rewrite our own stories". This act of taking back the narrative can best illustrate how Indigenous peoples with disabilities or those who have worked with disabilities are able to navigate oppressive government labels, assessments, and policies regarding being disabled. Understanding the person beyond their label or disfigurement can provide insight into the ways that Indigenous people view disabilities. This section will truly cultivate a response that can resonate with the reader, whether they are Indigenous and in search of information or non-Indigenous, who seek out different cultural perspectives and knowledge systems. Each reader will gain a new understanding.

Part III takes the approach from an interior perspective that needs to begin with '*Learning from within – including traditional knowledge*'. From what the previous themes revealed, this theme will add more insight by including the traditional knowledge and belief systems of various Indigenous groups. The information shared from specific a tribe, nation, or communal standpoint will add to the overall understanding of how this knowledge can influence those who seek to better understand their being different.

Part IV The knowledge presented within this book has in one form or another been impacted by colonialism, so this is an attributing section '*Challenging colonial authority – infusing regional ideals and concepts*'. Authorities have controlled, organized, and even limited Indigenous peoples through educational practices such as with boarding schools, assimilation policies, and language reeducation methods, which undermine Indigenous ways. This book will challenge institutional authority that has acted negatively towards Indigenous survival. Thus, it goes into the ways that need to be taken in order to move forward through the process. How these changes have impacted the current knowledge and belief systems will be explained in greater detail. So, this theme will capture the previous threads by looking from within as many sources and publications have done before.

Thus, taking control of Indigenous disabilities will make a new stance possible from Critical Disability Theory (CDT) and traditional colonial Critical Disability Studies (CDS). It will also give a multitude of new approaches as to how disabilities are brought forth from Indigenized perspectives, knowledge, and belief systems. These types of new approaches to understanding disability knowledge can provide a new Indigenous perspective that has often been ignored by settler-colonial academia and also negatively taught as a bad association through traditional knowledge systems that have been tainted by colonialism.

Finally, **Part V** will give a collection of *interpretations, narratives, and lived experiences of grassroots teachers and social service providers with* tribal knowledge from various Indigenous communities in Africa and India, adding their contribution to this global Indigenous response. This inclusion from areas that have not until now been included and given the opportunity to share their experiences regarding disabilities and learning disabilities provides a glimpse into areas that are often forgotten. This grassroots perspective will provide an insightful response to colonialism, how disabilities are understood from a tribal response, and how disabilities differ from those of the Western – colonized worlds. The information presented in this final Part will follow a plain language approach as these teachers and service providers, many of whom are self-funding within their tribes will give an inside look into who they are; where they are from, and how disabilities and learning disabilities impact them and those they help.

The primary objective of this book is to unravel the complexity of how disabilities are understood and considered through a multitude of approaches, by conveying them through a multitude of Indigenous lens and backgrounds. This is a way of reflecting on the Indigenous knowledge, root of their beliefs, and lived experiences of individuals/groups (nations/tribes/communities). By illustrating these sociocultural differences, we can truly relate to how disabilities are taught, and interpreted, as well as learn from these unique perspectives. Often disability studies from the predominantly White or institutional standpoint have grouped these responses into a melting pot, which exclude the richness and diversity of so many varied Indigenous cultures.

These grassroots teachers and service providers will thus grasp the uniqueness of all the members' cultures, who have participated in this book.

Accumulating areas of expertise – The influence of Indigenous traditional knowledge

This international representation of Indigenous authors has gathered, through these five threads, collectively comprises a narrative that will reach all those who seek out this book to read what has been shared. The authors including Elders share the knowledge systems of unique perspectives from their countries, not as a whole, but as a window into the differences, which could be the colonial languages (English and French) or that of their own hereditary use. By following a distinctions-based approach, readers will be able to see, hear, and understand the differences in knowledge systems as they pertain to the authors' specific geographical areas. These professionals will provide front-end access to Indigenous people, who have struggled with their colonial labels, classifications, and the assessments that renamed them. Every parent who struggles with intergenerational trauma and school phobia due to their own treatment will be able to rely on this source not only to combat the colonial stance on disabilities and being different but perhaps even see themselves in the writing. The knowledge shared might even help in their own healing and navigating their own trauma and daily struggles or that of their children (Absolon, 2016). There will even be in the negative impact of colonialism the dark viewpoint that can give clarity to those who have taken their own lives and for those parents who are left wondering what else could have been done to change this painful outcome.

These different perspectives and various intersectionalities add to the overall knowledge of disabilities and how they are perceived, taught, lived, and understood and demonstrate the emerging issues, and insights into interdisciplinary Disability Studies. This book captures Indigenous content into a single publication, thereby, becoming a first of its kind so fulfills a great need according to Hilary Weaver, John Gilroy, Lavonna Lovern, and Ella Callow, especially, an absolute need as both Indigeneity and disabilities are not conveyed within such a comprehensive handbook.

There is an absence of content dedicated to Indigenous disabilities in academic circles. Thus, the intersectionality of Indigenous and Disability is in great demand in academia. Universities and teaching institutes are desperate for content for teaching/learning under the United Nations' Convention on the Rights of Persons with Disabilities (CRPD) and the United Nations Declaration on the Rights of Indigenous Peoples (UNDRIP). The United Nations (UN) and the World Health Organization (WHO) are two superpowers in this area that have gathered all that has been written to formulate a database; yet, there is still so much missing – the stories, lived experiences, and knowledge systems from countries that have been excluded, segregated, and often limited such as the voices on the continents of Africa, Asia, and South America. This book provides that and brings forth the knowledge presented to those academics, professionals, universities, and associations in order to develop strategies within the emerging field of Indigenous Disabilities. The content will become most beneficial to journals, but also to professionals that rely on Indigenous content when working to aid Indigenous peoples – many of whom work in a colonial manner such as those who work in friendship centers, community lodges, and social networks, who can provide guidance when colonial interference has contributed enough to the cause and discomfort of being disabled.

Reconciliation allows us to reconnect through healing

The word and concept of "reconciliation" is one that has been tossed around as a colonial "fancy word" with no meaning, until real action and real change have taken place as the expression conveys "money talks and bullshit walks." This colorful metaphor can speak to a global understanding that "actions speak louder than words" as a way of understanding how settler-colonial words, actions, and promises have failed and continue to fail because of colonial actions that are still being implemented through education practices, healthcare approaches, and the use of racist wording and comments. Reconciliation has been used in settler-colonial academia, in directives that all aim to bring about change with healing and an inclusion of Indigenous peoples. Many Indigenous scholars, speakers, politicians, and even Elders have said that it is merely another word used by colonials to feel they are making a real change – a sort of piecemeal directive that will show a true acknowledgment and then healing of past colonial attitudes, policies, and ways that have limited Indigenous peoples.

However, Elders are optimistic of the future as they draw on their past in looking forward to what may come. This optimism gives strength in our darkest time, as we navigate through our own past to heal the trauma that many Indigenous people have endured. Through this process of healing from within with the guidance of these Elders, readers will be accompanied on their path of reconciliation. As one Elder will reveal, "the healing of one, is the healing of all", which speaks truth as through the ability to heal ourselves, we will be able to heal others, even those who have hurt us.

The truth of knowledge

The knowledge presented here will allow for some to come full circle in healing from being labeled as disabled and living a life ashamed of being different to fully understanding that our differences are what make us part of the human family. These differences – not disabilities will set us free.

> Our elders have maintained a tradition of transmitting knowledge, values, and history through oral tradition. We learn from the experiences of others. There is something beyond the story itself that takes hold of each listener's heart and remains in memory.
>
> (Skinner, 1999, p. 107)

This quote illustrates the fundamental reason that Elders are not only needed but are also essential for this book. Their stories will help the reader to see how disabilities are understood and perceived by becoming the basis for what the other authors will contribute. Storytelling is a cultural tool among Indigenous peoples, especially, the Elders. So, some shared pieces of oral history that came down through the generations, which provides a basis of their lived experiences and supports the knowledge presented. As storytelling is one of the main forms of communication reflected within this publication, some authors chose to rely entirely on oral history regarding their knowledge of disability from their community. Thus, the reader may often feel they are actually engaging in dialogue with an Indigenous author. It is a pivotal part, if not essential skill for Indigenous Elders, who can connect the reader through their tapestry of information. Readers will walk through their stories of how disabilities have impacted their lives or others they have known and reveal how they have lived, learned, thrived, and had to become resilient due to colonialism, outside influence, and the changing times. These individual stories bind us together as humans as the themes – threads of knowledge help us understand how our unique differences unite us in the commonality of how disabilities are interpreted through our collective response. This grouping of international Indigenous contributors will provide insight into the emerging field of Indigenous disabilities by including their countries, regions, philosophies, and educational differences that have yet to be brought forth in this area. This ensures that this contribution will become a leading resource guide as it provides cutting-edge research with traditional knowledge systems by members of those geographical areas.

Readers will, consequently, connect to the cultures and communities of the authors in ways that have not been done before. The knowledge presented will provide the reader with an understanding of how disabilities are understood by these tribes. It will offer an in-depth comprehensive overview to allow the voices of many to be read, heard, and understood by a world looking for clarity, and guidance on how disabilities and learning disabilities – learning differences are perceived.

When communicating with the authors, I asked them "What would you like to see or what is lacking in this topic of Indigenous disabilities?" Their submissions are all original because they wanted to contribute in a way that had not been submitted before. These will captivate the reader to go beyond what has been presented, argued, and debated within the field of disability studies and Indigenous disabilities, which is the pivotal difference between what has been written and what will come to be.

Impact of colonialism

The impact of colonialism is a contentious issue and how it has contributed to the current perception of disabilities by Indigenous peoples is ultimately the primary purpose of this book. Colonialism is often understood as a dark chapter; if not a dirty aside because of its contribution to a country's wealth and ability to grow and thrive. However, it also was the expedient to how it oppressed the poor, disabled, and marginalized by living off their backs. The word colonialism could also be interpreted as a "dirty" word among those, who were used to prop up society and the state of their oppressor. Only by diving into how colonialism has impacted the world's Indigenous people can we better understand how it has undermined people, and changed the cultural traditions and knowledge systems of colonized peoples. This leads us to how "disability knowledge" changed from a positive association in precontact days to a negative connotation so often referred to in postcontact as a "deficit" – a handicap. Only by looking at this approach, can we the reader(s) navigate our own experiences along this path towards disability-as-reconciliation.

Colonialism was not just the subjugation of people, but it also reared its head in the policies, direction, forcible relocation, and indoctrination of children's mindsets through educational and medical approaches. This persuasive indifference toward people, who previously had no contact and had no need for these changes contributed to later systematic trauma, abuse, labeling, and the internalization of self-loathing (Ward, 2023a). Two places among many where this took place that come to mind are the infamous Indian Residential Schools (IRS) in Canada and the Indian Industrial Schools (IIS) in the United States, where forcible relocation to boarding schools occurred, along with

Indian hospitals (Canada and the United States), where sterilization was conducted. Both these places contributed to the current situation in Canada and the United States and indeed in all other colonized countries and territories.

Changing the colonial mindset – Decolonization in action

Colonialism also disrupted the life and education of Indigenous peoples and continues to do so in the present day because of labeling. Rhea (2015) looked at how the British Empire was able to imprint their colonial mindset onto their Indigenous subjects as a method of controlling and limiting their educational freedoms (p. 91). Rabang et al. (2023) explains that "disability is usually defined in the media and Hollywood within the medical model. Hollywood has inappropriately stereotyped Indigenous cultures and disabilities cultures for many years" (p. 141).

One can extrapolate that this happened in Canada and the United States based on the Anglo-Saxon approach to imperialism. Rhea (2015) introduced the advice that "teachers and other school leaders are aware of the colonial mindset that influences their thinking, that they will unwittingly reinscribe the contemporary school experience with tropes of education that are painfully familiar to generations of Aboriginal[s]" (p. 92). This educational mindset could also coexist among other British colonies, even more so with postcolonial education systems (Rigney, 1999) such as residential schools (Hilton, 2011).

There is no shortage of stories, oral histories and testimonies, affidavits, eyewitnesses, and now unmarked graves surrounding these residential schools, which give accounts regarding all of the gross incompetence, inhumane treatment, and unethical, and criminal behavior that occurred, which engendered the situations faced by Indigenous peoples today. It can be easily understood that through these "specialized boarding schools" or as some Indigenous academics like to refer to them as "reconditioning – reprogramming", they became a stain on North American history. Many events occurred in them, but there is no need to drag on with the stories regarding the misery and violent acts of pure evil savagery.

By looking at a few fundamental notorious areas: unprofessional teachers, labeling and bullying, punishing, cognitive reconditioning, dehumanization of a child's mindset, and assimilation, we can comprehend the various sources that formulate a single directive that explains how this sinister part of history came about. It stems from the colonial mindset and birthed not only a cultural genocide but also the intergenerational trauma that many experience today due to these early interactions of reconditioning practices (Hudson, 2021).

The term "indoctrination" "originally had a neutral meaning, almost equivalent to educative teaching, but it gradually assumed the connotations of coercive teaching" (Puolimatka, 1996, p. 109). This later became known as "imperialism of the mind" (Curtin et al., 1978). The act of indoctrination became a crucial approach to educational development by religious leaders in colonized countries and elsewhere (Salleh, 2020). Indoctrination practices in non-Indigenous style schools, with a curriculum that adhered to colonial pedagogies, within a Eurocentric approach to learning are the root of the current situations faced by Indigenous peoples in Canada (Villanueva, 2021) today. This educational approach led to a specific form of oppression that was witnessed as brainwashing, abuse, torment, and other cruel methods to produce self-doubt within oneself in order to limit how Indigenous people viewed themselves as they were told to internalize their feelings. In this context, the indoctrination, or the annihilation of the Indigenous identity – distorting the mental, physical, emotional, and spiritual well-being of Indigenous children was primarily shaped by the IRS. Some of these schools were well known for carrying out acts of abuse such as mental or physical torture, and a series of medical, and dietary, as well as other types of experiments (Ward, 2023b).

Okazaki et al. (2008) examined how colonialism was used through educational formats – schools, as ways of subjugating Indigenous children by making them believe they were different, which was instilled into them by a colonial mindset. This oppressive approach to the difference "between the colonizer's "superior" or "more civilized" ways of life and the colonized people's allegedly "inferior" or 'savage' ways" (p. 92) manifested into an internalization of the mindset of inferiority by Indigenous peoples (McKinley et al., 2020).

Absolon (2019) gives a powerful perspective linking decolonization efforts with those of Western ways of learning so that "to de-colon-ize is to detoxify and cleanse from the internalization of a colonized mindset about what informs what we teach, and how we teach methods and theories of practice" (p. 17). The term "decolonization" is defined as a process to not only move away from colonized methods, but to also acknowledge the values of Indigenous knowledge and wisdom (Afonso, 2013) and bring together both Indigenous and non-Indigenous people to learn and respect Indigenous knowledge (Kim, 2018). Decolonizing the settler-colonial mindset will enable one to look beyond set practices that were established based on specific ideals, theories, and concepts, such as the Critical Disability Theory (CDT), Disability Studies (DS), and other methods so, that Indigenous knowledge systems can flourish beyond academic structures by allowing distinct insight to be applied, which can alter the perception of current academic/professional thinking.

Surviving residential schools – The precursor of intergenerational trauma

The forcible removal of Indigenous children and their relocation to get "free education" through the residential schools was policy in many colonized countries such as Australia (Murphy, 2018), Canada (Park, 2016), Finland, Sweden, Norway (Svonni, 2017), Russia (Kulikova, 2015), and the United States (Gram, 2016). Armitage (1995) gives a compelling look into the first organized comparative analysis of assimilation practices done on Indigenous children that were conducted in colonized countries such as Canada to make them become part of white society. Armitage exposes the assimilation measures within the welfare and adoption services, as well, including how the reeducational practices facilitated this approach from within the IRS – the primary method of assimilation of Indigenous children into Canadian society that purged them of their cultural identity (Niezen, 2017). Regan says, this "policy of assimilation as necessary to save and civilize Indigenous people" (2010, p. 98) and to plant the children into a new culture and society (Berry & Hou, 2016). Kong et al. (2021) recount that "being assimilated into the mainstream culture, in the end, [would make them] give up their own culture" (p. 99), which was the reason for implementing assimilation techniques in the Indian boarding schools. This supported "forced attendance at Residential Schools [was] designed to [implement] assimilation, systemic racism, [and the] extinguishing of rights" (Krementz, 2018, p. 26). The effects of assimilation are seen in many forms today, but most notably concerning Indigenous intergenerational trauma as "assimilation policies have left many Indigenous people alienated from their land and culture and, sometimes, their family" (Archibald, 2006, p. vi).

Indian residential school teachers – Misconduct and nonprofessional behavior

Papp (2016) looked at the necessity for "building good teacher-student relationships", (p. 6) to be "maintained through a style of teaching... in which the teacher demonstrates value and respect for the student" (p. 5). The teacher/student relationship is considered a sacred relationship that is built on trust and understanding through communication, which would ultimately lead to either a positive or a negative outcome (Baker et al., 2008) for the student. Particularly bad situations did happen in some schools, but it had more to do with the individual underqualified teacher and their stress about Indigenous children who seemed unable to learn as they had "disabilities" – meaning unable to learn.

Abuse comes in all types and approaches, but when a teacher uses their authority to condemn a child by making them believe they are subhuman, that they suffer from a learning disability, or they demand them to act like an animal only serves to negatively impact the child's psychological development and effects their long-term ability to function in society.

Barnes and Josefowitz (2019) stated that [IRS] children were subjected to

> verbal abuse ... [told they] were stupid or worthless ... subjected to unusual or humiliating punishments... forced to clean the stairs with a toothbrush or made to stand in a corner in urine-soaked clothing as punishment for bed wetting... deprived of food ... locked in broom closets, basements, or even crawl spaces for long periods of time... IRS students were thus frequently exposed to psychological abuse.
>
> (p. 69)

Non-Indigenous teachers coming from down south were harsh and lacked the ability to understand Indigenous students as they had never really been around Indigenous people before. Colonial teachers apparently understood the difference in teaching that they needed for Indian Schools, but most did nothing about trying to relate and teach with compassion. This led to abusive name calling, severe punishment for not complying with teachers, and all these issues resulted from a lack of teacher education training and their ability to learn from the students. They were unable to understand cultural differences of Indigenous students and seemed unable to love or show compassion for their students. However, there were some good and compassionate teachers, many of whom did not know how or were unable to change the IRS system/culture.

The inadequate quality of classroom learning experiences during the Residential School era engendered low-performance expectations placed upon Indigenous children, who were at substantial risk of receiving only a meager academic accomplishment, which resulted in low self-esteem and struggles in their social development. Barnes et al. (2006) showed that Indigenous children whose "English language development was weak and fragmented were at risk of having difficulties with basic literacy and subsequent poor academic achievement" (p. 24). These difficulties in reading, spelling, and speaking were labeled as merely a "learning disability", but in fact may have been a form of dyslexia (Siegel, 2003).

This restriction and inability to develop in a hassle-free environment contributed to the students' challenges of school achievement (DiPerna & Elliott, 2002) so the child's ability to learn and become an active member of settler-colonial society was restricted. These limitations of a student's abilities, exacerbated by labeling, bullying, victimization and subjected to other injustices, contributed to an overall impact on their psychological, emotional, physical, and spiritual well-being. Although not all students were subjected to these abuses and labels, many were and the voiceless cannot speak up to defend themselves.

Intergenerational school traumas

The bullying, labeling, and abuse of the Indian Residential School (IRS) later had much greater repercussions as it led to intergenerational trauma (MacDonald, 2019). Wesley-Esquimaux (2007) defined intergenerational trauma as

> the historical experiences of First Nations people, which disrupted the process of the Indigenous cultural identity formation, [which] continues to loudly resonate in the present, and that the harm done in the past has continued to manifest intergenerationally into the present.
>
> (p. 7)

Groth (2021) gives a stellar explanation of trauma "Transgenerational trauma (also known as intergenerational, multigenerational, or historical trauma), often overlooked in trauma training, results from decades of generational oppression, dehumanization, and racism or a familial history of trauma passed down from one generation to the next" (p. 24), especially, due to the IRS.

The limitations and consequences of negative IRS experiences imposed by teachers *and educators* are not only linked to teacher bullying, racism, and segregation techniques, but these also contributed to intergenerational school traumas and phobias (Milne, 2016). Thus, these later traumas brought on by physical or mental abuse or labeling (Partridge, 2010) were damaging as they led to abusive attitudes that were passed on to the children's offspring. These abuses even contributed to PTSD, and major depression, which can lead to suicide (Wilk et al., 2017).

The ensuing intergenerational trauma was the reason why parents would not teach their children their hereditary languages and customs out of fear of their children experiencing racism and retribution as they had done (Partridge, 2010). This fear was then transferred from parent to child and became an instinct for survival (Gaywish & Mordoch, 2018). Bourassa et al. (2015) stated how multigenerational experiences of colonization resulted in traumas that overall impacted the well-being of Indigenous peoples, even more so, those with disabilities, referred to as invisible disabilities (p. 12).

Historical intergenerational trauma from the settler-colonial era impacted Indigenous peoples and the continuous assault from the trauma, thus, disabled their ability to function within cultural norms, which resulted in PTSD (Gone, 2014). This impact on their mental well-being came from the attributing factors such as the labeling and abuse used by the residential school teachers (Kirmayer et al., 2014). It came at the cost of an IRS student's long-term stability (Wilk et al., 2017). As opposed to this, it is known that Indigenous children who connect with their culture have increased well-being and self-esteem that can reinforce their academic attainment and enable and develop their resiliency to discrimination, racism, and segregation practices. This, in turn, helps them avoid their own abusive behavior, substance abuse, incarceration, and/or suicide (Chandler & Lalonde, 2008). It also encourages their psychological and emotional renewal (Halseth & Greenwood, 2019).

Therefore, Indigenous children were forced to follow settler-colonial ways of learning, living, and most importantly become productive members of Canadian society. This proved to be wrong as the "IRS system was racist, and represented an explicit attempt to eradicate what were perceived as the defining characteristics of the Indigenous peoples" (Matheson et al., 2016, p. 567). What is surprising, though, is the denial of these types of actions and how they are dismissed as acts from long ago; even though, there are other leading factors such as adoption, health, education, legal, and many more types of services that still put Indigenous children and families at risk similar to what had previously occurred. These acts of violence have not stopped (MacKenzie, 2020).

Wesley-Esquimaux (2020) gives an alternative viewpoint that

> we should reiterate that it isn't always physical manifestations that create intergenerational dysfunction; it can also be the residual grief and intergenerational trauma that has not been identified and resolved from previous generations, which continues to surface in families and communities.
>
> (p. 69)

This would suggest that perhaps there are other attributing factors to family traumas that span beyond what has been previously stated. Colonialism has a long history of creating negatively impacting Indigenous peoples; trauma is but one effect and many more will be shared. How we move forward defines who we are as Indigenous peoples.

Breaking a child's spirit and causing PTSD may become a multigenerational school trauma, which results in a broken person, who must live out their life picking up the pieces and trying to get by on their own (Anaya, 2014). Söchting et al. (2007) explain this "Complex PTSD which include a series of 'blows' … on the developing child or adolescent's body and psyche in the form of psychological, physical, and/or sexual abuse within a context of inadequate emotional and social support" (p. 321). Gone (2013) looks at how Native Americans have demonstrated inexplicably high rates of traumatic experiences within the context of violence, poverty, and substance abuse that is twice as high as PTSD for the national U.S. adult population (Kessler et al., 2005). There are even final acts of suicide as there is no hope, except at the end of a rope. These troubling times cannot take hold of children, youth, and those who have had to bear the injustices due to what a foreign-colonial mindset revealed, labeled, and determined. We must rise up not only as the world's Indigenous peoples but for the greater good as we are all human after all.

References

Absolon, K. E. (2016). Wholistic and ethical: Social inclusion with Indigenous peoples. *Social Inclusion, 4*(1), 44–56.

Absolon, K. E. (2019). Decolonizing education and educators' decolonizing. Intersectionalities: A Global Journal of Social Work Analysis. *Research, Polity, and Practice, 7*(1), 9–28.

Afonso, E. Z. D. F. (2013). Rethinking the history of inclusion of IKS in school curricula: Endeavoring to legitimate the subject. *International Journal of Science and Mathematics Education, 11*(1), 23–42.

Amnesty International. (2023). Indigenous Peoples' Rights. Over. Doi: https://www.amnesty.org/en/what-we-do/indigenous-peoples/.

Anaya, J. (2014). *Report of the special rapporteur on the rights of Indigenous peoples*. New York City, NY: United Nations Press.

Archibald, L. (2006). *Decolonization and healing: Indigenous experiences in the United States, New Zealand, Australia and Greenland*. Ottawa, ON: Aboriginal Healing Foundation.

Armitage, A. (1995). *Comparing the policy of Aboriginal assimilation: Australia, Canada, and New Zealand*. Vancouver, BC: UBC Press.

Baker, J. A., Grant, S. and Morlock, L. (2008). The teacher-student relationship as a developmental context for children with internalizing or externalizing behavior problems. *School Psychology Quarterly, 23*(1), 3–15.

Barnes, R. and Josefowitz, N. (2019). Indian residential schools in Canada: Persistent impacts on Aboriginal students' psychological development and functioning. *Canadian Psychology, 60*(2), 65–76.

Barnes, R., Josefowitz, N. and Cole, E. (2006). Residential schools: Impact on Aboriginal students' academic and cognitive development. *Canadian Journal of School Psychology, 21*(1–2), 18–32.

Berry, J. W. and Hou, F. (2016). Immigrant acculturation and wellbeing in Canada. *Canadian Psychology, 57*(4), 254–264.

Bourassa, C., Blind, M., Dietrich, D. and Oleson, E. (2015). Understanding the intergenerational effects of colonization: Aboriginal women with neurological conditions—their reality and resilience. *International Journal of Indigenous Health, 10*(2), 3–20.

Chandler, M. and Lalonde, C. (2008). Cultural continuity as a protective factor against suicide in First Nations youth. *Horizons, 10*(1), 68–72.

Curtin, P. D. (1978). *African history*. Longman: Harlow.

DiPerna, J. C. and Elliott, S. N. (2002). Promoting academic enablers to improve student achievement: An introduction to the mini-series. *School Psychology Review, 31*(3), 293–297.

Gaywish, R., and Mordoch, E. (2018). *Situating Intergenerational Trauma in the Educational Journey*. Manitoba: University of Manitoba.

Gilroy, J., Uttjek, M., Lovern, L. and Ward, J. (2021). Indigenous people with disability: Intersectionality of identity from the experience of Indigenous people in Australia, Sweden, Canada, and USA. *Disability and the Global South, 8*(2), 2017–2093.

Gjertsen, H. (2019). Mental health among Sami people with intellectual disabilities. *International Journal of Circumpolar Health, 78*(1). https://doi.org/10.1080/22423982.2019.1565860

Gone J. P. (2013). Redressing First Nations historical trauma: Theorizing mechanisms for Indigenous culture as mental health treatment. *Transcultural Psychiatry, 50*(5), 683–706.

Gone, J. P. (2014). Reconsidering American Indian historical trauma: Lessons from an early Gros Ventre war narrative. *Transcultural Psychiatry, 51*(3), 387–406.

Gram, J. R. (2016). Acting out. Assimilation: Playing Indian and becoming American in the federal Indian boarding school. *American Indian Quarterly, 40*(3), 251–273.

Groth, E. (2021). *High school teacher understanding of student trauma and its impact in the classroom: A mixed methods study*. Doctor of Education in Education Policy, Organization and Leadership with a concentration in Diversity and Equity in Education and Global Studies in Education. Urbana, IL: University of Illinois Urbana-Champaign.

Hancock, A. M. (2007). When multiplication doesn't equal quick addition: Examining intersectionality as a research paradigm. *Perspectives on Politics, 5*(1), 63–79.

Hankivsky, O. (2014). Intersectionality 101. Vancouver, BC: Institute for Intersectionality Research & Policy, Simon Fraser University.

Hankivsky, O., & Cormier, R. (2019). Intersectionality and public policy: Some lessons from existing models. In *The Palgrave Handbook of Intersectionality in Public Policy*, 69–93.

Halseth, R. and Greenwood, M. (2019). *Indigenous early childhood development in Canada: Current state of knowledge and future directions*. Prince George, BC: National Collaborating Centre for Aboriginal Health (NCCAH).

Hilton, B. T. (2011). Frantz Fanon and colonialism: A psychology of oppression. *Journal of Scientific Psychology, 12*(1), 45–59.

Hudson, E. (2021). The cultural genocide of the Indigenous people of North America. *Journal of Interpersonal Violence, 23*(3), 316–337.

Kessler, R. C., Berglund, P., Demler, O., Jin, R., Merikangas, K. R. and Waters, E. E. (2005). Lifetime prevalence and age-of-onset distributions of DSM-IV disorders in the national comorbidity survey replication. *Archives of General Psychiatry*, 62(6), 593–602.

Kim, E.-J. A. (2018). *The relationships at play in integrating Indigenous knowledges-sciences (IK-S) in science curriculum: A case study of Saskatchewan K-12 science curriculum*. Doctoral Thesis: McGill University.

Kirmayer, L. J., Gone, J. P. and Moses, J. (2014). Rethinking historical trauma. *Transcult Psychiatry*, 51(3), 299–319.

Kong, Y., Atoyebi, J. and Tritthart, E. (2021). *Muses from the north*. Thompson, MB: University College of the North.

Krementz, D. H., Macklin, C., King, A., Fleming, T., Kafeety, A., Lambert, S., Laframboise, S. L. and Nicholson, V. (2018). Connections with the land: A scoping review on cultural wellness retreats as health interventions for Indigenous peoples living with HIV, Hepatitis C, or both. *Ab-Original*, 2(1), 23–47.

Kulikova, A. N. (2015). Problems of urban adaptation of Evenki youth: The case of Neryungri and Aldan regions, Republic of Yakutia [Sakha]. *Anthropology and Archeology of Eurasia*, 54(1), 53–67.

MacDonald, D. B. (2019). *The sleeping giant awakens: Genocide, Indian residential schools, and the challenge of conciliation*. Toronto, ON: University of Toronto Press.

MacKenzie, K. (2020). Unsettling White settler child and youth care pedagogy and practice: Discourses on working in colonial violence and racism. *International Journal of Child, Youth and Family Studies*, 11(3), 80–107.

Matheson, K., Bombay, A., Haslam, S. A. and Anisman, H. (2016). Indigenous identity transformations: The pivotal role of student-to-student abuse in Indian residential schools. *Transcultural Psychiatry*, 53(5), 551–573.

McKinley, C. E., Boel-Studt, S., Renner, L. M., Figley, C. R., Billiot, S. and Theall, K. P. (2020). The historical oppression scale: Preliminary conceptualization and measurement of historical oppression among Indigenous peoples of the United States. *Transcult Psychiatry*, 57(2), 288–303.

Milne, E. (2016). "I have the worst fear of teachers": Moments of inclusion and exclusion in family/school relationships among Indigenous families in Southern Ontario. *Canadian Review of Sociology = Revue canadienne de sociologie*, 53(3), 270–289.

Murphy, F. (2018). The whisperings of ghosts: Loss, longing, and the return in the Stolen Generations stories. *The Australian Journal of Anthropology*, 29(3), 332–347.

Niezen, R. (2017). *Truth and Indignation: Canada's truth and reconciliation commission on Indian residential schools* (2nd Ed.). Toronto, ON: University of Toronto Press.

Okazaki, S., David, E. and Abelmann, N. (2008). Colonialism and psychology of culture. *Social and Personality Psychology Compass*, 2(1), 90–106.

Papp, T. A. (2016). Teacher strategies to improve education outcomes for Indigenous students. *Comparative and International Education*, 45(3), Article 7, 1–14.

Park, A. S. J. (2016). Remembering the children: Decolonizing community-based restorative justice for Indian residential schools. *Contemporary Justice Review*, 19(4), 424–444.

Partridge, C. (2010). Residential schools: The intergenerational impacts on Aboriginal peoples. *Native Social Work Journal = Nishnaabe Kinoomaadwin Naadmaadwin*, 7, 33–62.

Puolimatka, T. (1996). The concept of indoctrination. *Philosophia Reformata*, 61(2), 109–134.

Rabang, N. J., West, A. E., Kurtz, E., Warne, J. and Hiratsuka, V. Y. (2023). Disability decolonized: Indigenous peoples enacting self-determination. *Developmental Disabilities Network Journal*, 3(1), Article 11, 132–145.

Rhea, Z. A. (2015). Unthinking the 200-year-old colonial mind: Indigenist perspectives on leading and managing Indigenous Education. *The International Education Journal: Comparative Perspectives*, 14(2), 90–100.

Rigney, L. I. (1999). Internationalization of an Indigenous anticolonial cultural critique of research methodologies: A guide to Indigenist research methodology and its principles. *Wicazo Sa Review*, 14(2), 109–121.

Salleh, M. A. (2020). The use of religion as tool for ideological indoctrination by Boko Haram: A critical discourse. *Journal of Critical Reviews, 7*(2), 806–810.

Siegel, L. S. (2003). IQ-discrepancy definitions and the diagnosis of LD: Introduction to the special issue. *Journal of Learning Disabilities, 36*(1), 2–3.

Sioui, G. E. (2012). The need for an Aboriginal auto-history. Canadian Institute for Energy Training. http://www.youtube.com/watch?v=YS6nGaggztE.

Skinner, L. (1999). Teaching through traditions: Incorporating languages and culture into curricula. In K. G. Swisher & J. Tippeconnic, III (Eds.), *Next steps: Research and practice to advance Indian Education* (pp. 107–134). Charleston, WV: ERIC Clearinghouse on Rural Education and Small Schools.

Söchting, I., Corrado, R., Cohen, I. M., Ley, R. G. and Brasfield, C. (2007). Traumatic pasts in Canadian Aboriginal people: Further support for a complex trauma conceptualization? *BC Medical Journal, 49*(6), 320–326.

Svonni, C. (2017). Reindeer gains: For centuries the Swedish government has regulated herding and education as a way of controlling the native Sámi population. *World Policy Journal, 34*(4), 20–23.

Villanueva, E. (2021). *Decolonizing wealth: Indigenous wisdom to heal divides and restore balance* (2nd Ed.). Oakland, CA: Berrett-Koehler Publishers.

Ward, J. T. (2023a). *Nòswàhanà-n Wìsakedjàk of Indigenous Elders' knowledge of disabilities, learning disabilities, and dyslexia through the lens of Indigenous disability methodologies.* PhD in Education, University of Ottawa Press.

Ward, J. T. (2023b). The Dark Side of Canadian History: A Two-Eyed Seeing Approach. In *The Palgrave Handbook on Rethinking Colonial Commemorations* (pp. 87–100). Cham: Springer International Publishing.

Wesley-Esquimaux, C. C. (2007). The intergenerational transmission of historic trauma and grief. *Indigenous Affairs, 4*(7), 6–11.

Wesley-Esquimaux, C. C. (2020). Inside looking out, outside looking. *First Peoples Child & Family Review, 3*(4), 62–71.

Wilk, P., Maltby, A. and Cooke, M. (2017). Residential schools and the effects on Indigenous health and well-being in Canada—A scoping review. *Public Health Review, 38*(8), 1–23.

Part I

The power, wisdom, knowledge, and lived experiences of Elders

Significance of Elders

The chapters in Part I capture the essence of the Elders, who have most graciously shared their insight with the reader. Their combined knowledge spanning over 300 years will profoundly impact readers. This is because in most publications, Elders are often not included, but with Routledge, we have been given the opportunity to show-case these significant people, who are internationally known within many circles. These Elders are from across the Americas: Canada (Algonquin, Cree, and Mohawk); the United States (Eskimo, Ihanktonwan Dakota, and Chickasaw) and representing the South of Venezuela and Colombia (Yukpa). These distinctive cultural depictions of how Elders are understood and what their challenges are will enable a greater understanding of their knowledge systems as oral testimony into the past, which is how we can grow into the future.

These Elders were and/or are at some point in their lifetime politicians, teachers, social workers, chiefs, emergency responders, counsellors, business entrepreneurs, professors, spiritual leaders, and psychologists. Most of all, though, they were there for those who needed help, providing guidance and support in times of great need by listening, speaking, and reflecting on topics that were and are controversial such as the American Indian Movement, Second Wounded Knee, Idle No More, and many other forms of solidarity that needed to be addressed and supported in great times of uncertainty. Their insights into the past are shaped by their struggles and this knowledge can provide wisdom, insight, and even clarity in times of confusion and have become a great inspiration for this book on Indigenous disability studies as their lived experiences transcend time.

Community connection

These authors are more than just merely contributors. They are the keepers of community knowledge and are often regarded as representatives of a nation, tribe, caste, or mob as they are chosen by their respective groups. It is with this action that Elders are held with high reverence and respect as they are chosen because of their own personal sacrifices and through their lived experiences we can see the essence of what it means to be Indigenous. The ability to connect with Elders can provide a glimpse into the lives they have lived as their knowledge systems are vast and deep with oral history that spans generations. They also share what they have learned as this process is part of who they are, so therefore these chapters are actually teachings as they will reflect about Indigenous

DOI: 10.4324/9781032656519-2

and disabilities through various topics that will provide clarity of knowledge. This will enable the readers to dive into this intergenerational knowledge system as we learn how Indigenous peoples view, interpret, and reflect on disabilities and learning disabilities. It is for this reason that this book on Indigenous disability studies begins with this section of Elders as Part I because in keeping with their ethics and protocols, Elders begin first and in keeping with this, these are their stories.

1 The colonial education system – Teaching Indigenous children with learning differences

Elder Annie Smith St-Georges

Introduction

Elder Annie Smith St-Georges is Algonquin from Kitigan Zibi First Nation located in the province of Québec and now resides in Gatineau. She is a traditional Elder related to William Ojigkwanong Commanda Morning Star, who taught and promoted her to become an Elder. She is active within the Indigenous Gatineau-Ottawa community. She is often accompanied by her husband, a Métis Elder, who supports her in all areas, so it is truly a team effort. She is a trained teacher and social worker (a healing profession), so she can communicate with people who require accommodation and healing approaches when learning. She has taught at several schools including Pierre Elliot Trudeau in Gatineau, which has a 22% Indigenous student population. She and her husband, with a few other teachers, established the first post-secondary learning institution for Indigenous people in Canada, which was known as College Manito. They championed, as well, in education, sharing knowledge, and engaging in dialogue, moving beyond the reconciliation and decolonization approach. So, she is a verbose public speaker and worked in the federal government, speaking in various federal government departments, the private sector, and represented Indigenous peoples abroad. Her profound impact is internationally recognized and her dedication to her topics gives insight into her strength as an Elder. There is no limit to her ability to stand up for what is right, regardless of where the wind blows. Her door is always open for all.

Education and language learning

Growing up, I only spoke Algonquin with my family. In Algonquin, 'no writing' existed, so writing was not exercised. However, this changed when I went to the Indian day school in Kitigan Zibi. My parents had also attended the same school, and both were brutalized and traumatized for not being able to read and write English. My father, Archer, was unable to read or write in English, but he was a 'very smart man.' My mother attended school until Grade 5, then left because of the way the teachers abused her. I understood that the disability labels, learning disabilities, and dyslexia made me only as functional as how society and the environment enabled me to be. I was sent to the Indian Day school on the reserve and later placed in the public school in Maniwaki because of how I was being treated. Teachers believed that a disability was not being functional, so the teachers had to learn to see the disabled students as functional. This labelling for me eventually became an intergenerational school trauma as it greatly affected my self-confidence and my family.

DOI: 10.4324/9781032656519-3

Labelling

As a little girl and all through my school years, I went through that process where I was abused emotionally and mentally, to break me. I didn't have any learning problems, but when I went to the Indian school, they started to label me as being disabled and unable to learn. In the second grade, in one incident, I got slapped at, screamed at, got abused, and told I was dumb and stupid. I got straps on my hand. I struggled throughout my time in elementary school. When I was in Grade 9, I was placed in a cooking class to be a lady to just stay home and be a good respectable wife. I felt frustrated at being placed in the typical position of a woman at the time. I was used to trapping, skinning, and making clothing from animal skins because our family was poor.

I was tired of being called stupid or having a learning problem. I do not have dyslexia. What I have is a language difference – a process, my brain processes in Algonquin first. I later recognized that this difference in language structure would appear to non-Indigenous teachers and co-workers to be a disability I was adamant about. I didn't have a learning problem or a learning disability. It's my language. It's my brain set – that's my culture, that's my way of speaking. That's who I am. This early interaction was why my teachers labelled me as disabled. This trauma affected me, so I felt hurt. I suffered all my life till I understood that my language was different. It is a direct language. We kind of sing when we talk, and it's very different from English and French. At one point in time, I rebelled and didn't want to speak French. I had no use for it. To me, it was of no use at that moment. I was told by the professor that I was hopeless. So, I had a challenge in learning languages.

There is a difference between Algonquin, compared to French or English, which have "a lot of these little 'le', 'la', 'de' words". It's 'the' which we don't need. The verbs and the adjectives don't necessarily follow depending on what you want. So, we don't have that elaborate English vocabulary with adjectives and beautiful colourism. So "English or French language amplify. I don't have that colourful language and the 'it's' and the 'er's'". Even today, I forget the 'is' and the 'er's' and the 'd's'. I tend not to use them in my writing and it's not my fault, because to me it's not important, and my language is a direct language. This language difference was why I thought I was labelled as being a difficult learner or a disability learner.

This difference in language structure impacted my schooling and all my struggles and traumatic experiences. One day, in high school, the school principal walked in and approached me. He kicked the chair out from under me, so I fell on the floor and got hurt. All the students were laughing. So, I said, "I have had enough of this, I took my books and went out of class. I'm going to a cooking class. I'm going to be going nowhere. I knew then I wasn't going anywhere". Once I had left, the director and everybody ran after me, saying "No, you're good, no. You're good, stay, stay." To which I replied, "I am not good. I'm a failure. I'm not good enough." I was so harassed, and the teacher was so harsh and called me a dummy. I went to school physically and mentally, but the kids laughed at me, and I didn't want to be laughed at.

I was laughed at well all my life and the language at home and the language in school were not the same. The teaching at home and the teaching at school were not the same. While attending an Indian school, no expert help was found for me, so these issues I faced could not be corrected instead of my being labelled. So, I suffered all my life until I acknowledged that my language learning was different, so I did not have a disability. At the Indian Residential School and then at the public school, with the teachers, I endured so much yet I overcame all these past injustices to become the person I am today.

At that time, I felt afraid to read in school as I would faint. I was the kid in the back of the room bending down, so the teacher wouldn't see me. This compelling inclination to just hide and become invisible is something that many people can understand. However, this school phobia resulted in ongoing anxiety that contributed to my shaking and stuttering because of the high level of stress.

After school

We lived in a small cabin-style home with my two brothers and parents. Even though we had no running water and were very poor, I had a happy life. I was protected. Those were the best times of my childhood. Speaking in Algonquin gave me strength and pride. During the time of continuous torment from teachers and classmates, William and dad, everybody would lift me to a higher state. That means, I was on media a lot. I met Pierre Trudeau, and they would bring me to these high-profile areas, and I would be in pow-wows. It was quite a different life compared to my time in high school off-reserve as the Elders would push me up and bring me up.

   After high school, I ran away because I was tired of being bullied by the teachers and labelled as having a 'learning problem,' so I left the reserve because of the way I was being treated. I walked off the reserve, which at that time First Nations living on reserves needed permission to leave from the Indian Agent,[1] which I did not have. As a result of this, an Indian Agent picked me up and brought me to Montréal where I enrolled in a social worker programme. This programme became a new opportunity for me because I was able to follow my passion for helping others, which led me to become a teacher with a degree in Early Childhood Education from the Université du Québec.

   Through these two programmes, I was able to teach in schools that did not have many Indigenous teachers at the time and led to my first posting at Manito College in 1973, which was the first and only post-secondary Indigenous school in Canada. I moved there with my husband Robert and our first child. I later taught at schools that had high numbers of Indigenous students, which contributed to my legacy as an educator as I bridged both Indigenous and colonial teaching approaches. My involvement as a teacher and later in government work led to my path of becoming an Elder.

Working and being (dis)abled

I later worked as a federal government worker and elementary school teacher. I also went to work at the Department of Indian Affairs in the late 1970s. I faced many challenges as an Indigenous woman, which was already difficult being Indigenous at that time in the federal workforce. Along with my many duties and responsibilities, while working at the Department of Indian Affairs, beside my Métis husband, I was faced with a slew of racist comments and jokes. During these challenging times, I had to rely on my husband because I had access to a new wonder – the internet. I would email my husband so that he could correct my letters and my spelling in either English or French without anyone knowing, which was an accommodation for me.

1 Indian agents were the law enforcement of then the Department of Indian Affairs, and they operated by controlling movement of First Nations on reserves. They had the legal authority to remove and return First Nations to their reserves or to another place if they were seen as being troublemakers.

During this time, I had two more children that my parents looked after for me, especially my son Yannick. He had a strong connection to his Algonquin heritage and was able to speak the language. I worked hard in the federal government, which enabled me to participate in programs and services despite my challenges with French spelling.

In the late 70s – 90s, it was uncommon to see Indigenous people working at the Department of Indian Affairs. My time in the government was stressful because I was often the only Indigenous (First Nation) person in the room, on the floor, or even within a section. As my husband looked white, he had no mistreatment as I did as I looked Indigenous being dark with long black hair. I endured racial slurs and comments from co-workers and managers, which became a daily routine.

However, my dedication and hard work got the attention of the Deputy Minister, who encouraged me to stay and push forward. He championed my progress as I was able to bridge traditional knowledge with that of the department's policies and implementing objectives. This led to my becoming part of a social committee that wanted to expand women vendors (non-Indigenous) to the departmental women's week. I was asked to organize all female vendors for the upcoming National Women's Day, which was such a huge success that it became the annual National Indigenous Peoples Day, which is celebrated every June 21st. Prior to that, Indigenous women had never been asked to participate as a vendor, so this event greatly encouraged their participation. Following the Oka Crisis of 1990 on the Mohawk reserve of Kanesatake, I also became instrumental in founding the Kumik Elders' Lodge in Gatineau as a place for healing and reconciliation. I knew there needed to be a place where people could come together to deal with trauma and grief.

Intergenerational school trauma

The labelling from school had a lasting impact on me and my family, which later impacted my role and duty not only as an Algonquin mother in passing on the culture, knowledge, and language but also in my work life. Even though my Algonquin language had mostly been lost, some of my children were later also identified and labelled with learning disability or dyslexia. However, I still believe that it's genetic. Thus, school phobias have a compound effect that can become intergenerational as they later can impact those around them in the family, who are the most vulnerable.

I compared my childhood experiences to those of my children's struggles. With the death of my son, Yannick, a suicide, who had endured challenges in school of not just being labelled as an 'Indian,' but also, we realized later he was bullied for having a learning disability – dyslexia. He was talented in drawing but struggled in the school system because he learned differently. Being Algonquin, he processed knowledge differently, which could have been interpreted by his teachers as dyslexia. I associated what happened to me with what happened to him – a striking resemblance as we both had to struggle learning English and French, while losing the Algonquin language because in the province of Québec, speaking French in school (primary and secondary) is compulsory. He had his mind mixed up – Algonquin and English languages so had trouble learning French. He was truly following the Indian way – in speaking, learning, living, everything, until he entered French school, where he had difficulties. His school experiences and the challenges he faced mirrored my own traumatic experiences – from teachers and even from co-workers. I feared for my children as I didn't want them to get hurt in the process and being belittled or labelled. I did not want them to go through the traumatic experiences that I had also encountered in school from a teacher, who was abusive, and did not expect much from the Indians.

I had experienced many challenges in life due to my being labelled with a learning disorder and due to having a difficult time learning language. This affected me all through my life, even while working in the government. Therefore, I tried not to let my children or the children I taught have to experience what I had gone through. I did not want teachers to label them 'disabled' because of the way they 'processed knowledge' and their 'thinking approach.' Or to get hurt, be belittled or labelled since a few of them were considered having learning disabilities – even though it's genetic. If they were seen as having dyslexia, I knew it inevitably would lead to teachers labelling and traumatizing them. Therefore, I also avoided teaching Algonquin to them because I wanted to protect them from the language difficulties I had had. This realization was passed on to my children, which meant a loss of some of their cultural identity. The additional intergenerational trauma of residential school abuse had been passed on from my mother as they had both gone to residential school, and then on to my children. Even though I had tried to protect them from these experiences, it was not easy. So, this revelation of disabilities, learning disabilities, and dyslexia shows the possible side effects from it.

Being labelled by teachers and a school director impacted my life. This notion by non-Indigenous teachers who believe that Indigenous students have a high proportion of learning disabilities provides one possible interpretation. From being both a student as well as a teacher, I saw how labels compound difficulties. I had been impacted so much that I was afraid of speaking publicly. I had been labelled and harshly treated all through life by non-Indigenous teachers in schools, professors in CEGEP and university, as well as management in the federal government.

Racism and segregation

These racist labels included assigning disability classifications due to performance issues and assessments and contributed to a lifetime of struggles and being belittled as a disabled Indian. These actions of assigning negative labels impacted my performance and emotional, physical, spiritual, and emotional stability was something I had to live with. The full extent of how I experienced racism and segregation in the colonial school system is a painful part of my life history that seemed to repeat itself while I was working with the Canadian government. I had recognized that my problems with learning a language were not a disability as from an Algonquin perspective, I was fine. Thus, I believe that labelling impacts the learning development of students.

There were many mixed marriages/relationships on a reserve, so the 'lighter-skinned' seemed to have less trouble succeeding than Indigenous kids even if they came from the same place. A racist divide existed because educational services and the degree of educational assistance one would receive depended on the colour of a student's skin. I know this from my lived experiences with the Indian Residential Schooling (IRS) system as a child, youth, and adult, and later professionally as a teacher. Those with a lighter skin tone often did not face the same type of abuse and had fewer learning differences/disabilities so they would make it. Thus, disabilities are looked for in darker skin students. As well, the ones of mixed heritage or lighter-skinned Algonquins had another advantage as many could speak both Algonquin, French and/or English, which was beneficial for working off-reserve. Therefore, they had a greater chance of overcoming the challenges and were better able to succeed as they were less burdened with learning disabilities.

That was considered an asset when attending school or working in the cities. They were able to better succeed in life and more able to move into positions of wealth when moving off-reserve to work in the government, or as a lawyer or in any other capacity because of their being bilingual. You will see them more in the higher levels. Working for the federal government was a challenge for Indigenous people; however, those of mixed heritage had more of an opportunity to succeed. Thus, skin colour was a factor in who was labelled with disabilities and who faced racism.

I witnessed segregation and racism within classrooms, especially towards students who were classified in the special education school. Even with the University of Ottawa leadership and members of their teaching and research community believed that because of their PhDs, they knew how to teach about Indigenous education from their research, data collection, and publications. I recall an event how learning disabilities and dyslexia are seen, understood, and felt by those who loosely label and criticize, Indigenous people. This situation began awkwardly, I was at a major meeting at a university where educators, and even the president with faculty members, had organized an event around Indigenous education. There was a non-Aboriginal guy making a presentation saying that "Indigenous people have learning disabilities." I knew that his statements were actually generalizing, which resulted in my taking action once questions were asked. I'm a person that is a pretty straight shooter, so I stood up right after he had made his presentation before anybody asked a question. I then confronted this audience of academics and told the group that:

> ...if I put you all in a Grade one situation in Algonquin ... At the end of the year; if we classify you, I know you'd be dyslexic, and have a severe learning problem. Maybe some of you might pass, but most of you might fail because our language is very different. The intonation, the way you express yourself, the nasal capacity of the language, it's different. If you don't have the proper pronunciation, you could be saying the wrong thing ... All of you here would probably fail grade one. You're saying that we have more disabilities than others, but if you learned Algonquin way, you'd be all disabled. Learning Algonquin because of the structure of grammar would be next to impossible to learn.

I provided my viewpoint, so the audience could understand the challenge and what a learning disability (dyslexia) would actually feel like, and how being labelled might feel. My intention is to provide a distinctions-based approach through an Algonquin lens into the difficulties in learning a new language structure, which may be mistaken for a learning disability. I attempted to convey the difference between learning a language academically and being immersed in it in your life – through a lived experience.

I hoped this would provide them with a better understanding and empathy for those labelled with a learning difference. This cultural lens perspective allowed the predominantly non-Indigenous audience to understand. My lived experiences and knowledge as an Elder allowed me to provide an alternative explanation to what had been raised by this non-Indigenous academic's scholarly claims based on his research. So, learning a different language is a language barrier not a disability, which makes all the difference between having a learning disability and not being labelled. They had labelled me as being disabled – unable to learn. I did not believe there was such a thing as dyslexia related to a learning disability. My belief of not having a disability thus impacted my life. In my way of understanding it, my learning/processing knowledge and speaking, writing, and reading were all part of my natural way so were not signs of a true disability, which colonial professionals would not understand.

Therefore, self-reflection is a necessary fundamental factor pertaining to disability and labels as labels contribute to a negative connotation, even if the original intent was to classify educational performance on how well students are able to work, learn, and apply their knowledge in the form of assessments and tests. I understood racism and disability from labels given to me and what I had witnessed. Attending the Indian school had made me resilient. A lot of our kids are still put in that situation that they have learning disabilities. They are labelled and classified as being disabled, which has been a recurrent thread for me since my time at the Indian school until today when meeting students in school.

My understanding of disability meant that I was not functional. I believed that the teachers calling us 'disabled' was, in fact, the same as being told "you are not functional" or "you are irrelevant." This characterization did not speak to me at all. I just saw that the problem was not a disability, but how the teachers and people of authority including directors and supervisors measured, labelled, classified, and understood these actions. You can see and understand the depths of my struggles. I was always worried that people would say I had a "disability". This fear or "insecurity became my handicap". I traced this phobia back to my early schooling. So, the impact of the earlier labelling on my self-confidence made me never feel secure. This intergenerational trauma of labels was forced upon people just because of how they process knowledge.

A lack of compassion by teachers and school administration as well as negative labelling made the challenges of learning worse that many students faced who were labelled harshly. When I worked in a school with Indigenous students, who had been singled out into a separate classroom in special education programs, I asked them what their dreams were, and what they wanted to become. As all of them had been labelled with learning disabilities, they said they were being prepared for menial jobs of cooking and cleaning. I also again saw the parallel between my own school struggles when they tried to push me into cooking classes because of my learning problem. That inspired me to listen to what my students had to say about their dreams, and their choices so that nothing would be a barrier to their success despite what society, school authority, or other small-minded views dictated their actions should be. However, my director did not believe that they could go on to higher education. So, working in this special education program with predominantly Indigenous students it also felt like the Indian school all over again, as the students' lives had already been predetermined by the non-Indigenous school administration. Even though, they were in special education, I knew some of them should be encouraged to go on to university or college. I spoke to them about their dreams and following their heart, which powerfully motivated them. I helped the students by listening to them and hearing about their dreams – what they wanted to do and not what the school director thought they could do.

I refused to lose this uphill battle, so demanded the director call a representative from the school board, who came, but did nothing. These students being treated differently empowered me to push their plight forward to have the school board allow them an equal chance. At the end of the school year, I told the students "Nobody can tell you the contrary. You can do it. I believe in you guys." I had pushed them to have confidence in themselves and go to college or university because I did not want them to encounter what I had gone through and be afraid to be who they were. This experience boosted my resilience because I believed in my students and not what non-Indigenous school officials deemed appropriate for them. I received messages a few years after I had left the school – one was in college and another was in a dream career she had wanted to be in. When thinking about this event, my interaction as a teacher was not merely to instruct my students, but to engage them and allow them all to rise up, instead of being condemned and limited by the school board.

It is, therefore, necessary for teachers to understand their students, their challenges, and their difficulties in the classroom, at home, or in society as ways of connecting instead of bringing division and providing misguided direction or pointless insults. Teachers think students are not interested, but their teaching methods may not actually target the students' learning approach, which only serves to distance the students. Teachers play a crucial role in the lives of their students and have the opportunity to positively mould and guide them, regardless of their learning differences or language background.

Teachers teach without compassion and etiquette. I knew that those students who had a darker skin colour or who were classified as 'different' or struggled with learning (learning disability) had a greater difficulty with their teachers. I saw the teachers as racist and had low expectations of their students. Teachers need to listen to the dreams of the youth, who are going in for doctorate degrees, regardless of their stumbles and the hard times that they have. Nobody is to judge who they are and where they came from. It is necessary for teachers, educators, and professors not to be racist and to support Indigenous students as they progress and let them follow their dreams. Teachers need to understand students and their diverse strengths, regardless of how they present themselves. Their actions, ideas, and dreams must be guided and supported just as I had supported mine going on to doctorate degrees.

This should be taken to heart by all teachers as more than just advice, but as knowledge told through the lived experiences of an Indigenous teacher, who endured what few non-Indigenous teachers would understand. Therefore, teachers from a racist stance, often without compassion have control of a little brown child that looks up to the teacher. The children live practically with the teachers more than with their parents and when that teacher has control of that little brain, they should empower that child, instead of breaking that little child. Every teacher should be considerate that everybody is an individual and precious. I believe that in the roles that teachers, administration, and public service employees play, what is missing is listening and inspiring students. Further to this, abusive labelling and racist language and actions have no part and are non-productive ways of educating, supporting, and stimulating young minds.

2 St. Anne's Indian Residential School – How labelling contributed to disabilities

Elder Peter Nakoochee

Introduction

Elder Peter Nakoochee is from a small island near Moosonee, located in Northern Ontario, but now resides on Fort Albany Indian Reserve. His grandmother had told him to learn English and that with an education, his life would be much easier than theirs. So, he took his grandmother's advice and used English to become a millionaire. He has worked in multiple occupations. When he moved to Moosonee, he became the mayor for two years, followed by the band manager in charge of community business for the chief and council. He was also the regional Indigenous relations officer for the Ontario government and owned the only general store in Moosonee (owned and operated by the Cree community). In Moose Factory, he was a finance director at Chapa Council, with the 'Mushkegowuk Council'. He was also appointed Commissioner by Bob Rae for the Ontario Northland Railway Communications. Peter's lived experiences as an entrepreneur, politician, government worker, and Indian residential school survivor led to his success in becoming a valued source of knowledge.

Time before time

My story is of a boy, who became a 'self-made millionaire'. My original Cree name was 'Ministik', which translates into 'island' because I was born in the bush at 'Hughes Goose Camp', on an island. From my lived experiences, I had knowledge passed down from my grandmother – a glimpse of a time long ago in a land that was divided that would, eventually, become known as Canada. In those days, my grandmother was young, so her grandparents had shared stories about that war. She explained how life was simpler in her community before the war between the French and the British. This early life reflected the dawn of first contact. During this time, there was much killing, and the continuous fighting led to people later finding cannonballs on and around where old Fort Albany was located. People took some of these cannonballs as souvenirs but did not know their history or what their journey was to get where they were my early life was hard, but when you are healthy and strong from walking and pulling to survive, you become used to living a hard life. This resilience built my character as I followed what my grandparents did to thrive.

DOI: 10.4324/9781032656519-4

Indian residential schools, hospitals, and tuberculosis

I grew up in Fort Albany, which had a population of about 501 and later rose to 1,000 as children came to attend St. Anne's Residential School run by Indian Affairs through the Roman Catholic Mission of the Oblates of Mary Immaculate.[1] I was sent to St. Anne's, where I was enrolled from Grade 1 to Grade 4. Although it was a school, the OMI missionaries provided donated clothing from southern charitable Roman Catholic organizations and churches. When my mother dressed me up in new clothes to go to school, all would change once I went back home for break wearing these old recycled, used clothes. Ones that were contaminated with TB were given to Native people in the community. She worked with the missionaries as a cook assistant and she saw that every time the missionaries wanted something, they washed it first. So, she would always wash everything that they got from the missionaries. This fear of getting tuberculosis (TB) was such a traumatic experience that I relate to the coronavirus and washing everything today.

In the 1960s, when the Indian Residential School was fully occupied, it included several buildings, the hospital, and a field where the cows and other livestock were fenced in. The area also included three lakes where the water was used by the residential school missionary staff and acted as a sewer lagoon that flowed into the main river that the Indian reserve accessed, but it was contaminated. This affected the community, as the river was the primary water supply – the place for cleaning clothes and fishing. I was only five years old when I noticed that Indigenous community members were being poisoned and dying of TB. The missionaries, who had been sent to help the 'Indians', in fact, contributed to their decline as it was believed they used TB as chemical warfare against the Indians in those days.

These missionaries also distributed contaminated blankets to the native people, who also got sick and died. From 1960 to 1975, by the time I was 17, the population of 1,500 was reduced to a mere 400 people. None of the missionaries died, nor were held responsible because they were isolating themselves away from the native people. This depopulation was a result in part of TB and other illnesses caused by contaminated water, where lots of people drank it and died and the fish died too as some people picked them up and ate them. We survived the chemical warfare that Canada had given us. We grew up and had fun at the same time, even though there was death all around. Luckily, some people survived who didn't drink from the river, the sewer line from the missionaries, right by the reserve. Thus, the Indigenous people of Fort Albany died because of the contaminated water, TB, or from the trauma at St. Anne's school or the hospital, which left many community members afraid of the missionaries.

Where I grew up, it only had six to seven man-made log houses owned by Cree families on the Island. These homes were built by cutting trees and bringing the logs to the OMI missionaries, who had a sawmill. In order to use this sawmill to prepare the wood to build their houses, the Natives had to give the missionaries half of their lumber. Some other families survived because their blood had high strong iron-rich protein from living off the land. They only had a few store-bought items such as bread, butter, and macaroni and cheese. They also relied on a few other non-food items such as rubber boots, mitts, winter coats and socks, and things like that.

---

1 The Missionary Oblates of Mary Immaculate or most commonly referred to as 'OMI' is a missionary religious congregation within the Catholic Church. It was instrumental in the operations of many Indian residential schools across Canada and in the North.

My knowledge of the OMI missionaries paved the way for my transition from traditional living on the land, speaking Cree and practicing our spirituality, to learning English, practicing Catholicism, and moving away from traditional educational practices. My feelings about the missionaries stem from a mixed perspective as a Catholic Cree, who condemned them for their abusive behaviours towards the people and the land yet praised their ability to convert the people including my family and myself. The Catholics preached to us about being good, while they abused us. This led to total confusion as I praised them yet condemned them at the same time.

In my previous Indigenous ways of life, nobody was hungry. Everyone was able to eat every day. However, it all changed once the missionaries came. They interrupted our culture – the traditional ways, the values, the norms, the beliefs. Life changed. The corruption of our natural way of life resulted in my witnessing first-hand something foreign – greedy people who become competitive people. Their competitive culture collided with and destroyed our sharing culture, the good life. This negative impact on my life transformed me and those around me making us dislike the missionaries, even though many people worked for them. Money and greed were the catalysts for Indian hospitals and residential schools since the Native students were taken to the Indian Residential School. The OMI threatened the family if the worker didn't make his children go to school, the family wouldn't see them again or receive rations. They would be fired, so people used to give up their children to go to school, whether they were healthy or sick with heart conditions, etc., and they let them go and then they were never checked up in the hospital.

This is what happened to my family as my father was threatened, he would lose his job at the nursing station if I did not attend. He let me go, so he wouldn't lose his job and his family, and so my sisters would have food. The children who were known to have TB, had been cured from it, or had other illnesses were sent to the residential school and mixed with others who were healthy, which negatively impacted the other students. So, more students were sent to the Indian hospital, if they were lucky. Those who did not make it died, or never returned home, nor did their families ever know what had happened to them.

People believed that as TB and other illnesses were purposely introduced into St. Anne's school and hospital, sickness was a financial benefit to the missionaries, the RCMP, and those who worked at the hospital since the federal government was covering the costs as a method of ensuring financial stability. I realized then that the RCMP hospital made money out of Native people when they got sick and then when they died, they made money out of it again. When I think about those things, it makes me want to take revenge on the elders. These traumatic experiences at school greatly impacted my life and would forever haunt me with nightmares.

Western education abuse from the notorious St. Anne's

With the colonial education at St. Anne's, there was verbal abuse and mental abuse. During the early interactions with my teachers, I was abused when my father registered me, on my first day of school. I was molested in a washroom – raped. That was the first bad experience I ever had in my life. I was also nervous at school because I did not speak any English at all and had never heard a White man speak except in church. I also got punished severely because the Grade 1 teacher had to ask me my name several times and I always answered "Ministik" as I did not understand what she was saying.

Twice, I was hit for no reason – disciplined, and my hands were so swollen, I could not eat. My friend Bennett buttered my bread and put it in my mouth, piece by piece. A religious brother handing out extra bread passed me, so Bennett explained that I was not able to speak nor lift my hands. So, the brother asked, "What happened to your hand?" I said, "I didn't understand what you said." I just saw him distributing bread so put up my hand. My hands were swollen, but I didn't shout in pain because I was afraid to. My friend, Bennett, told the brother "He got hit hard with a three-foot ruler that had steel lining so his hands got swollen."

Other students were stigmatized because of the way they learned so were also laughed at and mistreated. Then, my friend went missing. Disappearances were not uncommon as children ran away, and got caught and punished for their disobedience. Those who defied the teachers and school administrators were severely punished. I recall seeing students being stripped naked, covered with a blanket, and stood in the hallway, so everybody could see them to make them ashamed. It was a warning also to the other students that this is what happens to runaways. We were hostages in that residential school, working hard inside the basement cutting and piling wood, washing the floor, and cleaning toilets with toothpaste and a toothbrush. When scrubbing toilets, it took all night just to do one washroom, as it had to be spic and span.

I felt great isolation not being able to meet with my older brother in the school as we were not allowed to speak to each other in Cree. We had to speak in English. I did not know that, so I tried to talk to my brother, Abraham, but he wasn't looking at me or even waving. I wondered why he didn't acknowledge me. Not being able to talk with my brother was worse than the abuse. It was a traumatic experience because family relationships are essential in the Cree culture. This led a teacher punishing me right in front of the students to show them none could talk in Cree. I was struck with a belt. It was actually a kind of horse harness. However, my resilience kept me going. I had wanted to run away from that place, but I had heard stories of runaways being killed or severely punished. A student had told me that the teachers would cut your leg off, if you ran away and I had sometimes seen kids who had one leg missing, one foot missing, which prevented me from doing it. It made me stay there in shock. We survived. During this time, I faced the worst parts of schooling.

I had a difficult time writing and reading. I believed I was reading correctly, but instead I saw words reversed, (dyslexia) so I was punished. The nun who read my writing, my ABCs, didn't recognize my letters, so I got into trouble. She thought that I did these things on purpose to make her mad. So, she punished me for not writing the alphabet correctly. She thought I was acting out, which made her angry. When it was my turn to spell the words, I spelled and pronounced them reversed, so I was punished for not writing them correctly. The only learning problem that I believed I had was with my word/letter reversals. I said 's i' for 'is' to which the teacher replied. "No. That's not what is written." I could not change it because that's what I saw written. In fact, I was correct. My writing was not good at all. I was in trouble with my writing. Even though I was wrong, I still strongly believed I was correct. They didn't try to find out what was wrong with me, and why I wasn't able to spell or write properly. I was confused because if I was punished for not being able to learn, why didn't the teachers try to determine what was wrong with me and what was wrong with us those with mental or disability problems? They just thought we were troublemakers, that we were stupid, or crazy, so I believed I was insane and had a mental illness because the priests, teachers, brothers, and sisters taunted me, abused, labelled, condemned me because of the way I learned differently.

I realized that the teachers were unable to understand why I was struggling, which contributed to their abusive treatment of me.

So, she would hit me. She would always point with the same ruler that she used for punishment. I could not change what I said because that's what I saw written on the blackboard – all in reverse. I did not know what was going on as I had to relearn English even the numbers, which were also written down wrong. When the nuns, the teachers, asked me a mathematic question, I answered right, but when she told me to write it down, she said it was wrong. So, I was confused, and then, severely punished.

These learning difficulties resulted in the teachers promoting me grade after grade, even though I had difficulties. They labelled me as if I could not learn like the other students. This impacted my learning development. I was different and considered a mentally challenged. I wasn't disabled or weak because I was strong. I believed in my physical appearance and abilities in strength as I was taller than the other students. Thus, I disagreed with the colonial perspective of disability, which was non-functional. As I could read correctly, I believed that the teacher was perhaps wrong in her judgement. I was ridiculed by other students who made fun of me and called me names. They wanted to kill me because I was different from them. I was about age ten years old, when I was unable to write or spell properly, it was hard. They thought I didn't learn anything at all, but I was able to learn. I was able to speak English, but I couldn't write or spell English the way they wanted because the words I saw were backwards. So, this destroyed me. There I only had two friends. Even my own cousins laughed at me, I had no friends as the rest made fun of me.

What was worse was that my friends and my own family, my cousins, strung me up in the basement because I was different. This was the most difficult part of my experience – at the end of the rope. I was considered a mentally challenged person. The abuse, torment, and physical harm that I had undergone at school were traumatic, but what was more harmful was that my own cousins rejected me because I was unable to learn English. I received the worst treatment from my own family members. I had believed you look after your family. The horrific torment of being beaten by my own family – hung by my cousins was the most disturbing experience as family was a sacred bond, so the betrayal by my own family was the worst type of abuse I could endure. That experience had the most detrimental impact on my education. Family for me is a sacred and essential part of my Cree upbringing.

When I was hung, I actually died, but an angel came down to tell me *"It's not time so he sent me back."* I tried to hold on to the angel, but he held me back. I could feel him, stopping me. I couldn't go any further because when I tried to hang on to him, I couldn't. There was no solid thing that I could hold on to because he was a spirit, and I was a spirit. I didn't want to come back because I was already suffering a lot at school. Once I returned to life, I soon realized something was different. When I came back, I found out my English writing and spelling were different. I didn't know what happened or what was going on. Everything changed. I could see the numbers and letters properly. I had been healed. I was dyslexic then after I died, I didn't have dyslexia anymore. God/Creator's divine intervention had cured me of my disability. My struggles freed my 'dis', but my 'abilities' remained. My negative assessment of a mental illness was transformed, I was reborn without dyslexia – no spelling challenges! This deep spiritual intervention gave me renewed strength and faith, which enabled me to work through my many obstacles and move upwards and forwards in the Creator and Jesus, who for me was the same person. As I moved beyond the confines of St. Anne's and became a worker, I got married and became a prominent member of society. I overcame my difficulties and followed my aspirations.

This act of abandonment by my own family was worse than getting raped by the teacher. The compounding trauma and abuse by the students contributed to my suffering. This was intensified by the teacher's public humiliation of me, which worsened the students' attitude towards me. They thought that I did not want to learn anything at all, but I could learn. My traumatic school experience was challenging. I had been labelled, abused, hanged, beaten, bullied, and kicked by the missionary/teaching staff. I was starved for three days and punished for speaking my language for four long years, which resulted in my being placed in an isolation area, where I was treated like a wild animal in a zoo and tortured. They made me hungry, made me sing, and made me insane. I was considered mentally challenged. This level of abuse and trauma inflicted by this educational system made me believe that I deserved to be abused and labelled with a mental illness by my teachers because I was unable to read and write in English as well as the other children. My teachers made me feel as if I actually had a mental illness because I had, what I now believe was dyslexia. The teachers could not begin to understand my learning needs. Thus, I believed I was not 'normal' and I was different because of what the teachers told me, how they labelled me, and then punished me according to their views at that time, which impacted my development.

Teacher training – Unqualified

All my trauma was a direct result of my school experiences at St. Anne's. The teachers didn't have the knowledge of how to investigate – no common sense to try to figure it out. The teachers were not trained to deal with these learning challenges that I struggled with. They did not understand my challenges. When I realized I couldn't spell properly, it got me into trouble. They thought I was sick, and just promoted me, from Grades 1 to 4. I felt that my learning difficulties were actually a 'mental illness'. The teachers and missionary staff allowed this belief to develop, knowingly or unknowingly, which did not matter because the objective of the Indian schools, at that time, was to civilize the Indians by educating them – a policy of assimilation.

I believed I was broken or damaged, but I needed to know what was wrong with me as I was unable to read and pass Grade 4. The lack of adequate teacher training contributed to my belief that I had a mental illness because of my learning difficulties. This was reinforced by sexual, physical, and psychological torture at the hands of my teachers, which prolonged my belief that I had a sickness that could not be cured. Thus, students labelled with a mental illness were disabled inside them. Outside, they were strong. They were sent out to the opportunity class where teachers tried to help them or just put them aside, so they wouldn't disrupt the regular. I was put there several times because of the problem that I had. I wasn't trying to be bad. I was just unable to learn at the same level as the other students. This special classroom confused me because it was for students who had mental illnesses such as schizophrenia. As I was strong and able to do many things, I did not see myself with a mental illness. I had seen people with schizophrenia and how they acted in society and in school, and I knew I wasn't like that. My challenge was with the way my thoughts processed information – not how I acted.

Thus, my school experiences affected me and my family relations because they abused me for my inability to learn English. I had classroom difficulties, but the problem was also with the teachers, who had not been adequately trained to be teachers. They were not professionals as they really didn't know how to teach. They learned to be teachers, when they came to Fort Albany. They didn't have any professional excuse to become a teacher. It wasn't the teachers' fault because they had not been educated to be teachers. I did not condemn them because their lack of proper training made them unable to do the jobs they were supposed to do in their profession. They learned the things they needed to do. So, when they taught students with mental problems such as schizophrenia, the teachers mistreated them as they were not cooperative.

New life after school experience

Later on, I attended a day school program from Grades 5 to 8, then I set off to learn beyond St. Anne's. My grandmother told me "Why you need to go to school [is] to get educated to speak a different language so you understand them [White people], and you will use it to prosper." I took her advice and I later used that language [English] to become a millionaire I've been able to speak in English to become a mayor and was appointed Commissioner by Bob Rae for the ONR Communications. Learning to speak the English language enabled me to help those who needed it from my reserve, all the way to a provincial authority. That's why I'm able to speak English right now because my grandmother encouraged me to and said, "*You will have a better life. You will have an easy life.*" If it was not for her knowledge, I would be still living off the land and I never would have owned a store, become a politician, or got to where I am today.

For me, living off the land was a negative experience because it was associated with poverty and a lack of ability to achieve success. I knew my learning challenges in school contributed to my traumatic experiences, which enabled me to become the person I am today. Thus, I see education as a good thing, a positive step forward. My grandmother was telling the truth. Learning English became the difference between living off the land (bad) and working off the reserve (good) and building the infrastructure of the community, which is what I accomplished when I owned the store. Western education can help solve the economic despair of living off the land as a trapper compared to learning English and getting a job with greater economic opportunities. Thus, I moved beyond the traditional Cree lifestyle to make it in the new world. Learning English allowed me later to help people who needed help. I took up the educational values of non-Indigenous peoples, which gave me a prosperous life, so I could make money and succeed; whereas others who relied on the traditional ways of learning had to struggle. My learning English motivated by his grandmother's wisdom helped me overcome my trauma from school. Learning English enabled me to become economically independent and successful.

Family, church, and community

This family connection is a sacred healing bond that is bound to protect, care for, and respect everyone in the family regardless of any type of disabilities, physical appearance, or internal compacities. In my overall experience from my perspective as a Cree Elder, I believe family takes care of their own. So, everything is shared – food, all was shared when my grandmother was growing up. This sacred responsibility was based on the culture like the traditional ways, the values, the norms, and the beliefs. Even though I had this trauma with my own cousins turning against me, I overcame that so much, that now, I have an empathetic connection between disability and family care. This is not unheard of. When it comes to disability, mentally or physically, you are on your own with your family. I believe your family will look after you, so you are not destitute and not thrown away like garbage. Thus, this traditional approach towards family responsibility supported those with disabilities. People with disabilities are not seen as a burden and are not the job of the government. This was my understanding that the missionaries took care of those, who had spiritual ailments, diseases, or needed surgery, but once they were 'repaired', then it was the family's responsibility to help complete the healing. This was part of our culture to protect and take care of family members regardless of how they looked or functioned in society.

There are differences between 'disability – mentally or physically', as it affected me as a person, with learning disability due to my inability to learn, compared to my physical appearance, I wasn't disabled because I was strong. There are clear differences between these three types of disabilities that are actually three separate ones – physical as opposed to mental disabilities and clinical illness – they are all grouped together. My struggles with mental illness from classroom abuse by teachers and neglect by my cousins led me to believe that disabilities, learning disabilities, and dyslexia were mental illnesses. I believed I had a mental illness because of what they told me as I had internalized it. This caused significant psychological trauma because my teachers would abuse and label me according to their views and actions. What is wrong with us people? I was trying to understand this confusion within myself. My encounter with abusive teachers contributed to my low self-esteem as I saw both physical and mental disabilities as a bad thing because of how my teachers labelled and punished me.

However, in the Indian hospital, the missionaries took care of everyone regardless of physical or mental conditions. Then, when we got better, they even released those who had a disability or mental health disability, which added to my confusion because if a hospital released a person, with a mental problem/disability, then how could it be something bad? This was further supported by people who had been labelled with a mental problem, yet who were employed. This supported my confusion between physical and mental disabilities as both a bad and not such a bad thing to have, as I saw those labelled being able to work and make money.

Regardless, though, of what type of physical, mental, or clinical disability a person had, they were still all considered equally as functioning members of the community. Even the disabled ones were working, even the mental health, ones and the schizophrenics were working there too. People with disabilities – one arm missing, one leg missing – were still working in a special job that they were able to handle, and they got paid for, but not as much as the able ones. For instance, the ladies were paid less than a man and the disabled paid like a woman.

These people were able to work, even though they were classified as being disabled. They had a job despite being disabled – like potato cutting, looking after the vegetables, cleaning, when they had one hand, they attached an arm to them to be able to hold things through while they were filing away some axes or bucksaws. They were able to contribute to society, despite their physical appearance and mental capacity. Mental disabilities and clinical illnesses are interchangeable because they both depict how the brain reflects the challenges of learning, which also includes dyslexia.

Regardless of how people were classified or labelled, what mattered was looking after the community. That included serving in various positions that increased the autonomy of those who resided in Fort Albany and in Moosonee. My grandmother had spoken about how all had changed since the first contact. Then, later with the missionaries, the community, and the people who lived there all continued to change.

This notion of community bound me, especially as I knew I would return home for school break after ten months of school to be with my family. Family was the only place where I could be myself without fear of punishment, being labelled, or having to fear any type of abuse.

Spiritual healing/dream knowledge

I experienced an interesting divine intervention or spiritual healing. I recall my own outer body experience. The divine connects to reality to bring healing and interweaves Catholicism and Cree spirituality. These spiritual interventions are provided to those who endure much pain and hardship because they are the ones who will contribute to society. With my personal struggles with dyslexia, I experienced a series of incidents. One man accidentally shot himself, right through the stomach, so he was in St. Anne's hospital. The nuns were waiting for him to die, so they asked him if he wanted to live. He said, 'yes'. So, they operated on him and gave him painkillers. During his postoperative care, he lay in bed near a man who had schizophrenia, who was also recovering. He saw little black things come running around and go under his bed and pulling his blankets. He didn't want to die, and those little things went straight to grab him to die, so he stayed on top of the bed and hung on. When the priest came in to bless the man with the holy water, those little things ran off. This man shared his story about his experience with my uncle, which shocked me as he knew this man had never gone to church before because he was an atheist. This led me to interpret that people with mental illnesses such as schizophrenia are not disabled but in fact are possibly possessed by 'demonic spirits' or 'little devils'. I found out that this man had recovered from his injuries and decided to live and converted to Catholicism. That's how our religion became really, really strong because of those two people who talked about their near-death experience ... They strengthened our faith in the Roman Catholic faith.

My faith gave me the strength to fight off those 'demons' that were keeping me away from overcoming learning disabilities, mental illnesses, and dyslexia. I believed that people with schizophrenia might not have a medical problem because they were either possessed by the devil or had abilities to see or interpret what normal people could not. This powerful revelation occurred to me and the people I knew and enabled a glimpse into the spiritual connection between mental illness and disabilities. These connections were important as they helped me gain a new understanding of mental illness beyond what teachers and missionaries told me.

This new steadfast connection and dedication that I had – as the Native people – were still worshiping the Creator not knowing that the Creator and Jesus were different. He's the same God – that's what they believe. When you read the book about Him translated from English to Cree, it's parallel to the belief that we have in our Native religion. From my time away from my family, I saw those situations within a spiritual compacity, that's how we survived during the residential schools.

These divine interactions led me to understand what mental illness and dyslexia are within my own understanding. These challenges were directly linked to the Creator – as God and the angels look after me. There are lots of stories about punishment, abuse, and stuff like that. However, that's okay because the one that created us looks after us. Every time we suffer – we get paid for it. The Creator doesn't forget those things. When you have a strong belief in the Creator, you won't walk the wrong way. Even though you may suffer, you still keep walking with the Creator. If you walk the wrong way, you will suffer;

you will lose everything. Thus, if I had disobeyed the Creator, I would have become an alcoholic and probably would have died a long time ago.

This suffering at school made me resilient so I could move past my troubled school experiences and become the man I am today. However, my past still haunts me with flashbacks. Sometimes, my dreams are realistic. I dream that I am back at the residential school, and it doesn't stop, it doesn't go away, but when I woke up, I then realize the dream was actually a nightmare, a terror so I prayed *'please don't hurt me'*. I am a survivor and my faith in the Creator and Jesus is what gives me strength, especially during those troublesome evenings. I then remember that someone died for me and suffered greater than the way I suffered. That's why I survived. That's when you have a strong belief in the Creator.

3 Interpreting disabilities from a Mohawk perspective

Elder guidance when navigating the dreamworld

Elder Tom Dearhouse

Introduction

Elder Tom is Mohawk and Ojibway from the Kahnawake Mohawk reserve in the province of Québec. His father was Mohawk from Kahnawake, across the river from Montréal and his mother was Ojibwa from Garden River. Tom is a health, healing, wellness, and cultural justice Elder from Kahnawake, who resides in Salaberry-de-Valleyfield, Québec. He was born in Detroit, Michigan, in 1963 and grew up in Detroit away from his culture, his people, and their knowledge until he moved to Kahnawake. Growing up in Detroit as an urban Indigenous person was difficult, so connecting to his culture was mostly through the Friendship Center, which is where Tom's mother worked, and where his parents met. Due to his early urban Indigenous upbringing, whether he knew it or not, he spoke from the two-eyed-seeing[1] perspective.

Tom's education started with his mother's teachings from the Friendship Center, which continued while he attended elementary school, then to a private high school, which was known as the 'University of Detroit High School'. It gave him a worldview understanding that opened his eyes.

As he was unable to get a work placement for his Bachelor's degree, which was essential for graduating, he went into Social Work where he received a diploma in 1977, which gave him his calling. All this led him to become what he is today – an Elder in healthcare addressing the needs of community members in their desire to heal by bridging the traditional (Lodge House) and colonial (Catholicism and outside professionals) so that he offered services in response to the diverse needs of his community for members who live on-off-reserve and in the United States. Tom now works as a social worker on his reserve, while serving as an Elder in a multitude of capacities from education, healing, and spiritual both Mohawk and Catholicism. In these multi-roles, he is able to reach out and help many people in either Mohawk, French, and/or English language. As a young Elder, who embraced both traditional and colonial educational practices, he gave a unique perspective aligned with Mohawk community members, who reside on and off-reserve, from traditional or are mixed families, regardless of their political, spiritual, and cultural upbringing.

---

1 The Two-Eyed-Seeing approach was brought forth by Mi'kmaq Elders Albert and Murdena Marshall. This approach to viewing a topic or situation from a colonial and Indigenous perspectives to come, to a conclusion or resolution both viewing through this dualistic approach.

DOI: 10.4324/9781032656519-5

Early years – Mohawk learning

In 1976, my grandmother passed away, so I went to visit family in Kahnawake, which was not a place that I went often. A turning point in my life occurred in 1984 as my father's 79-year-old uncle's health had deteriorated. He was a double amputee confined to a wheelchair so needed medical care and continuous supervision as he was diabetic. As there was no one else he could rely on for support, I decided to help him for just a month, which soon turned into one year. That is where I am today as a social worker. When I moved into my uncle's house, I was there to take care of him, take him to the hospital, give him medication, cook and feed him, and take care of his house and other responsibilities as a social worker and personal support worker – all rolled into one with multiple duties. This allowed me to have a place to live and eat for free, but it was not easy at first. With patience and hard work, my uncle taught me how to cook, repair things around the house, and learn about my Mohawk culture and history. All this brought me closer to my Mohawk side as I learned how to speak Mohawk and learned through oral history. Taking care of family members is a well-known Indigenous cultural practice; however, what is uncommon is to have extended family members as caregivers, unless close members are unable or unwilling to do so, which is almost unheard of. Taking care of relatives, even if they are not directly related happens among many Indigenous societies. Family is supposed to take care of one another, but, occasionally, underlying issues make it necessary for other distant family to intervene. However, this relationship between my uncle and myself turned out beneficial for me as I could redeem my Mohawk side.

Involved in community

Although I was a social worker, due to my lack of experience in the field, there was not much work in my area. This led me to work in different other capacities where I was able to become involved in my culture and became an active community member. In 1985, I joined the Knights of Columbus, which was like a social club, which enabled me to meet more. The following year in 1986, I joined the fire department, which then led me to become a Certified Ambulance Technician in 1986, which combined well with my volunteer firefighting in the community.

The year it all changed

The tension between Kahnawake (Mohawk/English speakers) and Québec (French speakers) resulted in unresolved political unrest fuelled by miscommunication, poor federal and provincial relations, and their inability to conduct pre-emptive measures with negotiations. This led to the Oka Crisis of 1990, when Kahnawake was triple in size and the land was seized by the government. This history of miscommunication has never ended, so it was a very complex issue. Life got interesting and intense with the Oka Crisis,[2] as there were blockades and barricades set up throughout Mohawk territory. As part of the Emergency Response Team, the army set up militarized zones through checkpoints, my group was trained and prepared for incoming casualties. For many people, this was

---

2 See page 203 for Oka Crisis Reference.

a deliberate attack at gunpoint on their homeland, which resulted in a forcible retaliation. The French (Québec Government) has historically oppressed Indigenous peoples, especially those who do not support Québec's language act, Bill 101 regarding 'speaking only French' as Mohawks speak their own language and English. This defiance against Québec authority dates back to when the Mohawks arrived in Canada from their traditional territories – now the United States. There's an ongoing process with Canada's federal negotiators, but they have a mandate, probably not to settle or compromise. Kahnawake has come a long way through compromising on these things. Some things one can't compromise on.

This compromise of shrinking the Mohawk territory with its population density, while being surrounded by a non-Indigenous French-speaking population contributed to the traumatic situation. This resulted in my understanding the importance of both Mohawk and Canadian (French and English) histories. Thus, I developed my knowledge-gathering process towards reconciliation – essential for my community.

Reconciliation and rejuvenation

In 1993, I studied social work at Carleton University in Ottawa to go with my other skills as a personal support worker, volunteer firefighter, and emergency medical responder – all added to my expertise in helping my community and its members. As a social worker student, it made me look inwards at my past and reflect on my father having been an alcoholic, so this dysfunction had put shame on me when I was younger. I reflected on my younger days when I had failed mechanical engineering in Detroit, which had been a huge psychological blow. Realizing life in Detroit had not been for me, I began my path towards reconciliation – first by acknowledging my own faults, which is essential as a social worker. Moving forward and helping people would be a positive step ahead and with the strength and knowledge that I had obtained, I could become a driving force.

In 1994, I got my first job working at Kahnawake Shakotiia'takehnhas Community Services, within a drug and alcohol prevention program where my responsibilities were with the teenage group. The stress from that, along with that accumulated from the Oka Crisis, was too much for me so I took a break as many people were relying on the Community Services in the post-Oka trauma era. This time away from work allowed me to rejuvenate by taking courses, drug and alcohol prevention programs, and workshops on trauma, grief, intergenerational effects, and residential schools. I also worked for the Easter Door newspaper, which allowed me to connect with community events, members, and cultural activities, while helping those in need.

Eventually, I tried politics and ran against my cousin as a band council member, which I won and held from 1998 to 2000. This experience also referred to as a 'chief' was governed by the Grand Chief. This position made me aware of issues that were not always well presented. It gave me the chance to learn and contribute my knowledge, which was focused on health, well-being, community development, and reconciliation efforts. This opportunity opened the door for him to see all levels of community engagement, which I focused on when conducting trainings as a caseworker at Kahnawake Shakotiia'takehnhas Community Services. In 2001, I became a support worker for troubled youth, which was not an easy role, especially, when dealing with parents, who thought their kids could do no wrong. This challenging role also took its toll.

The red path

At this time, during a path of traditional learning, I began to gather from Elders, Grand-mothers, and Knowledge Keepers within the Long House – going to ceremonies and not just Mohawk, but just about anything that had a spiritual nature. Elders from the Long House gave me my first pipe in about 2002. Pipe ceremonies are used by various First Nations in a wide range of compacities surrounding sharing and honoring people. I was gifted a bowl by my brother, who is a faith keeper because I was on my path as a healer. I made a stem for it and then a bag that became my own unique pipe. The pipe is smoked in circles, sunrise ceremonies, and during fasts as a pipe is for all people. I use my pipe for healing and bringing people together, which is one of my roles in my community. This journey of self-learning and understanding provided me with what I was missing as it connected me with my Mohawk spirituality as a holistic source of strength and power that could be used for natural non-medicated healing. There were teachings given by Lakota Elders and members who participated in the American Indian Movement, who shared their knowledge, struggles, and resilience. Members were there from the Pine Ridge Reservation and shared their struggles during the 1970s.

I learned from traditional methods of healing such as drumming, sacred songs, sweats, pipe ceremonies, and even Sundance ceremonies – all had contributed to my growth and strengthened my connection to my people. This bonding of the old and young made my learning a fun and honorable way to be educated. These knowledge-gathering situations enabled me to further my fight towards reconciliation by weaving in traditional knowl-edge that has its own strength, wisdom, and healing capabilities. I recounted that I was one of only a few Mohawks social workers at the time, who implemented traditional approaches to healing when helping those with developmental delays – the handicapped, elderly, youth, and workers – all contributed towards strengthening the community in their own way and included some non-Indigenous workers. I also worked at the First Peo-ples Justice Centre as an Elder for cultural resources within the suburbs of Kahnawake, known as Montréal. There are a lot of smart people, but none have that wisdom to know and know how to explain it, but its life experiences combined with their mental ability, combined with direction. Those who share knowledge have their limitations because we must admit that we don't know everything, just have the faith to go through some things or our ordeals that we have to go through.

Giving back

I enjoyed working with a young Indigenous student who was doing his co-op with me at Kahnawake Shakotiia'takehnhas Community Services. He had lived with vari-ous Elders in their communities – Six Nations, Micmac, and with those throughout the United States. His story was similar to mine as both had struggled in school and dropped out, but through my advice and courage, he took courses, finished his high school and went on to pursue an undergraduate degree in social work, while work-ing for me. This mentorship linked both a traditional and academic perspective and areas of healing, well-being, and reconciliation that helped many Indigenous people in Canada as well as in the United States. The legacy of our youth and those who seek out an Elder's knowledge and guidance for the greater good will become leaders and heal-ers in their own right. This is why as Mohawk social workers, there is a great need to acknowledge the intergenerational problems and colonialism that have impacted our resilience. The ability to help those in need by organizing medical and health professionals within our ways of healing will go that much farther.

I chose this path to follow because of my personal struggles connecting with my Mohawk side and bridging the traditional knowledge of the Long House and from a colonial perspective, Catholicism. I believe that this is the best way to offer multiple ways of healing for those who seek out help. It's all about truth and reconciliation and healing. That's another part of my work. I work with families, former students, and grandparents who went to residential schools and suffered the effects. So, we're still seeing it several generations afterwards. That's my area of grief and healing and rebuilding the language or use of the language by reviving the culture and traditional methods. Among my other duties and responsibilities, I am also a traditional support counsellor, social worker, community legal advisor, pipe carrier, land-based teacher, conductor of ceremony and besides Mohawk, I speak English, French, Central Ojibway as well as Lakota.

The influence of colonialism and labelling

I have a distrust of colonial influences because of unresolved land disputes, which had reduced the land of Kahnawake. This resulted in many members such as myself having to move off-reserve, while they worked and had families on the reserve. This negatively affected its current economic, social, health, legal, cultural, and educational resources, and cultural connections. It further impacted the people's lives, by exacerbating the challenges of people as it hurt their well-being and self-esteem, especially those with disabilities.

As colonialism and the Indian agents enforced assimilation policies, Indigenous healing ceremonies were forbidden and had to be conducted in secret. It was a survival tactic for them, that when they practised their traditional ceremonies in their own language, they did it wearing the clothes they would attend Catholic services in. Sometimes there were people who were snitches or spies for the Indian agent, who would drop in. They were really trying to disrupt the ceremony, so the people had to be very cautious. This act of colonialism was done, we do it to ourselves that we adopt outside influence.

This clash of cultures created alternate ways of understanding those who learn differently, how we report, judge, and label people as not as good as others from the community. We're guilty of it ourselves by using labels or a different way of thinking that may not be the best way to treat our own people. One of the most destructive elements there are when helping people with disabilities, learning disabilities, mental health, and physical trauma is the impact of Western professionals, who use their positions of authority to label Indigenous people and assign negative stereotypes. This contributes to those who struggle being overwhelmed by fighting colonialism and this colonized thinking. Whenever we hear a doctor, psychiatrist, or someone in authority, a specialist, say '*this is the diagnoses*'. Sometimes that person will take it to heart, and they'll internalize it and think they have no hope, or very little hope of changing or any future in their life, and that's just coming from being a hurt person…an accumulation of hurts – part of the personality, part of the environment, family history.

There is a divide between 'Western professionals', who knowingly limit those who seek out help in this money-making profession, as opposed to other 'Western professionals', who embrace cultural diversity and allow their minds and hearts to open to see how mental health and people with disabilities are able to overcome situations that they are bound to. Professionals should provide alternative methods that include the Indigenous community and work with members as a way of completing the circle within a holistic pedagogy.

The impact of labels might not be seen as a detriment to these non-Indigenous professionals as they are not fully aware of how labels impact a person, who has already faced intergenerational traumas, abuse from Indian residential schools and or racism. Labels contribute to the impact of colonialism, accessing Western services, and racism can be seen and felt when trying to access these services that may not always be accessible to those who lose their 'Indian status', rejected by family or are caught between the traditional and western lifestyles with their mixed children.

Understanding disabilities within a two-eyed-seeing approach

I use the two-eyed-seeing approach from my shared knowledge and stories. This approach gives insight into both Indigenous and Western/colonial perspectives as they relate to Mohawk people, who reside on and off-reserve when accessing mental health, social, and educational services. This two-eyed-seeing focuses on what would be called alternative methods of teaching or learning. It might actually do very well in a different environment, as opposed to an office or clinical setting. This perspective of the varied healing approaches for learning disabilities and mental health draws on Mohawk and colonial methods to show the necessity of both to provide a balance that can shift in either direction. Thus, clients have different choices to follow, which enables a more flexible approach. These include meeting clients outdoors, in parks, inside a healing lodge, or at the person's home. This flexibility of providing healing within a traditional distinctions-based lens on the reserve or to provide alternative colonial methods in the city, all help in their capacity to provide the best of both worlds.

Colonial professionals have a history of labelling people who are different and do not fit into what society deems 'normal' behaviour. These people do not ask to be labelled but want to be included. This is more than just a Mohawk teaching. There are differences between Mohawk and colonial understandings of physical or mental differences, as many Indigenous peoples include a spiritual awareness, which includes everyone regardless of people's abilities. Indigenous philosophy sees the person as whole so does not assess, who they are or predetermine what challenges or limitations they will encounter.

One of the challenges I saw was what happens to people who rely on their parents or family members for support, and what happens to them when that member passes away? This big sudden void in the social structure can be overwhelming for anyone, especially for those who are not well-adjusted. How does anyone handle grief? I think it's more challenging for someone with autism or Asperger's to understand because no one's really taught, Does anyone really teach us how to grieve as kids? The more difficult grieving and healing that people with learning disabilities/differences have to go through as we see examples from different cultures. I know some are big into crying and wailing, emotional outbursts. It is a life experience that should be taught beforehand ideally because some people are stuck in grief and sometimes layers of grief. This combining of situations of unresolved grief can lead to healing from the bad things that happen by teachings of energy work, grief work, travel work, solar retrieval, etc. It's "based on the concept of having nine lives."[3] These issues add to an already overburdened lifestyle that has been compounded by abuse, traumas, and lived experiences. There is a need to offer help to those who struggle, so they can access ways of coping with loss and trauma.

---

3 This is a Mohawk philosophy (teachings from Kahnawake) of counting lives – everyone is born with nine lives but how they live determines their longevity.

Even those who are born differently such as a child with Down's syndrome bring happiness to families because, even though, they have been labelled as having a disability by Western standards, they are not considered as being disabled from a Mohawk understanding as they don't think they're different. Down syndrome children have the physical attributes, so they don't look the same – not sure about the mental functioning, but they bring families together and this gift brings if it's possible, more love between parents and couples and more attention. This is why people, who have been labelled as disabled, may act differently depending on their social and community connections. Thus, people with Down Syndrome from a two-eyed approach can be seen as disabled yet functional as they provide unconditional happiness to their parents to bring families together. This is an 'ability' and not a disability because they are seen as a gift. This can make all the difference between actually being 'disabled' as opposed to how society sees it and imposes a label that can be limiting.

Some people, either men or women, were seen as good counsellors because they understood both sides. It is these differences that make humanity interesting as we each have our own disabilities and abilities, but it is how we assess them that defines who we really are. Sometimes people are limited, but they are gifted in other ways. I found it interesting to explore, for instance a person who dreams a lot with mental illness, whereas Western understanding of bipolar and schizophrenia, it's not so clear. They're prescribed medicine.

We're fortunate in Kahnawake as we have people such as with Asperger's who have these gifts as they relate to learning disabilities. They might be socially awkward in some areas, but they're actually good in other areas. They might have been good at having lucid, vivid dreams. Working with a client who has these dreams and has gone through a lot of traumas in his life may have been working through things. This person needs to talk these out. He's finding his own answers through his dreams – his own way of working through his challenges.

There are some

success stories, and there's actually sad stories. People who have taken their lives. One man in his 50s suffered from a drug induced psychosis and then schizophrenia. He was financially stable with a disability and I helped him. Unfortunately, this man's family not being active in his well-being, added to struggles, which resulted in his taking his bicycle right up to the Mercier Bridge and jumping off the bridge. I didn't see it coming. No one could have predicted it. He didn't tell anybody. So, who knows what was in his mind? It is a real challenge working with people, who suddenly commit suicide, There's no way to predict a person's actions working with someone, where you can improve their chances of that success and work on factors that you can control the environment, their education, the services that you provide, the activities that you run etc. including the family. There must be an understanding of the individual and their struggle must be placed in the center and one works around it. Successes can be positively impacted by the participation of the community, but you have to make time to work harder to make them feel inclusive.

There are additional contributing factors such as involvement with doctors, psychiatrists, and family doctors and importantly, the family too needs to be, at the very least, knowledgeable about the illness, so they can be as supportive as possible. Family support is important, especially, in an Indigenous community as the family structure is embedded in the social fabric of the community. Although there are contributing factors that make it challenging to predict how people will react to intervention and remediation, these different characteristics can be an accumulation of multiple intersectionalities that interweave with a spiritual element of an individual to provide steps for healing.

Mohawk residents – 40–50-year-olds are put in the Douglas Hospital, and actually reside there, and then are taken advantage of being labelled. Someone actually lost their life there.

It was a rehabilitation institution that encouraged patients to come and go as they wished, but unfortunately, a young Indigenous woman disappeared and turned out someone hid in the bushes and took her life. This murder "made the newspaper story and headline for a while". However, the bigger picture is maybe the residents of Douglas, if they were labelled as mental illness clients are seen as less than or not as valuable.

The community and the family have to advocate for their family members, who are in this category, for lack of a better word – Asperger's, having a mental illness or dyslexia or some kind of delays. There is a need for advocating and finding someone in the medical profession, specialists, and psychiatrists. There's a psychiatrist with a heavy French accent whose background is as a transcultural or intercultural psychiatrist. He believes in including the community, and the culture, in the treatment, the psychosocial aspect, and dealing with when he prescribes the medication, but he believes the key part is the family. Where is the family support? Where are they at? And is the patient able to work part-time? What are their interests and activities? Are they part of their community or not? This cultural understanding is a way of bridging both the Mohawk and colonial methods towards recovery, healing, well-being, and reconciliation by combining both systems by the two-eyed-Seeing so that they can coexist, which allows the client to move back and forth between both systems.

Non-Western medicated intervention

Two-eyed-seeing has seers and healers from a traditional Indigenous perspective, which does not require medication, long-term hospitalization, or other methods that change the person or their ability to move beyond their situation. Indigenous philosophy, spirituality, and healing ways can provide alternative methods that are less aggressive because a spiritual component is utilized in conjunction with community practices and holistic engagement. However, with my lived experiences and two-eyed-seeing, I would also indicate that medication could help, it could be a gift that needs to be developed. These alternative medicine measures that are on the rise can provide a lasting positive effect.

Seers and healers have been a part of my community as a way of healing as many of them have followed their own path of struggles, hardships, and overcome these, which gives them a unique perspective based on their lived experiences, which can be offered to those who seek out help. Some of those seers and healers have endured their mental illness, schizophrenia, and bipolar disorder, especially when people are hearing things. One community member moved from victim to healer. This person described his start as a seer, who "had overcome personal struggles dealing with mental illness and trauma and always spiritually reached out to his mother' with his personal struggles. He also used tobacco and through his spiritual connections, he got to a place where he understood his difficulty a bit better. He actually helped himself and he was able to be in a role of helping others. He uses this life experience because there are people out there currently with symptoms of mental illness.

This person who had struggled as a seer used his gift in conjunction with tobacco to provide a spiritual connection, which enabled him to be in a state of mind, a place of harmony where he could understand what was happening and how to remedy it without relying on medication. The guy helped himself, which enabled him to go forth and help others as well in a role as a healer. This self-healing from within, by using tobacco and other holistic approaches, can be a way of providing non-medicated intervention. This can be puzzling to non-Indigenous, especially, white professionals within the medical field. Many people have been labelled and medicated as struggling with mental illnesses. There are root situations that occur, but if one doesn't address them, but only medicates them, or labels them, it undermines the individual, so they take on the label. This alternative healing with homeopathic medicine such as the use of tobacco alleviates and provides a non-colonial medication that can overcome their struggles.

I understand the unique abilities and talents that people have, when looking at the spiritual part because that's something that's not always looked at, in Western/medical approaches when you work on that – it gives an inclusive part. You are part of something like community. This ability to connect spiritually is lacking in colonial language, attitudes, and approaches, which try to understand people, who learn differently and express themselves in such a way that society judges them as different. It is difficult to be critical of a person's physical appearance, learning differences, and different abilities when the practice and teachings of spirituality are applied.

Kahnawake and the city of Montreal's health and well-being as partners provide additional services, while Indigenous people can still access traditional healing applications, such as sweat, smudging, using tobacco, etc. In addition to these services, the Mackay Center in Montreal offers programs for learning how to read and for those who are dyslexic. It provides funding opportunities for those who might not have access to specialized learning from grade school to pre-university and this successful place has enabled many community members to go in to be veterinarians, become doctors, or lawyers. These outside support facilities that they might not have access to, along with the community, that help struggling youth overcome challenges. This has given them the chance to showcase what they know, who they are, where they are from, and where they are going. The two-eyed-seeing embraces the values of Western and Indigenous interventions from the health and well-being applications towards disabilities and mental health.

While providing traditional teachings, I compared students who have been labelled as having a disability or mental illness, who have an extra sensory perception, so are able to sense weather patterns. So, they say when the rains come, the leaves flip over, like maple trees, but if you see the rain is coming, the winds pick up the leaves that ordinarily have the green facing up, and they'll flip over to the lighter green – that's not a coincidence. There is also the notion of smelling, senses, or knowing when it will rain with headaches. These abilities are seen as a gift. Some people know about medicines, and about what to do for high blood pressure, what to do for someone who got badly hurt, with a fractured skull, or for addictions. From a spiritual perspective, you ask a corn spirit to clear the mind and protect that person. The corn's natural healing ability will be passed on to the one who has asked it to share its medicine – its natural healing ability within the silk. This natural holistic knowledge or life science of the bush helps one adapt to one's natural surroundings, as they know what to do. I believe in the science and the medical that they're there for our help and if they needed anyone for any other help that they couldn't provide. I'd be there to help them. The two-eyed-seeing approach to both science and medicine is essential, as well as the application of the cultural teachings from an Indigenous community perspective, which is based on the spirituality of Indigenous and colonial.

Seers as teachers – Peacemaker and Hiawatha

Peacemaker, a Huron, brought peace to the Iroquoian peoples. He had a Mohawk name which is not supposed to be repeated, but it's Kariwi:io. Peacemaker met Hiawatha crying as he was wandering in the bush because his daughters had died. He needed someone to console him. Peacemaker heard his grief and told him that he had heard him and understood him. Peacemaker offered to wipe his eyes and offered him encouragement. Peacemaker had a speaking disability but shared his wisdom and knowledge with Hiawatha and listened to his misery about the loss of his daughters. Repeating what Peacemaker was trying to say aloud, enabled Hiawatha to overcome his trauma. This act of kindness and well-being qualified Hiawatha to become Peacemaker's interpreter, which he needed because of his speaking disability. The two became an integral part of the Great Law of Peace as, by accommodating each other's inability to communicate, they overcame both their disabilities.

Hiawatha needed to hear Peacemaker's message, so Hiawatha agreed to help him. This enabled Peacemaker's message to go out despite his severe speech impediment/stutter. Thus, Hiawatha communicated his message to him. This coming together of two different peoples, from different places, who had their own challenges/disabilities to work through was prophesied and they found an accommodation for themselves. Thus, the word of peace was spread throughout the Iroquoian peoples. Together, they would lead to the origin of the Iroquois Confederacy of the 50 Chiefs, which paved the way for governance and peace, that was later adopted by Benjamin Franklin as the model for the newly formed United States Constitution as Benjamin Franklin was a big proponent of the idea of consensus. Each person has a voice … one vote per person.

The message of Peacemaker was mainly that he was chosen by the Creator to bring the Great Law of Peace. This was later copied by other governments of other nations. This all originated from a man who stuttered, but who did not allow his speech impairment or disability to get in the way of what the Creator wanted him to do. That is quite powerful.

Trauma impacts learning disabilities – Healing and well-being impact mental illness

People with Asperger's considered a range of functioning are actually good in other areas, which shows how a learning difference can either be a disability or an ability, depending on the situation, lifestyle, and work environment. I believe learning disabilities come in a wide range of differences that include autism and mental illness, which can serve in both a negative and a positive way.

Again, by using two-eyed-seeing, which I gained in my schooling background one can have healing and hope by sharing this blend of both the traditional path as well as the colonial path regarding health, well-being, and 'the good path'. This enables one to function in either society that does not always accommodate people with learning differences. Once a person was wielding a knife at his mother, and she had to explain what his anxiety was, which allowed me to intervene and provide a holistic approach to de-escalate the event. Traditional healing such as offering tobacco could alleviate the situation by providing a safe space that enabled the person to understand their circumstances better. Thus, within colonial intervention, I could diminish the event, which could have transpired into a greater traumatic experience. Many people that I have helped had attended Indian residential schools or members of their family had, which contributed to their struggles with learning disabilities and mental health because of the traumas regarding their well-being of body, mind, spirit, and their emotions.

When healing a person, in either Indigenous ways or colonial ways, it is necessary for them to be in a safe space. This is a fundamental step towards healing and reconciliation as many of my clients have been victimized by labels related to disabilities, learning disabilities, and mental illness placed upon them during their time in Indian residential schools. Then, this trauma has been passed down to other family members. Some community members who reside off-reserve are still able to access services where they live or within the community. This connection to and way of identifying with one's own culture can be a strong driving force in healing. It is really all about truth, reconciliation, and healing too. I work with families who have endured so much as a result of the residential schools and it has impacted all community members. Their struggle for healing and the type of healing can vary whether it is colonial or traditional and by using both ways, and including Indigenous ceremonies is a good way of connecting with people on and off the reserve and helping those who need it.

4 Disability interpretation from colonial insight to Indigenous spirituality

A Ihanktonwan Dakota and Chickasaw realization

Chief Phil Jane Jr

Introduction

Phil Jane Jr. is a member of the Ihanktonwan Dakota in North Dakota and Chickasaw Nations of Oklahoma but was born at the Haskell Indian School in Lawrence, Kansas. He is an Elder and Hereditary Chief of the Hinhan Wicasa and Deloria Tiospayes of the Ihanktonwan Dakota, as well as an international speaker and treaty negotiator, he has engaged in dialogue building throughout the world and spoken at the United Nations. From 1980 to 1996, he was a professor at the Faculty of Education at the University of Lethbridge, Alberta, Canada where he followed in the footsteps of his grandmother, Ella Deloria, along with his cousin Vine Deloria Jr.

The process of becoming an Elder and later a Chief is by no means an easy task; there are many hurdles and struggles along the path as an Indigenous person. After leaving the Haskell Indian School, Phil followed a path to become an educator, at the National University in California where he pursued a master's degree in education, then later Public Administration at the University of Washington. This propelled him to become an Indigenous leader in human and community development like his father. It allowed him to bridge both worlds (colonial and Indigenous) in what he could see as a need for healing humanity which he refers to as "healing the hurts,"[1] – his motto. In 1982, he along with various Indigenous Elders and spiritual leaders from Canada, the United States, and Mexico created the Four Worlds International Institute, which later became the Four Worlds University that could connect Indigenous peoples from around the world by providing a safe place to learn, regardless of status.

Early years

My mother is a Chickasaw, while my father was Tankton Sioux, Ihanktonwan Nation. They met at the Indian school because the American government clustered together tribes from different states into one area for schooling. This coupling resulted in Phil's birth. I lived at the Haskell Indian School for my first three years. Much of my early experience with White people, primarily teachers, doctors, and other social service members were negative experiences that stemmed from the healthcare system as my mother had to rely on the advice of the medical staff, who she believed knew all about child-rearing. This trust almost led to my dying as an infant because of the recommendation of the White

---

1 This expression of 'healing the hurts' led to the 'Healing the Hurts Uncut' documentary by The Four Worlds International Institute. See video clip: https://www.fwii.net/video/healing-the-hurts-uncut

DOI: 10.4324/9781032656519-6

medical staff, which resulted in my malnutrition. This contributed to an intergenerational trauma from my mother to me so as to not fully accept what non-Indigenous colonial authorities deemed necessary, but they did not have a clue. Their belief in a colonial superior mindset contributed to my early struggles and health condition, which was a mistake that would not be repeated again.

I would like to clarify that there may be readers, who might take offense to some of my early interactions and teachings, especially regarding the Indian boarding schools or Indian industrial schools, which were similar to the Indian Residential Schools that Canada had. The Haskell Indian School was modeled after the 'Carlisle' which was an Indian Industrial School located in Carlisle, Pennsylvania.[2] My boarding school had brought in Indigenous people from various parts of the United States. However, if it weren't for this school, my parents would not have met and I would not be here today – to share my knowledge, testimony, and lived experiences with you.

How did these Indian boarding schools contribute to unity

The long-term impact of these boarding schools is referred to as an intergenerational trauma that greatly impacted all those who attended them. Many Indigenous peoples would meet for the first time there as they had left their traditional territories and come to one location. This would bring about a new unity as it caused all these different children to unite and bind together and protect one another. This coming together as a community with a shared experience of being traumatized and abused became the primary driving force to unite. Now, I am not trying to justify these schools. They were horrendous, but at the same time, we have to understand how these schools contributed in the long run by building an early resilience – as a strength for change. This change brought about Indian Nations coming together as they did as students in those schools. This unity formed the American Indian Movement (AIM) and included the National Congress of American Indians (NCAI) with many other organizations because of this coming together.

My experience in these early days allowed me to become the person I am today through many struggles, and these situations allowed me to navigate my own destiny when encountering racism; then colonialism through education, where we were, as Indigenous people trained to become like White people. This made me realize what it meant to be an Indian in the 1960s and 1970s in America, which was the time of the American civil rights movement. My perspective of being an Indian living in a world that was dominated by White colonial authorities, who believed their own mindset to be superior over anyone else's, became my driving force for the unity of Indigenous peoples through healing trauma, which was a direct result of their time at the notorious Indian boarding schools. This direction led me north to Canada, where I became a professor of education, so I could use my traditional Indigenous knowledge systems such as sharing circles for members in their healing and trauma process.

2 The connection between these Indian schools in the United States and in Canada originated in the Davin Report, 1879, as stated: Canada. Annual Report, 1880, Department of the Interior. "Report on Industrial Schools for Indians and Half-Breeds". Nicholas Flood Davin, March 14, 1879, reported when he visited several Indian Industrial schools including Carlisle to Prime Minister Sir John A MacDonald when establishing Canada's own Indian schools. What Darvin learned from Carlisle was how to deal with the "Indian problem" through education by assimilation when grouping Indian children in a boarding school.

Changing the colonial mindset

The mindset of colonial educators and medical professionals at the Haskell Indian school with the knowledge/beliefs of their White superiority contributed to my early experience as they tried to make us depend on their ways. This became a reoccurring factor that would repeat throughout my life. It was this superiority complex that the White teachers, doctors, and other staff members would reflect as "medical doctors thought they had become almost God, with their medical information." It was through this understanding that "somehow they knew better, through their knowledge system, about how children should grow, develop, and how [we] saw emotion, and understood emotion... this was very much frowned upon." This colonial mindset assumed that the school authorities and professionals knew about childcare, healing, and how children developed without knowing the Indigenous perspectives, including our natural development.

I knew then that one of the greatest challenges I would face was how the colonial mindset immortalized a superiority thinking that they knew better than the Indigenous peoples. This approach became "frowned upon because you have the rest of society and this idea of the intellect, which is the main thing we have as human beings, rather than realizing that we are both spiritual as well as physical beings." Conducting dialogue between Indigenous and colonial people was extremely difficult because "there's a challenge right there, especially if you come in and believe somehow, your culture is superior to another." This led to a divide between Indigenous and non-Indigenous primarily White Americans over education, healthcare, and social services, which impeded efforts towards reconciliation.

Education, at that time, was used as a tool for colonization, "colonial education, through its policy of assimilation, was taught by White teachers on a pedagogy that was not in sync with Indigenous ideals, lifestyle teachings, and philosophies." The education system taught in the Indian boarding schools was based on a "curriculum that was not appropriate for the students... this whole idea of kill 'the Indian' to save the child ... the philosophy was one needed to have this Western education to be successful." This American mentality resulted in Indigenous people believing that in order to become successful in the United States, one must have the necessary life skills to communicate effectively in the English language through the ability of speaking, reading, and writing, thereby displaying intelligence as good Americans.

Cultural differences vs colonial misunderstandings

Regarding this cultural difference, I can recall a situation amongst a group of

> Alaskan Natives, who spoke their languages. They had a teacher coming from down south in the US, who had never really been around Indigenous before... The students in the class were taught to be quiet unless, to ask a question directly and they're not as verbal. No back and forth ... The students were saying *'this teacher is so disrespectful. He doesn't give us time to share what we need to share'* and the teacher said, *'well, they can't be students as really they can't get to the point.'* But you know, had he listened to the whole explanation, he would have been able to understand what they were talking about, but because his mind had been conditioned to this inductive thinking.... it was very difficult.

Cultural misunderstandings are one of the most destructive approaches to teaching that can contribute to intergenerational trauma due to ill-informed teachers and racist beliefs about being different. A good example to draw on as to how different cultural perspectives can lead to ill-mannered behavior – during hunting time, Indigenous students will often leave school to help find food to feed their families. This has been reported and misunderstood by White teachers as their students being lazy or not interested in learning because they skipped classes, which was inaccurate because the teacher did not take into consideration the cultural habits of their students. It would be challenging to learn on an empty stomach, and malnutrition impacts many Indigenous peoples. Another good example is the interaction of non-Indigenous teacher and Indigenous student as the student looks down when their teacher addresses them, which in many Indigenous cultures is a sign of respect, not disobedience to authority. However, if non-Indigenous teachers would take the time to know their students, understand their cultural differences, and meet with community members to educate themselves, these types of cultural mistakes would be avoided.

This type of miscommunication can contribute to unwanted racist beliefs such as being labeled as a 'lazy student', which in fact could be just a cultural difference. This negative labeling such as learning disability due to cultural or learning differences only widens the diversity gap between different peoples as we share a perspective that "we all know, there is a very big difference between modern society and our society". Both have comparable differences and strengths in their own right, but each must be taken and understood on its own merits. We must acknowledge that the 'human family' is distinct and no society or "culture is superior to another ... We are unique, and every human being soul is unique... No piece of grain is the same on every beach in the world. There's never two pieces of sand the same." We must understand that our differences are what makes the human family unique as we all share a commonality to bettering ourselves, while embracing the ability to become more than who we are. The next generation will have to endure by moving forward on these past interactions as we are all human after all.

The White teachers, such as the one above, who taught Indigenous children in these boarding schools on the reservations yet had often no knowledge pertaining to the people they were teaching. This lack of cultural awareness contributed to the already racist educational teaching practices that had plagued Indigenous peoples. The teachers' and educational policy advisors' belief that Indigenous people could not comprehend the ideals needed to survive was emphatically wrong because "Indigenous people had a tremendous understanding of the environment... herbal medicines... and how to care for the lands they lived on". This difference contributed to how

> many children ... struggling with language, being unable to get any kind of education in terms of what we consider an academic education – the capacity to read well, to write -- these kinds of things because English was just not their language.

The processing of English did not follow the language structure that Indigenous people knew, which contributed to students being unable to read, write, and spell in this foreign format.

The differences in language structure

One of the differences in understanding language structure is how learning can be observed. The difference in language structure is based on how knowledge is processed within a cultural perspective and the abilities that are used to construct information pathways. The difference in language structure depends on the cultural differences, which can present the most challenge between Indigenous and colonial people. It is how, "the languages themselves are very different. They're opposites in a way ... the structure of the English language is very different ..., especially, if you come in and believe somehow, your culture is superior to another." These linguistic differences perceived to be superior over another would actually be misunderstood and result in challenges in teaching and learning, especially for children with learning disabilities. I must stress the differences between Indigenous people, who speak their own language compared to non-Indigenous who speak English; even though both are American yet have entirely different cultural and linguistical styles of language and learning.

It is these differences between two distinct language structures that reveal a great deal of information as, "native languages are primarily verb nomad languages. They see the world as a motion picture ... they see the whole picture method of learning English as a noun-based language that sees the world as a snapshot." This approach is entirely different from the ways Indigenous people learn. Therefore, from what I shared about my school experience, the teachers provided the learning structure that was to follow the curriculum of the American education system, which was 'a snapshot'. This approach explained how the English language replaced many Indigenous languages as many of us realized the benefit of learning English. During my schooling, while learning English, I realized that "I didn't want to be a half-wit." Many of us feared that not learning English could result in being labeled as 'disabled' or 'a half-wit' because of a language disability in the form of communication. I "wanted the same capacity in both" meaning I wanted to be able to communicate in the languages of my parents as well as in English, so that I would not be excluded from any society.

The fact remains that colonial language structure is very different, but the difference in how Indigenous children learned was not adapted from an Indigenous perspective, which could explain why some Indian children struggled to learn compared to White children. These differences in learning a new language also required a learning environment with family support, not abusive teachers forcing on them a culturally insensitive curriculum. By not fully understanding the differences in teaching people from two distinct cultures, how they processed information and what support structures were used in their families, could explain the reasons for these language struggles.

How we learn languages can connect us to our past. Thus, when I was in school and later within my own family, when "my wife really wanted my son to speak Thai, so she spoke only Thai to him. For the first several years, he spoke back to her in Thai and spoke English as well." How language bonds us is really important and can connect us in many ways as, "I think it's very important for children as well to learn the key concepts" as within languages, there is a way to understand and communicate. The significance of language learning reminded me of an idea I once had, which was to meet with Cree Elders and ask them,

> brothers or sisters, if you had to send your children on a 100-year journey and you were unable to be with them, what words, and concepts of the language would you feel you would really like to leave behind for your grandchildren?

Healing from within – A spiritual journey of self

Understanding the reason for education as a way of learning knowledge from both an Indigenous as well as from a Western perspective has led to a bridging of these two knowledge systems, as "they're opposites." However, each society has its own ways of learning and from a shared perspective within all the nations that I have encountered, I see they share a similar spiritual connection. It is this underlying factor that enables the ability to connect beyond what Western educators have deemed as essential within their learning structure. There is so much beyond what is taught in school. The world is rich in diversity, and the language structure can be a way of healing through a spiritual journey of oneself.

> Our contribution to humanity is our uniqueness, which is reflected in our different abilities... from time to time, you've had relatives who might have a disability.... Every single member of the community, even people with disabilities were seen ... as a precious gift from the Creator and everybody had a gift.... I think that we have this big split with Western science that... we know and understand, that we are spiritual beings as well as physical beings.

With this understanding that spiritual education acknowledges the variations within humanity, in particular, with the spirit or soul, whether from a spiritual, religious, moral perspective or from traditional knowledge systems. The fact remains that this is a big split with Western science. Our spiritual journey begins by understanding that "every human being is a soul ... a unique grain in the world." Thus, the spiritual connection of who we will manifest into the greater part of humanity is that "we're winning this spiritual struggle, the understanding that we are one human family." This is, especially, true for those with learning disabilities and physical disabilities, and it is what their family and community must show them. This connection taught in education could help in the healing process, regardless of how people learn, despite their challenges and no matter how they interact in society or what their limitations are within their physical and spiritual sides – one can see both sides of them. By looking at

> the difference between Indigenous philosophy that looks at the 'inner man'; as opposed to settler-colonial philosophy that often teaches us to see the deficits or negative attributes, which are usually outside the person, such as invisible disabilities or mental health problems, which are labeled with a negative classification within western education.

This could pertain to people with disabilities – different learning talents. Being aware of the complexity of Indigeneity as it intersects with history, education, language, parenting, and how one's identity through lived experiences and differences of knowledge systems can shape new perspectives towards inner healing.

> In one particular event that occurred to me when
>   Wounded Knee[3] happened ... we all had our beaded belt buckles and cowboy boots and, of course, I wanted to go braid my hair, but it's long and very curly ... My dad said, '*You know son, some people can wear braids, and some can't... you're one of those who can't.*

---

3 Wounded Knee also referred to as the Second Wounded Knee, lasted from February 27 to May 8, 1973, with approximately 200 Oglala Lakota or Oglala Sioux along with the AIM fought at the town of Wounded Knee on the Pine Ridge Indian Reservation in South Dakota.

I just wanted to embrace who I was from what I thought, but my actions did not matter as my father, who was an Elder, provided invaluable insight into the difference between inner and outer strengths and how our exterior appearance is a colonial way of thinking and has no room within Indigenous societies.

Strengths of Indigenous knowledge systems

I must say that the necessity to understand how different cultures share their knowledge can benefit others. This is something that Indigenous people have known yet been excluded from participating in,

> I am convinced that all these "California fires could have been avoided" because the Indigenous peoples were never consulted. They had a wealth of "knowledge about the forest … Had they been responsible for the … environment, I think we would have had a very different outcome because they knew about control burning".

There was

> a great loss of life, environmental disaster, and human suffering. The Indigenous peoples of California were not consulted -- a practice also seen in other colonized countries and during a dry season, the non-Indigenous people "literally massacred so many of those Indigenous people in California. It's one of the worst places ever" – they were nearly exterminated. Yet, the Indigenous people knew about drought from oral history. It would prove that without their knowledge systems of the land, climate seasons, and how agricultural life cycles occur that these natural disasters could have been prevented instead of consuming everything. All could have been avoided if Indigenous knowledge systems throughout the Americas had been validated or consulted. They were never asked to share in-conjunction with Western knowledge.

This inability to come together to work out our differences – "Indigenous people and settlers being able to work and live together in cooperation as a sort of harmony of respect and understanding is what Indigenous people understand." This occurred because "the colonial system of valuing knowledge misses out on the Indigenous ways of interacting with the land and with each other. This lived knowledge can be challenging for settler-colonial people to truly grasp, especially for researchers, academics, and professionals." This type of knowledge system shared through oral history and taught from a different language could have been applied to understanding disabilities from within tribes because Indigenous knowledge can be included. This inclusion by incorporating the knowledge system of a different and ancient society can only enrich the cultural experience of other societies and this infusion of knowledge system can bring about changes in ideas and create a *capacity* for dialogue. This type of mutual dialogue was not taken up during the Indian boarding schools, but it, eventually, took place across the United States and into Canada.

A need exists to include knowledge systems that can support the welfare of the human family. This need for coming together allows the entire "human family to realize that the way we're living is not the best way to live … it's just this path we're on is not going to take us where we want to go as a society." However, I am optimistic with the human family as "Western science is beginning to understand ... how abstract thought, creativeness, inventiveness, reason, memory" can all sponsor the growth of humanity. Through Indigenous participants, we can acknowledge that lived experiences taught in oral histories are essential as they can impact our own knowledge systems to become a way of bridging dialogue between different societies with cultural differences. This comparison of how other Indigenous people's approaches can not only be taken out of their own unique perspectives but can also be implemented in a wide range of social interactions ranging from lifestyles, learning development, teaching or adopting a culture or society's knowledge system, which can aid those who have been wronged – labeled as being different – disabled. This can help one see alternative perspectives through the understanding of those who have different viewpoints, not bad perspectives.

By looking into our past, in my travels, I viewed distinct knowledge systems such as the Inca Empire in Peru and Bolivia that had endured since the collapse of this mighty empire as a system that worked and is still valued in today's world. Travelling all over the Americas from the Eagle (North) to the Condor (South),[4] I saw how diverse humanity can change and this system is continuously transforming to meet the needs of the present, by connecting with the past so that we can embrace our future. This is how Indigenous people have influenced and participated as part of the human family. However, non-Indigenous people need to acknowledge Indigenous knowledge systems to ensure that a truly global harmony can occur as it will contribute to a dialogue and lead to an empathetic way of viewing and accepting diverse knowledge systems. This approach will provide the necessary steps towards diversity in education, spirituality, and human experiences as we learn differently by not allowing others to limit or disable our natural ways of learning. The importance of education is that understanding needs to be passed on to our children, whether this can be done in a public school, or ... our own Indigenous schools, I think that the spiritual education of children is just as important as intellectual education.

Final thoughts

My perspective on the involvement of Indian boarding schools in the United States and Canada is quite profound, having been born in one, and then attending one while growing up contributed to my early development. The overall long-term effect set me on a path of reconciliation and healing through resilience by my honoring the knowledge of where I came from, so I knew where I was going. This enabled me to combat the negative oppression that so many of my brothers and sisters had been impacted by because of the colonial education system. Seeing how people had been labeled, especially those with disabilities, would provide me with additional insight into the necessity for this process of reconciliation and healing. My lived experiences as the time to heal permitted me to build dialogue within a communal understanding that we must heal ourselves before we can help others as "the hurt of one is the hurt of all and the healing of one is the healing of all". I leave you with this, and we must become resilient in oppression yet be able to be open to dialogue so that the real process of healing towards reconciliation can begin.

---

4 This is to refer to the Eagle and the Condor Prophecy that during the 1490s would begin a 500-year period of slumber until an awakening by the Indigenous descendants. This could be a coming together in unity and sharing different knowledge systems for the greater good of the Americas.

5 An Eskimo's lived experience of disabilities – Elder, advocate, leader, and dialogue builder

Elder Percy Ballot

Introduction

Elder Percy Ballot is from Buckland, Alaska, which is located in the northwest Arctic of Alaska. It has a population of just over 400 with a small airport. They are the Buckland Tribe also called the Iñupiat, which is an Eskimo[1] tribe. He was adopted into a Christian family, and he has 7 children and 26 grandchildren with 2 more coming down the line in a few weeks, hopefully. He is the Vice Chairman of the Maniilaq Association, President of the Native Village of Buckland, Ruralcap Board of Directors; on the Alaska Native Health Board and the Northwest Region Federal Subsistence Board; on the Seward Peninsula Advisory Committee; and Past City Council member; on the School Board; and Search and Rescue; on the Alaska Housing Committee, on the Assembly of First Nations; and the Inuit Tapiriit Kanatami for the International Health Stirring Committee with Canada, Greenland, the United States, and Russia. He is also involved in many other things in all areas regarding health, economy, subsistence, environment, and housing. For 30 years, he was the Tribal President including on city council and a school board trustee.

One of his favourite things to do is create opportunities for others, especially kids and culture camps – taking them out is a special feeling when they first do this and share with elders, also to teach them how to prepare and eat what they get. This is hands-on learning that makes traditional knowledge a great way to experience the Eskimo way of life. Plus, he is involved with youth members to help the next generation. Anyway, he is a proud person, but most of all he is a family man. He lost his wife last year, but he has all his grandkids and everyone that he needs. He is 70 years old, and everybody calls him 'Tata', which means Grandpa no matter who it is as this is in their language. His Inupaiq name is Matchauq (after the first Black man Portuguese) who came up with Captain Cook. Buckland was named after a Professor Buckland from California who came up with them. He would like to pay tribute to Allen Geary & George Archie Washington, who used to take him boating and hunting when he was seven to nine years old at that time in my life, I did not have the means to hunt and these two men taught me the skills I needed to live off the land.

---

1 The word Eskimo is used within the United States and was used in Canada but changed to Inuit both are of the same people just different geography.

DOI: 10.4324/9781032656519-7

An Eskimo lived experiences

It is important to teach and help people whether with a disability or with education. We do a lot of things for children like culture camp, which teaches kids about safety and hunting and preserving our berries or plants or animals. I work with the city government and the school system, helping out where our tribe is needed and called upon to help the next generation – our children are the future of the tribe. Whatever we do, we just try to make life better for everyone. We all survived COVID by working together with other tribal governments, the city government, and the school. We all worked together by coming together. We lost a lot of people because of COVID and suicide, so we do a lot of mental health and well-being within the community.

We organize activities around loving yourself, learning about yourself, or by helping people. Every year, we have a celebration of life and other activities because we have funding from Victim Justice, so we can spend a lot of money doing activities about wellness for our kids and our elders who share their experiences as well as with other groups that come from out of town and all over including our relatives from Canada and other places. We have had NBA (professional players, gospel singers, retirement people), and those who are looking for wellness and being good for yourself in mind, body, and spirit.

Our beliefs about disabilities inspire the next generation

To understand how we see disabilities from our belief systems is by the saying '*never give up*'. That's the message that has been passed down all the time to never give up, no matter how hard things are. There is always someone to talk to, always someone to call, and always someone who cares for you. Then, when you are able to, you help those who need it too. This is our way of living. This is how our parents and our Elders lived. They lived in harder times, so we follow their approach to well-being and how they understood the challenges that arise. The strength of community is sacred. The youth today have much more free time than before when I was young, so we need to keep them occupied and focused on the challenges to come. We need doctors as well as our community is growing fast. We have our own teachers, nurses, and home care providers, for about 800 tribal members and others who live outside our communities.

We do have some youth with disabilities. Therefore, we try to let those who struggle at the bottom take part in our games, social and cultural learning because we make them part of our community. We do not exclude them because that is not our way of living. Our well-being is based on inclusion, compassion, and togetherness. Having fun is a community approach to learning as we all learn in a different way – not a disabled way. We have respect for everyone. That is who we are as a people.

The role of people with disabilities in our community

Even people with their disabilities have something they can do better than others. We must keep an open mind regarding their talents that might appear hidden because of the disability as everyone learns differently. It could be reading, writing, or making something as a builder or being an artist – everybody has a talent. These talents could be getting people to work together or to understand each other more. Everyone has their own gifts and talents which may be unique to use. We must keep an open mind that we are all different and our differences are our strengths. These abilities are what are needed for the future.

Whether you think you have a disability or not, that's ridiculous. Each one must share what they have, share their experience and their history – these will become their tools for success. Whether you have a learning or physical disability, you always have something you can give. We can learn so much from each other, about our challenges, and ways people have adapted to learn, thrive, and survive. My mother at 90 told me to use humour and be open. You have to have an open mind to be able to survive and live in this world.

The impact of colonialism: How language changed our lifestyle – The effects of abusive settler education

This is hard for me to write because I was put in a corner by a teacher when I was in grade 4 and told not to speak Eskimo or do any native dancing or fight back, which was a consequence of my early learning and development in these colonial schools. My brother Chester was sent away to a non-Indigenous family, and it took me 14 years to find him. I had to learn English to make enough money and then use my traditional learning to survive and help my community – my family. By learning English, I was able to find my brother and bring him home because I could leave the community and survive in non-Indigenous places.

Many children these days are bored and say they have nothing to do. Now, there is not much to learn and do like chopping wood, hunting, and fishing, but we must learn these traditional skills. Traditional hunting is a healthy way of living. By working with your hands, and mind, you become able to survive as you are self-sufficient. By working with our minds, we are able to learn and develop new skills for the future. Many children and youth of the new generation shop at stores so do not know what is in the food they eat. They think if it looks good, it is good, but there are many harmful chemicals in the processed foods today. Plus going to the store costs so much more money here in the Arctic. As well, many foods here are not good nor do they have the nutritional value for us as they are not our traditional foods.

The reliance on stores and on non-traditional education has contributed to disabilities as it disables the minds of our youth. Colonialism has created the mental disabilities of so many young folks. The environment of colonialism contributes to many of the consequences we face in our community, yet we still move forward despite our challenges. The community becomes dependent on someone else doing the work for them – the hunting, cooking, harvesting, learning, and so much more. Colonialism has contributed to our current situation and has impacted our way of life. It has disabled our youth by making them depend on television marketing and not relying on or learning their own traditional teachings and perspectives. Learning to think on your feet is as valuable as any other kind of colonial education, perhaps even better. Losing our way in life has become the biggest disabling effect of colonialism. We need our youth to do more for themselves or for their families as they face a big challenge. However, some do go on to college and university to become healthcare providers. Learning beyond their home on the land would build new ways of learning, help them gain new friendships, and other ways to develop themselves.

The effects of colonialism on our well-being

Drugs, fentanyl, and other heavy chemicals have contributed to an epidemic in our community, which has contributed to another form of disability by changing the mindset of our youth. They change them by disabling them, causing reactions, death from overdose, crime, and becoming hysterical. There was a time when I could leave my fishing equipment and gun in my boat without anyone taking it, but now, today, people steal and sell things just to keep taking these imported drugs. Our community is dry, yet people still sneak in alcohol, which has had huge impacts on the lives of those who drink and causes pain to their family members. This alcohol and drug use has contributed to a disabling of self and threatens the well-being of the entire community. The community is a family, so we are all impacted in one way or another. This is yet another challenge of colonialism and another battle we must face and fight. This is our battle right now.

The power and strength of humour

Having a sense of humour gets me through the hardest times. My mother told me that 'you should all use humour to get people all together to battle the things that go on in your head when they're overcoming a challenging issue or needing somebody to talk to'. I think humour, in general, brings people closer together. Humour can be a way to relieve the stress and anxiety of life by making a way to express our anger, sadness, and even confusion. I have been through a lot, I have a wooden leg, survived a heart attack, and had cancer. I have three fingers on my right hand, so as a young man, I connected with a lot of bad things that happened to me. We live in a part of the world that is -50c, which is part of who we are as Artic people, so humour helps us through the difficult times as a way to address mental health issues. I used humour to battle the things that I struggled with and it helped me to understand my own challenges. Plus, humour brings people closer together on a basic human level of communication for healing and it is a way of recognizing a new way of learning through laughter.

I am 70 and I don't really call myself an Elder yet. The real Elders are up there in their 80s and 90s, so I still have a ways to go. I am more of a junior Elder at this time, but getting there as we all have our places in society. Moving upwards is a gradual direction that comes with time, with struggles in the good times and the bad times – as a journey through the passing of time.

6 Perspectives of disability in the Yukpa peoples of Venezuela and Colombia from an Indigenous psychological perspective

Elder Rodolfo Andres Jauregui Ojeda

Introduction

Elder Rodolfo Andres Jauregui Ojeda is an Elder, working as a psychologist. He has the unique ability to help in a meaningful way, in a culturally friendly capacity by building dialogues between the Yukpa and the city of Cúcuta. He understands the racism, and the socio-cultural and economic challenges that the Yukpa people face, and his understanding of who they are and where they are from enables him to build on those relationships. His understanding of disabilities is just one of the many ways that he can help these people, as a form of reconciliation of mind, body, and spirit. Words of wisdom and knowledge are shared by Yukpa Elders (Nery Achita, Sergio Romero, and Natalia Romero) with whom Elder Rodolfo has relationships. As an Elder, himself, he can truly represent the Yukpa.

Who we are as Yukpa Peoples

The Yukpa people, originally from the mountainous regions of Venezuela and Colombia, have maintained their traditions and ways of life for generations. We will explore the perspectives of disability within these Indigenous communities from a psychological approach, highlighting their beliefs, attitudes, and practices that influence the way they understand disability. According to the Senior Chief of the Uchapetatpo – Yukpa community, Yonilda Sierra, the origin of the Yukpa people was as follows:

Anütatpo owayaina

Nana yukpa Caribe Piño Juwarapa Ep Anutatpo Owayaina kumoko amoretocha. Ep anukat oshipi. Weetaño Juwar yojet manuracha. Kumoko pap jakurarshi yünanopap ep yün jaküptusha we yan Manüracha. Jokurarhipa we yünajkap.

Manüracha Yümür pa nutot, onari kaj amoretocha Yukpa yunanukop oripa etpe küpa. Jaküror oripa etpe küpa otün kutaw amoretocha toramshikan shoman kwtaw amoretocha toramshikan shoman kwtow Yukpa oshipi tuwektaj. Tariopaj nan nataramat owayaipo kümoko wonka pory nan ekunekap tuwej. Owaya nan jano Yukpa. Yonilda Sierra.

The English translation would be:

We, Indigenous peoples, are from the Caribbean family. Our origin is told in this way: Amoretocha -- God is the one who gave us life through a tree called Manuracha, in our story. Amoretocha, God, sends the woodpecker to make the figure of the Yukpa Indigenous man and woman, so that they can work on the land.

DOI: 10.4324/9781032656519-8

The woodpecker listens to Amoretocha, God, and selects that Manuracha tree and pecks it. By pecking that wood, the woodpecker carves out the figure of the Yukpa woman and man. That is our origin, that is where Amoretocha, God, interrupted life. At that moment, the woodpecker carves out the figure of the Indigenous Amoretocha so, God is in charge of blowing on the figure. That is when the life of the Yukpa Indigenous people begins. Right then, life was formed Thus, we recognize through that tree, that is why the Indigenous people get strengthened and value nature.

The Yukpa have developed a traditional knowledge system and practices that are intertwined with the natural environment and their spiritual beliefs. Disability, within this worldview, is, therefore, perceived as a natural variation in human diversity. Individuals with disabilities are considered bearers of special wisdom so are valued for their unique contribution to the community.

It is important to highlight that the Yukpa Indigenous community comes from the Serranía del Perijá of Venezuela, and as such, unfortunately, are the victims of the migrant phenomenon. They have currently settled in the city of San José de Cúcuta, Colombia, and have been there for approximately five years, on the edge of the adjacent Táchira River, down to the Francisco de Paula Santander international bridge. The families became involved in the economic activities around the river such as offering a canoe service across the border, as a mechanism to generate income for their support ("work") – mainly carried out by the women on the Colombian side; some others, mainly young people, participate in the transportation of merchandise on bicycles or on their backs in order to gain income. Here is a image of the Yukpa community after relocation with Elders Rodolfo on the left and Nery Achita in the bottom middle surrounded by children (Figure 6.1).

However, with the pedestrian opening up of the international bridge in October 2021, their work decreased significantly, as the volume of people crossing the river decreased. Now, the historical productive systems of the community surround such natural exploitation as hunting, fishing, and fruit gathering. These, though, are not viable in their place of settlement, so the scourge of begging has returned to the streets of the city and even to the Norte de Santander area. Currently, the populace in the city of Cúcuta is organized at the community level into two groups, each with its own traditional authorities.

To conclude, the main characteristic of the Yukpa people is their nomadic ways in the same territory. This is why, currently, due to the situation of the migrant phenomenon, they are settled in San José de Cúcuta. This area is made up of 2 settlements: the Manuracha and the Uchapetapo, which together number around 450–600 people. Some of them are pendulous, that is, they come and go from Colombia to Venezuela. This phenomenon has generated many varied needs in the community such as:

- A lack of income for support
- Poverty
- Weakening of cultural identity
- Begging
- A lack of cultural recognition

These are the most relevant to the extent that they affect the biopsycho-social development of its members and generate a survival alert in the face of the great deficiencies that afflict them.

Figure 6.1 Photograph of the Yukpa community at the festival of life, 2022.
Source: Photographer: Juan Camilo Carrero Vasquez, Yukpa Community in Cucuta, Colombia

Yukpa beliefs, understanding, and teachings about disabilities beliefs and attitudes towards disability

Within the Yukpa communities, disability is not seen as a limitation, but only as a difference that enriches the community. People with disabilities are respected for their connection to the spiritual and are given important roles in ritual and healing practices. These people are believed to possess special abilities to communicate with the gods and spirits, making them essential intermediaries. Therefore, each member of the community develops activities according to their abilities, so they complement each other as a whole.

Disability is not understood as discrimination, but on the contrary, the community process is strengthened by generating space for participation that enhances the community's objectives and achieves the proposed goals in the different areas of life's plan.

The role of people with disabilities in the community

According to Sergio Romero, community leader and guarantor of healthcare processes:

> within the Yukpa community, people with disabilities occupy significant and respected roles. These people are believed to possess spirit communication skills and play a crucial role as intermediaries between the earthly world and the spirit world. Additionally, they are valued for their wisdom and knowledge, and are consulted in important decisions for the community, such as rituals and healing practices.

Teachings and learnings about disabilities

Teachings about disabilities are passed down orally from generation to generation. Yukpa Elders play a vital role in this process, sharing their knowledge and experiences with the younger generations. These stories not only convey the acceptance and valorization of people with disabilities but also pass on the traditional practices of support and care that the community provides to these individuals.

Nery Achita, Elder of the community, states:

> It is important that we all understand that we are in this world for a purpose that only God knows. We cannot discriminate against each other or disparage each other's work just because it is different. We all have a place in this community and we accept each other as we are.

Natalia Romero, Chief of Children in the community, shares that:

> since there are boys and girls, the Yukpa strive to understand their role in the community and are taught that mutual respect is important, helping those in need and working as a team to move the community forward are an agreement that the Yukpa learns from an early age.

How Colombian society– Colonialism – impacted the Yukpa

The arrival of the Yukpa people in Cúcuta, a city located in the northeast of Colombia, occurred mainly due to the forced displacements and internal migrations that occurred in Venezuela, as a result of the acute political and economic crisis that the country was and still is experiencing – violence and pressure on the natural resources on the original land of the Yukpa. Internal displacement led Indigenous communities, including the Yukpa, to seek refuge in urban areas in search of safety and better living conditions.

Consequences of Spanish colonialism: Changes to the Yukpa knowledge about disabilities

During the Spanish colonial period in Latin America, including the regions inhabited by the Yukpa, significant changes occurred in Indigenous perceptions, understanding, and knowledge about various aspects of life – including disabilities. The introduction of the colonial system influenced their beliefs and practices regarding people with disabilities; although it is important to note that these changes were multi-faceted and varied depending on the local circumstances and specific interactions with the colonizers.

The arrival of Spanish missionaries and colonizers led to the imposition of Christianity on the people and European beliefs about illness and disability. This may have affected traditional Yukpa beliefs and practices, as they introduced new perspectives on disabilities based on the European worldview. Under the colonial system, people with disabilities, like other marginalized groups, could have been stigmatized and marginalized by colonial society. This had an impact on how the Yukpa perceived and treated people with disabilities; although these dynamics varied widely by region and specific community.

Despite the tensions and conflicts inherent in the colonization process, there were also cultural interactions between the colonizers and Indigenous peoples, including the Yukpa. These interactions could have led to an exchange of disability-related knowledge and practices; although this area of study remains underexplored.

In addition to the above, not only Spanish colonialism, but the entire social and media impact of post-modernity impacted the Yukpa community, creating unknown scenarios for them, such as contact with new technologies. Its consequences are relative to the use given to them, but it is important to highlight that the people have suffered from being linked to these trends. Despite this, they continue to fight to keep their traditions alive. The policies and actions of the state have also become more inclusive to try to benefit and guarantee the basic rights of the population, but everything is insufficient because the needs are constant and so great, and the solutions are temporary.

Their housing systems have also been affected by the entire colonization process they have experienced. Today, being a city, they do not have the minimum guarantees for healthy housing or recreation spaces that allow children and adults to enjoy and strengthen their cultural environment. Their roofs are made of plastic, which, with the added hot sun and rainwater, does not have the consistency to remain firm. Thus, in any event, they collapse, leaving the house exposed to the inclement weather. The walls are made of the strongest guadua bamboo and the floor is made of mud, which when it rains, turns into a puddle with any number of viral risks. The Yukpa are no longer in their lands, so out of their comfort zone so out of what they know – their protection. They are away from their lands, far away, in search of better opportunities, like everyone else. They know how to move forward, but they have not had the chance to move forward because they have not even been able to achieve decent housing conditions.

Conclusion

This is the reality of many Indigenous people, who fight to stay alive in the midst of a predatory and inhumane society. Their innocence, their songs, their cultural acts, their ways of understanding life and the environment are a wisdom that cannot or should not be lost due to apathy and abandonment. On the contrary, we must preserve their origins, preserve the Yukpa culture, and of everything that began.

We have explored the perspectives of disability in the Yukpa peoples of Venezuela and Colombia from an Indigenous psychological perspective. We have learned that disability is perceived as a natural part of human diversity in these communities, and people with disabilities are valued and respected for their spiritual connection and significant contributions to the community. It is imperative that psychological professionals recognize and respect these cultural perspectives when providing support and services to people with disabilities in Indigenous contexts.

From an Indigenous psychological perspective, it is essential to recognize and respect the traditional beliefs and practices of the Yukpa peoples regarding disability. Indigenous psychology advocates a culturally sensitive approach that values and preserves Indigenous worldviews. By integrating Indigenous beliefs and knowledge into psychological interventions, supportive practices can be fostered that are authentic and effective for people with disabilities within these communities. The image below is of the Yukpa community in the celebration of women and life (Figure 6.2).

Figure 6.2 Photograph of Elder Rodolfo wearing this traditional ceremonial hat, 2021.

Source: Photographer: Juan Camilo Carrero Vasquez, Yukpa Community in Cucuta, Colombia

Part II

Reframing the narrative – Navigating self-representation

The chapters in Part II navigate how Indigenous authors understand who they are, where they are from, and where they are going as a way of self-development. The authors have been drawn from different parts across Mother Earth, Canada, the United States, Colombia, Mauritius, Nepal, and Algeria. Each provides a unique perspective that provides an insightful understanding of the chapters as the reader unfolds these readings.

Transcendent identifies

The knowledge shared by these authors gives an understanding of their Indigeneity as it crosses territories, time, and specific contexts. They offer insight through reflections of self-representation, through a traditional knowledge of teachings, and how they view themselves. Identity is a complex and ever-changing path to understanding oneself that is confronted by a multitude of intersectionalities and dimensions that all contribute to the identity of self. This can impact how people view themselves as privileged within a marginalized group or belonging to one tribe over another, but, also, how their choices for change can impact them, their families, and how they situate themselves as caregivers to those who struggle. In understanding how these authors view themselves we can as Indigenous people look within as being Indigenous is an ever-changing perspective that has been plagued with colonialist measurements, a lack of access to cultural teachings, not being able to connect with communities, unable to learn tribal languages, and even in our appearance. All of these indicators shape not only who we are as Indigenous peoples but also how we define ourselves in this ever-growing world that has been predominantly colonized in one form or another. However, it will never take away our inner spirit, which is pure and unique. Regardless of how Indigenous people view themselves, their actions, voices, teachings, beliefs, and knowledge systems will progress as will their understanding of disabilities, which is an ever-changing word and meaning. Just like colonialism, disability studies and the belief systems that contribute to this developing field changes with each story, language, and region, which will influence and inspire change in this global representation of Indigenous disability studies.

Listing from within – A realization of the power of change

Who we are and how we are connected have been the fundamental beliefs shared by many Indigenous peoples on Mother Earth. It is this global link that binds us as Indigenous people for many of us have been changed as a result of colonialism, yet we are resilient to this change and rise up to face challenges. The authors within Part II give us a glimpse

DOI: 10.4324/9781032656519-9

into who they are by key periods in their history that will allow us to navigate our own viewpoints as we discover who we are as Indigenous people in this post-colonized world. These contributors have given unique perspectives related to labels and self-identification as they walked their own path of rediscovery. This approach to following the red path as a way of finding oneself has been used through various Indigenous territories such as a walkabout in Australia; *miskâsowin askîhk* is Cree for (finding oneself on the land). Whatever the approach, it is within us to self-heal our hurts as a form of well-being. There are some who smudge tobacco or walk in the bush or sit in a sharing circle and share their thoughts. What the authors have revealed has impacted them as much as it will impact those who read their words. The power of change is one of many ways Indigenous people can navigate their own narrative by reframing who they are, so they will know where they are going.

7 To see or not to see

Am I blind or is that just another colonial label

Kevin P. Morgan

Introduction

My journey led me back to my Métis roots, my culture, and my traditions where I discovered my authentic self and a true sense of belonging. During my career, I held various senior management leadership roles in the Canadian Federal Public Service. In 2015, I obtained a Master's in Leadership Studies Organizational. A leadership project focussed my energy on attracting more Indigenous people to career opportunities within the federal government's National Capital Region (NCR). Recently, I stepped back from some of my Indigenous recruitment, development, and retention-related leadership roles to support the next generation of Indigenous leaders who bring with them new vision and ideas to the ongoing advancement of these programs. However, I continue to provide consultation and advice to new leaders, while leading and co-facilitating Indigenous training, learning, and knowledge-sharing opportunities. I also continue to share my lived experiences on bringing my whole and authentic Indigenous self to work as an Indigenous leader, and as an Indigenous person with a disability.

My earliest years

Many Indigenous languages of Turtle Island do not have a word that describes the concept of "disability"; in fact, many Indigenous peoples around the world look at a disability as a gift from the Creator. The Online Etymology Dictionary (2023) indicates that the origins of the word "disability" date back to the 1640s and meant "incapacity in the eyes of the law". Therefore, the term disability is arguably an overarching term founded on a colonial construct that does not align with the traditional views of many Indigenous peoples, as it comes from a deficit-oriented perspective (Roberts, 2022). For many Indigenous peoples, one's capacity is not limited to one's physical attributes, but more to one's overall health – that is their emotional, spiritual, physical, and intellectual well-being and the balance among these attributes, as well as the way we engage with others and the world around us.

As I have lived on the traditional and unceded lands of the Anishinaabe Algonquin Peoples since 2011, I have come to learn that in Anishinaabe culture, people receive their names through ceremony and the name they receive reflects the gifts they carry or their responsibilities within the community (Ineese-Nash, 2020). As a result, Anishinaabe children often learn early about their role within the collective based on their capabilities, their unique gifts, and what teachings they bring to the community. As a Sixties Scoop[1] survivor, I did not uncover my ancestral roots, traditions, and culture until my mid-30s.

DOI: 10.4324/9781032656519-10

These were not the traditional views or teachings that I had been exposed to in my earliest years, yet they now form an important cornerstone of my sense of self.

Born in October 1967, I was adopted by a progressive Irish family in mid-1968. My adopted father was a first-generation immigrant from Ireland, and my adopted mother, a second generation. I grew up in an ever-growing suburb called Coquitlam, located approximately 40 kilometres outside of Vancouver, in British Columbia. While Coquitlam, today, is recognized as one of the most culturally diverse communities in Canada, in the late sixties, this was not the case. After its incorporation in 1891, early 1900s growth in Coquitlam revolved around Fraser Mills, a state-of-the-art lumber mill located on the banks of the mighty Fraser River. This attracted French Canadian migrants experienced in the Québecois logging culture. Post-World War II, Coquitlam's population growth exploded, and continues today; however, growth during my formative years arguably started with many immigrants of Western European descent. My maternal mother travelled West from Winnipeg at age 15 to the north shore of Vancouver to give birth because back home, she faced a great deal of discrimination and harassment as a teenager, unwed, Indigenous mother-to-be. She, of course, could not have known that I too would face persistent discrimination, harassment, and bullying in my most formative years and throughout my youth, not only because I looked different than most of the other children, at that time, but also because I was born legally blind.

I was reportedly a very happy-go-lucky toddler, although, perhaps renowned for periodic mischief and the odd tantrum. I recall seeing photos of me in my earliest years walking around in shorts with suspenders, no shirt, rubber boots, and a fake corn-cobb pipe-in summer. I also learned to whistle as a toddler and would not hesitate to share this craft with anyone, who would care to listen to me. It seems to me in retrospect that until I knew I was legally blind, and until I learned that I was adopted, life seemed good. However, grade school and my inability to read chalkboards quickly exposed my visual "disability". A year's worth of missed classes to undergo every eye exam under the stars, and sitting isolated at the front of the class, from time to time with a pirate-like patch on my weaker eye, contributed to my earliest foundational and colonial-based understanding of what I thought of at that time as "my disability". Classroom photo days reinforced the fact that for years, I was the only kid in my class who did not have a white complexion; although, my parents told me that my origins were of Spanish and Irish descent – a convenient lie to protect me and perhaps them, my intuition and likely engrained Indigenous culture, suggested to me that this was not the truth.

While I grew up only several kilometres from the Kiikwetlem First Nation, whose traditional territory surrounds the Coquitlam River watershed, I did not have any exposure to my or other Indigenous cultures or peoples until young adulthood. Yet, while I consider my upbringing as fortunate, even privileged, when I reflect on the history and lives of many Indigenous peoples in Canada, without a grounded understanding of my ancestral and cultural origins, and the Indigenous teachings I know and live today; I grew up with a deep sense of disconnection and lack of belonging. Moreover, as a young boy growing up in a world where the colonial definition of a disability prevailed, where a disability was something that needed to be compensated for and that prevented one from pursuing certain interests, hobbies, and careers, I had no idea what capabilities or unique gifts I had been given nor how I might someday use them to benefit others. Contrarily, I grew up with the impression that my blindness was a weakness and something that should be hidden from others so I would not be preyed upon or taken advantage of, and that the world was a very competitive and unforgiving place, so I needed to be driven and fearless, if not to excess, close to in order to demonstrate my worth and to fit in.

The start of a new way of being

In my early thirties, I learned who I really was, and it forever changed my life. Admittedly, the journey started because my wife wanted to learn more about my biological family's medical history to determine if our boys were at risk of losing their sight too. However, when she shared a letter that my birth mother had sent her, inviting me to reach out and make contact, my childhood desire for cultural connection and belonging was immediately refuelled, and with little hesitation, my personal and cultural journey of discovery had begun. In the months and years to follow, I met my birth mother, who all those years had been living in North Vancouver, only 16 km as the crow flies from my family home in Coquitlam. Her half-brother, who has been an Indigenous Correctional Program Officer with Corrections Canada for many years, took me under his wing at that time and became my cultural teacher, exposing me to the teachings of our and other Indigenous peoples. Through his lived experience and knowledge, I came to learn that I am of Ojibwe, Cree (Oji-Cree), and French descent, with my ancestral roots firmly planted in the Red River Valley, in Manitoba, Canada – the home of the Métis peoples, and that my ancestry could be traced further back to the Chippewa of North Dakota, United States.

Not only did my second uncle invite me into the family with open arms, mind, and heart, but he also exposed me to the foundational teachings of the Oji-Cree, Métis, and other Indigenous peoples through participation in cultural events and ceremonies. First, I was accepted into the community as a member of the Fraser Valley Métis Association (FVMA). I still remember attending my first FVMA Harvest Dinner and Dance. My mother, whom I had met in person only earlier that year had gifted me a traditional Métis ribbon shirt, which she had hand sewn, which I proudly wore as I immersed myself in Métis cuisine, music, regalia and, of course, my first kick at Métis jigging. I fondly recall participating in the 2006 Pulling Together Canoe Journey, a seven-day canoe journey down the mighty Fraser River to help raise awareness for Indigenous youth at risk and build better relations between the Indigenous and policing communities. The journey itself was majestic and taught me about the life-sustaining importance of the river and its tributaries to many Indigenous communities, while our overnight stays at several First Nation communities including Kwikwetlem, Katzie, and Musqueam exposed me to some important traditional cultural protocols and ceremonies, as well as the welcoming nature of Indigenous peoples and the richness of their cultures. In the years to follow, my second uncle would expose me to several other cultural events and ceremonies of significance, including smudging, Pow Wows, and Sweat Lodge Ceremonies held on the traditional and unceded lands of the Squamish, Tsleil-Waututh, and Sts'ailes (formerly Chehalis) First Nations.

Indigenous leadership and disabilities in the federal public service

My personal explorative foray into Métis and other Indigenous cultures engendered my desire to give back to the communities and peoples I served through my career with the federal government. While I started small, through involvement with local employee equity and diversity committees, my interest and passion continued to pull me towards leadership roles on regional and national committees responsible for Indigenous recruitment, development, and retention, as well as Indigenous employee networks that support Indigenous employees' transition into the federal workplace and then create a sense of community and support within. In 2015, my master's in leadership studies organizational leadership project focussed on what my federal employer might consider doing to attract more Indigenous people to non-entry-level career opportunities within our NCR. Over recent years, I have stepped back a little from some of the leadership roles I held, as I am a strong believer that renewal through leaders with new visions is integral to the continued evolution of our programs; however, I continue to provide consultative advice to our new leaders, lead and co-facilitate Indigenous training, learning and knowledge-sharing opportunities, and provide the occasional keynote speech.

How my colonial concept of disability evolved to where it is today

In 2008, I went on a business trip with my then-director and current-day colleague-at-a-distance and friend, Allan. Allan is of the Maakwa Clan and a member of Apitipi Anicinapek First Nation, formerly known as the Wahgoshig First Nation, in Northeastern Ontario, Canada. While our trip was under the auspices of intergovernmental relations with our provincial partners, the North American Indigenous Games that year was held on Vancouver Island, in Cowichan, British Columbia, close to our meetings so, we, therefore, decided to make a quick stop for "a looksee" on the way home. Later, that afternoon, we were sitting in a long ferry lineup at the Swartz Bay Terminal in Sydney, Victoria, and Allan, unannounced to me, snapped a quick photo of me looking out over the Saanich Peninsula in a contemplative state. Shortly after returning home, I received the photo from Allan, along with a note that read "for a man who cannot see, you have great vision". This was the first time, I started to think of my visual disability as a gift from the Creator. It was the first time I can recall that I did not think about my blindness as an impairment, making me different in a lesser manner than others, but rather as part of a whole person, one who perhaps could live with harmony of mind, body, and spirit and with others and all our relations. Although I did not fully comprehend the significance of Allan's simple, yet thoughtful gesture, nor the impact it would have on me as I continued my personal and cultural journey of discovery, Allan's gesture would have an increasingly profound effect on the way I lived my life (Figure 7.1).

Figure 7.1 Photograph of the author – "For a man who cannot see, you have great vision" 1997.
Photographer: Allen Doriff at Swartz Bay Terminal, Victoria, British Columbia

Furthermore, as I continued to learn about and practice traditional Métis and First Nation's core values and beliefs, such as the teachings of the Medicine Wheel[1] and the Seven Grandfather Teachings,[2] my historically Eurocentric conceptualization of my disability continued to dissipate. Also, the language I used to communicate around it, and related issues, became less distinctions-based, that is, less founded upon the dichotomy between normal and those considered as failing to meet the standard of normalcy (Norris, 2014), and more upon the Cree word *kakanaticichek*, meaning "the gifted ones", "the special people". While my adopted parents encouraged me to be the best I could be in every aspect of my life, there was always a persistent undercurrent, as well as the occasional discussion, about what my legal blindness would prevent me from doing, rather than what I could do with the gifts I possessed. As "language embodies the way a society thinks" (Little Bear, 2000, p. 78), it is only through significant personal and cultural growth over many years that I have come to understand how growing up in a world that labelled me as handicapped, or more recently, disabled, contributed to my feelings of isolation and low self-esteem and often left me wondering who am I? What is my value? and Where do I fit into our society?

Today, however, I understand that I possess certain gifts that are highly valued by society and that these gifts can and should be shared with others. Perhaps, it is because I cannot see the eyes of those in an audience and, therefore, feel less intimidated when public speaking than others, but I have been told that I am a strong orator, capable of capturing the hearts and minds of others through spoken word. Since Allan first shared with me, others have come forward as well and told me that I possess strong "vision" – that is, "the act or power of the imagination", "mode of seeing or conceiving", and "unusual discernment or foresight" (Merriam-Webster, 2023), something that if well channelled can arguably unify and inspire others towards a sense of shared purpose and direction. Today, I embrace these and other gifts with a sense of curiosity, honour, respect, and humility, and seek to engage others in a manner that will help me better understand the special gifts they possess.

My lived experience with leadership and *dis*ability within the federal construct

The Federal government, in my opinion, has made great strides over the last 25 plus years ensuring that persons with disabilities, including Indigenous peoples, feel more respected, valued, and at ease bringing our whole and authentic selves to the workplace and we are better able to optimize our contributions. In my earliest days of equity, diversity, and inclusion-related activities, the government focussed primarily on ensuring that our labour force matched labour market availability figures. In other words, it was more about having the right number of bums in seats necessary to ensure federal employees were generally representative of the public we serve, as opposed to really understanding and valuing the gifts that (Indigenous) persons with disabilities bring to the workplace. Yet, with all the advancements, I have experienced and lived; the federal government's

1 The medicine wheel is represented by four elements, which are mental, physical, emotional, and spiritual. This First Nations concept is based on a spirituality and cultural perspective that aim to teach these four areas when representing self as a sort of self-assessment.
2 The Grandfather Teachings or Grandmother depending on the location will be revealed in greater detail in Chapter 7 is based on the Indigenous concept of seven sacred teachings comprising humility, bravery, honesty, wisdom, truth, respect, and love.

legislated responsibility to accommodate persons with disabilities continues to make use of certain languages, such as *"identify and remove barriers"*, and *"make reasonable accommodations for equity-deserving groups"*, language founded upon good intentions, but arguably, language that still seems reminiscent of a more colonial mindset and understanding of persons with disabilities. As I am legally blind, I have an accommodation plan, which outlines my *limitations* and recommends accommodations, and while I find the plan helpful, I await the day when my employer truly understands my gifts and seeks to have me work in an area where these gifts will be optimized and leveraged for the betterment of the Canadians we serve.

For many Indigenous peoples, relationships are thought to be reciprocal and egalitarian in nature, as opposed to the Eurocentric perspective where humans sit at the top of the hierarchy of all living things and are capable of subjugating all for their own purposes. Differences among many Indigenous peoples, while recognized, are respected, and valued, and do not result in relationships founded upon inequality or power imbalances, but rather on mutual respect of these differences, or gifts, and a mutual understanding that we are all interdependent and interconnected. I have experienced this on many occasions throughout my career in government, most specifically, when collaborating with my Indigenous colleagues. For example, our Indigenous employee network meetings always exude a sense of interconnectedness and kinship, community, a give-and-take among all participants, regardless of individual job classification, group, and level; position or tenure within the network, department, or government; educational attainment; or other differentiating factor that may still bestow a sense of hierarchy, power, or prestige on some government officials in boardrooms across the country. As a young child, I was undoubtedly influenced by my adopted father's many idioms, including *"if you want something done right, do it yourself"*. Today, through immersion in my and other Indigenous teachings, I feel a greater sense of relatedness to all others and the world around me – a sense that we are all in this together and that together we are stronger. While I have seen an increased engagement of employees at all levels during my career, the historically hierarchical nature of government, while a necessity given the size of the federal public service, and something that arguably promotes accountability, still has much room for increased use of a more participative style of management (Kim, 2002); if we are to continue to create space for Indigenous people with disabilities, and all others, to share their unique and valuable insights and ideas.

Growing up without my culture in my most formative years left me feeling for the longest time that I was solo on this journey we call life, that the world we live in is highly competitive, and that someone like me with a visual *dis*ability needs to be ultra-competitive in all that I do in order to seek out my deserved place and prove to others what I was capable of achieving and the worth I could bring to others. In retrospect, the success of this approach was always immediately noticeable, but more often than not, short-lived. In my youth, it enabled me to compete at a high level in my preferred sports – including competitive running, which led to my participation in the Track City International Classic in Eugene Oregon, United States, and the Harry Jerome Track Classic, in Burnaby British Columbia, Canada. I also feel that my competitive nature contributed to my relatively strong academic achievements throughout my grade-school years and beyond. When I first joined the Federal government in 1997, in an entry-level junior program officer role, my competitiveness contributed to my success in obtaining several promotional opportunities leading to my first leadership role, as well as entry into my employer's middle-management development program.

However, as I started to obtain leadership roles of increasing scope and responsibility, the character traits that I had arguably overdeveloped as compensation for what I perceived as *my* disability, and my lack of a strong cultural foundation, started to reveal some cracks. As you might suspect, someone with an excess of courage might just be considered rash, or even reckless from time to time (Crossan et al., 2013), while drive "[a]t its worst, it can be undirected, unfocussed energy that feeds on itself – constantly requiring additional physical and emotional investment to sustain it" (Seijts and Young, 2019). I recall taking a self-assessment test entitled the Leadership Character Insight Assessment (LCIA) (Crossan et al., 2018), a test designed to measure leadership character and provide leaders with practical insight for leadership development. In short, the LCIA, while revealing relative strengths in certain leadership traits including collaboration, humanity, integrity, justice, accountability, and transcendence, also exposed an excess of courage and drive, and deficiencies in humility and temperance. These results fuelled a great degree of self-reflection – after all, a deficiency in humility from an LCIA-perspective meant that my ego-driven behaviours could result in selective listening, difficulty admitting errors or failures, arrogance, overconfidence, complacency, and even hubris (Crossan et al., 2012) and from the perspective of the Seven Grandfather Teachings could equate to a lack of compassion, calmness, meekness, gentleness, and patience (Nottawaseppi Huron Band of the Potawatomi, 2022). Thus, my deficiency of temperance, a character trait arguably embedded in the Seven Grandfather teachings on "humility" could ultimately mean that I suffer to a degree from a sense of "short-termism", the need for instant gratification and the inability to see the possible constraints in a situation (Crossan et al., 2012).

Interestingly, when I first joined the Public Service, I was handsomely rewarded for my excesses of courage and drive, while managing to stay out of any career-ending issues resulting from my deficiencies of humility and temperance. In fact, in the earliest days of my career, my lack of humility seemed to have been misinterpreted as a confident leader, and my deficiency in temperance, as someone who was just passionate and really cared about the work we do and the results we achieve. This should not surprise us, as the definition of "leadership excellence" has evolved greatly over time, from "the great man theory" (pre-1900), to trait theories that highlight natural talents (1900–1948); to contingency theories that focus on the situational variables leaders face (1948–1980s); to the transformational theories (1978-present) and multifaceted theories (1990-present), that integrate aspects from both the transactional (founded on trait and behavioural issues) and transformational schools of thought (founded on visionary and entrepreneurial elements) that exist today (Van Wart and Dicke, 2016). While there is arguably a relative dearth and fragmentation of materials available that speak to the best leadership style to apply within the federal construct, I would argue that today, balance is key. Today, the world we live in is more challenging; the problems and opportunities we face are much more interrelated and complex and arguably require leaders to call upon and leverage all the Seven Grandfather Teachings and Eleven Dimension of Character Leadership traits in the right mix, and proportion, at the right time.

Finding balance and bringing my whole and authentic self to my leadership practice

Finding balance and harmony within, and with all living things around me, including within my public sector leadership practice, has been a lifelong journey. It has not been easy, nor passive, but rather a challenging active pursuit of a better, more peaceful way of life, where understanding of self and self-acceptance is central to my personal and professional growth. In the earliest days of my journey, the ceremony was integral to getting me on the right path. The Sweat Lodge Ceremonies in which I participated provided me with opportunities to cleanse and heal, as well as reground myself during times of adversity. The feasts we shared afterwards provided me with a sense of cultural connectedness in community and a heightened connection to the physical and spiritual worlds that I had not experienced in my youth. These ceremonies provided me with greater insight into my cultural roots and helped me build a greater sense of identity. It is said that when we are sitting in a Sweat Lodge, we are sitting at the centre of the Four Directions and inside the lodge, we seek the help of the Creator and the spirits. As a 60s Scoop survivor,[3] albeit one raised with all the trappings of middle-class life, I did not carry a great sense of self or place in either my formative or early adulthood years, yet the Sweat Lodge Ceremonies did just that. They gave me a greater sense of self and place.

In 2007, I participated in a Sweat Lodge Ceremony held on the traditional lands of the Squamish First Nation, in West Vancouver, British Columbia, as part of a one-week course co-facilitated by the Canada School of Public Service and the Squamish First Nation called *Mikawiwin: Leadership and Aboriginal Affairs*. While protecting the sacredness of this experience, I feel compelled to share that an eagle came to me in that ceremony. Its wings seemed to flap vigorously around my head, yet with an opposing sense of grace, beauty, and gentleness that seemed to entomb me. The beauty of this experience brought me to tears, yet it would only be years later, when reflecting on the reoccurring sightings and visions of eagles and their symbolism, that I would understand how they have and would continue to inform and guide the rest of my life's journey. It is taught that "when we lay down our tobacco, *Migizi* [(the Eagle)] comes down to gather our prayers and then soars high up into Ishpeming (above) to bring them to the Gchi Manidoo [(the Creator)]" (Sault Ste. Marie Tribe of Chippawa Indians, 2020), and perhaps that day, unannounced to me, my prayers for peace, wholeness and self-acceptance were answered, even if not yet fully embraced.

Shortly after this experience, I participated in the Pulling Together Canoe Journey. During this week-long journey down the mighty Fraser River, we stopped and camped at six different participating First Nation communities along the way. We finished the final leg with a landing on Jericho Beach, situated on the unceded traditional territories of the xʷməθkʷəy̓əm (Musqueam Indian Band), Sḵwx̱wú7mesh (Squamish Nation), and səlilwətaɬ (Tsleil-Waututh Nation), located between downtown Vancouver and the University of British Columbia. During the landings at each First Nation community, protocol required leading canoes to circle clockwise, in the order for the Four Directions, until all canoe families had caught up and then all would gather facing the beach, while the canoe landing ceremony took place, which requires the leader in each canoe family to ask permission to come onto the land of the host community. During each of these ceremonies, except for the final landing at Jericho, eagles circled above, seemingly putting myself and others on notice to be courageous, to stretch our limits, to be patient with the present and know that the future holds possibilities that we may not be able to see.

3 Sixties Scoop – The large-scale apprehension of Indigenous children in the 1960s from their homes, communities, and families of birth – often without their parents' or band's consent – and their subsequent adoption into predominantly non-Indigenous families across the United States and Canada (Johnson, P. in the Canadian Encyclopedia. The "Scooping" of Indigenous Children, 1951–1980s. *https://www.thecanadianencyclopedia.ca/en/article/sixties-scoop.)*

First, in the Sweat Lodge, and then during the Pulling Together Canoe Journey, where my first two mesmerizing and spiritual encounters with eagles took place, seemed to be suggesting that the eagle spirit was calling for, or guiding me, perhaps even symbolic of who I am at my core and the unknown gifts I possess. After all, eagles are known to be a source of inspiration to many Indigenous peoples for their ability to see the big picture as well as focus on the smallest of details (Squamish Lil'wat Cultural Centre, 2013). Ironically, when I was young, people used to tell me that I was "as blind as a bat", yet neither they nor I knew at that time that in many Indigenous mythologies, the bat represents rebirth – the ability to transform our former selves into a newborn being, as well as wisdom, as they can perceive things in an uncommon way. The prominence and symbology of eagles have continued to reveal itself periodically, even in more recent times. In 2021, my family and I moved from downtown Ottawa to the quaint village of Aylmer, in Gatineau on the unceded lands of the Algonquin Anishinaabe peoples.

While affordability and downsizing due to the departure of our oldest boy were at the root of this move, there were times when I questioned this decision. Yet, the first spring after our move, a kettle of eagles circled in the skies about our house for nearly ten minutes, with one even performing an overhead flyby near our driveway as my youngest son and I looked up in awe. Golden and Bald Eagles have been sighted by bird enthusiasts along the Eardley Escarpment, one of the richest and most fragile ecosystems in nearby Gatineau Park; however, our neighbours told me that they had not seen them in our neighbourhood. An ornithologist could surely provide further insight into eagle behaviours in and around their natural environments; however, I have not heard of sightings of this nature near our home in Aylmer, nor did some quick online research reveal any similar sightings in the years before or since. Moreover, an ornithologist would not likely weigh in on the experience I lived during the Sweat Lodge on Squamish First Nation lands, nor why since (and not before), these types of sightings have occurred with some degree of frequency and uniqueness.

Where this journey has brought me and how it impacts my ways of being and leading

My ongoing journey of personal and cultural discovery has continued to positively affect my perceptions of self, most specifically, my views on my blindness, and more recently, the gifts I have likely always possessed, which have continued to reveal themselves over the years. First, I have long since stopped trying to either hide or compensate for my *disability*. Previous efforts to do so were exhausting and counterproductive, as they not only reinforced the colonial perspective of disabilities being epistemologically deficit-oriented, and differences among people being dichotomous in nature but also because they prevented me from optimizing the good that could come from the gifts I possess. In both my professional and personal life, I used to feel as if I had lived in two worlds, or perhaps, between two worlds – the Indigenous world that I have embraced over the last 20-plus years, and the Western world, into which I was born and was raised. Unfortunately, this opposing way of being diminished the Indigenous energies and ways of being that I possess that could have been used to cope with and thrive on when facing life's pressures. It undermined my efforts to engage modernity in a consistently positive and constructive way, while at the same time developing and maintaining my Indigenous values that are important for my health and well-being and others with whom I interact daily (McCoy, 2009).

While at work, there remains a need for me to self-identify as a person with a disability to receive appropriate accommodation plans, such as adaptive screen-reading software. I, like many other Indigenous peoples, do not see myself as disabled, which makes the whole self-identification and accommodation process seem awkward, uncomfortable, and incongruent with my cultural norms. Certainly, I do acknowledge that my lack of vision does place some limitations on my ability to perform certain tasks, but by no means today do I feel that my low vision lessens in any way the contributions that I am able to make to my family, my community, and the Canadians I have helped serve through my public sector leadership role. Admittedly, I do not feel as though I have faced much direct or overt discrimination or harassment in the workplace as a result of my indigeneity or blindness, however, there are times when I feel that I may have been affected by "othering" – an underpinning sense that others do not quite look at me the same way as they do their non-Indigenous and fully abled colleagues. Within the federal construct, any examples I would share would be relatively opaque and only serve to highlight the degree to which the government organizations in Canada have continued to advance their drive for equity, diversity, and inclusion in the workplace. However, outside work, the true nature of some people's misunderstanding and underestimation of the capabilities and gifts possessed by (Indigenous) persons with disabilities is more evident. For example, as an avid runner and recent pursuer of duathlon sport, I often wear my bright yellow athletic shirt with "Blind Runner" emboldened on the back, and without fail, whenever I do, I get comments from runners, cyclists, and other passers-by such as "well done", "keep it up", "way to go" and the like, comments which were scarce at best when I did not wear the t-shirt. While my feelings on this require continued reflection and self-examination, the somewhat patronizing tone in which these comments are delivered could reasonably be translated as "you are doing amazing for an (Indigenous) person with limitations". Then, given the myriads of walking, running, and cycling paths that surround the Outaouais region in close proximity to the Parliament Buildings near where I work, it would be fair to say that these comments are also coming from other Federal Public Servants, and that, therefore, the "othering" phenomenon exists within the Federal construct too, even if it is much more difficult to detect.

While there remains much work to do to ensure that Indigenous leaders with disabilities are not only appropriately represented in Canada's federal workplaces, but that they can also bring and apply their whole and authentic selves and leadership practices to all that they do. Today, I feel as though I live a life that recognizes Indigenous ways of being and systems "as their own sovereign system within a world that formerly thrived off Indigenous systems" (Online: Indigenous Motherhood, 2018). No longer do I stand with one foot in the Indigenous world and the other in the Western world, but rather today I am more firmly grounded in my Indigenous identity and capable of bringing my fundamental and core Indigenous values, morals, and beliefs to all that I do. This means that my leadership practice today embodies Indigenous leadership principles including the concept that leadership is more than just serving others, but rather a more circular, holistic, and connected approach, grounded in a sense of spirituality. It has a greater communication through storytelling, a longer-term perspective, less focus on hierarchy and more on circularity and community, and the continued desire to be authentic to one's Indigenous ways, while being respectful of ingrained colonized mainstream practices that still permeate much of our workplaces (Althaus and O'Faircheallaigh, 2019). Interestingly, there is evidence that some of these traditional Indigenous leadership practices are regaining standing and currency in the continued evolution of Westernized mainstream approaches to leadership (Julien et al., 2010).

While I am still on a journey of self-discovery, today, I know who I am and much about the gifts I possess. I cannot see however, I have been given the gift of vision and the ability to convey my visions, with increasing frequency, and with clarity and conviction, helping others to come together for a shared purpose, or to soar high and achieve their individual dreams and aspirations. Today, I am comfortable being perfectly imperfect and realize more than ever that the increasingly complex and interrelated nature of the challenges and opportunities we face in today's work environment calls upon me as a leader to continue to develop and sustain a leadership practice grounded in competency, character, commitment, and perhaps most importantly, community.

References

Althaus, C., and O'Faircheallaigh, C. (2019). *Leading from between: Indigenous participation and leadership in the public service*. McGill-Queen's Indigenous and Northern Studies. Number 94 in series.

Crossan, M., Gandz, J., and Seijts, G. (2012). *Developing leadership character*. Ivey Business Journal, Issues, January/February. https://iveybusinessjournal.com/publication/developing-leadership-character/.

Crossan, M., Mazutis, D., and Seijts, G. (2013). In search of virtue: The role of virtues, values and character strengths in ethical decision making. *Journal of Business Ethics*, 113(4), 567–581.

Crossan, M., Seijts, G., and Gandz, J. (2018). *Leadership character insight assessment*. Sigma Assessment Systems Inc.

Indigenous Motherhood. (2018). "Walking in Two Worlds" Can Be Seen as a Colonial Idea. (August 23). https://indigenousmotherhood.wordpress.com/2018/08/23/walking-in-two-worlds-can-be-seen-as-a-colonial-idea/. Accessed August 2, 2023.

Ineese-Nash, N. (2020). Disability as a colonial construct: The missing discourse of culture in conceptualizations of disabled Indigenous children. *Canadian Journal of Disability Studies*, 9(3), 28–51.

Julien, M., Wright, B., and Zinni, D. (2010). Stories from the circle: Leadership lessons learned from Aboriginal leaders. *Leadership Quarterly*, 21, 114–126.

Kim, S. (2002). Participative management and job satisfaction: Lessons for management leadership. *Public Administration Review*, 62(2), 231–241.

Little Bear, L. (2000). Jagged worldviews colliding. *Reclaiming Indigenous Voice and Vision*, 77, 85 108.

McCoy B. (2009). 'Living between two worlds': who is living in whose worlds? *Australis Psychiatry*, 17(1), S20–S23.

Merriam-Webster (2023). https://www.merriam-webster.com/thesaurus/vision. August 23, 2023.

Nottawaseppi Huron Band of the Potawatomi (2022). Seven grandfather teachings. https://nhbp-nsn.gov/seven-grandfather-teachings/#:~:text=He%20was%20taught%20the%20lessons,Honesty%2C%20Humility%2C%20and%20Truth. Accessed July 23, 2023.

Norris, H. (2014). Colonialism and the rupturing of Indigenous worldviews of impairment and relational interdependence: A beginning dialogue towards reclamation and social transformation. *Critical Disability Discourse*, 6, 53–79.

Online Etymology Dictionary (2023). https://www.etymonline.com/search?q=disability. August 21, 2023.

Roberts, M. (2022). Indigenous disability awareness month – A conversation with Dr. Rheanna Robinson and Lisa Smith. Rick Hansen Foundation. https://www.rickhansen.com/news-stories/blog/indigenous-disability-awareness-month-conversation-dr-rheanna-robinson-and-lisa.

Sault Ste. Marie Tribe of the Chippewa Indians (2020). Anishinaabe teachings of the eagle (Migizi). Newsroom. Cultural News. (August 26). https://www.saulttribe.com/newsroom/209-cultural-news/6938-anishinaabe-teachings-of-the-eagle-migizi.

Seijts, G., and Young, M. K. (2019). Leadership Character Blogs 2019. Ian O. Ihnatowycz Institute for Leadership. Ivey Business School. https://www.ivey.uwo.ca/media/3790504/2019leader_character_blogs_bklt.pdf.

Skwxwú7mesh Líl̓wat7úl Cultural Centre/Squamish Lil'wat Cultural Centre. (2013). The Eagle. https://shop.slcc.ca/. Accessed September 22, 2023.

Van Wart, M., and Dicke, L. (Eds.). (2016). *Administrative leadership in the public sector*. Routledge.

8 Reframing the narrative—Navigating self-representation

Indigenous Deaf people

Melanie McKay-Cody

Introduction

Indigenous Deaf people have their own history and culture. In Indigenous Deaf communities across North America, the term "disability" is rarely used because the term does not fit them. Like many hearing Indigenous scholars across different disciplines, writing about "disability" in Indigenous scholarship today reveals a similar Native perspective. For example, Dr. Locust (hearing Cherokee), who I had the honour of working within the early 1990s, stated in her work "there are many Native American languages that have no word for 'disability' or 'handicapped' " (Lovern & Locust, 2013, p. 52). Ward (2022) emphasizes, "For Indigenous peoples, disability is a foreign term, steeped in colonial ideologies" (p. 338). There are other scholars who discuss "disability" and "impairment" as alien, which conflicts with their traditional beliefs (Connell, 2007; Hickey, 2008; King, 2010; Rivas Velarde, 2018; Watson, 2002). Interestingly, even Shakespeare wrote of the balance of disability as a social identity. Indigenous people with impairments experience a separation of living with impairment and the interpreted disability from Western construct based on the ongoing prevalence of European ideologies and colonization. Indigenous people balance their contributions to both family and community in addition to handling their disability. It is a unique balancing act that shapes their personal perspectives (1996).

Lovern and Locust (2013) state:

> While the term "disability" is currently used in Western cultures
> to refer to physical and mental differences, the term
> "Handicapped" is used in some of the Native American voices.
> The terminology difference represents not only a difference in time,
> as some interviews were conducted beginning in 1960, but also
> a difference in the translation used by some Native Americans.
>
> (p. 75)

The sentiment expressed here holds true for Indigenous Deaf peoples, who have long experienced being called by different, degrading names most of their lives. In Indigenous Deaf communities, we rarely bring up the term "disability" because it does not align with who they are. The term and concept belong to Western scientific research. Through the deeply entrenched influence of the Western research community, the term has come to apply to Indigenous communities who, for a variety of reasons, absorbed Western influence into their education and ways of thinking about Indigenous Deaf people. Unfortunately, both sides suffer from a lack of familiarity regarding their own Indigenous Deaf, who

DOI: 10.4324/9781032656519-11

reside on the reservation or live in urban communities. In their work, Lovern and Locust (2013) describe how "Native Americans have had to find a place in their societies for the new Western concepts of disability" and how children are accepted in the village but are likely being "segregated out [into] the education system and labelled 'mentally or physically disabled'" (p. 90). Many Indigenous Deaf people undergo a life experience adjacent to those who attend Deaf residential schools across the nation. Castleden (2002), who is an American Sign Language (ASL) interpreter in Canada, witnessed and wrote in her case study, "Deafness is often equated with mental disability or confused with other disabilities" (p. 164). For that reason, Indigenous Deaf peoples dislike the term "disability," as it also triggers educational and personal trauma from Deaf residential schooling.

Decolonizing medical and clinical influences

As Castleden (2002) outlines the medical model from the pathological framework in literature, deafness is identified as a disability that Lane described as "a broken part that needs to be fixed" (1999). It is well known that Western doctors and specialists tend to see Indigenous Deaf people as "problems that need fixing"; circumstances, which lead to erroneous negative clinical and medical approaches in treatment because they are not perceived as "normal." It is widely known in Deaf communities that 90% of the Deaf population are descended from hearing parents who have little to no knowledge or exposure to deafness before the medical diagnosis (Bat-Chava, 2000; Castleden, 2002; Haualand & Grønningsµter, 2003; Leigh et al., 2022; McKay-Cody, 2019; Nguyen, 2008). This leads to hearing parents misunderstanding that deafness is not just a medical phenomenon but a cultural and linguistic experience. They want their child to be hearing with the assistance of medical technology and often try to steer them into operating within the dominant culture; a culture which has, for centuries, disregarded the needs and desires of the Deaf. This is all to avoid the label of "disabled" and is seen in hearing culture as a way of saving the child. However, whether this common chain of occurrences is an act of mercy or not is highly controversial, as it alienates and demonizes those who do not benefit from a hearing and "able" dominated society. At its root, did Indigenous Deaf people ask to be fixed? After all, their primary concerns, as a community, often tend to relate to accessibility and visibility rather than being "fixed." Some Indigenous Deaf people made their own decisions to have medical replacements like cochlear implants, while others were forced into these procedures and replacements (CI), by their own parents because their family wanted them to function as hearing people. Often, it was the medical establishment that manipulated the parents and families to have their children get implants.

These systems take advantage of the grief these confused and under-informed parents feel after discovering their child has become deaf. However, as made evident by first-hand accounts from the Deaf community, this is an inhumane bandage that ignores the underlying causes and greater issues. Eventually, after years of using CIs, many children want the devices removed from their heads as they were placed inside of them without their consent. Indigenous Deaf people in their teens or into adulthood often want CIs removed, but the cost is astronomical and out of reach for many. Resources about Indigenous Deaf peoples and cultures, including materials on the traditional Indigenous ways of teaching the Indigenous Deaf, are lacking on both reserves/reservations and in cities. Early intervention programs regarding the teaching of Indigenous Deaf ways of knowing and being would be helpful; however, there is no training or funding available for Indigenous

Deaf people to establish necessary mentorship networks and resources for families on the reserves/reservations. As a result, parents often find themselves within an echo chamber where the only path presented to them is through the lens of the hospitals, clinics, and Indian Health Services that view deafness from the Western scientific perspective.

Historically, Indigenous Deaf people have fought to remove the stereotypes placed on them by medical doctors and clinical specialists. From the perspective of the traditional Native ways, there is nothing wrong with being culturally Indigenous Deaf, so in spite of medical and clinical practices, thousands of Indigenous Deaf people opt to separate from the Western influence in regard to the concept of deafness. Through "cultural teaching," a combination of Deaf Culture and Deaf Education from their own Deaf residential schools, these Indigenous Deaf adults and children are able to accept their deafness. After "graduation," they reclaim their identities and unlearn what they learned at their deaf schools. Many reclaim the Native ways and re-identify themselves as Indigenous Deaf people. Unfortunately, there are many more Indigenous Deaf people who are lost due to a long history of linguistic and cultural genocide.

In the old days, the Indigenous Deaf played important roles contributing to Indigenous societies. They were recognized for their skills and talents regardless of their hearing status. For instance, John Clarke, a Blackfeet Deaf artist from Browning, Montana, had a skill for sculpting wildlife animals, to the extent that several of his sculptures are in galleries and museums around the nation. Presently, Dennis Long, a Navajo Deaf rug weaver who crafts Navajo style rugs, has many of his works housed in galleries and museums as well. He was taught by his mother, who is well known within the Navajo rug-weaving community. Nancy Rourke, a Kumeyaay Deaf artist, has become notable for her mural artwork. Several Indigenous Deaf people dance in Pow Wows because their parents provided support in cultural teaching.[1] Several Indigenous Deaf people have emerged with doctoral degrees and fixed inaccurate literature about their people, including publications on how the concept of "disability" is understood in different lights. Too often, people of the majority do not recognize that there are accomplished Indigenous Deaf people across a sea of disciplines, who have gone entirely unnoticed by the outside community.

The root of the problem is that medical doctors/specialists and clinical pathologists are exclusively of a Western scientific mind, directly inherited from European practice, ideology, and influence. They are overwhelmingly part of the hearing majority, making these people more likely to place negative, degrading, and minimizing labels on people, such as "hearing impaired," "hearing loss," or all other classifications based on the word "hearing." Why not turn the tables? If Deaf people used terms such as "signing impaired" to label non-signing hearing people, the negative connotations would clearly shine through. In the traditional Indigenous culture, there are tribal signs describing deafness that have no relation to "disability" at all. These particular sign languages are from different tribes, usually signing "Deaf," "HEAR NOT," or "SPEAK NO" (McKay-Cody, 2019). In past tribal stories and some literature, Indigenous Deaf people were given tribal names meaning "MAN or WOMAN Deaf."

---

1 The significance of this cultural tradition is that those who danced in the Pow Wows were the ones who received familial support in cultural teaching; the separation of the Indigenous Deaf from their families during residential schooling means many do not have the privilege to learn. Many hearing Indigenous people do not sign or have the ability to share traditional knowledge.

Community-engaged research

In the middle of the 1990s, it was the beginning of a wind of change in research to fit Indigenous ways rather than rely on centuries old Western theories. Well-known authors, Kovach, Smith, and Wilson, in their articles influenced the next generation of Indigenous researchers using a different approach called Indigenous Methodologies (Kovach, 2009; Smith, 2001; Wilson, 2008). In the time since, it has spread widely in Indigenous research communities around the globe. When examined, it becomes clear that this methodology fits the hearing Indigenous populations, but often falls short when it comes to the Indigenous Deaf community. Deaf communities are inherently visual-minded, and, by extension, Indigenous Deaf people tend to use sign languages and think with a more visual focus. McKay-Cody coined the term "Indigenous Deaf Methodologies" to refer to a set of research approaches that are more applicable to this specific group of people. Indigenous Deaf Methodologies enable a fresh start on emerging community-engaged research between the researcher and the Indigenous Deaf community.

This research is still ongoing and is designed to empower the community to look at their communal needs by using both ASL and North American Indian Sign Language (NAISL). In Native communities, whether Deaf or hearing, signing in NAISL is known as Hand Talk and is an integrated part of cultural communication with respect to their signed narratives. These narratives range from traditional stories to their learning journeys in reclaiming their tribal sign languages that have been lost to many tribes. The exception being tribes in Western regions where Plains Indian Sign Language, Great Basin Indian Sign Language, and Southwest Indian Sign Language[2] are still in use among hearing and deaf signers.

Regarding NAISL, there is another name that has been coined within community-engaged research and the field of linguistics. In these settings, where sign languages are being used worldwide, the term "shared-signing communities" has become frequently used (Bickford & McKay-Cody, 2018; Kisch, 2012). ASL lacks Indigenous contextual signs, though, with some gestures being made up by non-Native educators based on how food, clothes, furniture, and other aspects of the world are understood through the white lens. For that reason, Indigenous Deaf people within shared-signing communities incorporate ASL, the "national sign language" (Zeshan, 2008) they learned from Deaf residential schools, and cultural context signs from NAISL into their linguistic identity. In today's world, Indigenous Deaf people have created and Indigenized numerous signs to fit their communal performances, such as ceremonies and signing circles (Freeman, 2017). These signs refer to cultural elements, such as food, in a way that complements the culture.

There is a plethora of various linguistic and cultural identities within the Indigenous Deaf community. Most of the members are Indigenous Deaf people who have been exposed to the Deaf culture from Deaf residential schools in multiple locations around North America. The D/deaf dichotomy, for clarification, refers to two different identities. Capital D "Deaf" refers to a group of people who are culturally Deaf meaning they grew up in Deaf residential schools or public schools with a large population of Deaf children and use sign language as a primary language in their lives. This is often the national language, which is ASL in the United States. Lowercase D "deaf" refers to people who were not exposed to Deaf educators or Deaf role models during their upbringings. These individuals were not active members of a Deaf community when they were growing up

---

2 These three sign languages are language varieties of NAISL.

and cannot be considered members of the cultural community. There is a large amount of literature on the D/deaf dichotomy, and it is an acceptable term for use in Deaf communities (Cue et al., 2019; Deafhood Foundation, 2017; Holcomb, 2012; McKay-Cody, 2019; Reagan et al., 2021; Stapleton, 2015; Woodward & Horejes, 2016). Other members tend to be Native and non-Native interpreters, parents of Indigenous Deaf children, Elders, and others who work together for common goals to educate the public about this population. Teaching within these groups becomes a consensual agreement and community-wide endeavour, with members educating the outside world about the Indigenous Deaf through presentations and outreach projects to different agencies and universities.

The use of American Sign Language and North American Indian Sign Language

As usual, many hearing Indigenous scholars mistook and misinterpreted sign languages, mostly based on assumptions without consulting with the Indigenous Deaf community. A passage in Lovern and Locust's (2013) book about ASL and American Indian Sign Language (AISL) states, "One skill that is debated frequently is that of teaching hearing impaired persons American Sign Language (ASL)" (p. 103). Following the earlier discussion about medical terminology, the authors of this piece should have had more awareness regarding hearing- and disability-forward labels, especially, given the recent date of publication.[3] First-hand knowledge is a necessary influence within these discussions. In my work, I came to know that Dr. Locust used Hand Talk and we communicated through that shared language in the early 1990s. She had learned it from her father, who had acquired it in the military from soldiers from various tribal nations. However, hearing people are generally ignorant to the differences between ASL and NAISL and fail to realize that language confusion can occur with Indigenous Deaf children. Bilingual education does not exist on the reserves/reservations as there are a lack of Indigenous Deaf educators who are familiar with both sign languages.

Of course, there is a large amount of misinformation where the origins of sign languages are concerned. Lovern and Locust (2013) mentioned, "The remedy for this situation might be to teach the family to use ASL, but the cost of such a program could be prohibitive" (p. 103). According to my knowledge, there are certain states that hire people to go out to the homes of hearing parents with deaf children or provide classes over Zoom to teach ASL. A widespread issue is that hearing people with no background in Indigenous Deaf education make decisions on who needs to learn ASL or AISL. Problematic statements such as,

> In many tribes a few members remain that know and use AISL. In many cases, this sign system AISL is much easier and faster to learn, is more functional and might be appropriate in a rural or an isolated family situation: it could also create a rich source of communication for Native Americans with hearing loss.
>
> (Lovern & Locust, 2013, p. 103)

It is very minimizing to use a phrase such as "few members" as there are more signers, who already know NAISL. Additionally, younger generations of both hearing Indigenous and

3 The term "hearing impaired" is no longer in use except among deaf persons who grew up in mainstream public schools without exposure to Deaf Education, Deaf Culture, or Deaf role models.

Indigenous Deaf people are reclaiming their tribal sign languages. Today, sign language documentation and revitalization are an emerging field and Indigenous Deaf children are starting to bring back tribal sign languages in their learning journeys.

"Two Worlds" is for hearing, not Indigenous Deaf peoples

"Walking in two worlds" is a frequently used phrase in hearing Indigenous literature, but does it do justice when communicating the experiences of Indigenous Deaf peoples? According to hearing Indigenous scholars, the first two "worlds" of a traditional cultural identity and a dominant cultural identity are applicable to Indigenous Deaf people. Hearing Indigenous people have to live within both the world of the English-speaking majority with its overbearing cultural influence and the world of their own tribal community with its own spoken language and rich cultural influence.[4] The other two worlds represent Deaf communities. One world is that of the Deaf community and culture of the United States, where ASL, the national sign language, is acquired from the Deaf residential school system (Zeshan, 2008). The last world regards Indigenous Deaf culture, with its own language and cultural identity. The combination of these four worlds—or identities—is what underlies the layered experience of every Indigenous Deaf individual. This is a unique identity developed and established by the Indigenous Deaf people themselves since 1994. It is tied to their Indigenous ways of knowing, being, and doing. Just in the last two years, Indigenous Deaf people have developed their own cultural context signs and Indigenized traditional teaching for Deaf residential schools and Deaf communities.

It must be understood that it is hearing Indigenous scholars who emphasize the concept of "two worlds" (Locust & Lovern, 2013, p. 206). For example, "Walking in two worlds represents a unique position for the individual who either must or chooses to interact in the Western world while maintaining her Indigenous world" (Locust & Lovern, 2013, p. 206). As another example, Dauphinais et al. (2009) stated, "Indigenous Americans come from cultures rich in traditional knowledge, survival, resilience, and healing. Most Indigenous Americans experience 'living in two worlds,' that of their traditional or tribal culture and that of the dominant culture" (2009). From non-Native Deaf cultural perspectives, "juggling two worlds" (McKee and Hauser, 2012) really seems to only encompass two sets of binaries: Deaf/hearing and ASL/English or American/Native culture and English/Indigenous spoken language. Neither of these sets, even overlapped, truly encompass all the Indigenous Deaf experience, though. It would be more accurate to say that the Indigenous Deaf do not walk in two worlds, but instead walk in four. There has been an observable pattern of hearing scholars neglecting to acknowledge the experience the Indigenous Deaf have with all of the aforementioned identities overlapping. These articles do not include or consider this intersectionality when addressing language learning and teaching concerns involving Indigenous Deaf children and adults.

---

4 It is worth mentioning that this only applies to Indigenous Deaf people in an ideal situation as many face language barriers and do not have communication in their homes and among their community members. Some families create gestures and establish a set of "home signs" to communicate within the household. In some tribes, signs vary from clan to clan depending on location.

Created by Dr. Melanie McKay-Cody
Designed by Nicholas Sanchez, 2019
Remade in HD by Christina Kelly, 2024

Figure 8.1 Circle of Interconnection.

Source: Created by Melanie McKay-Cody and designed by Nicholas Sanchez, 2019

Learning within Indigenous shared signing communities

Indigenous Deaf people are not the only ones who are a part of Indigenous shared-signing communities. A multitude of other groups are involved including the parents of Indigenous Deaf children, Native and non-Native ASL interpreters, the children of Indigenous Deaf people, and some specific professionals who work with the community. They all shared the Circle of Interconnection which fits the 5Rs (respect, responsibility, relationship, relevance, and reciprocity) an approach commonly utilized by Indigenous Deaf people for learning traditional knowledge (https:tiht.org) (Figure 8.1).

The Circle of Interconnection created by McKay-Cody as a result of community-engaged research and input from participants. For more information about Turtle Island Hand Talk, an international organization serving Deaf, Hard of Hearing, Deaf-Blind, and hearing Indigenous people, please visit tiht.org.

This community-engaged research and sharing of traditional knowledge began in 2017, consisting of Indigenous people from different tribes in North America. Kirkness and Barnhardt (1991) created a 4Rs framework consisting of respect, relevance, reciprocity, and responsibility; however, other Indigenous scholars added a 5th R, standing for relationship. The 5Rs approach has since become standard. Ward (2021) described the 4Rs framework in his article on the education system. Additionally, using the 5Rs, McKay-Cody's work concentrated primarily on Indigenous Deaf people and the distinct needs within Indigenous Deaf communities. Within the Indigenous Deaf community, the reasons for their struggles are widely known. This negative view primarily stems from the influence of past research, which heavily relied on rehabilitation studies involving members of the Indigenous Deaf community. This ultimately contributed to the amount of inaccuracy in scholarly work and literature regarding these people. Non-Native scholars across a wide range of disciplines have exploited them to a great extent and published research rife with ethical violations. The innocence of the community was taken advantage of regarding how the research was to be conducted, causing profound communal trauma. They were not consulted about their rights and how data was collected. Stemming from educational trauma mentioned earlier from Deaf residential schooling, many Indigenous Deaf people do not have good literacy and their understanding of English, especially, in dense academic and legal forms, has presented challenges for them.

During the community-engaged research program, workshops were provided to these groups to increase awareness about exploitation and provide education regarding their rights to protect their data. Discussion on the term "disability" had come up a few times and participants expressed why they felt that concept had no value within the group and why such terminology shouldn't be in use. This also applies to Indigenous interpreters who are members of shared-signing communities; as well, cultural education and understanding are of the utmost importance because they contribute their services to the Indigenous Deaf community. Fortunately, as they spend time within the community, they come to possess the knowledge of Indigenous cultural context signs. The opportunity to engage with Indigenous-themed workshops, meetings, and presentations can provide interpreters with the ability to interpret for community members more effectively. Sometimes, interpreters who are CODAs[5] have first-hand experience living with Indigenous Deaf parents in a household grappling with cultural and linguistic genocide and communication barriers.

Conclusion: positive steps for the future

With the decolonization of medical and clinical methods, Indigenous communities need to step forward to build a bridge from unknown territory to an exchange of traditional knowledge about each group. Cultural understanding and a recognition of community needs are of substantial importance to these Nations. As of today, McKay-Cody, the author of this piece, is working alongside the Native people in an effort to correct these circumstances. Native people are educated on and actively involved in the gathering

---

5 Child/Children of Deaf Adults; hearing children raised in a Deaf household.

of data, which can then be used to assess the needs of each host Nation's community. These strategies will aid in figuring out how the repercussions of colonization can be improved through decolonization, the breaking down of language barriers, and an increase in culture-forward and visually accessible teaching approaches from Indigenous lenses.

"Disability" is not a word in our signed or spoken tribal vocabularies; it is only a concept that can be understood through Western-constructed ideologies. A necessary revisit of the literature of different academic fields regarding the Indigenous Deaf must continue to be conducted. Additionally, discussion and research into how better accessibility for Indigenous Deaf peoples can be employed in tribal colleges and universities where networks of Indigenous staff and faculty exist. There is a dire need to revitalize programs, specifically, the new Native Interpreter training program with coursework in Native topics coursework.[6] There is a desperate need for Native interpreters, who could act as a bridge between hearing and Deaf Indigenous people. In order to maintain the journeys and life experience of community members, learning about the diverse cultures that exist within these communities at home and in educational and public settings is of extreme importance. Indigenous Deaf Education is a blend of Indian and Deaf Educational methodologies using Indigenous ways of teaching. Restoring the culture in this way would also give hearing Indigenous people the opportunity to learn from their Indigenous Deaf counterparts and come to understand their ways of doing, being, and knowing (and vice versa). With a touch of compassion in addressing the ongoing effects of history within these cultures, implementing these ideas to uplift these communities should be an obvious positive step forward.

Acknowledgements

I would like to thank Christina Kelly for her assistance in editing this article and John Ward for his support in getting this article included in the handbook. I send my gratitude to those Indigenous Deaf people who shared their signed narratives and experiences; it was a necessary contribution for this to be a fruitful paper.

References

Bat-Chava, Y. (2000). Diversity of Deaf identities. *American Annals of the Deaf, 145*(5), 420–428.

Bickford, J. A., and McKay-Cody, M. (2018). Endangerment and revitalization of sign languages. In L. Hinton, L. Huss, & G. Roche (Eds.), *Routledge handbook of language revitalization* (pp. 255–264). New York, NY: Routledge.

Castleden, H. (2002). The Silent North: A Case Study on Deafness in a Dene Community. *Canadian Journal of Native Education, 26*(2), 152–168.

Connell, R. (2007). *Southern theory: The global dynamics of knowledge in social science*. London, UK: Routledge.

Cue, K. R., Pudans-Smith, K. K., Wolsey, J. A., Wright, S. J., and Clark, M. D. (2019). The Odyssey of Deaf epistemology: A search for meaning-making. *American Annals of the Deaf, 164*, 395–422. https://doi.org/10.1353/aad.2019.0017

Dauphinais, P., Charley, E., Robinson-Zañartu, C., Melroe O., and Baas, S. (2009). Home-school-community communication with Indigenous American Families. *NASP Communiqué, 37*, 19–26.

---

6 Ideally existing cross-departmentally within one university as well as collaborating with different universities and tribal colleges/universities where Indigenous students are enrolled.

Deafhood Foundation (2017). To D or not to D: Deafhood Foundation's Position Paper on Naming Deaf People. https://www.deafhood.org/positions

Freeman, R. R. (2017). The talking stick way: An Indigenous research methodology for engaging diverse global conversations. MA Thesis. University of Oklahoma.

Haualand, H., and Gr°nningsµter, A. (2003). Uniting divided worlds: Identity, family, and education in the life projects of Deaf and hard of hearing young people. *Disability Studies Quarterly*, 23(2), 75–88.

Hickey, H. S. J. (2008). Claiming spaces: Maori (Indigenous persons) making the invalid valid. In M. Levy, L. W. Nikora, B. Masters-Awatere, M. Rua, & W. Waitoki (Eds.), *Claiming Spaces: Proceedings of the 2007 National Maori and Pacific Psychologies Symposium*, 23rd–24th November 2007 (pp. 62–67). Hamilton, New Zealand: Māori and Psychology Research Unit, University of Waikato.

Holcomb, T. K. (2012). *Introduction to American Deaf culture*. New York, NY: Oxford University Press.

King, J. A. (2010). Weaving yarns: The lived experience of Indigenous Australia with adult-onset disability in Brisbane. Doctoral Dissertation, Queensland University of Technology.

Kirkness, V. J., and Barnhardt, R. (1991). First Nations and higher education: Four R's – respect, relevance, reciprocity, responsibility. *Journal of American Indian Education*, 30(3), 1–15.

Kisch, S. (2012). Demarcating generations of signers in the dynamic sociolinguistic landscape of a shared sign-language: The case of the Al-Sayyid Bedouin. In U. Zeshan & C. de Vos (Eds.), *Sign languages in village communities: Anthropological and linguistic insights* (pp. 87–125). Nijmegen, The Netherlands: Ishara Press (De Gruyter Mouton).

Kovach, M. (2009). *Indigenous methodologies characteristics, conversations, and contexts*. Toronto, ON: University of Toronto Press.

Leigh, I. W., Andrews, J. F., Miller, C. A., and Wolsey, J.-L. A. (2022). *Deaf people and society: Psychological, sociological, and educational perspectives* (3rd Ed.). New York, NY: Routledge.

Lovern, L. L., and Locust, C. (2013). *Native American communities on health and disability borderland dialogues*. New York, NY: Palgrave MacMillan.

McKay-Cody, M. (2019). Memory comes before knowledge – North American Indigenous Deaf: sociocultural study of rock/picture writing, community, sign languages, and kinship. Doctoral Dissertation, University of Oklahoma.

McKee, M. M., and Hauser, P. C. (2012). Juggling two worlds. In P. V. Paul & D. F. Moores (Eds.), *Deaf epistemologies: Multiple perspectives on the acquisition of knowledge* (pp. 45–62). Washington, DC: Gallaudet University Press.

Nguyen, L. T. (2008). Born into a hearing family: A guide for hearing parents with Deaf children. MA Thesis, Californian State University Sacramento.

Reagan, T., Matlins, P. E., and Pielick, C. D. (2021). Deaf epistemology, sign language and the education of d/Deaf children. *Educational Studies*, 57(1), 37–57.

Rivas Velarde, M. (2018). Indigenous Perspectives of Disability. *Disability Studies Quarterly* 38 (4) Fall 2018. https://dsq-sds.org/index.php/dsq/article/view/6114/5134

Shakespeare, T. (1996). Disability, identity, and difference. Exploring the divide: Illness and disability. In T. Shakespeare (Ed.) (2006). *Disability rights and wrongs*, 94–113. Florence, KY: Routledge.

Smith, L. T. (2001). *Decolonizing methodologies: Research and Indigenous peoples* (2nd Ed.). New York, NY: Zed Books Ltd.

Stapleton, L. (2015). When Being Deaf is Centered: d/Deaf women of Color's Experiences with racial/ethnic and d/Deaf identities in college. *Journal of College Student Development*, 56(6), 570–586.

Ward, J. T. (2022). Chapter 22. Reframing disabilities: Indigenous learners in Canadian educational systems. In Hilary N. Weaver (Ed). *The Routledge International Handbook on Indigenous Resilience*, 335–348. New York.

Watson, N. (2002). Well, I know this is going to sound very strange to you, but I don't see myself as a disabled person: Identity and disability. *Disability & Society*, 17(5), 509–527.

Wilson, S. (2008). *Research is ceremony, Indigenous research methods*. Winnipeg, Canada: Fernwood Publishing.

Woodward, J., and Horejes, T. (2016). d/Deaf: Origins and usage. In G. Gertz & P. Boudreault (Eds.), *The SAGE deaf studies Encyclopedia* (vol. 1, pp. 284–287). Thousand Oaks, CA: Sage Publications.

Zeshan, U. (2008). Roots, leaves, and branches: The typology of sign language. In R. M. de Quadros (Ed.), *Sign Languages: Spinning and unraveling the past, present and future* (TISLR 9, Brazil, December 2006, pp. 671–695). Petropolis, Brazil: Editora Arara Azul.

9 Neurodiversity from an Indigenous perspective

Honouring the Seven Grandfather's Teachings

Lexi Giizhigokwe Nahwegiizhic

Introduction – My journey

In this chapter, I hope to show you the critical differences in how our modern Western society views neurodiversity and my cultural perspective. As a young child, I thrived in school. My passion for learning was observable from kindergarten when I read books several grades higher than my level. By grade 2, I developed a knack for English grammar and spelling. In grade 7, I was chapters ahead of my peers in math class as I taught myself the material from the textbook. In my early primary years, school was easy for me. However, as the workload got heavier with each grade, I started to struggle. I noticed that I had to put in more effort than my peers to complete the same level of work. When I tried asking my teachers for help, they refused to listen. They did not have time to focus on a student doing well, as they had several barely passing students. My teachers told me that my grades could afford to drop a few percent. And so, they did.

By the time I reached high school, I was reasonably confident I was living with dyslexia, just like my father. He also had a gift for mathematics, but we often made similar mistakes in our arithmetic, flipping positive and negative integers when writing down equations and mixing up the order of numbers. Eventually, my high school had me tested, and I was officially diagnosed with dyslexia. The school offered me some accommodations, but they were insufficient to keep up with the pace of my classes. I had to advocate for myself at the beginning of every semester. Some teachers were open to accommodations, while others felt I was abusing the system. Many did not bother to ask what I specifically struggled with, instead subjecting me to stereotypes and myths. Being Indigenous only made the stereotypes worse. I recall one teacher remarking, "I thought you were different from the other [Indigenous] kids; I thought you were smart." My spirit was crushed. In their view, I could not be bright, living with a neurological development disorder, or be intelligent and Indigenous.

With my grades falling and my struggles mounting, my mental health plummeted. No one would listen when I asked for help, not even my school psychologist reached out. At 17 years old, I was admitted to a children's mental health program at the closest city hospital, two hours away from home. I was diagnosed with depression and generalized anxiety disorder. When I returned to school, I was treated differently. I felt as though my teachers were avoiding me. I barely attended the last few months of my senior year. It was a lonely and challenging year.

I was 18, when I received a diagnosis of Attention Deficit Hyperactivity Disorder (ADHD). I finally had some medical terminology to describe my experience of the world, although most people would continue to subject me to inaccurate stereotypes. My natural

DOI: 10.4324/9781032656519-12

gift for learning started to feel like an obstacle. How could I succeed when it felt impossible to receive an education? I began to question my abilities to learn. Maybe, I was not as bright as I had once thought. It was too late to change my mind on post-secondary education. I was already enrolled in a program and was expected to succeed. My entire First Nation reserve was cheering me on.

In 2017, I left my home and moved to Ottawa to complete a Bachelor of Science in Neuroscience and Mental Health. I wanted to know what made my brain different from my peers on a scientific level. After four years of study, I completed my Bachelor's. I felt I had a better biological understanding of the brain, but I could still not talk to others about how I experienced the world. I was still subjected to the same stereotypes and discriminatory remarks. Even with all my education, I was seen as *different*.

One day, I realized I was not the problem. I was living in a world where I was not accepted for who I was. The people around me did not see me as equal but as an anomaly. I was less of a human being in their eyes because I did not see the world from their perspective. The gifts that I carry – my strong attention to detail, my ability to absorb and learn information, and my mathematical talents – were all overshadowed by areas where I struggled: poor time management, forgetfulness, and sensory overstimulation. To survive, I had to learn to hide my "deficiencies" and mask my behaviour to appear "normal" in the public eye.

While I did become good at masking, it came at the cost of my mental health. I no longer knew who I was, my passions, or where I wanted to go in life. My behaviour was cold and bitter towards most people, pushing heavy judgement on how they lived their lives. I lost all control over my emotions, spiralling into fits of anger when someone noticed cracks in my psychological armour. I was tired of pretending to be someone that I was not. I knew I could not hide behind the mask for much longer without losing the few people I had left in my support system.

My first step towards change was evaluating what my mask looked like. Who was I trying to be? And how did it differ from who I was? Aside from my neurological differences, the most significant contrast was my cultural identity. I had grown up on my reserve as a proud Indigenous individual. I loved listening to stories from Elders and learning sacred traditions. My mask hid my spirit. In the city, it was not safe to identify as an Indigenous woman. We were, and still are, targeted for violence and sexual harassment. I felt safer when identified as a neurotypical, heterosexual white-passing woman instead of a neurodivergent, two-spirited Indigenous woman. My mask was in complete opposition to my authentic self. It was clear that I had to reconnect with my spirit and culture.

Along my journey, I noticed a striking difference in how I viewed people from cultural and societal aspects. Culturally, I focused on the strengths of other people. I was taught that each person is unique, blessed with gifts from the Creator, and must use them to fulfil their purpose on Earth. Societally, I focused on the deficits of other people. I noticed when someone did not fit the standard model of how to be a functioning human. Medical diagnoses cast a negative light by labelling individuals with disabilities. It's common to ask, "What's wrong with you?" and receive an answer with several medical disabilities, dysfunctions, disorders, or differences. All of which are seen as unacceptable and life-limiting.

If the Western World could adopt an Indigenous perspective, where one expects individuals to have different strengths and focus on what makes them unique, society would treat people better. Instead of relying on a medical model to define a person's capability, rather just use their spirit and gifts. Rather than looking for what is wrong, notice what is exceptional. Drop the individualistic way of thinking. Indigenous cultures have always focused on what is best for the community, as the notable strategy for survival was to work together.

In recent years, there has been a growing awareness and understanding of neurodiversity and neurodiverse conditions. The Internet culture has allowed individuals to speak about their experiences and broadcast their messages worldwide. Unfortunately, misinformation and ignorance also run rampant over the Internet, threatening to undermine any hope of mutual understanding between different types of people. While there are several different models to define neurodiversity, I prefer to use a biological definition.

What is neurodiversity?

Imagine our society as a giant puzzle. Each person is represented as an individual puzzle piece. No two pieces are identical; their combination of size, shape, colour, and pattern is unique. Some pieces are the same shape but not the same size. Other pieces have the same colours but use the colours in a different design. Even with their differences, every detail is essential, and no puzzle piece is more important than another. When correctly arranged, a beautiful picture is painted across the surface, telling a story with the collective attributes of every piece.

The unique attributes that comprise each puzzle piece describe the diversity among the elements. Simply put, diversity is the differences among a group, whether a group of people or puzzle pieces. Neurodiversity describes differences between brains; how the brain processes and interprets information. Structural and functional differences between brains give us our unique characteristics and personalities.

The brain is a complex organ, undergoing constant change starting around four weeks of embryonic development and continuing throughout life (Nicholls et al., 2012). With over 100 trillion neural connections across approximately 85 billion brain cells, there are endless opportunities for diversity to flourish within our neuroanatomy (Bear et al., 2016; Pellicano and den Houting, 2022). Differences in our genetic code, availability of nutrients, exposure to toxins, and imbalances in neurological chemical messengers are only some factors that impact our brain's structural development (Chiaradia and Lancaster, 2020). These structural variations change the brain's functions, resulting in unique perceptions of the world we share. Just as no two puzzle pieces are created identically, our brains are unique, and all are equally important in building a societal picture.

Historically, we associate neurodiversity with two classes of individuals: neurodivergent, an individual whose brain functions differently than the standard accepted norm, and neurotypical, an individual whose brain does not have functional differences (Pellicano and den Houting, 2022; Shah et al., 2022). While neurodiversity was initially defined to explain the neurological differences in individuals diagnosed with Autism, as the scientific literature continues to grow, many advocates have expanded the definition to include other Neurological Development Disorders, including ADHD, Obsessive Compulsive Disorder (OCD), dyslexia, and Tourette's Syndrome (Boyd et al., 2018).

Interestingly, many medical diagnoses that classify an individual as neurodivergent cannot be described by a single biological basis (Botha and Gillespie-Lynch, 2022; Meredith, 2014). That is to say, a specific set of genes does not cause these conditions but instead is grouped based on shared characteristics considered "abnormal." For example,

Down Syndrome is a genetic disorder in which an individual has an extra copy of one of their chromosomes, a structure that carries long strands of DNA (Hartwell et al., 2017). Individuals who are diagnosed with Down Syndrome have an extra copy of the genes of chromosome 21. The single biological basis of Down Syndrome is the presence of additional genetic material. On the contrary, many neurological development disorders are diagnosed based on observational traits viewed as "deficits" to normal functioning (Russel, 2020; Pellicano and den Houting, 2022). Currently, no brain scanning or imaging technology can detect and identify the presence of these disorders (Dyck and Russell, 2020; Ribeiro et al., 2022). The same goes for genetic tests. Without a clear biological basis for these disorders, explaining the "why" behind a diagnosis is difficult.

The idea of a "normal" or "dominant-prevailing" brain is a Western concept that evolved from the Victorian era. Sir Francis Galton, a scientist and mathematician from the late 1800s, spent much of his life working on "improving the human condition" through selective breeding (Gillham, 2001). After collecting data on the health and intelligence of thousands of individuals, Galton used statistical measures to define desirable traits to produce more vigorous offspring (Botha and Gillespie-Lynch, 2022). After he died in 1911, his work was later picked up by other scientists and government bodies that used his ideas to justify forced sterilization and discrimination among individuals deemed "unfit" to bear children (Pegoraro, 2015; Rutecki, 2011). Traits such as IQ, race, age, disability, physical endurance, and societal class are only some of the examples of the criteria used throughout the United States and Europe in the 1930s to evaluate a person's worth (Farber, 2008). In 1935, the Nazi regime also created programs to control the genetic makeup of future generations (Farber, 2008; Reilly, 2015). Although much of the United States and Europe revoked their policies for forced sterilization following World War II, undocumented sterilization continued to surface until the 1970s (Reilly, 2015). The 1900s were a dark period in World History, embedding the practice of classifying human traits and behaviours as normal and not normal within several leading nations.

There is no such thing as a default brain; every brain is unique. However, society has classified certain behaviours and abilities as "normal" (Lawson, 2010; Shah et al., 2022). Some of these features include:

- **Intellectual abilities:** able to read and write proficiently in one or more languages
- **Social aptitude:** able to comfortably interact with peers, hold conversations, and function in large or complex social settings
- **High tolerance to sensory stimuli:** able to navigate high levels of sensory information, such as intense light, loud noises, and sudden movement
- **Adaptability:** able to perform well in competitive settings and deal with change.

Some literature is moving away from the dichotomy of labelling individuals as neurodivergent or neurotypical (Dyck and Russell, 2020). As awareness for neurodiversity continues to grow, individuals who would have considered themselves "neurotypical" recognize some neurodivergent traits within themselves. This is not to say that the person should have a medical diagnosis of a neurological development disorder, but rather that these traits are equally distributed among the population (English et al., 2021; Russell, 2020). When we view the world through a lens of diversity, recognizing that no one is normal and everyone has unique needs, we strive for a society of inclusion and belonging.

Seven Grandfather Teachings

There is a teaching that is shared among several Indigenous cultures. The Seven Grandfather Teachings, also known as the Seven Sacred Teachings, guide us in thinking and behaving to live a good life. Following these teachings, we treat all other living beings as equals. We see the individual as an essential part of Creation and respect their journey. The Grandfather's Teachings tell us to stay open-minded to the perspectives of others, listening for opportunities to learn from their wisdom.

I believe the answer to accepting and integrating neurodiversity within our society is embracing the Seven Grandfather's Teachings. We will never be at peace until we acknowledge all beings as equal. I'd like to mention that the following descriptions are my interpretation of the teachings. Among the various tribes of individuals that comprise all Indigenous Peoples, our stories and details will differ. That is not to say that one version is more accurate than another; all teachings are considered authentic. The storyteller's perspective is not constant and will lead to different teachings.

Dibaadendizowin – Humility

The first teaching is humility, dibaadendizowin.

> DIBAA – low; EN – to think; DIZO – of oneself.
> To think low of oneself.

Humility is to know that we are a part of the greater whole. We consider ourselves equal with all Creation, the plants, animals, insects, medicines, Mother Earth, and the universe. We are not arrogant or think too highly of ourselves.

Gratitude is the key to being humble. When we are humble, we recognize that everyone is on their journey. No one knows everything, not even the elders. Expressing appreciation for other living beings allows one to acknowledge the greater whole.

Gwayakowaadiziwin – Honesty

The second Grandfather's Teaching is honesty, gwayakowaadiziwin.

> GWAYAK – proper, in order; AADIZI – to live a certain way.
> To live a proper life.

Honesty is to see and accept yourself for who you are and how the Creator made you. When you live an honest life, you are true to yourself. You do not pretend to be someone you are not. You accept the gifts given to you by the Creator and use them to their fullest abilities.

Honesty allows us to see the world without distortions. In modern society, hiding from the real world has become common. Without being able to accept ourselves, we are unable to accept others. Instead, we focus on areas deemed "ugly" and "unwanted." Wearing a mask to hide our true identity is a mentally draining task. By accepting ourselves, we stop worrying about how others view us and, in turn, stop viewing other individuals negatively.

Manaaji'iwewin – Respect

The third Grandfather's Teaching is respect, or integrity, manaaji'iwewin.

> MANAAJI – to go easy on.
> To go easy on others.

Respect is to acknowledge we are all sacred beings, brothers, and sisters of Creation. All living beings are subject to the rollercoaster of life. We all have to deal with hardships, overcome challenges, suffer losses, and experience pain. When we treat another individual with respect, we acknowledge their experience of life and treat them as family. We offer them our help, celebrate their successes, and support them when they ask. Our relationships with other living beings are the foundation of our community. In return, we pool our resources and work together to overcome obstacles.

Respect is not limited to other human beings. All life should be respected: plants, animals, water, Mother Earth, the moon, and stars; all of us are connected through our experience of life. We need to take care of one another to survive. Give yourself a reality check – imagine what the world would look like if one of our sacred beings were to disappear. How would we survive without clean water or air? The answer is we wouldn't.

Zoongide'ewin – Courage

The fourth Grandfather's Teaching is courage, or bravery, zoongide'ewin.

> ZOONGI – to be strong; DE – heart.
> To have strength of the heart.

Courage is to do what is right, not what is easy. You must be brave to face danger and transform the fears that stop you from living a good life. There will always be threats in your environment, people, and animals who wish to hurt you. Running away will not make you stronger. Whether you win or lose, you will emerge stronger and wiser.

It takes courage to support those who have wronged you in the past. We must be brave and trust that something good will come from facing our fears in difficult situations. Choosing to turn away from someone in need is to view them as being less than you instead of an equal.

Nibwaakaawin – Wisdom

The fifth Grandfather's Teaching is wisdom, nibwaakaawin.

> NIBWAAKAA – to be wise.

Wisdom is to know how to use your gifts. When you are wise, you recognize that all beings are unique and have a purpose. The gifts you carry are to be used for the benefit of all. You tell the Creator you are not grateful for your life by not using your talents. When you compare yourself to others, you live a life based on something you wish you were, not what you are. To live wisely is to live your life based on your unique gifts.

Wisdom also entails a willingness to learn. We are constantly learning. To learn, we must listen. We listen to ourselves, watching for areas of self-development. We listen to our bodies for signs of not living in balance or needing help. We listen to the opinions and wisdom of others, keeping an open mind for opportunities to learn. We listen to Mother Earth to witness her beauty and power over us.

Zaagi'idiwin – Love

The sixth Grandfather's Teaching is love, zaagi'idiwin.

ZAAG – to love; IDI – reciprocal, each other.
To love each other.

Love is to know peace. We must love ourselves and others unconditionally. When we love unconditionally, we express trust in the Creator. All life starts with the Creator; as equals, we are not entitled to pass judgement or decide who is worthy of love. Doing so only serves as a distraction from our journey. We have limited time in this World and much to accomplish. We find inner peace when we learn to let go of judgement and love unconditionally.

Debwewin – Truth

The final Grandfather Teaching is truth, debwewin.

DE – heart; WE – sound, voice.
I speak to you from my heart.

Truth is to know and follow all of these teachings. Speaking the truth means speaking from the heart. When we stay humble about our place in Creation, we speak to others with respect. When we are honest with ourselves, we learn to listen to the wisdom of others. We build the courage to engage in difficult conversations when we love unconditionally.

It is easy to hide the truth. We can treat living beings with less consideration to conceal their significance. We can hide our true selves and pretend to be someone we are not. We can limit our understanding of life by ignoring the knowledge of others. However, in doing so, we will not live a good life. We will always look over our shoulders, looking for cracks in our masks and fighting our true spirit. We will not understand the world well and see life's beauty. Our bodies and minds suffer the consequences of a broken spirit.

Accepting and following the seven teachings teaches us to view every living being as unique, purposeful, and meaningful. There is no labelling of "normal" and "abnormal." All of us are connected through the experience of life. Living a good life makes us a small piece of a larger puzzle. All the other details around us, although different, are equally important. With just one piece missing, the puzzle will forever be incomplete.

Maintaining a view focused on diversity is challenging to uphold in large societies when facing strenuous situations. When resources become limited, we are conditioned to care for the majority before considering minorities. It is a battle we are all too familiar with today: the fight for minorities to have equal representation when compared to the majority. In these large societal groups, diversity is viewed as an anomaly. Being different from the majority means you are an outcast who must try to survive in a society not built to support you. However, in small groups of individuals, diversity is a strength. Being different means contributing unconventional skills and providing new perspectives to the community.

The importance of neurodiverse individuals in smaller communities

Before Europeans' migration and the New World's creation, Indigenous tribes flourished across North America (Witgen, 2012). In contrast to modern societies, these tribes were much smaller in population and widely distributed across the land. Neighbouring tribes did not always share cultural traditions, as they were often independent of one another. However, they did share a mutual respect for all of life.

Neurodiversity is a critical success factor for small communities as it increases the population's resilience. A more comprehensive range of perspectives, experiences, and ideas among the members allows for more significant innovation and problem-solving. Community involvement is crucial for the survival and growth of smaller populations. Everyone has a role to play in the survival of the community.

Consider how different gifts could benefit a community:

Strong attention to detail, highly empathetic, and an overtly honest individual would make a powerful healer. They would excel at taking care of ill members and crafting medicines. They would also be very trustworthy.

A different individual who is charismatic, has high energy and thinks "outside the box" would exceed as a leader. Their ability to think unconventionally allows them to generate new ideas and see different perspectives. Their energy would enable them to connect with their people and dedicate themselves to the community.

A highly observant third individual who focuses intently and works better independently would make an exceptional hunter or gatherer. Their ability to observe the plants and animals would provide valuable insight into how much of a particular resource is safe without causing shortages. They would be more in tune with the land, striving to take care of it as much as it takes care of the community.

Notice how there is no mention of what areas an individual may face difficulties in each of these examples. Assigning tasks based on strengths allows members to thrive in their work. There would be no concerns about not being good enough for the community, as everyone is expected to contribute in the best way possible. There will always be individuals with gifts that make them better suited to a particular role but that does not make the gifts of others any less important.

Reflecting on the future

Reflecting on my journey, I noticed that the people from my community did not see me as different. They viewed me as a talented and strong community member and have never stopped cheering me on. The institutions from the Western World made me feel ashamed of my gifts. The public school systems and workplaces thought it was necessary to standardize the human brain, one of the most complex and diversified organs.

Indigenous Peoples survived and thrived on the land for thousands of years before the European settlers crossed the Atlantic Ocean and entered North America (Forster et al., 1996).

Figure 9.1 Looking within as I follow the seven Granfather's Teachings, 2024.

Photographer: By Lexi Giizhigokwe Nahwegiizhic

Their teachings and traditions, such as the Grandfather Teachings, gave them the skills to live harmoniously with other beings. The small communities presented a platform for diversity to flourish, where all gifts were accepted and valued. The Western World struggles to embrace all types of diversity because people are determined to fit their spirits into an impossible standard norm.

We will never live in peace until we accept all life as equal. As long as one life is valued as more important than another, there is no love, respect, or humility. We cannot learn from one another if we do not appreciate each other's wisdom. Without the courage to be ourselves, we are forced to hide behind masks of dishonesty. And without the remaining teachings, we lose sight of the truth. It is through this approach that we must rise and look beyond our challenges and by using the Grandfather's Teachings will this help, as I have reflected in myself by looking within (Figure 9.1).

References

Bear, M. F., Connors, B. W., and Paradiso, M. A. (2016). Chapter 2: Neurons and Glia. In Jonathan Joyce, Linda G. Francis, Tom Lochhass, and Tish Rogers (eds) *Neuroscience: Exploring the Brain* (4th Ed., pp. 23–54). Wolters Kluwer.

Botha, M., and Gillespie-Lynch, K. (2022). Come as you are: Examining autistic identity development and the neurodiversity movement through an intersectional lens. *Human Development*, 66, 93–112.

Boyd, L. E., Day, K., Stewart, N., Abdo, K., Lamkin, K., and Linstead, E. (2018). Leveling the playing field: Supporting neurodiversity via virtual realities. *Technology and Innovation, 20*, 105–116.

Chiaradia, I., and Lancaster, M. A. (2020). Brain organoids for the study of human neurobiology at the interface of in vitro and in vivo. *Nature Neuroscience, 23*(12), 1496–1508.

Dyck, E., and Russell, G. (2020). Challenging psychiatric classification: Healthy autistic diversity and the neurodiversity movement. In Taylor, S.J., Brumby, A. (eds) *Healthy minds in the twentieth century: In and beyond the asylum* (pp. 167–187). Palgrave Macmillan.

English, M. C., Gignac, G. E., Visser, T. A., Whitehouse, A. J., Enns, J. T., and Maybery, M. T. (2021). The Comprehensive Autistic Trait Inventory (CATI): Development and validation of a new measure of autistic traits in the general population. *Molecular Autism, 12*(1), 1–23.

Farber, S. A. (2008). U.S. scientists' role in the eugenics movement (1907–1939): A contemporary biologist's perspective. *Zebrafish, 5*(4), 243–245.

Forster, P., Harding, R., Torroni, A., and Bandelt, H. J. (1996). Origin and evolution of Native American mtDNA variation: A reappraisal. *American Journal of Human Genetics, 59*(4), 935–945.

Gillham, N. W. (2001). Sir Francis Galton and the birth of eugenics. *Annual Review of Genetics, 35*, 83–101.

Hartwell, L. H., Goldberg, M. L., Fischer, J. A., Hood, L., Aquadro, C., Karagiannis, J., and Papaconstantinou, M. (2017). Chapter 3: The chromosome theory of inheritance. In *Genetics: From genes to genomes* (2nd Ed., pp. 80–119). McGraw Hill Education.

Lawson, J. (2010). An investigation into behaviours which challenge at university: The impact of neurotypical expectations on autistic students. *Good Autism Practice (GAP), 11*(1), 45–51.

Meredith, R. M. (2014). Sensitive and critical periods during neurotypical and aberrant neurodevelopment: A framework for neurodevelopmental disorders. *Neuroscience and Biobehavioral Reviews, 50*, 180–188.

Nicholls, J. G., Martin, A. R., Fuchs, P. A., Brown, D. A., Diamond, M. E., and Weisblat, D. A. (2012). Chapter 25: Development of the nervous system. In *From neuron to brain* (5th Ed., pp. 531–564). Sinauer Associates.

Pegoraro, L. (2015). Second-rate victims: The forced sterilization of Indigenous peoples in the USA and Canada. *Settler Colonial Studies, 5*(2), 161–173.

Pellicano, E., and den Houting, J. (2022). Annual research review: Shifting from 'normal science' to neurodiversity in autism science. *Journal of Child Psychology and Psychiatry, 63*(4), 381–396.

Reilly, P. R. (2015). Eugenics and involuntary sterilization: 1907–2015. *Annual Review of Genomics and Human Genetics, 16*, 351–368.

Ribeiro, F., Shumovskaia, V., Davies, T., and Ktena, I. (2022). How fair is your graph? Exploring fairness concerns in neuroimaging studies. *Proceedings of Machine Learning Research, 182*, 1–20.

Rutecki, G. W. (2011). Forced Sterilization of Native Americans: Later twentieth century physical cooperation with national eugenic policies? *Ethics & Medicine, 27*(1), 33–42.

Russel, G. (2020). Chapter 21: Critiques of the Neurodiversity Movement. In Steven K. Kapp (eds) *Autistic Community and the Neurodiversity Movement: Stories from the Frontline.* (pp. 287–303). Palgrave Macmillan.

Shah, P. J., Boilson, M., Rutherford, M., Prior, S., Johnston, L., Maciver, D., and Forsyth, K. (2022). Neurodevelopmental disorders and neurodiversity: Definition of terms from Scotland's national autism implementation team. *The British Journal of Psychiatry, 221*(3), 577–579.

Witgen, M. J. (2012). Part I: Discovery. In *An infinity of nations: How the Native new world shaped early North America* (1st Ed., pp. 23–28). University of Pennsylvania Press.

10 Navigating my indigeneity through colonialism and how disabilities impacted my knowledge systems

A Muiscas and Teusacá experience

Angela Patricia Mora Rodriguez

Introduction

The 'Indio patirrajado' was on my mind when trying to put this story together. It has always been there, and it has been used by my family for many years now. I'm pretty sure I have heard it in several instances, so it is an essential part of the vocabulary of many people and is continuously used by all sorts of people in the town where I was born and raised. We all know what it means. For those of you who do not know, an 'indio patirrajado' is a way of referring to those who are, in a certain way, 'ignorant' or who are 'uneducated'. I guess I never wondered why this came to be a reasonable way of referring to people, objects, or situations, but as with many things in life, I learnt it, and I used it whenever required. For example, when I would see someone cutting me off on the highway and being disrespectful, I would just shout: 'Uy, qué indio' or 'Indio patirrajado tenía que ser!' and I just moved on, saying this in several situations. It doesn't matter if you're referring to a man or a woman; they are just 'indios' regardless of their gender.

I remember whenever my mom would hear my brother burping rudely at the table, she would say: 'No sea indio!' She really used the word and its variations often. I guess she heard it from her own mom, who constantly spent a lot of time looking out the window, thinking about the bad things her neighbours were doing, and when we would go visit her, she would just angrily refer to them as the 'indios esos'. These people we call 'indios' are nameless; they don't deserve to have a name because we deem their actions to be rudimentary, and therefore, we are better than them, so why would you name those that are not worthy? You just actually want to forget them and complain to the next decent person about this ignorance that crosses our paths. I will come back to this concept of 'Indio' later on.

Now, you might be asking yourself why this is important in this book and why this all matters. I will tell you how, as a linguist and lover of languages, this term makes sense in the current panorama of the Indigenous peoples in Colombia. This is nothing new, but rather something that has been normalized by generation after generation in that country. It is so normalized that it took me years to think about this and come to terms with it. It took me going through college, living in different parts of the world, and moving to Canada to finally realize that it was all connected, that I am connected, and that I cannot identify as an Indigenous person because of the stigma that this has created in me and my way of looking at things, but mainly because there is so much yet to discover. I know so little about my past and family members that I do not feel like I'm worthy of this. However, not everything is lost, and hopefully, through these pages, you can understand

DOI: 10.4324/9781032656519-13

why this is such a complex topic to cover and that you might understand that this is just coming from my experience and knowledge.

Who I am – A self-navigation

My name is Angela Patricia Mora Rodriguez. I was born and raised in Colombia. My name does not hold any special meaning; it just refers to angels, so my mom (Blanca Cecilia) thought that would be cute. My dad (Teodoro) wanted a different name, but I guess my mom won. In my family, we do not choose names because of ancestral traditions or because we have a firm belief in names and their meaning. Names are chosen based on religious purposes. I almost did not make it into this world, so I guess my mom was relieved when I was born, so to say, 'normal'. My whole life, she has explained how she does not know how I might have survived. You will see, I had an unplanned pregnancy after a miscarriage, so my mom found out about me late in her pregnancy, and I caused so many complications to her and her body. She was put on bed rest for months; she would bleed daily, and she needed to be carried everywhere.

Doctors were not very positive about this pregnancy, so they prescribed different drugs and vitamins to be religiously taken so that it wouldn't end up in a miscarriage. As soon as people close to my mom heard, they recommended visiting a 'sobandera' who would be able to help my mom. A 'sobandera' was an older lady commonly known in the community because she would perform massages and would provide teas and natural remedies to people to cure diverse illnesses. She was, in a certain sense, a 'curandera' (think of her like a shaman) because of her deep connection to Mother Earth and the inherited knowledge she had of the world. She had learnt it from her parents or grandparents and would gladly help people in need. My mom needed almost daily massages so that I would 'stick'.

My parents blindly trusted this woman, who had no medical training, who probably couldn't read, and who perhaps was unable to write. Still, to this day, they swear that this lady helped my mother through that difficult pregnancy. You see, a doctor's advice is not as strong or as believable as the knowledge produced by the community and the ancient rituals that our parents and grandparents acquired over generations. This lady was incredibly powerful and respected, and my parents put all their trust in her hands. I would like to think that many other Indigenous children are alive because of this, that these children and every life is valuable with or without a disability. Disabilities do not mean the same when we live on a farm or when we are Indigenous. They mean that children become productive adults and learn about the land, trade, or about curing others. They, however, have less access to mainstream education and end up living in remote areas of the country. Perhaps, the lady who helped my mom during her pregnancy lived with an invisible disability, and perhaps she knew more than I ever will.

Growing up and looking back at this, I realize that she was probably an Indigenous lady, but she would never be identified as such as the value it holds is useless and detrimental to the image people had of her. She was probably a person who was raised by farmers and who earned a living taking care of her patients. I am convinced that she was never rich as she would barely charge her patients (picture paying her 2,000 Colombian pesos or $1 Canadian). She was probably a super religious person, who would use the name of the Lord to cure people while using knowledge that is older than the belief in God or religion. She was looked down upon by many but was required to be available at odd times, weekends, holidays, early in the morning, or late at night, etc. The job she performed has slowly been forgotten and replaced by Eastern medicine, pharmacies, and sadly newer generations have not acquired any knowledge to keep the tradition alive.

A cultural thing

People like her were all around me; they were part of the community. We respected them, and they had the final say in several health aspects. A doctor wasn't as respected as they were. My own grandfather (on my dad's side) was also a 'sobandero', and people would visit him to get their ankles and wrists fixed whenever someone had hurt them or twisted them. I still remember the smell of the cream he would use and how much that smell meant to me. He would have several visitors from all paths of life. My grandfather was a labourer; he would earn some coins working in the fields. He never learnt how to read or write, and he could barely sign documents. He came from a town called Guatavita, where the Guatavita Lake can be visited. This lake holds great significance for Indigenous people, and it was considered a sacred ritual place for the Muiscas and their people. Unfortunately, I know little about my grandfather's family but here is to honour him and his legacy (Figure 10.1).

I am sure that my grandfather's lineage can be easily traced back to these Indigenous groups and that if we were to find out, we would learn so much about our history, but most of this data has been lost forever. Here in Canada, many Indigenous groups are seen; you get an ID to say that you have an Indigenous background, and depending on your status, you can go to college, get special accommodation in certain cases, and be proud of your status. However, for my grandpa, things were different; he moved to a larger city and raised seven children in what my dad described as a poor and food-insecure home. So, being Indigenous was worthless. He had incredible knowledge about herbs, remedies, and the human body, but for society, he was illiterate and had a job that could barely sustain my dad, my aunts, and my uncles.

Figure 10.1 Family photo of my sister, mother, and grandfather (Teodoro Mora Sr), 1985.

Source: Photographer: By Teodoro Mora Jr.

I often think about him and what he represents to my family and, especially, to me. I could spend hours listening to his stories about the fields he grew up in and the people around him, and I would memorize the words he used. He was a great storyteller, but unfortunately, I never heard the end of many of those stories. I truly felt sadness when he passed away. I felt like with him, my childhood and a part of our history died. I would never smell the cream he used to treat patients again, and I would never get paid again to go and buy a soda for him. I would never hear the story about the white tissue and the lady (everyone in the family wonders about this one). Most importantly, the people from his neighbourhood wouldn't have anyone to talk to and to get advice from regarding herbs or they wouldn't get their hands or ankles fixed. His passing meant that a piece of the community was lost as well.

My grandma, his wife, didn't have it easy either. Just as many young Indigenous girls still are, she was sold to the highest bidder at the age of 14 and forced to marry a man in his forties. She ended up having six children and working in the fields. She was born and lived in La Calera in Bogota, where the Teusacá people lived and prospered. She was born to farmers and ended up having a harsh life of labour (she would clean and wash for the richest people to grab some coins and feed her children). According to my grandpa, he stole her away from her husband because he knew she was the one for him, and he decided to bring her and her children to Zipaquirá (meaning land of the Zipa – City of our father), where my dad was born.

All the children went to school, but life was hard, and most of their memories are filled with violence (because that's how people were raised before), fear of God (as Catholicism had replaced all the original Indigenous systems), and poverty because both my uneducated grandparents struggled to make ends meet (my grandpa would drink his pay and my grandma had to be creative to put food on the table). I often wonder how different my life would have been if my parents had had better opportunities, not because I had a bad life but because they suffered and sacrificed so much because of this darkness that surrounded them in their early years. This is also not new for Indigenous communities. There's the risk of alcoholism, violence, prostitution, addiction, etc., and somehow, it is always taboo or rather normalized, to the point in which this is completely normal behaviour.

I always heard my aunts and uncles had different last names than my dad, but it never clicked in my brain because, after all, they were simply family. Only when I grew up, I dared ask, and my dad, as openly as he could, told me all these stories. Much of the pain he lived through his childhood still follows him to this day. He does keep a bit of the knowledge acquired from my grandpa and grandma, but he will never be the 'sobandero' or the storyteller my grandpa was, but I feel a bit of him lives on in my dad. It is such a shame knowing that my grandparents (both maternal and paternal) had to go through this rough life, and I regret not listening before, not asking before, and not understanding what this all was. A part of our history is gone forever, and unfortunately, my children and their children will know less and less about where I come from.

Education

I am proud to say that my mom and dad made such an effort for me and my siblings to be educated, to learn, and to have a better future. I was born and raised in Zipaquirá, Colombia, a small town relatively close to Bogotá. I attended the same school my sister and brother did before me; we even got to be taught by the same teachers at one point.

This was one of the first times, I heard about Indigenous people, but I did not learn a lot about them. I learnt why my town was called Zipaquirá, the anthem that was specially written for the town, and I learnt that a long time ago, some people lived in the area before the land was 'discovered'.

I have lost most of this knowledge as we rarely discussed these things or had an in-depth conversation regarding the Indigenous people or their work to build Colombia from the ground up. When I was little, everyone would call them 'indiecitos' or little Indians, 'Little Indians' always comes to mind with these memories. These 'indiecitos' were a by-product of colonization. They occupied and knew about the land, but I spent years learning about Cristobal Colón (Christopher Columbus) and his ships (they are engraved in my head), learning about wars and dates. I often remember that tales are told by the winning parties, so my learning of Indigenous affairs was heavily influenced by the history textbooks made in Spain or mass-produced in Latin America. It was just a chore to learn about it for school, and my younger self never thought more about it.

The saddest part is that I do not remember much about Indigenous culture because that was not seen as important or educational. I remember that we dressed up as Indians (with the popular costume with a feather and khaki clothes), and that was my understanding of Indigenous culture. As I grew up, I started learning a bit more about Indigenous groups and cultures in Colombia. We would draw maps, do some research, and make some presentations during class.

My earliest memory of an Indigenous person was Pocahontas, and honestly, she still is for many people Disney's Pocahontas with her carefree ways of living, her love for John Smith, and the fact that every princess needs a prince. I found her to be boring and a mere made-up story. She was one of my least favourite princesses. I saw in her nothing that would stand out, nothing worth mentioning, and I surely didn't like her singing. Nowadays, I see her with different eyes. I see how people never wondered about Pocahontas' position in her community, her knowledge of flora and fauna, or the fact that she had mentally mapped the whole forest in her head. I see how, again, language and history are shaped. This story was narrated to teach us about her and her legacy but ended up being another Disney princess love story. Just as disappointing as the teachings we have of Indigenous communities. Now that I think about it, how do I expect curricula or our culture's ways of thinking to change if all we have to educate children are Pocahontas and mass media?

While I was a student at school, on the news, I would always see children in neglected communities – mostly Indigenous and farm children had to struggle to get quality education. They, like my grandma, were still suffering the same destiny: lack of quality education, resources, and opportunities. Young girls in remote areas still have to live life as young brides, and boys were recruited by the armed forces, narcos (drug traffickers), and guerrillas. These Indigenous children were interviewed and were praised for all the effort they made (some walk for hours, skip meals, and are victims of forced labour) because education is the key to success and their pain is not important as long as they make it back to school. It is a never-ending cycle that Colombian society is not even close to fixing. What's supposed to take you out of this poverty is what the good people in our society do. Most of these children were not much into learning, as what they learnt was not practical in the fields. They knew how to milk a cow, work on the crops, and cure others using natural remedies. For them, school did not offer options for their real-life context; they still went back to their lives and could not dream of a better future.

When I graduated from high school, it was time to choose where and what I would do with my life. I often think I was too young to have chosen. I knew nothing, and I wasn't ready for what was to come. My father said I should choose something I liked because if I did that, I would be happy and would succeed. So, I chose languages and teaching, mainly because I had spent years learning English, and I thought that I wanted to know more about what languages do and how they work. I chose a private University, and I don't remember having ever seen an Indigenous classmate (or at least they never introduced themselves as Indigenous). I think I only saw one person who came from the Amazon Forest on campus, and I only knew because they were wearing traditional clothes, and everyone just stared. There were no Indigenous groups or communities to join. In all fairness, there were some electives that could be taken, but I never felt an interest. I felt I would be out of place or that I would be looked down on for this. I was ignorant even when I knew where I came from and what this meant.

Now, everything is alright if you are a 'normal' child, but whenever there's a disability, you will struggle even more. Disability is a word Colombia is not very familiar with. For Colombians, being disabled is linked to being unable to move like everyone else. The words 'invisible disability' are new to everyone, as we navigate through autism, learning disabilities or simply Down Syndrome and minorities seem to be emerging. Few schools have accommodations for disabled students and interestingly enough, I had faced disabilities my whole life, but I never thought about them. You see, disabled people have been in the shadows for generations and generations, been undermined, and have been neglected. Now, if you are Indigenous, poor, and disabled, you are doomed. Most of these children learn a trade, they take care of animals, learn how to cook or manage stores and they just do what they can with what they have. Most will also end up living in orphanages as their parents are unable to cope. Almost all mental disabilities are referred to as 'retardo' (being retarded) and due to the lack of knowledge and opportunity, these children are more often, than not always, undiagnosed.

College was not the best thing that ever happened to me. I made many mistakes, and I felt like I truly did not know what the future had in store for me. I was young and dumb. I often look back on it and realize it was not a safe space. It was a space in which thinking outside the box was often frowned upon. Teachers would only like you to reuse their knowledge to complete tests and assessments. I thought after many years, I would find what I was looking for when I moved to Canada and decided to go back to school – only to find that you were punished even more for not following what the teachers wanted. In fact, students were ridiculed, and the teachers would threaten me and my colleagues with the famous 'D' for diploma. Disability is more accepted here in Canada, but academia still has a long way to go in order to recognize the difficulties that arise for both 'normal' and 'disabled' students. I hate these labels that always separate people based on conventions, and I hate that education is still so behind in understanding the struggles of growing up, figuring yourself out, and, most definitely, the struggle of finding your passions.

I can only imagine what it is to live with a disability, in Colombia in college. I only had one classmate who would use a wheelchair, but he would always be placed in buildings that had no elevators, ramps so were difficult to access. We all loved having classes with him. We would definitely get the best and newest buildings after he went to talk to the faculty secretaries who would say something on the lines of 'Oops, we kinda forgot'. Another classmate with a disability was one hell of a person. She was blind and needed accommodation, but she would walk with us, and we would assist her. She didn't have anyone to help her navigate the University, so we would all be her eyes. She is one of the smartest people I have ever known, and her disability for her was completely different. I never knew any Indigenous students, and as expected most of them had no access to education. How could they afford education, if they could not afford daily food? clothes? and in some cases a home?

The only thing that college gave me was a desire to learn more about others, about languages, and about travelling the world. I have found great people, bad people, and people who, like me, just wanted to find themselves. In Canada, I got to meet with a group of Indigenous students at the University. They would candidly talk about their experiences, share their knowledge with others, and teach others about their communities, families, and friends. It was an amazing experience to share with others, but I still could not find myself in that group. I was not Indigenous enough. I didn't look Indigenous, and I did not know about my family traditions or our history. I was not an Indigenous person from Canada, so I felt I was not part of the group either. I felt ashamed of not knowing about this, about not knowing myself, and not being recognized as Indigenous. No matter what you do, you are never part of the circle; you are not what you should be to fit in. I blame my ignorance, and I blame my education. However, I blame myself for not taking the lead, for figuring things out late, and for missing 'a window'.

The places where you are supposed to learn are the places in which you end up leaving more of your heart, dreams, and ambitions. The worst places to get to know the real you. The words I heard, the texts I read, and the people I've met shaped me differently, and I am only glad to have been given opportunities and a future. Many others before me have not had this chance.

What is it to be Indigenous?

Writing these pages, I couldn't stop thinking about my country and its people. This is the right time to redeem myself and others before me. It is the time to understand where I come from and what having Indigenous roots really means to me. However, the real question is, what makes a person Indigenous or not? I needed to rethink myself to answer this question. After all, I had to separate myself from the experiences that others have had and from the preconceived notion that I had in my mind about being Indigenous.

When asking myself this question, I started to think about the big things like not knowing the Indigenous languages or not knowing all the Indigenous groups that inhabit Colombia. It was sad to think that I know more about other countries' histories and traditions and that I have taken lessons to learn Algonquin, but that I still haven't worked on learning more about my own country. Then it hit me. I value others' Indigenous values and knowledge because I was always ashamed of mine when I lived in Colombia. I was ashamed of others talking about me and referring to me as Indigenous because of the poor connotation we give our own people and because of all the bias and wrong ideas we have had implanted in us from childhood. My town, my family, and my upbringing made me what I am today, but to be honest, I have also had to build myself together again. I had to defy myself to erase behaviours that were no longer useful to me or my new chosen family. I had to understand that my family's upbringing had been challenging and that they probably had done the best they could to raise me and my parents. You see, I always blamed others for what I didn't have or what I hadn't learned, but I realized that there's no one to blame. There's only the responsibility to learn and respect ourselves.

Then, I thought about my body and how fashion and the social media have taught me that Indigenous features are not attractive and not worth celebrating. I realized that being Indigenous also had to do with how I perceive myself and my body, how my dark hair and hazel eyes have felt unattractive during these years. How my nose and eye shape don't quite fit with the usual beauty standards, but my pale skin does (it is one of the reasons why people think I am not even Colombian). Since living in Canada, I have learnt that these features that I am not comfortable with are part of being Indigenous, that my features are to be celebrated, and that my body is a temple, and as such, it is to be loved and celebrated. I have learnt that my body tells the story of many before me and the lives they used to live. I still need to get used to this way of thinking, and I really need to appreciate who I am and what makes me.

For me, being Indigenous is a self-discovery journey. It's a feeling and it's a state of mind. All these aspects were essential to me when writing this paper as I navigated through my memories and past. It was important to remember that my experiences were part of a collective group of people and that some of them will never have the chance to explore these aspects of their lives. I had to believe in myself and my experiences to really understand what others before me had gone through. I had never felt Indigenous before, and I still think I'm not quite Indigenous (whatever that might mean), but I do have a better understanding of the struggles many communities have. I know I can effectively think about the pain that institutions have caused on Indigenous lives and the effects this has had on many different people around me (especially those with disabilities). I guess being Indigenous makes me more aware of others around me, makes me think of the greater picture, and has made me realize that I am not to be ashamed of what I am or where I come from.

Conclusion

I truly believe that being Indigenous for me has a special meaning that others might not share. As a Colombian with Indigenous roots, being Indigenous is a learning process, a constant reminder of my roots and the history of my country, and a reminder that being Indigenous is a part of many of us. There is just so much more to discover and rediscover, but still, it is tempting to think that one day, my children and their children will feel proud of their roots and their ancestors because I decided to take the lead and go down this path. I would love for them to understand the amount of cultural richness Colombia has to offer, the vast knowledge of flora and fauna our elders used to have, and how our traits tell the story of our past.

11 Navigating disabilities from a Mauritius perspective

Vijaye Lutchmee Davi Jaypal

Introduction

Mauritius is a beautiful volcanic island located in the Indian Ocean, just over 1.130 kilometres east of Madagascar, off the southeastern coast of Africa. It has a surface area of just over 2,000 km^2 with a population of 1.3 million. The official language is English, but French is more widely spoken, and the local dialect is Creole, strongly influenced by the French language. This mixture of languages is due to the history of Mauritius, influenced by the French, and then the British. The island was uninhabited before its first recorded visit during the Middle Ages by Arab sailors. In 1507, Portuguese sailors came. Mauritius was then colonized by the French from 1715 to 1796, then by the British from 1814 to independence in 1968. My father-in-law, the late Mr. Rameshwar Jaypal actively participated in the Historical Constitutional Conference of 1965 at Lancaster House, U.K., with 25 other Cabinet Ministers and Members of the Legislative Assemblies of the Mauritian delegation, which led the country to its independence on March 12, 1968. The country became a republic on March 12, 1992. Mr. Rameshwar Jaypal was elevated to the rank of the Commander of the British Empire (CBE) in 1977.

Although Mauritius does not have any recorded Indigenous population, the island is made up of its own people with the intermixing of different ethnic groups, which makes us uniquely different. I will provide my perspective on disabilities in Mauritius as an Indo-Mauritian, whose great grandparents came from India. Almost half a million indentured labourers arrived from India at Aapravasi Ghat to work in the sugar plantations between 1834 and 1920. The Mauritius' ethnic composition is a product of over two centuries of European colonialism and continued international labour migration from India, China, Africa, and Southeast Asia. There are five broad ethnic categories: Franco-Mauritian, Sino-Mauritian, Indo-Mauritian, Afro-Mauritian, and Creole-Mauritian, which all co-exist peacefully as one nation. The majority of the population in Mauritius are Hindus making Mauritius the only country in Africa with Hinduism as the main religion. The longstanding practice of ethnic endogamy has contributed to the persistence of ethnic and social class distinctions over time. Their culture and lifestyle have absorbed pieces from their former colonization countries.

Understandings and beliefs about disabilities in Mauritius

Beliefs, understanding, and teachings about disabilities in Mauritius have evolved over time. Historically, disabilities were often viewed with a stigma and misconceptions. People with disabilities were sometimes seen as cursed or as burdens on their families.

DOI: 10.4324/9781032656519-14

However, there has been a gradual shift towards a more inclusive and empowering approach in recent years.

In Mauritius, various religious and cultural beliefs influence the understanding of disabilities. For example, Hinduism, which is practiced by a significant portion of the population, teaches the concept of karma and reincarnation. This belief system can sometimes lead to the perception that disabilities are a result of past actions or karma. However, it is important to note that these beliefs are not universally held and that attitudes towards disabilities are actually diverse within the Mauritian population.

The role of people with disabilities in the Mauritian community

People with disabilities play an important role in the Mauritian community. They possess unique talents, skills, and perspectives that contribute to the overall development and well-being of the society. However, due to societal barriers and discrimination, their full potential is often underutilized.

In recent years, there has been a growing recognition of the importance of inclusivity and equal opportunities for people with disabilities in Mauritius. Efforts have been made to promote accessibility, provide reasonable accommodations, and challenge stereotypes and prejudices. By embracing diversity and creating an inclusive environment, the Mauritian community can greatly benefit from the talents and contributions of people with disabilities.

Teachings and learnings about disabilities

Teachings and learnings about disabilities in Mauritius have evolved over time. In the past, disabilities were often hidden from public view, and individuals with disabilities faced significant challenges in accessing education, employment, and healthcare. However, with the implementation of inclusive education policies and awareness campaigns, there has been progress towards a more inclusive society.

The government has implemented policies to ensure equal access to education and employment opportunities for people with disabilities. Thus, Mauritius has made efforts to promote inclusive education and provide support services for students with disabilities. Additionally, various organizations and advocacy groups have been working to raise awareness about disabilities and promote inclusivity in all aspects of society. Some advocates provided a few suggestions on how to improve the lives of people with disabilities and make a positive impact. This requires a multi-faceted approach that addresses various aspects of the people with disabilities well-being:

- Accessibility: Promote accessibility by ensuring that public spaces, transportation, and buildings are designed to accommodate individuals with disabilities. This includes ramps, elevators, braille signage, and audio announcements.
- Education and Employment Opportunities: Advocate for inclusive education and employment policies that provide equal opportunities for individuals with disabilities. Encourage vocational training programs and support initiatives that help them develop skills and find meaningful employment.
- Healthcare and Support Services: Advocate for improved healthcare services specifically tailored to the needs of individuals with disabilities. This includes accessible healthcare facilities, specialized equipment, and support services such as physiotherapy and counselling.

- Awareness and Sensitization: Raise awareness about the challenges faced by persons with disabilities and promote inclusivity in society. Encourage campaigns, workshops, and events that foster understanding, empathy, and acceptance.
- Legal Protections: Advocate for the implementation and enforcement of laws and policies that protect the rights of individuals with disabilities. This includes anti-discrimination laws, accessibility standards, and social welfare programs.
- Community Engagement: Encourage community involvement and support networks for individuals with disabilities. Promote the creation of inclusive spaces where they can socialize, participate in recreational activities, and build meaningful relationships.

Legislation

In Mauritius, there are several legislations and regulations in place to protect the rights of persons with disabilities. The main legislation is the Disability Act 1996, which provides a comprehensive framework for the rights and welfare of persons with disabilities. This act covers a wide range of areas, including education, employment, accessibility, and social welfare.

Under the Disability Act, it is illegal to discriminate against persons with disabilities in various aspects of life, such as employment, education, and access to public facilities. The act also requires public and private institutions to provide reasonable accommodations to persons with disabilities, ensuring that they have equal opportunities and access to services. The Disability Act in Mauritius was enacted to ensure the rights and inclusion of people with disabilities in all aspects of society. It aims to promote equal opportunities, non-discrimination, and accessibility for individuals with disabilities.

Compared to other legislation, the Disability Act in Mauritius is comprehensive and addresses various aspects of disability rights. It emphasizes the importance of reasonable accommodation, which means making necessary adjustments to ensure equal access and participation for people with disabilities. The act also establishes a National Council for Disabled Persons to oversee the implementation of disability policies and programs.

By enacting this legislation, Mauritius is taking a proactive approach towards creating an inclusive society. It recognizes that people with disabilities have the right to live independently, participate fully in all aspects of life, and enjoy equal opportunities. The Disability Act in Mauritius is an important step towards achieving these goals and ensuring that people with disabilities are not left behind.

- Protection of Rights: The Disability Act serves as a legal framework to protect the rights of people with disabilities. It guarantees their right to education, employment, healthcare, accessibility, and participation in all spheres of life. It ensures that individuals with disabilities are not discriminated against and have equal opportunities to fully participate in society.
- Inclusion and Empowerment: The Disability Act promotes the inclusion and empowerment of people with disabilities. It recognizes their unique talents, skills, and contributions to society. By providing legal protection and support, the Act aims to create an inclusive society where individuals with disabilities can live with dignity and independence.
- Accessibility: The Disability Act emphasizes the importance of accessibility for people with disabilities. It requires public buildings, transportation, and services to be

accessible to individuals with different types of disabilities. This includes provisions for ramps, elevators, accessible toilets, and other accommodations that enable people with disabilities to navigate and use public spaces independently.

- Education and Employment: The Disability Act focuses on ensuring equal access to education and employment for people with disabilities. It mandates inclusive education policies, reasonable accommodations, and support services to enable students with disabilities to access quality education. It also prohibits discrimination in employment and promotes the inclusion of individuals with disabilities in the workforce.
- Awareness and Sensitization: The Disability Act promotes awareness and sensitization about disabilities in Mauritius. It encourages educational campaigns, training programs, and public awareness initiatives to challenge stereotypes, misconceptions, and prejudices surrounding disabilities. This helps foster a more inclusive and accepting society that values diversity.
- Implementation and Enforcement: The Disability Act establishes mechanisms for the implementation and enforcement of disability-related policies. It sets up a National Council for the Rehabilitation of Disabled Persons (NCRDP) to oversee the implementation of the Act and monitor the progress made in promoting the rights and inclusion of people with disabilities.

In summary, the Disability Act in Mauritius is essential to protect the rights and promote the inclusion of people with disabilities. It ensures equal opportunities, non-discrimination, and accessibility in various aspects of life, including education, employment, healthcare, and public spaces. By enacting this legislation, Mauritius aims to create a more inclusive society that values and respects the rights and dignity of all individuals, regardless of their abilities.

Additionally, the NCRDP Act 2003 established the NCRDP. The NCRDP is responsible for coordinating and implementing policies and programs related to disability issues. Furthermore, the Equal Opportunities Act 2008 protects persons with disabilities from discrimination and ensures their equal treatment in various areas, including employment, education, and access to goods and services. The Rights of Persons with Disabilities Act was enacted to align the country's laws with the United Nations Convention on the Rights of Persons with Disabilities (UNCRPD).

The Rights of Persons with Disabilities Act aims to promote, protect, and ensure the full and equal enjoyment of human rights and fundamental freedoms by persons with disabilities. It recognizes disability as an evolving concept and emphasizes the importance of respect for the dignity, autonomy, and independence of persons with disabilities. One significant difference between the Rights of Persons with Disabilities Act and the previous Disability Act 1996 is the shift in focus from a medical model to a social model of disability. The new act emphasizes the removal of barriers and the promotion of inclusion and accessibility in all areas of life for persons with disabilities. The Rights of Persons with Disabilities Act also establishes the National Committee on the Rights of Persons with Disabilities, which is responsible for monitoring the implementation of the act and advising the government on disability-related matters.

It is important to note that laws and regulations can change, and it is always recommended to refer to the most up-to-date information or consult legal professionals or relevant authorities for the latest updates on disability-related legislation in Mauritius.

Impact of colonialism in Mauritius – changing of language, ideals, or concepts of disabilities

Colonialism had a significant impact on various aspects of Mauritian society, including language, ideals, and concepts of disabilities. Mauritius was colonized by various European powers, including the Dutch, French, and British. Each colonial power brought with them their own language, culture, and beliefs, which influenced the understanding of disabilities in Mauritius.

During the colonial era, the dominant colonial powers imposed their language and cultural practices on the local population. This often resulted in the marginalization and erasure of local beliefs and practices. The colonial powers also brought their own understanding of disabilities, which was often influenced by Western medical models.

How colonialism changed the understanding of disabilities

Yes, colonialism did change the understanding about disabilities in Mauritius. The imposition of colonial ideals and concepts, including the Western medical model of disability, had a significant impact on the local understanding of disabilities. The traditional beliefs and practices of the Mauritian population were often marginalized or replaced by the colonial perspective.

The Western medical model of disability views disabilities as individual deficiencies that need to be fixed or cured. This perspective often overlooks the social and environmental barriers that contribute to disability and focuses solely on the individual. The colonial influence also led to the establishment of institutions and systems that segregated and marginalized people with disabilities.

However, it is important to note that the impact of colonialism was not entirely negative. The introduction of Western medical knowledge and practices also brought advancements in healthcare and rehabilitation services for people with disabilities. These advancements have contributed to improving the lives of individuals with disabilities in Mauritius.

Conclusion

In conclusion, beliefs, understanding, and teachings about disabilities in Mauritius have evolved over time. There has been a shift towards a more inclusive and empowering approach, recognizing the importance of equal opportunities, and challenging stereotypes and prejudices. People with disabilities play a vital role in the Mauritian community, and efforts are being made to promote their inclusion and participation.

The impact of colonialism on the understanding of disabilities in Mauritius was significant. The imposition of colonial ideals and concepts, including the Western medical model of disability, changed the local understanding of disabilities. However, it is important to acknowledge that colonialism also brought advancements in healthcare and rehabilitation services that have benefitted individuals with disabilities.

Overall, the understanding of disabilities in Mauritius continues to evolve, influenced by both local and global perspectives. Efforts to promote inclusivity and challenge societal barriers are crucial in creating a more equitable and inclusive society for all.

12 Reframing the narratives of Indigenous person with disabilities and creating inclusive spaces through advocacy

Pratima Gurung

54 million Indigenous people with disabilities (UNPFII Report, 2013) and 28 million Indigenous women with disabilities (UN Women Factsheet, 2020) live around the globe with multiple marginalized intersecting identities. Thus, they routinely encounter historical, structural, systematic, and indirect discrimination in their daily lives. These identities are mostly associated with 'Indigenous peoples' as their first identity, 'a person with disability' as a second identity, 'woman' as third identity and 'Indigenous person/woman with disability' as fourth and many more identities and categories. Often, these multiple identities/social categories overlap and interconnect, which stimulate and become aggravated by the social influences around them leading them towards oppressive identities and exclusion, which distinctly affect their lived experiences.

The Convention on the Rights of Persons with Disabilities (CRPD), the ILO Convention No. 169, the United Nations Declaration on the Rights of Indigenous Peoples (UNDRIP) and the Convention on the Elimination of all forms of Discrimination Against Women (CEDAW), as well as General Recommendation 39, are the five most relevant international normative frameworks for respecting, promoting, and fulfilling the rights of Indigenous people and women with disabilities all across the globe. However, these groups have less awareness about their rights and have no awareness or less awareness about the multiple identities that exist and impede their exercising their rights, with their association and their impact on their daily lives. The intersections of normative frameworks and lived realities on the one hand and, the state discourse around one 'dominant identity', on the other, are constructed and influenced by society which shapes into a narrative. So, these realities and evidence are excerpted from the global literature as well as from the lived experiences of Indigenous people and women with disabilities in different qualitative studies that were conducted by the National Indigenous Disabled Women Association Nepal (NIDWAN) from 2020 to 2023 due to the impact of the COVID pandemic, violence, participation, climate change impacts, and others.

Indigenous people continue to live with the constructed worldview. On the one hand, they practice their unique traditions with distinct social, cultural, economic, and political characteristics separate from those of dominant societies with whom they coexist. On the other, they have experienced centuries long policies of assimilation and structural discrimination as pointed out by Hodson (2002) and these world views are co-opted and assimilated into the state-led dominant worldviews, which are directly and indirectly imposed on the disabled. As a result, they struggle for their own existence, identity, and establishing their language and culture within themselves and beyond with a broader movement. Consequently, the distinct experiences and issues of Indigenous people with disabilities remain occluded within disability, Indigenous movement, and policy debates.

DOI: 10.4324/9781032656519-15

As with Indigenous peoples globally, they often do not view a missing or differently functioning body part, sense or capacity as a 'problem' requiring 'fixing' (Avery, 2018; Bevan-Brown, 2013; Walsh, 2020). Instead of an Indigenous person with 'a disability' having to be 'made normal', in most parts of the world, the family and community often ensure that the person is accepted, included and able to participate in social and cultural life (Avery, 2018; Walsh, 2020). Even the notion of disability is often perceived by Indigenous and other marginalized groups to be a harmful, political label imposed upon them by colonizers, which brings feelings of deficiency, inferiority, stigma, and shame so, thus, in fact, creates 'disability' (Imada, 2017; Ineese-Nash 2020; Walsh, 2020). These constructed narratives exist in the society we live and Indigenous peoples are part of these realities.

Another example of health, Indigenous people with disabilities do not enjoy equitable access to information on health, health-related intervention, limited mobility assistance, or services related to social habilitation and rehabilitation (UNPFII Report, 2013). This inequity is affirmed in the ill-health suffered by Indigenous peoples such as some diseases, which include blindness due to trachoma and diabetes, hearing loss, heart disease, leprosy, tuberculosis, and sexually transmitted diseases (Briscoe, 2003). These occur frequently among Indigenous communities that lack basic housing and health infrastructure or access to health services. Generations of Indigenous people globally suffer from starvation and malnutrition, leading to disastrous effects on physical and intellectual development as well as a heightened susceptibility to a myriad of immune system diseases and disabilities. Malnutrition persists in remote communities, compounding other social determinants of chronic ill-health (Martin, 2011), so it results in a reduced quality of life, and food starvation for people with disabilities, who must seek for alternative ways to exist (WFP-Nepal Report, 2021) – so they have more rapid deaths than ordinary people. This highlights the impact of preventable impairments that issue from poor nutrition, as well as accidents, and injuries (Danuletti, 2000). Some excess incidence of impairment among Indigenous people is caused by injurious behaviors such as maternal ill-health, because of drug and alcohol abuse during pregnancy (Salmon, 2007). These effects are magnified by the lack of access to information and to health systems, and health-promotion strategies directed at smoking, alcohol and drug abuse, exercise and nutrition as well as, Indigenous knowledge, health systems and practices that existed in the past, which are gradually not being promoted. Hence, it is imperative that disability definitions and measurements (such as screening and diagnostic tools) be informed by Indigenous people's conceptualisations and experiences, such as taking into account the social, cultural, historical and other determinants of ill-health and disability, such as colonization, dispossession, marginalization, racism and trauma (Lau et al., 2012; McCausland & Dowse, 2020).

Many Indigenous people cannot access resident/family, disability-related cards or certificates to obtain government-provided services. Therefore, this results in the community not being recorded for accessing social security, health insurance and social services. The issue of distance to health services and access to health systems further makes Indigenous people with disabilities limited in their access to health services. The underlying cause for this disparity rests on awareness, education and access to health systems for Indigenous peoples. This is a challenge, as the right to health in the context of Indigenous people with disabilities is still characterized by discrimination and marginalization.

Similarly, as far as Indigenous peoples' issues are concerned, they are derived from the widespread impact and their understanding of development. The vulnerability of Indigenous people is contributed to by the potential discrimination and exclusion that they faced during the development process by state and non-state actors. In the name of development, Indigenous communities are affected by harmful development and business projects like hydropower projects, electricity transmission lines and factories, which forcefully evict Indigenous peoples and local communities from their traditional land without respecting their free prior and informed consent. These also cause brutal attacks and gross human violations that engender exclusion and an isolation of Indigenous peoples. This brings a higher possibility of being at risk and a prevalence factor of disability exists and gets escalated. Such threats can be observed in every aspect of life, but the more vulnerable conditions are more poignant among persons with disabilities. Many communities are unaware that co-optation and assimilating the understanding of Indigenous values, philosophy and community-led intervention mix with development rights. In some self-aware communities, they create their own development pathways such as exchanging information, skills, tools, resources and sharing their struggles, and ideas. This helps them rediscover their inherent strengths, to shift the power and frame their own Indigenous-led worldview and narratives for a just society. However, in many instances, the social participation of Indigenous people with disabilities in such engagement in their own environment and their own group, and even in the system of society and state is still often neglected.

Studies in many countries reflect that disability rates are higher among women and also among Indigenous women and girls (Burlock, 2017). This is because they face gender discrimination, poverty, malnutrition, violence, work pressure and disproportionate care burdens including a lack of access to sexual and reproductive health services. They also suffer from depression and anxiety, a great exposure to violence and harmful practices, and a male-centered household distribution of resources. Women have low education, receive low health-related services and have no or minimal participation and engagement in both the public and private spheres.

Indigenous people and women with disabilities in Nepal

Nepal is no exception to the aforementioned various related anecdotal evidence and data. In Asia, Nepal is progressive enough to debate and discuss regarding the protection and promotion of the rights of Indigenous persons with disabilities. About 45 million Indigenous people with disabilities live in the Asia Pacific regions in extreme poverty so at high risk (Asia Pacific, 2015) and there are 700,000 Indigenous women with disabilities in Nepal (NIDWAN et al., 2022). There are many contributing factors placing Indigenous people at the higher rates and risk of disability. These factors are not limited to their greater level of poverty, lower living standards, poor quality of prevention, a lack of suitable rehabilitation services, increased exposure to environmental degradation, climate change impacts, natural and other disasters, conflict and a higher rate of being victims of violence (including sexual violence and rape), dangerous working conditions and accidents as well as foreign employment and higher rates of illiteracy, an inadequate nutritional level, lower immunization coverage, higher unemployment and underemployment rates and lower mobility, and less early intervention. NIDWAN (2022) reveals that "81% [of] Indigenous Persons with Disabilities and Indigenous Women with Disabilities have poorer access to public facilities. Girls and women with disabilities face a higher risk of violence than those without disabilities". However, "we do not have a reliable data on the violence faced by an Indigenous Woman with Disabilities. The lack of data on this issue is not only alarming but also exposes the truth about how this minority group has been largely neglected by the government and the other national and international organizations" (para 2). Despite the higher rates of disability among Indigenous communities, there is an under-reporting of disability data, and very little or no attention is paid to the issue both from disabled communities and state intervention (UN, 2024).

There have been some intervention from Indigenous people with disabilities like the NIDWAN that gathers, unites and debates about the Indigenous person and women with disabilities – with community-led initiatives and issues and policy interventions; however, these are yet to be addressed in an effective manner. There has still remained a gap in the nexus of gender, disability, Indigenous and culture-related initiatives including collective rights to ensure and promote the rights of Indigenous peoples and women with disabilities. There is a dearth of Indigenous-designed and culturally meaningful assessment tools available internationally, which results in less debate and discourse from an Indigenous perceptive in the context of Nepal and Asia. The understanding and internalizing of the intercultural and intersectional approaches in the policies and programs has left a space for discourse.

Understanding disabled identity intersects with stigma, prejudice, social norms and values, discrimination, limitation, barriers, and exclusion and many more; whereas Indigenous identity intersects with culture, language, connection to land, identity, colonization, historical discrimination and exclusion, oppression, human rights violations, collective ways of life to name a few. On the other hand, gender identity connects with deep-rooted patriarchal values, systems and culture, structural elite groups/caste/power relations, dominance, and hegemony, traditions and stereotypes, beliefs and cultures that have existed for centuries. How the people coexisted with these myriad and multiple layers of values and systems remains baffling and a dilemma or unknown in most instances, and we are not in a position to demand their argument. The complex negotiation of each single identity and its complex intersections in individual lives, at the institutional level and the state level remains mainly undebated. Furthermore, the existing cumulative structural and historical discrimination that multiple identity holders have undergone remains an unexplored topic, which is the root cause of the denial of rights, disparity and discrimination. Therefore, framing the narratives from their marginalized voices and creating inclusive spaces for amplifying their voices is key for Indigenous people with disabilities.

Gaps, issues and priorities of Indigenous people and women with disabilities

Having intersections of racism, ableism, sexism and structural issues, Indigenous people with disabilities are diverse and distinctly related to historical injustices compounded by marginalization from economic opportunities and exclusion from societal participation. Historical roots and the intergenerational impacts of colonization, the Indigenous worldview and epistemologies are less debated in the public domain because of the problematic nature of state. The state's dominant silos approach and worldview is highly important and flourishes while the Indigenous worldviews are assimilated and co-opted during the process which hinders further marginalization in all development processes and mechanisms.

There are dilemmas of Indigenous people with disabilities to thrive, especially, with a gap between the grassroots to global levels. The UN Expert Group Meeting on Indigenous People with Disabilities highlights some of the gaps such as:

- A knowledge gap at the grassroots level
- A risk of cultural and social assimilation

- Social perceptions of disability among different Indigenous communities
- The situations of Indigenous women and girls with disabilities
- A lack of access to services and support in most areas
- Insufficient statistical information on Indigenous people with disabilities and the need to invest in disaggregated data (UN Expert Meeting Report, 2016).

These gaps have identified other prominent discussions such as climate change, humanitarian issues, armed conflict situations, the prevention of Indigenous disabilities before birth, support for Indigenous persons with disabilities, respect for their autonomy and making clearer definitions regarding social services for Indigenous people with disabilities in light of the need to avoid the risk of assimilation, a lack of awareness on intersectionalities, as well as indirect and structural discriminations – these are some of the gaps and issues.

The UNPFII Report 2013 highlights some of the prominent issues of Indigenous people with disabilities like a lack of relevant, available and reliable data. They face discrimination and exclusion in all areas of life, preventing their realization of their rights, which results in extreme inequalities. Exclusion is compounded by multiple dimensions of discrimination. For example, in situations where education and other services are not culturally appropriate or accessible. Circumstances such as sex, age, location and ethnicity can aggravate such forms of exclusion. The right to self-determination is a central right for Indigenous people and includes rights to autonomy or self-government and also to participate and be actively involved in external decision-making processes. The right to self-determination should be respected by all external stakeholders, while supporting the elaboration and implementation of all laws, policies and programs, so that the needs, and rights of Indigenous people with disabilities should be taken into account.

The right to participate in decision-making processes is reaffirmed by both the UNDRIP and the CRPD. This right should be respected in relation to relevant decision-making processes by all governments. Similarly, consultation processes taking place in Indigenous communities should include the participation of people with disabilities. The right of Indigenous peoples to determine their political or organizational systems should be exercised with the full participation of those members with disabilities, taking into account the cultural barriers that women tend to face in such processes. Many Indigenous people with disabilities are excluded from participating in and benefiting from culturally and otherwise appropriate development. Many live in poverty and lack food and clothing, equal access to appropriate quality education; health services; work and employment; social protection, sanitation; assistive devices including mobility aids and health and rehabilitation services, among others. Existing services may lack adequately trained providers, as well as proper physical or accessible buildings, and may be located at great distances from those living on Indigenous lands, or in rural or remote areas. The lack of appropriate services can also contribute to higher rates of institutionalization of Indigenous people with disabilities, removing them from family, culture, traditions, community and society.

Indigenous people with disabilities also face a broad range of challenges in relation to access to the justice system, including physical inaccessibility to police stations, domestic or traditional courts and accessible proceedings which are not conducted in relevant languages or where appropriate assistive devices or technology are unavailable. Access to information and appropriate services, including forensic services, appropriately trained law enforcement and medical services in instances of criminal cases, to support their access to justice are often lacking. A lack of support and services for families with Indigenous children with disabilities has led to the displacement of families from their communities and often to the separation of children from their families and communities. In many societies, Indigenous people suffer intergenerational trauma caused by, among other things, forced assimilation and the removal of children from their families, thus, Indigenous children with disabilities continue to be at high risk of being separated from their families.

Available evidence shows that girls and women with disabilities are at a higher risk of violence than girls and women without disabilities and that Indigenous women are often disproportionately victims of sexual violence. In terms of realization of their rights, as well as access to redress, and remedies for human rights abuses, Indigenous women with disabilities often face a complex set of barriers related to gender, Indigenous identity, and disability. According to a 2013 survey, conducted by the UN Office for Disaster Risk Reduction and partners, a high proportion of people with disabilities die or suffer injuries during disasters.

The risk of exposure of Indigenous people with disabilities to disasters and emergencies is also elevated because they often live in areas of particular risk related to climate change, the environment, militarization and armed conflict and because of the impact of extractive industries. They also have the right to full and effective participation in all aspects of life. The realization of this right requires accessibility in terms of physical environments, transportation, information and communications, and access to other facilities and services open or provided to the public, both in urban and in rural areas. All these issues discussed above are some of the major ones of Nepalese Indigenous people and women with disabilities that exist, and these issues are not discussed among many Indigenous people with disabilities.

Reframing the narrative of distinctness: What does it mean to us?

Racism, ableism, sexism, classism and colonialism are all associated with Indigenous people and women with disabilities as an interlocking system operating at several structures such as the individual, interpersonal, institutional and cultural levels.

> As a marginalized multiple identities groups, we are dominated by certain groups based on our ethnicity, race, gender, class, religion, language, accent, attire, and on other categories in the public forum and in our work and institutions associated with our several identities that we hold, which are subtle and direct. In the process of conversation, the sense of domination, exercising of power and the influence of their voices gets engaged and influenced and we are not in a situation to argue and counter argue on the defined statements, therefore, we often remain an observer with left out issues and agendas.[1]

These reflections from an Indigenous women's group with disabilities highlight the usual practices towards Indigenous peoples and the process of defining and understanding how dominant narratives are framed in social-political discourse at the individual level, so decolonizing to understand the multiple identity groups is necessary. This means reframing

---

1 Participant in the discussion of the research conducted by NIDWAN on the Situation of Indigenous Women with Disabilities in Nepal, To the CEDAW on GR on Indigenous Women and Girls,79th Session, Geneva, 18th June 2021.

the narratives with the intersectional nuances and interventions to be Indigenous community owned, and not merely being community based is critical. It is foremost central to express the distinct challenges Indigenous people and women with disabilities continue to face in a changing society through self-advocacy.

Likewise, at the interpersonal level, the focus on an individual's actions, behavior and language interact with other different individuals, who integrate the Indigenous systems, tradition, and values that shape and set the mindset, perceptions and opinions based on the actions, behavior and language of peoples and policy planners, who have a set constructed and dominant worldview. Therefore, Indigenous designed, owned and led discussion should be ensured to set the conversation and narrative. Self-advocacy through reframing the Indigenous-led narrative in the actions and utterances of people on their own behalf with intervention is crucial.

Correspondingly, at the institutional level, the system, rules, policies, procedures, and practices, which are written or unwritten, within an institution define who is eligible and can fully participate. Processes, systems, and structures are defined by people mostly in power who often are not from an Indigenous community. Often, most Indigenous people do not have a history of engaged in these systems, structures and state mechanisms, so they are engaged in their own traditional customary practices and institutions, which promote Indigenous knowledge worldview and do not fall under the state's norms and systems. These systems are discouraged and demoralized by the state and are on the verge of extinction, so Indigenous people and the Indigenous person with disabilities at the institutional level get further confined to scale up their intervention. Many Indigenous communities all around the globe practice oral traditions that are transformed from generation to generation, which are equally unfamiliar to the state-led processes, which are written policies, and further limit them in exercising their rights and values.

At the cultural level, the dominant worldviews, narratives, cultural messages, and norms are framed directly and indirectly to serve to maintain power and privilege, by creating the set of standards about right, normal, beautiful and so on. As we develop a critical consciousness and work to help address and dismantle racism, sexism, ableism, and other forms of oppression, it is important that we apply a distinct systems approach to our work and begin to analyze, uncover, and change the ways that oppression is affecting the individual, or interpersonal, institutional and cultural levels. If we include Indigenous peoples' past and present experiences, it may also help address racism and stereotypes and improve relations and trust between Indigenous and non-Indigenous people (Miller, 2017; Trofimovs & Dowse, 2014). This is critical as it will enable us to look through a gender lens from the Indigenous worldview in an equitable manner. Subsequently, distinctness through Indigenous-owned and framed by Indigenous ways of knowing, being, seeing and doing is essential as it connects the ecosystems in a holistic approach to reframe the narratives within and beyond. For Indigenous people, planet and state operate in relatedness. Everything and everyone are related and their belief is that people, objects and the environment are all connected, which is reinforced by law, kinship and spirituality, so one understands each and every oppressive identity.

Learning from within and beyond for Indigenous people and women with disability rights

To effectively reframe the distinct narratives of Indigenous people and women with disabilities in Nepal, NIDWAN has been framing the issues and concerns from the ground, generating evidence through recognition, affiliation and programmatic intervention at five levels. First at the national, local, provincial and federal levels. Similarly, it has been linking the national level work at the national, regional and global levels to create inclusive spaces for learning and linking policies with global evidence to ensure and exercise their rights. Second, through self-advocacy which includes knowledge of self, knowledge of rights, communication and leadership. The third action is stories as power, for collective voices for collective actions through finding one's voice and articulating the circumstances in order to work for social change in the communities. Fourth action is a cross-movement collaboration with different entities and in a different normative framework and the fifth, is linking the local to global advocacy with documentation and a normative framework (Gurung, 2020).

In a nutshell, the understanding of the nexus of disability and indigeneity in a cohesive and comprehensive form within and beyond the structure, which is essential as Indigenous peoples' values, are connected with entire the ecosystem, significant policy, legislative and essential system reforms, which means learning about Indigenous people must be carried out by the government and relevant stakeholders in the way of respecting, ensuring and empowering Indigenous people with disabilities about their rights, first through policy implementation and intervention; second, the reorientation and discourse on decolonizing, intercultural epistemologies, Indigenous values and self-determination development to all policy planners; third, engaging within and beyond the social movements and defining their distinct narratives through preserving and promoting Indigenous cultures, identity and values; and fourth, a capacity for building up Indigenous people and mainstreaming them in the state mechanism by creating inclusive spaces.

With the trajectories of within and beyond progress, challenges, Indigenous people and women with disabilities as right holders are cocreating their inclusive spaces and struggling within and beyond the movement to incorporate their distinct identity and intersectional lens by demanding, asserting and claiming rights on the ground of *"Nothing About us Without Us"* with state and relevant stakeholders. So, it is urgent to create inclusive spaces for all of us ensuring no one is left behind.

References

Asia Pacific Declaration on the Rights of Indigenous People with Disabilities. (2015). First gathering of Indigenous people with disabilities from Asia and Pacific Region.

Avery, S. (2018). *Culture is inclusion: A narrative of Aboriginal and Torres Strait Islander people with a disability*. Sydney: First Peoples Disability Network.

Bevan-Brown, J. (2013). Including people with disabilities: An Indigenous perspective. *International Journal of Inclusive Education, 17*(6), 571–583.

Briscoe, G. (2003). *Counting, health and identity: A history of Aboriginal health and demography in Western Australia and Queensland 1900–1940*. Canberra: Aboriginal Studies Press.

Burlock, A. (2017). "Women with disabilities" Statistics Canada website, Retrieved 2 April 2018.

Danuletti, M. (2000). *Meeting the needs of Koorie people with a disability: Developing and implementing strategies for improving service equity and access*. Melbourne: Department of Human Services.

Gurung, P. (2020). Our lives, our story: The Journey of the voiceless towards advocacy in Nepal. In *Global perspectives on disability activism and advocacy, our way*, Eds. Karen Soldatic and Kelly Johnson. Interdisciplinary Disability Studies (pp. 145–160). Routledge.

Hodson, D. (2002). Introduction comparative perspectives on the Indigenous rights movement in Africa and the Americas. *American Anthropology, 104*(4), 1037–1049.

Imada, A. L. (2017). A decolonial disability studies? *Disability Studies Quarterly, 37*(3).

Ineese-Nash, N. (2020). Disability as a colonial construct: The missing discourse of culture in conceptualizations of disabled Indigenous children. *Canadian Journal of Disability Studies*, 9(3), 28–51.

Lau, P., Marion, C., Blow, R., and Thomson, Z. (2012). Healing for Aboriginal and Torres Strait Islander Australians at risk with the justice system: A program with wider disability & society35 implications. *Criminal Behavior and Mental Health*, 22(5), 297–302.

Martin, S. (2011). Starvation fears in Aboriginal lands. *The Advertiser, September*, 1(1).

McCausland, R., & Dowse, L. (2020). The need for a community-led, holistic service response to Aboriginal young people with cognitive disability in remote areas: a case study. *Children Australia*, 45(4), 326–334.

Miller, A. (2017). Neighborhood justice centers and indigenous empowerment. *Australian Indigenous Law Review, 20*, 123–153.

NIDWAN. (2021). Indigenous Women and Girls in Nepal: A Brief Overview. Nepal. https://nidwan.org.np/ development-research/indigenouswomen-and-girls-in-nepal-a-brief-overview/?doing_wp_cron=1643362864. 97347807884421630859375.

NIDWAN. (2022). Indigenous Women and Girls in Nepal: A Brief Overview available at https://nidwan.org.np/2022/01/14/indigenous-women-and-girls-in-nepal-a-brief-overview/

NIDWAN et al. (2022). Special Rapporteur on violence against women, its causes and consequences (January, 31). https://www.ohchr.org/sites/default/files/2s022-03/Joint-Nepal.pdf

Salmon, A. (2007). Dis/abling states, dis/abling citizenship: Young Aboriginal mothers and the medicalization of fetal alcohol syndrome. *Journal for Critical Education Policy Studies*, 5(2), 271–306.

Trofimovs, J., and Dowse, L. (2014). Mental health at the intersections: The impact of complex needs on police contact and custody for Indigenous Australian Men. *International Journal of Law and Psychiatry, 37*(4), 390–398.

United Nations. (2016). Expert group meeting on Indigenous persons with disabilities. July 7-8. (pp. 1–21). ILO Headquarters, Geneva.

United Nations Human Rights Council, the Special Rapporteur on the Rights of indigenous Peoples (2024). https://www.ohchr.org/en/calls-for-input/2024/call-inputs-indigenous-persons-disabilities.

United Nations Economic and Social Council, Permanent Forum on Indigenous Issues. (2013). Study on the situation of Indigenous persons with disabilities, with a particular focus on challenges faced with regard to the full enjoyment of human rights and inclusion in development. E/C.19/2013/6.

United Nations Women. (2020). Fact sheet on Indigenous women with disabilities. https://www.unwomen.org/en/digital-library/publications/2020/04/fact-sheet-on-indigenous-women-with-disabilities

Walsh, C. L. (2020). Falling on deaf ears? *Listening to Indigenous voices regarding middle ear infections and hearing loss*. PhD dissertation. Australian National University, Canberra, Australia.

World Food Program. (2021). A study on access to food of indigenous peoples with disabilities in Nepal, WFP Report, Nepal.

World Health Organization. (2017). Mental disorders. http://www.who.int/mediacentre/factsheets/fs396/en/

13 Old meets new – Moving forward with the colonial mindset of disability – A Kabyle perspective

Boussad At Yaagun (Djerbid)

Introduction

Djerbid Boussad was born in 1933 in Algeria when the French ruled their country during their colonial reign in Africa. I am first and foremost Kabyle, which is now known as the Amazigh people because in pre-contact their tribe changed its name. From a young age, I only spoke Kabyle and learned French during the colonization. I fought for the liberation of my country in 1962. I left Kabylia to continue my studies in France, where I benefitted from the education, and access to new developments, which enabled me to not only embrace who I am as a Kabyle person but also to be able to obtain a foreign education that I could use for a job and start a family. These were all essential to survive as a subject in the French empire. This chance to obtain the necessary skills as a Kabyle was most advantageous because the Kabylia people are often poor. Thus, I became a school director not only for me to rise up but also to enable other Kabyle youth to have a similar opportunity.

The history

The Kabyle traditional territory is located about 100 km from the capital Algiers. The Kabyle people are part of the Berber ethnic Indigenous group that reside in the Kabylia in northern Algeria that spreads across the Atlas Mountains, east of Algiers. They represent the largest Berber population of Algeria and the second largest in North Africa. Kabylia is a mountainous coastal region in northern Algeria and the homeland of the Kabyle people.

To understand the complexity of disability in my people, we must first look at the historical approach towards being colonialized by multiple foreigners. As I said previously, the Kabyle is who we truly are. However, with the forced assimilation by the Arabs, we had to convert to this new way of life by speaking their language, learning their religion, and customs to survive. This process made us change from Kabyle to Amazigh. The next colonialist aggression was from France in the 1830s and although many of the Kabyle people speak Arabic and now French, we are still at our core Kabyle people and proud of it. Learning Arabic and French gave me the opportunity to excel in school and obtain a higher position as a school director/principal, which enabled me to help so many people including Kabyle children. This approach to relearning language could be constructed as a form of (re)colonialization by reprogramming students to relearn a different and even complex language structure that would negatively impact Indigenous and those who struggle with reading challenges – dyslexia (Figure 13.1).

Some Kabyle live off their land and others harvest olives. Very few families live off their possessions because they live and farm in poor areas as the French took most of the rich soil that was excellent for growing crops. This is why so many Kabyle live in poor

DOI: 10.4324/9781032656519-16

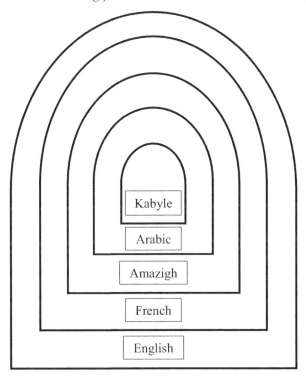

Figure 13.1 Recolonizing through language.

conditions and even more moved to France for a better life as many learned how to speak French. Even today, Algerian French speakers are considered as better than the natural French speakers from France.

Pre-colonial times – before the French arrived

In pre-colonial times, we called on the Elders, who had experience and knowledge as they were holders of such information and guided our people as natural leaders in spiritual, mental, physical, and emotional growth. Our Elders guided the development of the Kabyle through their wisdom of the past then enabled us to move forward and confront new challenges with knowledge, insight, and resilience. Much of who we are as Kabyle people comes from the oral history of Elders and collectively, we move forward in dialogue as a people.

The influence of colonialism on the Kabylia people

After colonization, education was generalized. Many children benefitted, which is why there are many Algerian immigrants in Canada, France, etc., who just had the chance to attend school. In Algeria, medicine became free after independence, which helped so many people who had medical troubles such as speech, loss of hearing, or deformities. It was at this time, in 1960, that I first heard of the term dyslexia, which impacted many students as the schools in Algeria had a mixture of Kabylia, Algerians, and French and later Africans, and so there were lots of human and animal losses when France was training to keep their colonial grip on their foreign territory. Colonization deprived the Algerian population by exploiting them but also obtained good lands that had originally been occupied by various Indigenous peoples.

There was a group of 22 men from all tribes, who gathered near the capital of Algiers to start a war as the new Arabic nation of Algeria began against the Indigenous peoples and yet again, against their foreign colonial oppressors who wanted to have them removed. Yet, the Arabic Algerians still limited the Indigenous peoples of the land, which is why, so many Indigenous peoples moved to France, their former oppressor, and to other colonized countries such as Canada and the United States.

The end of French colonialism and the beginning of Algeria

It wasn't until 1962 that Algeria became independent and opted for the Arabic language. Arabic has become the national language, but the majority of Kabyle adults do not know or understand Arabic. We are called Arab, yet we have always been Kabyle in our hearts, minds, bodies, and spirits. Arabic has been taught at school since 1962, but the Kabyle only learned Arabic as a foreign language because, at home, the most used language is Kabyle (mother tongue). Tamazight which means 'freeman' is able to learn both Arabic and French without any legal problems. Personally, as I was a civil servant, I needed training in Arabic to get a promotion, which was why I learned the Arabic language for a better job, but always in my *ul* 'heart', I am Kabyle.

How disabilities are understood from a Kabyle perspective

From my point of view, any child regardless of their situation is a gift from heaven.

Kabyle parents take very good care of their children who live with all kinds of disabilities and protect them against winds and fatigue from the different colonial representations, which were often the cause of people with disabilities learning differently.

The Kabyle people believed in traditional medicine before colonization. People living with disabilities were accepted by others in their families and the community at large as equals. Traditionally, in Kabyle culture, people who have a disability are taken care of by the family and by the village. It is this approach to a communal acceptance that makes our cultural inclusive of differences. In the case of children with disabilities, learning happens naturally like other children; although, with additional patience and method, as we expect each person has their own development. Sometimes the teachings may not achieve the desired goals, which is expected. Education is compulsory, but there are parents who judge the usefulness of education for their children as they know, who their children are, and what they are capable of doing. This lived experience is far better than a colonial label that impacts the child and follows them throughout their lifetime. The Kabyle believe in inclusion education by including all people as part of the human family. This approach to learning became a uniquely Kabyle perspective as it includes all students, but it went against the Algerian educational values. It is this equal footing with others – those who learn and look different yet are never excluded from learning. Society yes, in the Algerian mindset, but not in the Kabyle communal understanding.

They preferred that their children tend livestock and do housework rather than send them to school, as children have been victimized by teachers, who only see the differences of certain children. Instead of allowing their children to be further traumatized, some parents choose to have them in a safer place, away from abuse, name calling, and subjugation by teachers only because they learn differently.

Amazigh (Tamazight) words and expressions used to explain differences *not* disabilities

In the Amazigh language, there are suitable words to call people with disabilities:

- Amuḍin/tamuḍint would be 'sick' – in our culture, which is not used negatively but simply to put things into perspective.
- Ur ksan ara as in 'you shouldn't blame him/her, it's not his/her fault'.
- Ad yelli Ṛebbi di laawen – is would be like 'may the gods help him/her'.

These words and expressions are attributed with pure innocence, with no malice or bad intentions towards the individual. It even happens that they are attributed to divine powers. for example, there was a blind woman in our village who was attributed with fortune telling. She was blind but not disabled as she was able to see into the unknown, so this gift was a positive cultural responsibility.

My time as a school principal

The next two examples are testimonies from my father, as he was then the director of an elementary school in another village. During the early years of Algeria's independence in the 1960s, the newly independent country began to build an education system in French and Arabic but excluded Tamazight, the Indigenous language of North Africa, which is that of my ancestors. This new system was rudimentary at the time and did not include any tools or support for the kids with disabilities. This approach to education in post-France colonization had excluded the Kabylia approach, which included all members.

There was a deaf student, who had no accommodation or teaching adapted to his needs, so he could not follow classes and received poor grades. At the end of the year, during the class council, his teachers suggested that they make him repeat the year. My father had suggested that instead, they should let him move to the next class so that he would continue to be with his peers of the same age, especially, since he had no chance of succeeding even after repeating, as the school had no resources for his situation. By allowing this student to stay among friends, his self-esteem and well-being would not be subjected to being traumatized due to an inability to learn. There is more to schooling than education, we must nurture and look after the children in our care as educators beyond what regulations dictate.

There was another student girl who couldn't see the blackboard clearly. I suggested to her father to have her examined to get glasses. Once she had glasses, her results subsequently improved significantly. I have found that working with students gave me the chance to understand who they were and what challenges they might endure, which allowed me to advise and provide guidance in terms of support.

The role of teachers in the Algerian education system

From the Indigenous point of view, some children are born with disabilities, but we accept them as they come and as they are. According to my understanding, these children are lucky if they can find a teacher, who can support their linguistic, cultural, and social differences; if not, these challenges would become disabilities and learning disabilities if not provided alternative curriculum, therapy, and specialized teaching. All these factors play in the child's learning and development. As some teachers have more knowledge than others, it all depends on what type of teaching the child may encounter.

For example, when I was a school principal, there was a very intelligent child. The Arab teacher, who was an Iman and taught the Qur'an, was not a trained teacher, which resulted in the teacher assigning a label as crazy on a child because the child was alter and well beyond the grade level, he was in. I just told him that he was a very alert child, and learned faster than the whole class, several repetitions of this were needed so the teacher just had to adapt without judgement. This religious teacher was not ill-intentioned, he only judged from the way the child responded so thought he was crazy, when he was in fact the opposite and quite intelligent, beyond the confines of the classroom. In today's schools, this child would be considered as gifted, possibly autistic.

For children, who were unable to assimilate better, there was the system of repeating a year and of tripling for students who were unable to adapt at the same pace as the others. Children with disabilities could have the chance to be integrated into a normal class depending on the management of the director of the establishment and the school staff; however, they did not expect miracles from them given their learning challenges. Before independence (1962), people living with disabilities were dependent on their parents as the authorities did not help them, but after independence, there was an improvement in this direction. Social services took care of the disabled and those who had served conditions and required specialized trained staff.

More is needed in the ability to learn languages as the right teacher can make all the difference in providing support, mental health, and well-being. The role of a teacher is not to merely teach but to support the natural development of their students, so they can achieve their next educational level. For children, who had to retake a class or grade, this was not a punishment for failing, but a way to learn more of the course content as the student needed a better understanding. This approach to repeating a grade did not appear as a form of negative association due to learning, but as a way to acquire more knowledge of a topic, which would thus allow the student to learn more without feeling they had failed because of being held back. This way was understood as a trauma-free approach and allowed the well-being of the students to not be affected due to their learning difficulties. In the community, inclusive learning was the basis in schools as they did not separate 'the dis' from 'the abled'. Children could learn together and not feel that they were different because of segregation based on learning differences as in Western cultures.

Recolonization of the Indigenous people of Algeria

So before, when children first went to school, they learned French in the 3rd grade, and then they started to learn Arabic. From grades three to six, after their 1962 independence from France, the language curriculum changed to learning Arabic in the first year and French in the 3rd grade. This switch from French to Arabic then reversed was confusing for many, especially for the Indigenous children, who learned their own language, French, Arabic, and now English, which has replaced French. Children who struggle with reading, writing, and spelling or those with dyslexia face even greater challenges. Although all children are treated equally, those who face language challenges are at a disadvantage, even more so, with the Indigenous groups as they are again colonized due to a colonial approach to learning another foreign language. What is even worse is that Indigenous children must learn to speak Arabic and English in order to obtain success, plus look and act like an Arab. Our Indigenous children must act and look the part of an Arab by becoming an actor to secure a chance of moving forward out of poverty, which is a common factor among Indigenous peoples in Algeria. This is due to the government's act of de-Indigenization by removing all Indigenous influence in the military, police, and other forms of power, which resulted in many tribal members moving out of Algeria and resettling in France and in Canada, given the familiar French language.

The challenges of Algeria on the Kabyle peoples in moving forward

The scientific knowledge level as achieved by the Western educational systems is considered by our culture as viable and would be beneficial, especially, if adapted to our culture. However, the Amazigh and Kabyle cultural issues lay with the North African regimes that promote an ideology that is based on the Arabic and Islamic culture, and this is a great obstacle for our people.

Conclusion

To conclude this contribution as a reflection of my lived experiences, wisdom, and insight from my own Kabyle perspective on disabilities, I share this oral testimony as a method to share with the world about who we are as a people and how we include all peoples regardless of how they learn or act. I am a Kabyle man who came from a proud background deeply rooted in traditions, language, and history, which is a part of who I am and how the Kabyle people represent ourselves. Additionally, we place the family at the center of our society as sacred and important for our future and take great pride in this. In following this approach of family, I would like to honour my wife's mother with her photo. Her resilience as a proud and strong Kabyle woman can be seen and traced in my family today as she wears traditional clothing and adorns facial markings (Figure 13.2).

Figure 13.2 Photo of Jida Aini – Kabyle traditional women – my wife's mother, 1990.

Source: Photographer: Djerbid Boussad in Kabylia

Part III

Learning from within – Including traditional knowledge

The chapters in Part III provide a distinctive cultural depiction of how traditional knowledge is used as a way to learn from within so that we can grow and share our experiences by moving forward together. Examples are presented from around the globe including Australia, South Africa, the United States, Canada, Taiwan, and the Democratic Republic of the Congo that will provide insight into leadership, empathy, support services, psychosocial, oral history, and how natural learning abilities can empower people. The authors dive into the essence of being Indigenous from a wide range of knowledge and belief systems that support and encourage development in a multitude of approaches.

Traditional knowledge as ways of knowing

The authors in this Part III have all contributed within their own perspective on how using traditional knowledge as a way to understand our past, to see our present that enables us to look to the future. Traditional knowledge and belief systems are the fundamental bond understood by many cultures, especially to those who still practice it, as a way to connect with our past self through the stories, histories, and ways of life of our ancestors. Knowing where you came from can be a powerful tool in moving forward and by making this connection, we can connect to our humanity on a deeper level. This is a perfect place to include an ageless knowledge system that can help those who seek out ways of deeper understanding. This can allow for the infusion of past knowledge of oral history to be used in a different format, one that can reflect current situations and ways of communicating through models, templates, and how to assess a person within a culturally friendly environment by excluding the settler-colonial negative outcomes of victimization. How we infuse traditional knowledge into our systems can help in the braiding or weaving of new perspectives in this ever-changing world by including Indigenous content in disability studies. Thereby supporting a truly Indigenous disability studies outlook that will benefit all those who read, listen, and understand what has been shared.

DOI: 10.4324/9781032656519-17

14 The importance of Indigenous sign languages on the cultural empowerment of Deaf Indigenous people

Rodney Adams and John Gilroy

Introduction

Similarly to Indigenous spoken languages, Indigenous sign languages have been impacted by colonial ideologies of normalcy and European imperialism. These ideologies have threatened Indigenous languages with extinction. Global colonial agendas of domination of Indigenous lands from the 18th century have meant the education of Indigenous children with hearing loss using Western educational methods prohibited the use of Indigenous signed languages. This paper argues for the revitalization of Aboriginal and Torres Strait Islander sign languages as part of the global advocacy movement to imbed Indigenous languages in community and school education curricula.

Background

The rate of disability in the Aboriginal and Torres Strait Islander population is around twice the rate compared to the non-Aboriginal population. Aboriginal and Torres Strait Islander people with disabilities experience the worst rates of disadvantage and poverty in Australia (Biddle et al., 2013). This is also true for the rate of hearing loss amongst Aboriginal and Torres Strait people which is estimated to be 43% (Australian Bureau of Statistics, 2019). The rate of deafness is predominately caused by the high rates of Otitis Media and other ear infections.

The colonial ideals of whiteness and audism are the antithesis of the traditional practice of disability inclusion, which resulted in many Aboriginal children, who experience deafness also experiencing social exclusion in the wider community. Traditionally, deaf Aboriginal and Torres Strait Islander people were not considered different from their hearing peers and Indigenous communities worked to be inclusive of people, who were deaf. Indigenous communities around the world have an established sign language for people who are deaf. Marmion et al. (2014) reported that Indigenous languages are at the core of vibrant Aboriginal and Torres Strait Islander cultures, essential to individual and community social and emotional well-being. Similarly, Gilroy and Emerson's (2016) analysis of the data from the Longitudinal Study of Indigenous Children concluded that, in order to thrive during their development, children who are at risk of developmental delay require support to engage in their kinship and culture.

This paper challenges commonly held ideologies about normalcy, disability, and human diversity in the context of deafness in Indigenous communities. The experience of our identity as Aboriginal and Torres Strait Islander people, and our experience of

DOI: 10.4324/9781032656519-18

deafness, has been framed and shaped by our past. Under the influence of our culture, being Koori men, who experience deafness/hearing loss, we know the cultural benefits of revitalizing Indigenous sign languages, and by utilizing the Cultural Interface in school education, assess resolutions that may reduce the continuing impacts of colonization. The paper examines the exploration of revitalization attempts, the normalization of sign languages, and a reduction of the impacts of deficit ideologies.

Cultural interface: theoretical overview

Gilroy and Donelly (2016) have suggested that much of the research about Indigenous people with a disability is driven by the desires and wants of non-Indigenous researchers and their Western research institutions. The research of Indigenous people with a disability functions as an enterprise that serves the capitalist interests that underpin colonization. The research enterprise focused on impairment and sought out biomedical justifications for the social marginalization experienced by Aboriginal people. Gilroy et al. (2013) stated that:

> There are volumes of knowledge, a whole epistemological library in fact, on Indigenous people with a disability. This knowledge is not owned by Indigenous people, rather this library operates as a resource for non-Indigenous researchers and government decision makers to legitimate themselves as the controllers and bearers of the 'truth' on disability.
>
> (p. 116)

Indigenous (Avery and First Peoples Disability Network, 2018; McEntyre, 2020; Smiler, 2014) and non-Indigenous disability scholars (Meekosha & Soldatic, 2016; Soldatic, 2015) are incorporating decolonizing methodologies into disability research to fight against the Western research enterprise. Decolonization is a metaphysical approach to deconstruct and challenge the hegemonic structure of traditional Western academic practices in Indigenous communities. Such an approach aims to prevent further deterioration of Indigenous cultures and values by locating Indigenous voices at the centre of research planning, practice, and praxis. This methodology has seen a significant shift from academic and research institutions, and other agencies of power, determining what is 'knowledge' and profiting from the knowledge of Indigenous communities.

We use Gilroy's (2009) and Gilroy and Donnelly's (2016) modified version of Martin Nakata's (1997) Indigenous Standpoint Theory, the Cultural Interface, as a decolonizing framework for disability research. The cultural interface is the domain where the trajectories of Western knowledge systems intersect with Indigenous knowledge systems, establishing the conditions that influence the everyday lives of each Indigenous person. At the interface, the values, ideologies, and practices of pre-colonial times influence the behaviours and perceptions of each Indigenous person, as do current Western philosophies. The interface is both a physical and metaphysical world, where it is not always possible to locate every viewpoint or practice as traditional or not traditional. Gilroy and Donnelly's (2016) model blends the Cultural Interface with the United Nation's International Classification of Functioning to ensure the intersections of the experiences of colonialism, disability, and Indigeneity are acknowledged.

Indigenous sign languages: the Interface of deafness and indigeneity

Signed and spoken languages have coexisted in Indigenous communities for millennia, demonstrating the resiliency of human languages (Davis, 2010). Kusters et al. (2020, p. 1) states that "sign languages are languages that use the visual – kinaesthetic and tactile – kinesthetics modalities". Indigenous sign languages are languages that are used by both hearing and deaf Indigenous people and have been passed down by multiple generations. Aboriginal Elder, Janie Long Perrier (Green et al., 2011), similarly explained how sign language is taught in his family:

> The old people taught us sign language; they handed it down to us. They held that knowledge from the Dreaming and they handed it over and passed it on to us. Now we want to pass it onto our children.
>
> (p. 1)

In many Indigenous communities, sign languages evolved naturally alongside spoken languages in alternative or primary means. In Australia, it appears that many Aboriginal and Torres Strait communities may have used a sign language prior to colonization (Butcher, 2015). Evidence for this assertion comes from the notes and records of early explorers and linguists (Kendon, 2013). A point further supported that sign languages were not only widespread throughout Australia but 'varied inversely with an increase in distance between them' (Umiker-Sebeok & Sebeok, 1978, p. 26).

Sign languages were once used by all Indigenous Nations across the Australian continent (Gilroy, 2012). An analysis of historical colonial reports and research have documented 'gesture languages' across Australia as far back as the late 1800s. So extensive were sign languages in north-eastern Australia alone, that 18,895 sign language items were recorded (Umiker-Sebeok & Sebeok, 1978). Of these, half are single lexical items and half are sentence-length texts. The rest are longer texts ranging between four and five pages long with approximately 500 signs each, with some of this work illustrated on 4,000 feet of film with another 400 feet of recording of mimes.

So prominent was sign language use in Indigenous communities of Australia and North America that it could be said that such a practice was foundational in such communities and served as an example that deafness was not viewed as a deficit, but instead an asset for community harmony and an expansion of the multimodality communication systems extensively used throughout (Kendon, 2020). On the North American continent, Plains Indian Sign Language (PISL) was used extensively covering an area of 1.5 million square miles from Canada to Mexico and from the Mississippi to the foothills of the Rocky Mountains Plain (Davis, 2010). Evidence of the intergenerational transmission of PISL dates back 1,500 years, with signs still used in PISL evident in rock art from this period (McKay-Cody, 2019). PISL was used by more than 40 Indigenous nations, among both deaf and hearing people, to communicate and to transmit cultural knowledge. Indigenous sign language was important in traditional storytelling and in communicating ancestral lore, national history, and family lineages. It was also used for religious purposes such as prayers, origin narratives, and imperatives (Davis, 2010). In Australia, corroborees examined by West (Umiker-Sebeok & Sebeok, 1978, p. 429) revealed that the sign languages used in such instances revealed more information about its purposes 'in scope and specificity' than that of the spoken language adaptation. An indication that the functions of sign languages can at times exceed those of spoken languages, which accentuates the benefits that the Deaf Gain can contribute to the socio-economic development of all communities.

Linguicidal effects of colonization on Indigenous Deaf children

By nature, colonization inherently alienates peoples' connection to their lands and is accompanied as well by violent attacks on Indigenous people's connections to their spoken/signed language, their culture, and kin (Gaby & Woods, 2020; Schofield & Gilroy, 2015). The Australian, 2019 Hearing Health Plan (Australian Government Department of Health, 2019) makes no mention of Indigenous Sign Languages or how it can be utilised within Indigenous communities. The Hearing Health Plan focuses on learning Auslan and training interpreters in the target language. Marmion et al. (2014) Indigenous language survey revealed that most respondents, who were Indigenous (91%), believe that connection with traditional language is critical for their identity and well-being. The massive funding generated for programs that seek to eliminate ear diseases such as Otis Media are examples of the deficit models so entrenched within Western pedagogies. These linguicidal practises have done much harm with an exclusively phonocentric approach to the education of deaf children, leaving many with language deprivation (Gulati, 2014) and funding towards the revitalization of Indigenous sign languages lacking any real substance.

If 'Ableism is a product of settler colonialism', then a by-product of settler colonialism is Audism. Audism has its roots in Social Darwinism and the Justinian Code that perpetuates the deficit models so prevalent in Western philosophy. In deaf education, this came to a resolution at the Milan Congress in 1880. The effect of the resolutions made at the Congress was a global hastening of the already existing trend to eradicate sign language education programs for deaf children in favour of oral programs (Moores, 2010). The first resolution stated, "given the incontestable superiority of speech over signs in restoring deaf-mutes to society, and in giving them a more perfect knowledge of language that the oral method ought to be preferred to signs" (Moores, 2010, p. 309). This is a stark comparison to Indigenous communities in both Australia and North America, where sign languages flourish alongside spoken languages as it had done for thousands of years.

The linguistics field has shown contempt for the lack of revitalization efforts of Indigenous Sign Languages, reflecting Gilroy's and Smith-Merry's (2019) concept of racial-ablism that defines the intersection of disablism and racism as a practice in Western science and hegemony. Similarly, Adams and Crowe (2020) describe this as an audist bias within the field of linguistics that has favoured the documentation of Indigenous spoken languages over Indigenous sign languages, with worrying outcomes on the documentation and existence of Indigenous sign languages. Alongside 'hegemonic whiteness' (Gaby & Woods, 2020, p. 268), the implications of this bias are twofold when 'hearing hegemony' (Cue et al., 2019, p. 418) is combined to impact Indigenous communities, who suffer high rates of hearing loss, leaving its population with high levels of language deprivation.

Navigating the landscape of Deafness and Indigeneity

Simms et al. (2008) stated that "the politics of authority structures, racism, audism, and oppressive language and academic policies often work against deaf students.... to acquire language, an academic foundation, and a healthy cultural identity" (p. 394).

People who experience deafness can acquire a healthy identity in what Ladd (2003) refers to as the process of deafhood. Aside from the forces of racism, Indigenous people who are deaf often combat the oppressive forces of phono-centricism with its focus on Western pedagogies that hearing is the foundation of language and literacy development. Phono-centricism perpetuates 'hegemonic ideologies and practices that disadvantage' (Maher, 2021) people who are deaf with a focus on non-visual forms of communications. This is a direct contradiction to the traditional practises of Indigenous communities. Likewise, McKay-Cody (2019) refers to the 'gravity of oppression' to portray the multiple layers of bias, from hearing professionals who oppress the deaf, to deaf White people who internalise these biases and then oppress Indigenous deaf people and their sign languages.

A consequence is that deaf Indigenous people suffer from the double effects of racism and audism, which are compounded by what Stauffer (2015) calls 'ethical loneliness'. A condition undergone by persons, who have been unethically treated by both human beings and political structures, and who emerge from that injustice to find the world deaf to their testimony. So, ethical loneliness is the process of being abandoned by humanity compounded by the experience of not having a voice.

Gilroy et al. (2018) research of the treatment of Indigenous people in the colonial news media identified incidents where deaf Indigenous people experienced ethical isolation in the colonial and Australian court systems. One example is a deaf Indigenous man who was scarcely supported in the provision of information against a European person who was suspected of selling alcohol to Indigenous people. The evidence of the 'deaf and dumb blackfellow' with his signs interpreted by a Chinaman was immediately dismissed as 'ludicrous' because his testimony was unreliable (Gilroy et al., 2018, p. 41).

Impacts on well-being

By tradition, languages are a key element of Indigenous peoples' individuality and cultural expression so vital to their well-being (Gilroy & Emerson, 2016; Marmion et al., 2014; Sivak et al., 2019). There needs to be a greater acknowledgement that Indigenous sign languages are part of this tradition. The resurgence of Indigenous languages, with reference to Indigenous sign languages, is a means of inspiring Indigenous communities to reclaim their culture, identities, sense of belonging, and enhance communication between families and generations. In the framework of deafness, there are widely reported difficulties with socio-emotional well-being and psycho-social development, and a higher prevalence of mental health difficulties for people who are deaf (Dammeyer & Chapman, 2017; Murray et al., 2019). Reports that children with hearing loss are one and a half to two times more vulnerable to experiencing mental health problems compared to hearing children in Queensland are also prevalent worldwide with the prevalence of mental health problems of 40% in Deaf children compared to 25% in their hearing counterparts in the UK (NHS, 2005). While suppositions for these complexities are numerous, most relate to alterations in the language access and experiences of children with hearing loss, and how it relates to their capacity to use language to negotiate social relationships and develop a positive sense of well-being (Adams & Crowe, 2020).

Gilroy and Smith-Merry (2019) describe the intersection of racism and disablism as 'racial-ableism', whereby the hegemony of race operates simultaneously with the hegemony of normative functioning. Peoples' experiences of racial-ablism contribute to poor mental health and self-confidence. Adams and Crowe (2020) express concerns related to language and well-being that continue beyond the individual to communities and societies as well. It has been described that many hearing people, up to 87% in one study, held a negative mindset towards people with hearing loss (Hauser, 2019). Similarly, Avery and the First Peoples Disability Network (2018) reported that many Aboriginal people with disability experience racism and disablism on a regular basis, contributing to the experience of a double disadvantage. Such attitudes have wide consequences for people who are deaf, in terms of access to employment and leisure activities, which further compound the problems they experience. For example, looking at Black deaf populations in America only 38.2% were employed, compared to 69.6% of Black-hearing people (Garberoglio et al., 2019). The effect of such attitudes can be labelled as audism, where the notion of superiority is based on the ability to hear. Like other forms of oppression, such as racism or sexism, audism stigmatises people who are deaf, limiting their potential. While there is very little data on deaf Indigenous people worldwide, Aotearoa has statistics that indicate that Deaf Maori experienced the highest mortality rate (2× that of other groups) and had some of the highest rates of mental health when compared with other demographics in the study (Smiler et al., 2023).

Furthermore, comparisons can be drawn with disability discrimination in Indigenous people, leading to 'racial ableism', an experience where both disability and cultural discrimination lead to a greater inequality between disabled Indigenous people and non-Indigenous members of the population. This issue is further exacerbated by the higher rates of disability among Indigenous people (Gilroy & Smith-Merry, 2019). Also, a far greater inequality exists when it comes to social, health, and well-being compared to other population groups (Avery & First Peoples Disability Network, 2018).

Adams and Crowe (2020) examined the implications of disablism and audism, which is magnified by the attitudes of those around them that perpetuate the stigmas associated with such a disability. This includes the deficit model so widely practised and embedded in Western institutions (Fogarty et al., 2018). For example, in NSW, Aboriginal students are up to 36 months behind in learning (AECG NSW & NSW DET, 2004) and are exacerbated when deafness is part of the equation. With the high rates of hearing loss among Indigenous populations, this has serious consequences, with children who experience mild to moderate hearing loss lagging behind their peers (Sung & Carew, 2019). For deaf Indigenous people, a focus on their assets, such as their Indigeneity (including their language), can strengthen their everyday lives living with welfare issues (Gilroy et al., 2018). The experience of navigating both mainstream and Indigenous cultures and the marginalization that follows leads Indigenous deaf people to be considered 'invisible and well-hidden people' (McKay-Cody, 2019).

Deaf gain: combining traditional and Western teaching pedagogies

The concept of 'Deaf Gain' was embedded in many traditional Indigenous communities and the importance of the revitalization of Indigenous sign languages becomes crucial to cultural continuity. In modern contexts, Bauman and Murray, (2010, p. 210) coined the term 'Deaf Gain' to reframe "deafness not as a lack, but as a form of human diversity capable of making vital contributions to the greater good of human society". Deaf Gain is an approach to combat the forces of audism that malign deafness as a deficient characteristic of modern societies. Kusters et al. (2020, p. 297) examined how "deaf people are regarded as bringing particular contributions to diversity" and thus to Deaf Gain.

The opposition to the use of Sign Languages in current educational practises in Western pedagogy is a contrast to the normative practises of traditional Indigenous communities.

Historically, Indigenous languages were oppressed to such an extent that Indigenous Sign Languages were used as a survival mode to avoid the scrutiny of punishments for those who used their own spoken languages. For example, residential schools in North America were governed by White communities where paternalistic and racist policies and legislation ensured that Indigenous students became suppressed from knowing their own languages (Smith, 2012). To combat the linguicism of such residential environments and to overcome the limitations of speaking and listening with an array of different languages because of the influx of different tribes, students used PISL to overcome these communication barriers. While traditionally, PISL was used in the plain regions of West America, it also became a language to transmit cultural values in residential schools. At the Carlisle Indian Industrial School that was established in 1879, hearing Indigenous students 'use Plains Sign Talk to take advantage of their teacher's misunderstanding of their communication systems and push back against the curriculum that sought to strip them of their identities and languages' (Klotz & Cross, 2019). As PISL was used so prominently by tribes of the plains, as it was transmitted from one generation to the next, it became 'nativized' (Davis, 2010, p. 186) in its use so that Indigenous students at the Carlisle school normalised its practise there.

The use of PISL in residential schools by Indigenous students mirrored segregated laws during the period 1890s–1960, where people of colour were also suppressed but with a totally different response. While the majority of deaf White schools tried in vain to prevent the onslaught of oralism, approximately 81.25% of Black Deaf schools continued to use American Sign Languages (Tsegay Moges, 2020), which further enhanced Black American Sign Language as a powerful dialect, while it remained uncontaminated by the segregation laws that preserved and protected their use. The concept of Deaf Gain is, at its core, empowerment for people who are deaf, whether Indigenous or non-Indigenous. Efforts to revitalise Indigenous Sign Languages around the world have served to raise awareness of the purpose, vitality, and profound impact that access to these Languages have on well-being.

The combination of the revitalization of the minority languages movement by both Indigenous and Deaf communities resulted in a greater focus on Indigenous Sign Languages and the declaration by the United Nations of the annual "International Day of Sign Languages" celebrated every year since 2018. Regardless of the lack of opportunities to learn Sign Languages during school for deaf and hard-of-hearing students, Auslan interpreters remain the third most in-demand language interpreters behind Arabic and Mandarin (Chinese) (Deaf Australia, June/2021).

Learning Indigenous spoken languages has multiple benefits that include economic, educational, health, and social welfare (Walsh et al., 2014). Although the advantages of Indigenous sign language use have rarely been investigated in Australia, inferences can be drawn from the advantages of Indigenous spoken language use and sign language use. Oster et al. (2014, p. 3) findings suggest cultural continuity is essential to 'being who we are' and the use of Indigenous sign languages could play an important role in the transition to cultural empowerment with both deaf hood and Indigeneity being allowed to develop (Adams & Crowe, 2020). For deaf Indigenous people, the navigation of dual identity between cultural empowerment and self-determination into two worlds can be difficult. Asserting their identity within the Deaf world, as well as their Cultural world, means a construction of an identity where their ability to express themselves requires self-knowledge and determination to negotiate a place where their identity in both worlds is respected (Kirsten & Mckee, 2007).

The use of sign languages fosters the development of cognitive processes unique to using a visual language, improved capacity for visual-gestural communication, and access to alternative ways of thinking and expressing ideas. The launch of the Illustrated Handbook of Yolŋu Sign Language in 2020 is indicative that sign language plays a prominent role in language documentation for future generations. When used in the context of Indigenous Knowledge, sign language unveils a rich smorgasbord of tools that can empower deaf Indigenous in a way that 'solutions primarily in technology and pedagogy' can't (Roche, 2020, p. 164), and any attempt to force assimilation into hearing culture by means of hearing technology (Horejes & Heuer, 2013) alone will not suffice. The assumptions that hearing devices will conclude with positive language outcomes, and henceforth education, are adequate for 'standalone' approaches for deaf children but are not based on evidence (Hall et al., 2017).

Examples of the benefits of teaching Indigenous Sign Languages in schools as part of the revitalization of Indigenous languages are demonstrated by an Indigenous-managed intensive language learning retreat by the Plains Indian people in the United States. They teach people to communicate in Sign Language and a Cree spoken language to connect with ancestors and reinforce positive well-being (Narine, 2019). Over the last few years, communicating in PISL is now encouraged in the Crows Reservation's Wyolga Elementary School and the University of Oklahoma (Bickford & McKay-Cody, 2018). Oneida Sign Language is another example of how revitalization is being used to create greater self-worth among its language groups in Canada and the United States. Similarly, from 2013, Hawaiian Sign Language was brought to the attention of researchers and linguists at an International Language Conference and can be traced back to 1821, before the colonization of American Sign Language almost a 100 years later (Perlin, 2016). Efforts to promote its use among the Indigenous population involve greater documentation via multimedia avenues.

Deaf epistemologies, or 'Deaf ways' as the deaf way of thinking or viewing the world (Holcomb, 2010; Ladd, 2003), when combined with the Indigenous way of knowing, provide deaf Indigenous people with empowerment, and assist in the development of healthier identity within the deaf and Indigenous contexts (Cue et al., 2019). Current pedagogies in education, with phono-centricism, embedded as its foundation, give justification to the 'illusion of inclusion' (Glickman & Gulati, 2003, p. 8) where deaf students are functionally excluded from participation in mainstream education, through the exclusive use of auditory teaching methods.

A different delivery model, which encompasses a holistic approach as a requirement of cultural continuity (Fogarty et al., 2018) and not "seeing deaf people as having a deficit and lacking full sensory faculties" (Cue et al., 2019, p. 398), is needed. Maher (2021) argues that the challenge to the 'hegemony of phono-centricism' is needed to provide a more inclusive experience in education and this should be a consideration in its application to deaf Indigenous children.

Evidence of social and emotional problems among Australia's Indigenous young people can be found in health, employment, the justice system, and education (Blignault et al., 2016) with the statistics indicating that deaf youth are at greater risk. A greater focus on the linguistic rights of deaf Indigenous people to use their natural sign languages is needed particularly to elevate Social and Emotional Well-being outcomes. Like Black deaf students, the intersection of Deafhood and Indigeneity is needed as it impacts educational success (Awad, 2007). In addition, Article 13 of the Declaration on the Rights of Indigenous People (United Nations, 2007) states that "Indigenous people have the right to revitalise, use, develop and transmit to future generations their histories, languages" (p. 5) – including Sign Languages.

Conclusion

As Indigenous people, we located ourselves at the cultural interface in writing this paper. Gilroy and Emerson (2016) reiterated that Indigenous people, who experience disability, must undergo a dual identity/socialization process to achieve their full potential. The experience of this dual identity is compounded by the hegemony of colonialism and audism that maintain Whiteness and full-hearing as normative. Our resistance to colonial assimilation and White oralism (Tsegay Moges, 2020) can be reinforced by the revitalization of Indigenous Sign Languages, with comparisons to the positive impact other spoken Indigenous languages have had on identity and self-determination. Ensuring that both hearing and deaf Indigenous students are being instructed in their traditional languages both safeguard the future of the languages and shows that language revivals are inextricably connected to traditional cultures (Oen, 2018). For such individuals to flourish, recognition of the intersectionality of audism, linguicism, and systemic racism is crucial to developing a common consciousness, thus empowering themselves in their cultures and language.

Sign Languages have long been seen as an asset to Indigenous communities. Rather than being viewed as a communication deficit, as Western ideologies profess, the clarity and simplicity of Sign Languages, as a natural way of communicating, provide benefits to both hearing and deaf people. Their use in residential schools for both deaf and non-deaf to combat colonization, and to provide a common communication pathway, demonstrates that a continuation of their traditional way of life was essential in the past and remains so for Indigenous people today. Such cultural continuity encompasses Indigenous Sign Languages as a Deaf Gain, a form of human diversity, and an important contribution to our understanding of Indigenous languages and their identities.

The connection with traditional languages as a vital component of well-being has been stated (Marmion et al., 2014) and the act of Indigenous sign languages' revitalization is an essential tool that indicates their value to both deaf and hearing communities (Adams & Crowe, 2020). Teaching Indigenous sign languages to Indigenous deaf students will ensure that Indigenous cultural continuity is maintained the same as it does with non-deaf, as 'language is the most efficient means of transmitting, maintaining, and even reviving culture' and to ward off and avert the spiritual, emotional, and physical impacts that loss of language can have (Whalen et al., 2016).

References

Adams, R., and Crowe, K. (2020). The revitalisation of Indigenous sign languages. In. *Foundation for Endangered Languages Conference, FEL-XXXIII*. Sydney, AU: University of Sydney.

AECG NSW and NSW DET. (2004). The report of the review of Aboriginal education. Yanigurra Muya: Ganggurrinyma Yarri Guurulaw Yirringin. gurray. Freeing the spirit: dreaming an equal future. NSW Department of Education and Training: Sydney.

Australian Bureau of Statistics. (2019, December 11). Test suggests 43% of Aboriginal and Torres Strait Islander people have hearing loss. ABS. https://www.abs.gov.au/articles/test-suggests-43-aboriginal-and-torres-strait-islander-people-have-hearing-loss.

Australian Government Department of Health. (2019). Roadmap for Hearing Health - Hearing Health Sector Committee: Supporting all Australians who are deaf or hard of hearing to live well in the community. Department of Health: Canberra.

Avery, S., and First Peoples Disability Network. (2018). *Culture is inclusion: A narrative of Aboriginal and Torres Strait Islander people with disability*. First Peoples Disability Network: Sydney.

Awad, G. H. (2007). The Role of racial identity, academic self-concept, and self-esteem in the prediction of academic outcomes for African American Students. *Journal of Black Psychology, 33*, 188–207.

Bauman, H-D. L., & Murray, J. J. (2010). Deaf studies in the 21st century: "Deaf-gain" and the future of human diversity. In M. Marshark & P. E. Spencer (Eds.), *The Oxford handbook of deaf studies, language, and education*, Vol. 2, pp. 210–225). Oxford University Press.

Bickford, A., and McKay-Cody, M. (2018). Endangerment and revitalization of sign languages. In. L. Hinton, L. Huss and G. Roche (Eds.), *Routledge handbook of language revitalization* (pp. 255–264). Routledge: New York.

Biddle, N., Yap, M., Gray, M., and Research Australian National University. Centre for Aboriginal Economic Policy. (2013). *Disability*. Centre for Aboriginal Economic Policy Research: Acton.

Blignault, I., Haswell, M., and Pulver, L. J. (2016). The value of partnerships: Lessons from a multi-site evaluation of a national social and emotional wellbeing program for Indigenous youth. *Australian and New Zealand Journal of Public Health, 40*(1), S53–S58.

Butcher, A. (2015). The origins of alternate sign languages in Australia: Could they include hearing impairment? *Indigenous Sign Languages, 16*, 26–39.

Cue, K. R., Pudans-Smith, K. K., Wolsey, J. A., Wright, S. J., and Clark, M. D. (2019). The odyssey of deaf epistemology: A search for meaning-making. *American Annals of the Deaf, 164*(3), 395–422.

Dammeyer, J., and Chapman, M. (2017). Prevalence and characteristics of self-reported physical and mental disorders among adults with hearing loss in Denmark: A national survey. *Social Psychiatry and Psychiatric Epidemiology, 52*(7), 807–813.

Davis, J. (2010). *Hand talk: Sign language among American Indian nations*. Cambridge University Press: Cambridge.

Deaf Australia. (2021). Media Release – Census 2021. Deaf Australia: Sydney.

Fogarty, W., Lovell, M., Langenberg, J., and Heron, M.-J. (2018). Deficit discourse and strengths-based approaches: Changing the narrative of Aboriginal and Torres Strait Islander health and wellbeing. Lowitja Institute: Carlton South, VIC.

Gaby, A., and Woods, L. (2020). Towards linguistic justice for Indigenous people: A response to Charity Hudley, Mallinson and Bucholz. *Language, 94*, 268–280.

Garberoglio, C. L., Stapleton, L. D., Palmer, J. L., Simms, L., Cawthon, S., and Sales, A. (2019). Postsecondary achievement of Black deaf people in the United States. U.S.A Department of Education, Office of Special Education Programs, National Deaf Center on Postsecondary Outcomes: Washington, DC.

Gilroy, J. (2009). The theory of the cultural interface and Indigenous people with disabilities. In. New South Wales. *Balayi: Culture, Law and Colonialism, 10*, 44–59.

Gilroy, J. (2012). The participation of Aboriginal persons with disability in disability services in New South Wales, Australia [unpublished doctoral thesis on the internet]. University of Sydney.

Gilroy, J., Colmar, S., Donelly, M., and Parmenter, T. (2013). Conceptual framework for policy and research development with Indigenous persons with disability. *Journal of Australian Aboriginal Studies, 2*, 42–58.

Gilroy, J., and Donelly, M. (2016). Australian Indigenous people with disability: Ethics and standpoint theory. In. S. Grech and K. Soldatic (Eds.), *Disability in the Global South: The critical handbook* (pp. 545–566). Springer International Publishing: Cham.

Gilroy, J., and Emerson, E. (2016). Australian Indigenous children with low cognitive ability: Family and cultural participation. *Research in Developmental Disabilities, 56*, 117–127.

Gilroy, J., Ragen, J., and Meekosh, H. (2018). Chapter 3. Decolonizing the dynamics of media power and media representation between 1830 and 1930: Australian Indigenous peoples with disability. In. K. Ellis, G. Goggin and B. Haller (Eds.), *Routledge companion to disability and media*. (pp. 35–49). Routledge: New York.

Gilroy, J., and Smith-Merry, J. (2019). Why Aboriginal voices need to be front and centre in the disability Royal Commission. The Conversation: Sydney. Doi: https://theconversation.com/why-aboriginal-voices-need-to-be-front-and-centre-in-the-disability-royal-commission-115056.

Glickman, N., and Gulati, S. (2003). *Mental health care of deaf people: A culturally affirmative approach*. London: Routledge. Green, J., Woods, G., and Foley, B. (2011). Looking at language: Appropriate design for sign language resources in remote Australian Indigenous communities. *Sustainable data from digital research: Humanities perspectives on digital scholarship*. Custom Book Centre.

Gulati, S. (2014). Language deprivation syndrome lecture. In. *American Sign Language Studies program*. Edited by Harvard Medical School Center for Language Studies and the Program for Liberal Medical Education. Rhode Island.

Hall, W. C., Levin, L. L., and Anderson, M. L. (2017). Language deprivation syndrome: A possible neurodevelopmental disorder with sociocultural origins. *Social Psychiatry and Psychiatric Epidemiology*, 52, 761–776.

Hauser, P. (2019). Prevalence of Audism in the United States. In. *Audism Conference. College International de Philosophie*. Centre Alexandre-Koyré: Paris.

Holcomb, T. K. (2010). Deaf epistemology: The deaf way of knowing. *American Annals of the Deaf (Washington, D.C. 1886)*, 154, 471–478.

Horejes, T., and Heuer, C. (2013). Negotiating deaf bodies and corporeal experiences: The cybernetic deaf subject. *Societies (Basel, Switzerland)*, 3, 170–185.

Kendon, A. (2013). *Sign languages of Aboriginal Australia: Cultural, semiotic and communicative perspectives*. Cambridge University Press: Cambridge.

Kendon, A. (2020). *Sign languages of Aboriginal Australia: Cultural, semiotic and communicative perspectives*. Cambridge University Press: Cambridge.

Kirsten, S., and Mckee, R. (2007). Perceptions of Māori deaf identity in New Zealand. *Journal of Deaf Studies and Deaf Education*, 12, 93–111.

Klotz, S., and Cross, H. (2019). The historical work of cultural rhetorics: Constellating Indigenous, deaf, and english-only literacies. *Consellations*, 2.

Kusters, A., Green, M., Moriarty, E., and Snoddon, K. (2020). *Sign language ideologies: Practices and politics*. De Gruyter: Berlin and Boston, MA, 3–22.

Ladd, P. (2003). *Understanding deaf culture in search of deafhood*. Multilingual Matters: Clevedon.

Maher, A. J. (2021). Disrupting phonocentricism for teaching Deaf pupils: Prospective physical education teachers' learning about visual pedagogies and non-verbal communication. *Physical Education and Sport Pedagogy*, 26, 317–329.

Marmion, D., Obata, K., & Troy, J. (2014). *Community, identity, wellbeing: the report of the Second National Indigenous Languages Survey*. Australian Institute of Aboriginal and Torres Strait Islander Studies: Canberra.

McEntyre, E. (2020). But-ton kidn doon-ga: Black women know – re-presenting the lived realities of Australian Aboriginal women with mental and cognitive disabilities in the criminal justice system. Unpublished Doctor of Philosophy thesis. University of New South Wales: Sydney.

McKay-Cody, M. (2019). Memory comes before knowledge-North American Indigenous deaf: Socio-cultural study of rock/picture writing, community, sign languages, and kinship. The University of Oklahoma: Norman.

Meekosha, H., and Soldatic, K. (Eds.) (2016). *The global politics of impairment and disability: Processes and embodiments*. Routledge.

Moores, D. F. (2010). Partners in progress: The 21st international congress on education of the deaf and the repudiation of the 1880 Congress of Milan. *American Annaul Deaf*, 155, 309–310.

Murray, J. J., Hall, W. C., and Snoddon, K. (2019). Education and health of children with hearing loss: The necessity of signed languages. *Bulletin of the World Health Organization, 97*, 711–716.

Nakata, M. (1997). The cultural interface: An exploration of the intersection of western knowledge systems and Torres Strait Islander positions and experiences. Brisbane, AU. James Cook University.

Narine, S. (2019). Plains Indian sign language set for a revival at six-day camp. In. *Windspeaker.com*. Alberta.

NHS. (2005). Mental Health and Deafness: Towards Equity and Access. (pp. 1–35). Doi: https://signhealth.org.uk/wp-content/uploads/2020/10/Towards-Equity-and-Access.pdf

Oen, C. (2018). Fighting to save Indigenous sign languages. Doi: https://intercontinentalcry.org/fighting-to-save-indigenous-sign-languages/.

Oster, R. T., Grier, A., Lightning, R., Mayan, M. J., and Toth, E. L. (2014). Cultural continuity, traditional Indigenous language, and diabetes in Alberta First Nations: A mixed methods study. *International Journal for Equity in Health, 13*, 1–11.

Perlin, R. (2016). The race to save a dying language. *The Guardian*, 10 August.

Roche, G. (2020). Abandoning endangered languages: Ethical loneliness, language oppression, and social justice. *American Anthropologist, 122*, 164–169.

Schofield, T., and Gilroy, J. (2015). Indigeniety and health. In. T. Schofield (Ed.), *A sociological approach to health determinants* (pp. 99–120). Cambridge University Press: Cambridge.

Simms, L., Rusher, M., Andrews, J.-F., and Coryell, J. (2008). Apartheid in deaf education: Examining workforce diversity. *American Annals of the Deaf, 153*(4), 384–395.

Sivak, L., Westhead, S., Richards, E., Atkinson, S., Richards, J., Dare, H., Zuckermann, G., Gee, G., Wright, M., Rosen, A., Walsh, M., Brown, N., and Brown, A. (2019). Language breathes life-barngarla community perspectives on the wellbeing impacts of reclaiming a dormant Australian Aboriginal language. *International Journal of Environmental Research and Public Health, 16*(20), 3918.

Smiler, K. (2014). Ka puāwai ngā kōhungahunga turi. A study of the nature and impacts of early intervention for Māori deaf children and their whānau. Victoria University of Wellington.

Smiler, K., Bowden, N., Sheree, G., and Kokaua, J. (2023). Kei Aaku Ringa Te Mana Motouhake O Ngaati Turi. An independent report commissioned for the Taangata Turi Waitangi Tribunal claim.

Smith, L. (2012). *Decolonizing methodologies: Research and Indigenous peoples*. Zed Books: London.

Soldatic, K. (2015). Postcolonial reproductions: Disability, Indigeneity and the formation of the white masculine settler state of Australia. *Social Identities, 21*, 53–68.

Stauffer, J. (2015). *Ethical loneliness: The injustice of not being heard*. Columbia University Press: New York.

Sung, V., and Carew, P. (2019). Hearing loss still a challenge for kids. In. *Persuit*. The University of Melbourne: Melbourne, VIC.

Tsegay Moges, R. (2020). From White Deaf people's adversity to Black Deaf gain: A proposal for a new lens of Black Deaf educational history. *JCSCORE, 6*, 68–99.

Umiker-Sebeok, D., and Sebeok, T. A. (1978). *Aboriginal sign languages of the Americas and Australia: Volume 1; North America Classic Comparative Perspectives*. Springer: Boston, MA.

United Nations. (2007). Declaration on the rights of indigenous peoples. United Nations: Geneva.

Walsh, M., Marmion, D., and Troy, J. (2014). Re-awakening Australian languages: Economic, educational, health and social benefits to the community. In P. Heinrich and N. Ostler (Eds.), *EL XVIII Okinawa: Indigenous Languages: Their Value to the Community*. Foundation for Endangered Languages: UK.

Whalen, D., Moss, M., and Baldwin, D. (2016). Healing through language: Positive physical health effects of indigenous language use. *F1000research, 1*.

15 Learning from traditional knowledge

Basotho Indigenous epistemology of disability

Maximus Monaheng Sefotho

Introduction

The Basotho nation emerged as the Sotho people, who have developed a unique culture over time. Basotho are found in Lesotho, with some in South Africa, Zambia and Zimbabwe. The Basotho are known to embrace peace and promote good health. This is deeply embedded in their culture through the daily practice of greeting each other and showing a "high degree of social concern" (Matŝela, 1979, p. 102). The Basotho greet each other by asking one another about their state of health, wishing to ascertain that each person is in good health. Thus, Basotho are known to have a well-developed ethics of care that is non-discriminatory. Traditionally, chiefs were responsible for people in their communities through Indigenous ways of governance. As a communal people, Basotho chiefs had social responsibilities towards all members of the community without discrimination. Yet, little is known about the Basotho philosophy on disability; however, people with disabilities were also members of communities. While Lesotho became negatively influenced on how to perceive people with disabilities, traces of cultural practice, which should have been disseminated through Indigenous education exist.

Disability, as human experience, is variably viewed from diverse Indigenous cultural contexts. Generally, people with disabilities suffer discrimination and marginalization (Johnstone et al., 2022). However, a closer inspection of Indigenous epistemologies reveals that societies disregard their Indigenous knowledge systems and develop anti-disabled campaigns. People with disabilities were traditionally the responsibility of chiefs, who looked after them, so the chief would be the first to know when they were sick ('Mamothibeli Sehlabo, 2023/10/29 – individual interview). There were few people with disabilities among Basotho, but they were there ('Mamothibeli Sehlabo, 2023/10/29 – individual interview). A nugget of wisdom from a collection of Sesotho proverbs is *Sehole ho 'Ma-sona, se setle* (a child with a disability is beautiful in its mother's eyes; Sekese, 2011). The mother is constantly hopeful that the child will eventually be like other children ('Mamothibeli Sehlabo, 2023/10/29 – individual interview). Motherly love is more profound towards such a child. The word "sehole" seems to have lost its affirming meaning as interpreted from the vantage point of current discourses of disability. Pitso (1997) provides synonyms of sehole as "helehele; lathalatha; leoatla; nkahlama; obuobu; otseotse; phathakalle; phathaphatha; phauphau; phooaphooa; selehe; sephoqo; sethoto; setlaopa; setlatla; thelethele; tŝaetŝae; tŝethetŝethe" (p. 248). All these have very derogatory meanings and should not be used to describe any human being. Nowadays, a more acceptable term seems to be "Sekooa", meaning a person with a disability or "bokooa", meaning disability. However, Pitso (1997) provides its synonyms as "sehole, sekulane [a sickly

DOI: 10.4324/9781032656519-19

person] or seqhoala [an injured person]" (p. 250). According to 'Mamothibeli Sehlabo, 2023/11/03 – individual interview, sekooa is a person who has been ill for a long time and decapacitated by an unknown disease. The disease has debilitated the body, so the person has no bodily strength and therefore cannot perform any work. This poses a serious lexicographic and semantic gap for the Sesotho language in relation to disability. More debate and consultation would benefit the disability lexicon in Sesotho (Figure 15.1).

However, considered from the illocutionary (the intention of the speaker) use (Caponetto, 2021), "Sehole" in Sesotho is positively appraised for accepting a person as being no different from any other. Illocutionary acts are communicative actions (Hornsby, 2002), which are "the intention-based nature of illocutionary acts" (Sbisà, 2009, p. 33). They demonstrate the intention of the speech acts. The Sesotho proverb: *Sehole ho 'Ma-sona, se setle* (a child with a disability is beautiful in its mother's eyes) promotes the illocutionary (the intention of the speaker) use of a mother who accepts her child with a disability as like any other human being. This same attitude was evident in how traditionally the chiefs were accepting of people with disabilities and devised ways of how to support them. Chiefs used Indigenous ways of accumulating resources to support people with disabilities under their care. *Tŝimo-ea-lira* was a field designated as a source of food production to feed people under the chief's care (Manyeli et al., 2023). The chief would mobilize work parties traditionally known as *matsema* (plural) and *letsema* (singular) to produce food from *Tŝimo-ea-lira*. Members of the community volunteered their labour to till the land, sow and harvest the crops (Lebeloane & Quan-Baffour, 2008). This spirit of care and benevolence permeated the Sesotho culture and spread even into healthcare. The underlying philosophy of Botho/Ubuntu drives these inclinations to care for one another. Ebersöhn (2012) explains this practice of pooling together resources to care for

Figure 15.1 Mamothibeli Sehlabo – Custodian of the Sesotho culture.

Source: Photographer: Maximus Monaheng Sefotho

one another as "flocking" (p. 30). A Botho/Ubuntu philosophical principle propelling flocking emerges from a Sesotho proverb: *Bana ba monna ba arolelana hlooho ea tsie* (The children of the same homestead/community share the head of a locust). The significance of this proverb is that people would share the little they have as long as each one has something to benefit from. During times of great hunger and famine, people ate even such things as locusts to survive. Another proverb supporting this is *Sejo-senyane ha se fete molomo (Half a loaf is better than no bread)*.

The objective of this chapter is to reflect on how learning from the traditional knowledge of the Basotho Indigenous epistemology of disability can contribute to the global understanding of disability.

African Indigenous communities

African Indigenous communities can provide a lens for understanding disability from their contexts. Diverse as she is, Africa is paradoxically one. It is a continent made of many nations, about 54 of them, with diverse cultures and languages. In their diversity, African nations are known for their communality epitomized by botho/ubuntu. The philosophy of botho/ubuntu propels a way of life based on interdependence. The African proverb, "Motho ke motho ka batho ba bang", means *a person is a person through other persons* underpins a sense of communality within African communities (Setlhodi, 2019, p. 1). Botho has been a way of life among African people, and a unifying factor that fortifies a sense of togetherness (Figure 15.2).

Figure 15.2 Thaba-Bosiu cultural village in Lesotho.

Source: Photographer: Maximus Monaheng Sefotho

The Indigenous communities of Africa could be understood through the concept of indigeneity. "'Indigeneity' has come to also presuppose a sphere of commonality among those who form a world collective of 'Indigenous peoples' in contrast to their various others" (Merlan, 2009, p. 303). The term Indigenous is equated with struggling for identity, culture and recognition as well as a lack of resources for survival (Guenther et al., 2006). "'Indigeneity' is an image self-constructed by the subordinate under restrictions set by the superordinate discourse" (Guenther et al., 2006, p. 24). Indigeneity, therefore, challenged whether "Learning from traditional knowledge through the Basotho Indigenous epistemology of disability" is indeed possible. I argue that this is possible once the superordinate discourse recognizes and validates knowledge systems from the subordinate discourses such as the understanding of disability from the Basotho cultural perspectives. The importance of indigeneity is in giving a voice to the voiceless and being a political instrument that they can use to be heard and their resources being protected. Indigeneity is perceived as a resource that allows for recognition of the Indigenous people (Ioris, 2023).

Traditional ecological knowledge

Traditional ecological Knowledge emerges from the "Indigenous groups['] offer [of] alternative knowledge and perspectives based on their own locally developed practices of resource use" (Berkes et al., 2000, p. 1251). "…Traditional Ecological Knowledge [is] a cumulative body of knowledge, practice and belief, evolving by adaptive processes and handed down through generations by cultural transmission, about the relationship of living beings (including humans) with one another and with their environment" (Berkes et al., 2000, p. 1252). In this chapter, traditional ecological knowledge is used as a lens to interpret and understand an evolving body of knowledge, practice and belief as they pertain to disability from the Basotho perspective.

The Sesotho lexicology of disability suffers scarcity of words, and precision in describing disability, as well as the variety and diversity aligned to a plethora of disabilities in existence. Very little disability-related words are available in Sesotho. The synonyms of Sehole (a person with a disability) provided by Pitso (1997) include a reverse definition of Sehole as Sekooa, a newer definition of a person with a disability, really not different from that of Sekooa. The Semasiological meanings of the two words do not adequately differentiate them. Semasiology (from Greek: σημασία, semasia, "signification") is a discipline of linguistics concerned with the question "What does the word Sehole or Sekooa mean?" There seems to be an impasse on the side of the disability community in Lesotho to provide direction towards clear descriptions of different disabilities known to humanity. Extensive research is required in this regard to allow harvesting lexically appropriate descriptions of disability in Sesotho. While traditional ecological knowledge about disability is there, communication and dissemination of knowledge about it are close to non-existent.

For example, the current surge of neuroscience cannot be expressed through the Sesotho language as there are no equivalent words. Firstly, at a more general level, there are no words to explain what neurons and neurology denote in Sesotho. Cregenzán-Royo et al. (2022) observed a similar phenomenon in Cameroon, where parents and caregivers could not explain Fragile X syndrome as no explanatory models existed. Secondly, words such as neurodiversity have no parallel words in Sesotho to explain them. Thirdly, to explain differences to an ordinary Mosotho based on certain genetic or chromosomal conditions, such as Fragile X syndrome, would be very complex (Jin & Chen, 2015).

Autism spectrum disorder (ASD) also presents serious linguistic challenges, disadvantaging most marginalized communities who would traditionally care for anyone within the spectrum. It would be difficult to explain to ordinary Basotho that a person with autism doesn't necessarily have an intellectual disability.

This is where the challenge of the word sehole becomes evident as it is too generic. From the Sesotho cultural perspective, a person who seems to have any difference in their mental demeaner falls into two categories: It is either such a person is considered a sehole or Lehlanya, meaning a mad person. To bring into the mix, issues of neurodiversity would fall flat as language would not be available to explain it. At the level of behaviour, differing cultural interpretations may lead to further confusion with parents not understanding and accepting why their child behaves differently from other children (Freeth et al., 2014).

Epistemologies of disability

Challenging the disproportionality of epistemologies of disability is critical for establishing more diverse understandings and inclusive perspectives on disability. Epistemologies of disability are as diverse as cultures within which such philosophies of knowledge are found. "Epistemologization" of disability provides frameworks similar to "race, class and gender" (Nielsen, 2008, n.p.) for interpretation of the meanings of disability and how people with disabilities are treated (Hamraie, 2015, p. 115). Henri-Jacques Stiker's History of Disability (Stiker, 2019) "explores the notion of disability as difference since antiquity" (Hamraie, 2015, p. 117). Stiker (1999) sparked the debate on disability with what he referred to as avoidance indicating that:

> It has to be explained at the outset that in French, we are obliged to use the word handicap to cover what is understood by the term disability in current Anglo-Saxon usage. The word handicap has been adopted and adapted in French as the least bad generic term. Protest as one might against this, a language is nevertheless made by language users, the people who speak it. It is not worth agonising over it further.
>
> (p. 352)

However, it is important to emphasize that difference is fundamental to facilitating understanding and accepting epistemologies of disability that may be different from our own. Difference is neither bad nor good, it is just difference and must be accepted as such. Disability epistemologies, therefore, ought not to "...equate dis-ability with in-ability" (Kudlick, 2003, p. 769), but "...to integrate disability naturally, even positively into its understanding of humanity without trying to control or cure it" (Kudlick, 2003, p.770). Epistemologies of disability around the world must facilitate an understanding of disability, be inclusive rather than exclusive and treat knowledge construction about disability in equitable ways. In order to achieve this, Nijs and Heylighen (2015, p. 146) observe that Rod Michalko, a blind sociologist "advocates for recognizing the situated knowledges emerging from disability experience". In this manner, epistemologies of disability should be legitimate and developed from legitimate experiences and not vicariously. Therefore, the Basotho Indigenous epistemology of disability is used as one such experience that represents how Basotho epistemologize disability. From the botho perspective, each person is considered human, Sebopuoa as Molimo, meaning a creature of the creator, who must be afforded human dignity and respect without discrimination.

Basotho Indigenous epistemology of disability

Generally, epistemology concerns itself with the nature, scope and sources of knowledge. If Lesotho's inclusive education policy precedes universal declarations such as Education for All (UNESCO, 1990) and the Salamanca Statement on Special Needs Education (Johnstone & Chapman, 2009, p. 133; UNESCO, 1996), what informed the nature, scope and sources of knowledge about disability? The chapter embraces epistemology as the philosophy of knowledge, or the study of knowledge itself, what it is and how it is possible. An example of the Basotho Indigenous epistemology of disability is captured by Johnstone and Chapman (2009, p. 133) in the following quote:

> Inclusive education, as understood in Lesotho, is a practice whereby students with physical, sensory, or intellectual impairments that affect learning (i.e. students with disabilities) are educated in regular schools. Lesotho's 1989 policy was somewhat radical, preceding universal declarations such as Education for All (UNESCO, 1990) and the Salamanca Statement on Special Needs Education (UNESCO, 1996). Lesotho's neighbour, the Republic of South Africa, adopted an inclusive education policy only after the demise of apartheid.

Leshota (2011), validates the above by poignantly pointing out that:

> From the reading of Mariga and Phachaka (1993, p. 30), it is evident that inclusion is not new, and that it existed in some form in the past, represented as a voice of previous knowledge that tends to lie on the margins of inclusive discourse. Within this voice of previous knowledge are learners, parents and teachers who appear to be rich sources of Indigenous knowledge, belief and practice. Their experiences are nominally acknowledged, yet theirs could not be inclusive discourse because power and knowledge did not constitute it, and it was not implemented, controlled or built by those who knew and had power. This is, I argue, a voice that has been denied an opportunity to be heard.
>
> (p. 120)

Interwoven into contemporary Lesotho culture of care and epistemology of disability emerges "King Moshoeshoe II's charitable social organization Hlokomela Bana (Care for People)" (Johnstone & Chapman, 2009, p. 133). The correct translation of Hlokomela Bana should be "Care for Children", the mistranslation is welcome as it encompasses everyone and is in reference to people with disabilities. Basotho practiced an "Indigenous tradition of care and protection" (Matŝela, 1979, p. 141). Families cared for one another, communities cared for one another and national general health was important under the practice of *botho* (Theron et al., 2013). The Basotho Indigenous epistemology of disability is premised on the philosophical principle of *botho*. Botho is a metaphysical term that denotes a "moral humanbeinghood" (Gaie, 2007, p. 30). Botho is morality itself (Gaie, 2007). The inferences from botho as morality are diverse, but the most fundamental is the consideration of botho as "the good personality" (Gaie, 2007, p. 32). Botho, therefore, is a founding principle of how Basotho practice botho towards everybody, including people with disabilities. Premised in botho, the Basotho Indigenous epistemology of disability is perceived "...as an ethic that prescribes living in a harmonious way with others, usually forbids doing something that one foresees will cause someone severe anxiety, fear and other negative emotions and feelings" (Metz, 2010, p. 87). This includes people with disabilities. While Mariga and Phachaka (1993) correctly note that disability has been arbitrarily considered a curse, punishment and bringing shame to families where children with disabilities are born, many positive examples abound in the Sesotho culture. Khatleli et al. (1995, p. 6) note that people with disabilities in Lesotho are generally not discriminated against but are considered full members of their families.

Basotho ethic of care

African Values/Ethics as Setho/Isintu (Dube, 2009) are foundations of the Basotho ethic of care. Basotho is generally known as a caring nation. This is evident from their hospitality to others even if they are unknown to them. Traditionally, travelling throughout Lesotho, there was no need for one to worry about where they would find a place to sleep a night or two to get to their destinations. People used to just arrive unannounced, and they would find a family to stay the night with. Systematic caring through traditional practices such as Letsema (communal work teams) is intricately interwoven into the fibre of the Basotho way of life. Letsema is an intentional communal practice of participating in work altruistically to benefit others and not self (Mokolatsie, 2019) (Figure 15.3).

Letseka and Letseka (2021) advise that "Botho/Ubuntu presupposes humaneness… and is taken to encapsulate moral norms and virtues such as kindness, generosity,

Figure 15.3 Prof. Lauren Lindstrom, given a Basotho blanket as a sign of care, a Basotho hat as protection.

Source: Photographer: Maximus Monaheng Sefotho

compassion, benevolence, courtesy and respect and concern for others" (p. 141). These principles are found to articulate the Basotho ethic of care in that they all address health and well-being. The ethic of care also forms part of the cultural Basotho education through the initiation process that inculcates in the young men a sense of the obligation of care to "protect the health, safety and well-being of citizens" (Rathebe, 2018, p. 1). Basotho ethic of care aligns with the Sustainable Development Goals (SDGs), Goal 3: Good Health and Well-Being. A nation that well cared for is likely to enjoy good physical and mental health.

Conclusion

The Basotho way of life is indicative of acceptance of people with disabilities. Thus, I have demonstrated the importance of learning from the Indigenous knowledge systems, in particular from the Basotho epistemology of disability. The central concept of *botho* provides a seedbed for the ethics of care, especially for people with disabilities. Although the Sesotho language is not sufficiently rich enough to have terminology that matches that of the English language, the Sesotho way of life supports people with disabilities despite linguistic discrepancies. However, this gap is fertile ground for research. Therefore, the traditional knowledge of Basotho Indigenous epistemology of disability can indeed contribute to the global understanding of disability as knowledge constructed from non-dominant discourses.

References

Berkes, F., Colding, J. and Folke, C. (2000). Rediscovery of traditional ecological knowledge as adaptive management. *Ecological Applications, 10*(5), 1251–1262.

Caponetto, L. A. (2021). Comprehensive definition of illocutionary silencing. *Topoi, 40*, 191–202. https://doi.org/10.1007/s11245-020-09705-2.

Cregenzán-Royo, O., Brun-Gasca, C. and Fornieles-Deu, A. (2022). Behavior problems and social competence in Fragile X Syndrome: A systematic review. *Genes, 13*(2), 280.

Dube, M. (2009). "I am because we are': giving primacy to African indigenous values in HIV&AIDS prevention". In *African ethics: an anthology of comparative and applied ethics*. Edited by: Murove, M. F. 188 – 217. Pietermaritzburg, South Africa: University of KwaZulu-Natal Press.

Ebersöhn, L. (2012). Adding 'flock' to 'fight and flight': A honeycomb of resilience where supply of relationships meets demand for support. *Journal of Psychology in Africa, 22*(1), 29–42.

Freeth, M., Milne, E., Sheppard, E., and Ramachandran, R. (2014). "Autism across cultures: Perspectives from non-western cultures and implications for research," in F. R. Volkmar, S. Rogers, R. Paul, and K. Pelphrey (Eds.). *Handbook of Autism and Pervasive Developmental Disorders*, (Hoboken, NJ: Wiley), 997–1013.

Gaie, J. B. R. (2007). The Setswana Concept of Botho: Unpacking the Metaphysical and Moral Aspects. In J. B. R. Gaie & S. K. MMolai (Eds.), *The Concept of Botho and HIV/AIDS in Botswana* (pp. 29–44). Zapf Chancery Publishers Africa Ltd. https://doi.org/10.2307/j.ctvgc61hd.5

Guenther, M., Kenrick, J., Kuper, A., Plaice, E., Thuen, T., Wolfe, P., … and Barnard, A. (2006). The concept of indigeneity. *Social Anthropology-Cambridge, 14*(1), 17.

Hamraie, A. (2015). Historical epistemology as disability studies methodology: From the models framework to Foucault's archaeology of cure. *Foucault Studies, 19*, 108–134.

Hornsby, J. (2002). Illocution and its significance. In S. L. Tsohatzidis (ed.), *Foundations of speech act theory* (pp. 195–215). Routledge. https://doi.org/10.1080/14330237.2012.10874518.

Ioris, A. A. (2023). Indigeneity and Indigenous politics: Ground-breaking resources. *Revista de Estudios Sociales, 85*, 3–21.

Jin, X. and Chen, L. (2015). Fragile X syndrome as a rare disease in China - Therapeutic challenges and opportunities. *Intractable & Rare Diseases Research*, 4(1), 39–48.

Johnstone, C. J. and Chapman, D. W. (2009). Contributions and constraints to the implementation of inclusive education in Lesotho. *International Journal of Disability, Development and Education*, 56(2), 131–148.

Johnstone, C. J., Sefuthi, N. and Hayes, A. (2022). The democratization of inclusive education: Political settlement and the role of disabled persons organizations. *Comparative Education Review*, 66(4), 688–708.

Khatleli, P., Mariga, L., Phachaka, L. and Stubbs, S. (1995). Schools for all: National planning in Lesotho. In O'Toole, B., & McConkey, R. (Eds.). *Innovations in developing countries for people with disabilities* (vol. 10, pp. 135–160).

Kudlick, C. J. (2003). Disability history: Why we need another "other." *The American Historical Review*, 108(3), 763–793.

Lebeloane, L. D. M., & Quan-Baffour, K. P. (2008). Letsema: A way of inculcating and preserving African Indigenous Knowledge in the youth through formal education in the 21st century. *Journal of Educational Studies*, 7(2), 43–49.

Leshota, P. L. (2011). *A deconstruction of disability discourse amongst Christians in Lesotho.* (Doctoral dissertation, University of South Africa).

Letseka, M., & Letseka, M. M. (2021). Basotho community elders' views on botho/ubuntu as a moral concept. *Indilinga African Journal of Indigenous Knowledge Systems*, 20(2), 141–153.

Manyeli, T. F., Thabane, S. and Mahao, P. M. (2023). 10 community solidarity and intergenerational relationships in the care of older people in Africa. In Twikirize, J. M., Tusasiirwe, S., & Mugumbate, R. (Eds.). *Ubuntu philosophy and decolonising social work fields of practice in Africa* (pp. 137–149). Routledge.

Mariga, L. and Phachaka, L. (1993). Integrating children with special needs into regular primary schools in Lesotho. Report of a Feasibility Study, Ministry of Education, Maseru, Lesotho.

Matŝela, Z. A. (1979). The Indigenous education of the Basotho and its implications for educational development in Lesotho. Doctoral Dissertations 1896- February 2014. 2193. https://doi.org/10.7275/8n2y-cc36. https://scholarworks.umass.edu/dissertations_1/2193

Merlan, F. (2009). Indigeneity: Global and local. *Current Anthropology, 50*(3), 303–333.

Metz, T. (2010). Human dignity, capital punishment, and an African moral theory: Toward a new philosophy of human rights. *Journal of Human Rights*, 9(1), 81–99.

Mokolatsie, C. N. (2019). Revisiting virtue ethics and spirituality of Botho: A study of an Indigenous ethic of character formation in the moral thought and practice of Basotho (Doctoral dissertation).

Nielsen, K. E. (2008). Historical thinking and disability history. *Disability Studies Quarterly, 28*(3), n.p.

Nijs, G. and Heylighen, A. (2015). Turning disability experience into expertise in assessing building accessibility: A contribution to articulating disability epistemology. *Alter, 9*(2), 144–156.

Pitso, T. T. (1997*). Khetsi ea Sesotho: pokello ea mantsoe a lumellanang le a hananang'moho le maele le mabitso a batho.* Cape Town: CTP Printers.

Rathebe, P. C. (2018). The role of environmental health in the Basotho male initiation schools: Neglected or restricted? *BMC Public Health*, 18(1), 1–8.

Sbisà, M. (2009). Uptake and conventionality in illocution. *Lodz Papers in Pragmatics*, 5(1), 33–52.

Sekese, A. (2011). *Mekhoa le maele a Ba-Sotho.* Sesuto book depot.

Setlhodi, I. I. (2019). Ubuntu leadership: An African panacea for improving school performance. *Africa Education Review*, 16(2), 126–142.

Stiker, H. J. (1999). Using historical anthropology to think disability. In Holzer, B, Vreede, A and Weigt, G. (Eds.). Disability in different cultures: Reflections on local concepts. 352 – 380. Bielefeld, Germany: Transcript Verlag. Stiker, H. J. (2019). *A history of disability*. University of Michigan Press.

Theron, L. C., Theron, A. M. C. and Malindi, M. J. (2013). Toward an African definition of re-
silience: A rural South African community's view of resilient Basotho Youth. *Journal of Black
Psychology*, 39(1), 63–87.
UNESCO. (1990). *World Declaration on Education for All*. Paris: UNESCO.
UNESCO. (1996). *Learning: The treasure within*. Paris: UNESCO. Report of the Delors Commis-
sion on Education for the 21st century.

16 Half man of Spring Bayou

Understanding and living with mild cerebral palsy through traditional Indigenous knowledge

Jean-Luc Pierite

Introduction

To overcome the impacts of intergenerational colonization, Indigenous peoples center revitalization of language and culture. Internationally, fostering collaboration between Indigenous community members and non-Indigenous health workers impacts a decline in the prevalence of cerebral palsy in births of Indigenous children. To promote collaboration from the front-line community perspective, Indigenous community members can take a multidisciplinary approach to access literacies and technologies in digital design and fabrication, life sciences, and language documentation. International networks focused on collaboration provide infrastructure for knowledge sharing and codesign which have the broader impact of confronting challenges related to colonization. In the United States of America Gulf South context, traditional stories can provide alternative empathetic perspectives to communicate concepts around healthcare and diverse abilities in community members. For the Tunica-Biloxi Tribe of Louisiana in particular, the traditional story of Tanap, a medicine keeper, provides social and personal context of overcoming challenges and affecting change within local and global ecosystems.

The chapter is based upon work within the North American Indian Center of Boston (NAICOB), which is based in Jamaica Plain, Massachusetts, United States of America. NAICOB is an over 50-year-old organization that started as the Boston Indian Council. NAICOB is the oldest urban Indian center in Massachusetts. Urban Indian communities resulted from the adoption of termination policies in the 1950s by the United States Congress. The forced urban relocation and assimilation necessitated community organizing to provide cultural and social services. The Boston Indian Council originally was based in a funeral home in Dorchester, Massachusetts. After a fire that left only the pow-wow drum, the community decided to continue its work in a new location. In 1991, the Boston Indian Council reorganized as NAICOB and has remained in its current location of 105 South Huntington Avenue, Jamaica Plain, Massachusetts for over 40 years. In 1976, the organization was designated as a liaison for Commonwealth of Massachusetts residents who are members of tribes outside of the current borders and who maintain historical government-to-government relationships with the state.

Indigenous presence in Massachusetts and the broader New England region extends to time immemorial. One of the earliest treaty relationships between settler colonists and Indigenous peoples is the 1621 "Treaty with (the) Massasoit." Still, this agreement was reached after decades of slave trade impacting Indigenous peoples in the Northeast. An earlier attempt at termination within Massachusetts was implemented through "The Enfranchisement Act of 1869." Despite this, two federally recognized tribes – Mashpee

DOI: 10.4324/9781032656519-20

Wampanoag Tribe and Wampanoag Tribe of Gay Head (Aquinnah) – remain extant. Additionally, the Nipmuc Nation continues through their lineal descendants and two tribal bands. The Greater Boston area is within the traditional Indigenous territory of the Massachusetts Nation who continue in part through their lineal descendants, Massachusetts Tribe at Ponkapoag. At least 30 other tribes and first nations outside of the state borders hold historical relationships and ancestral ties to the land. So, the work of NAICOB requires constant diplomatic navigation of all of these relationships as well as all identifying Indigenous peoples who reside within the Commonwealth of Massachusetts.

In the Gulf South between the waters of Lake Pontchartrain and the Mississippi River, there is a community known as New Orleans East. The main highway connecting the suburb to New Orleans itself is known as Chef Menteur Highway. As my memory fades into the story, there are at least two accounts of why this road is known by that name. Both center around the Choctaw distrust of dishonest people. It could either be named for Louis Billouart de Kerlérec, a former governor of Louisiana, or of an unnamed Choctaw chief who spent an exile with his family in the bayous near the Rigolets. In either case, land and memory are embedded within the languages and names are often taken for granted. It was in this community at Methodist Hospital that Jean-Luc Pierite was born. Jean-Luc's mother Donna M. Madere Pierite exclaimed the first words to be heard outside of the womb, "He's Indian." Jean-Luc was born into the Tunica-Biloxi Tribe of Louisiana. Although Jean-Luc was born beyond his expected due date, he also began life with a condition of mild cerebral palsy.

Living with mild cerebral palsy, Jean-Luc had his left ankle broken at an early age. As he grew, books dominated leisure activities in lieu of the outdoors. Jean-Luc's father Michael R. Pierite was an avid reader who kept a bookcase full of science fiction, fantasy, and horror. One book that Jean-Luc became attached to was a collection of Lewis Carroll's work with a red dust jacket trimmed with gold lettering and a picture of Alice's white rabbit. Reading and stories were such a part of Jean-Luc's life that his mother recalls him carrying the red book with him. One day, at a car dealership, Donna noticed that her son was focused on the pages. When she asked what he was doing, he responded that he was reading. Testing his abilities, she asked him to read to her. It was this early sign and others that resulted in testing for special education for gifted and talented programming in New Orleans Public Schools. Donna herself was a French and Spanish teacher who also taught English as a Second Language to the Vietnamese migrant community. Even as a teacher, it was through the testing that Donna became aware of the resources available to Jean-Luc through adapted physical education and physical therapy. Further, Donna would confront racism and discrimination even from her peers in public schools who denied that her family was indeed Native.

Beyond the resources in school, Jean-Luc had a second form of education by spending time at his grandparents's houses, both around the corner in New Orleans East and in the neighboring City of Kenner. Donna's parents were Stanley A. Madere, a World War II veteran, and Marria L. Normand Madere, a physician's assistant who worked in a physical therapy clinic. Michael's parents were Joseph A. Pierite, Jr., the first tribal chairman of the Tunica-Biloxi Tribe of Louisiana, and Fannie L. Ben Pierite, the first Choctaw woman to graduate from a four-year college in Mississippi and the first Choctaw woman to teach in a White school in the same state. It was through grandparents' teachings in language, culture, and history that Jean-Luc began to understand his family's position within the local landscape.

Grounded in history and culture, Jean-Luc continued to dream about impossible creatures and fantastical adventures. Sometimes, these would reveal themselves. At Audubon Zoo, a newly installed Louisiana swamplands exhibit featured a sculpture that would frighten and fascinate Jean-Luc. This figure had the head of an owl and the body of a frog. It stood erect with the aid of a cane which was draped with Spanish moss and empty cans. The sculpture represented the Honey Island Swamp Monster. Just along the Northshore of Lake Pontchartrain, the stories and representation of this creature spoke to a world of traditional Indigenous knowledge in conflict with the refuse and waste of modern life. It would not be the only guardian of local ecosystems that Jean-Luc would spend time dreaming and imagining stories.

One day, Joseph Pierite drove Jean-Luc to visit his cousins who lived in one of eight Choctaw communities that would make up the tribal lands of the Mississippi Band of Choctaw Indians. Joseph drove a Ram pickup with a realistic hood ornament. Joseph would joke with Jean-Luc as they passed cars along the I-55 interstate highway. Each car was swallowed by the Ram and left behind on their ride from the waters of Louisiana to the rolling hills of east central Mississippi. There was one moment when the joking stopped, and the truck's radio was turned down for Joseph to have the full attention of Jean-Luc.

> I'm going to tell you a story. I will only tell you once. You don't ask me any questions about it. There is this man in the back of our (Tunica-Biloxi) land in Spring Bayou. He is half a man. He has one arm, one leg, and half a face. He is all covered in hair and lives up in the trees. What happens is that if you have a little boy in the house, that half man will come down and take him away. I heard him before because I could hear him scratching on the screen windows. What happens next is that the half man teaches the boy how to wrestle. If the boy can throw that half man down on the ground, then he will teach the boy about all the plants. That boy will become the best doctor in the world.

Jean-Luc's cousin Diana Michelle Ben lived in Standing Pine with her grandmother Helen Ben Young. Michelle would hear of similar yet distinct stories of children being put to a test by little people who live deep in the pine woods. More than oral tradition passed down, Michelle had her own experiences. One night when Jean-Luc's grandmother Fannie was visiting her sister Helen, Michelle received a message to wake up and go outside. When she exited her home, she saw children that glowed in a white light. The children asked for Michelle to go and play with them. When Michelle got too near to the pine woods, she ran back to the house which she found to be completely locked. Fannie woke up to let Michelle in, but the same sequence happened for a second time that night. Despite not going to the pine woods, Michelle became a nurse.

Back in New Orleans, Jean-Luc navigated school life facing teasing about his gait and questions about his ethnicity. Often, Jean-Luc dreamed about living on tribal lands with his cousins and their friends. These tensions resulted in a need to leave New Orleans to pursue ambitions. This was not fully realized until after Jean-Luc completed a Bachelor of the Arts in Humanities at Dillard University with a co-major in Mass Communication and Japanese. Jean-Luc's passion was in helping his family revitalize and preserve the language and culture of their communities. This was the reason for delving into communication technologies and foreign languages. Following Dillard University, Jean-Luc returned to school at Full Sail University in Orlando, Florida where he completed an Associate of Science in Video Game Design at Full Sail University. After Jean-Luc completed that program, Hurricane Katrina wiped much of the landscape of New Orleans. In those moments and days that captured national attention, Jean-Luc confronted a situation in which much of his former life was erased by the storm and broken levees. In the following years, Jean-Luc would go from the San Francisco Bay Area to Washington, D.C., in pursuit of jobs and contract work until he returned home to his family in 2008.

Jean-Luc's family relocated just outside of Tunica-Biloxi tribal lands in Marksville, Louisiana. The Tribe is careful not to refer to these lands as a reservation as they are the remnants of an original Spanish land grant to an ancestor of Jean-Luc's who was the Biloxi chief Bosra. While the tribe had held onto this land since the original land grant, it came at the expense of life and the impacts of racism and discrimination. The Louisiana Purchase was written to stipulate that the United States would maintain nation-to-nation relationships with Indigenous peoples as did France and Spain. In reality, the pursuit of federal recognition for Jean-Luc's tribe was over 180 years. Through this time, the Tribe had a diaspora of satellite communities in Chicago, Illinois, and Houston, Texas, resulting from families looking for employment and more equitable living conditions. The annual tradition of the Fête du Blè or Green Corn Ceremony would anchor the Tribe and rekindle otherwise distant kinship. It was at these ceremonies that old family stories and traditional tales would be shared by those who held onto the knowledge.

One day when Jean-Luc was working for his tribe at the Paragon Casino Resort, Jean-Luc noticed several of his cousins gossiping and laughing about something called Pachafa. Recognizing the name as something either Choctaw or Mobilian (a universal trade language shared in the Gulf South), Jean-Luc asked what his cousins were talking about. It's some bigfoot that lives in Spring Bayou, responded one cousin. By this time, Jean-Luc had been working with his mother and sister, Elisabeth M. Pierite, on language educational programming. By this time, Jean-Luc knew the name of his grandfather's half-man, which was Tanap. But here was another creature inhabiting the local ecosystem. Or, maybe it was the same creature under a different name. After all, the Tunica-Biloxi are descendants of Tunica, Biloxi-Choctaw, Ofo, and Avoyel who intermarried with Louisiana French and Creole peoples. There could be many names for one or more things. In any event, something was there in Spring Bayou and it was spoken of across communities.

After a stint in tribal politics and a campaign for a tribal council seat, Jean-Luc would move again to Massachusetts to pursue a law program at the University of Massachusetts Dartmouth. Following a semester of study, Jean-Luc returned to work at Mohegan Sun in Uncasville, Connecticut. Through these times, Jean-Luc maintained ties with home and participated in yearly pow-wows. In 2013, Jean-Luc would settle in the Greater Boston area. In March of 2014, Jean-Luc started a temporary position as an executive assistant for Neil Gershenfeld at MIT's Center for Bits and Atoms. It was there that Jean-Luc learned about digital fabrication which shared some of the design and fabrication skills that he was acquainted with through sign shops and coding. Confirmation of the path for Jean-Luc would come about during an office visit by Neil's brother Alan who was the cofounder of E-Line Media. The connection was through the video game "Never Alone (Kisima Ingitchuna)" which E-Line had collaboratively developed with the Cook Inlet Tribal Council, a host of a community-based digital fabrication laboratory or fab lab. In May 2014, Jean-Luc joined The Fab Foundation which is a nonprofit dedicated to fostering the growth of the International Fab Lab Network. Coincidentally, Jean-Luc was concurrently invited to his first Institute for Collaborative Language Research or

CoLang at the University of Texas Arlington which itself hosted a fab lab. In both cases, Jean-Luc became involved in international networks that center collaboration between academics and local communities. These loosely connected distributed networks helped Jean-Luc articulate the skills and educational programming sought by himself and other Indigenous peoples, especially those in the Gulf South.

Stories reveal themselves over time. A half-man in Spring Bayou wrestling with a young boy could be illustrated in how we as adults grapple with the trauma and emotional baggage of childhood. In the place of plants and medicines, we can look to the local and virtual ecosystems for what is needed by family and community. While there is a decline in births affected by cerebral palsy in Indigenous peoples, these oral traditions which center on language and culture help us understand the living conditions and life pathways for children and impacted adults. In reflecting on my Tribe's tradition, I learned to contribute within the context of my own abilities. In this way, the traditional Indigenous knowledge systems and stories are a living body of knowledge.

17 The strength, wisdom, and resilience of traditional knowledge as a cultural approach to modern-day living in Northern Canada – an Inuk perspective

Noah Papatsie

Introduction

Ullaasiaq/Ullaatsiavakkut means 'Good morning' and Qungappasi Tammmik means 'Smiles all round'. I greet you in my language, which is who I am. I am the third youngest in my family but was raised with traditional and modern-day knowledge. My grandparents had to move from the northern areas, called Puvirnituq, where they were born and raised in Northern Québec to a new territory. It brought a lot of change, especially after they got sick and other issues arrived. I was raised with a knowledge of disability as my grandfather was blind and my aunts and uncles had physical disabilities. Some members of my family had post-traumatic stress disorder (PTSD) due to their treatment by non-Indigenous teachers and people who viewed them differently because of the way they lived, and others were wheelchair bound with mental health, hearing impairments, and other challenges that they had to endure.

I was raised in Iqaluit with seven sisters and one brother. At a young age, we were always taught how to use tools and knowledge to understand our language more. Life changed there for me after my family grew with marriages, in this fast time frame. My sisters and brothers-in-law needed to find jobs and schooling for everyone, which became a busy time. I learned hunting skills with my brothers-in-law. I was fortunate enough during this time, I was being taught traditions and languages to take on leadership as I grew up. I went to school at Gordon Robertson Education Center now Inukshuk High School. During that time, food was scarce, and we needed food for home and for the rest of the family depended on us, especially the young and the elderly.

I started a family during the 1990s when I was 25 years old. As I needed to support my family more, I took some courses and landed a job in 1990 with the Inuit Broadcasting Corporation as a Technical Producer for a children's program called Takuginai= 'Look and See'. I took some additional broadcasting courses here in Iqaluit and became a staff member for this network by starting at the bottom and working my way up to being the Executive Producer.

I then had an accident that raised my knowledge of inclusion. While I was working away from home in a community west of the territory on Cambridge Bay, during a festive season, I was filming an interview for work. A co-worker did not see what I was doing so, as I was working on other lights, he turned on the lights and bam the lights went out. I was hurt and had issues trying to finish the film. I went to see a doctor as soon as I got back and was told my right eye was gone so no more vision. They needed to work on my left eye. That is when my advocacy started as I had to wait for five years for an answer before I could get surgery. While waiting, I was not going to just sit and wait so I took my

DOI: 10.4324/9781032656519-21

life by the horns and worked my way up to getting better myself as no one was assisting me waiting for answers from the doctors.

My new lease on life

I took some training for services that I needed to use for my new life. Independent living skills such as braille, computer training assistive technology, and walking with a guide dog became my new life challenge. I did not allow this change in my lifestyle to stop my progress. I would continue to learn, work, and meet members from various organizations in Nunavut and across Canada. This new lease on life brought me to areas of Nunavut that I had not known which would, eventually, allow me to build new relationships with various members who I now call friends. As I began a new chapter in my life, I worked as an Inclusion Canada Board Member by helping with intellectual disability issues and families. I helped abroad with IRIS International Research and Developmental Inclusive Society, Heritage Canada, Elections Canada, the Trans Canada Trail and more here in Iqaluit as the Local President for Maliaganik Legal Aid Tukisiniarvik and President for the Board for the Coalition Nunavut District Education Authority. I was also a City of Iqaluit Councillor for 2013/2017/2019/2021 and created the Disability Group and I was on various boards in Iqaluit city development.

Understanding and beliefs of disability

Well, we all used to work together as one and still need to do so, especially, in remote places as we each are leaders of different communities. Therefore, we need to do it more and as for Mayors and Premiers, they need to support the territory more traditionally how it was meant to be. Together, everyone welcomes each other, making sure the leader is aware of what's happening. Everyone engages in betterment daily to assist each other. Single parents and caregivers were people, who supported each other without any question. By applying the community phrase – "the more we work together, the better we will become". Even equipment was made and used to assist the families, who required necessary adaptions for accessibility.

People with disabilities within community

Everyone has a unique experience that must be developed naturally within their own element. Some are advocates, support workers, and even some are politicians, but most are advocates as our services are not there with new technologies and workforces to assist each other as in an abled world. The services need a huge revamp because when Nunavut was created, disability networks, associations, and governmental bodies were not supported and needed to grow and develop. Through this growth period, there was a need for more services and resources, but this did not happen due to a lack of support such as with educators, translators, and all that was needed to respect those who needed our help to continue to provide better services to help each other. Working with various community organizations, services and in association with territorial and federal representatives would help in the gradual process of providing the types of things that all Inuit people could benefit from. This cooperation process could be shared with all people of Canada and with our brothers and sisters beyond our territory, as we share a common connection with people who face their own challenges of disabilities.

Working from within the community allows for a gradual learning process and sharing this approach enables all people, who have been impacted by physical and mental disabilities to access all services, equipment, and specialized training in education as a user, but also helps those who must be trained as service providers. What occurs in one Inuit community can be adapted to another one and what we learn from another territory or outside of Canada can help us to improve what services, education, and ways of learning can change that can benefit all Inuit community members even beyond our territory.

Teaching and learning about disability – How traditional knowledge can be a guide

We cannot judge each other, no matter what the state of the person is, without knowing the entirety and we need to work together as one for the greater good of all people. Things cannot be done in a day. We need to take our time to ensure a good practice will follow, by giving the needed attention to those who seek out help.

By always giving someone an opportunity, we can engage in a better process of working together for more of an inclusion approach and allow for different knowledge and belief systems for our youth and the next generation to give them all that they need. It is this boost as a support service that is greatly needed as well as to be accessible in a different way by different people. There is always a way to overcome the challenges of the modern day, by looking at our past when moving forward. There will always be challenges tomorrow, but it is how we act today that will set up how we view and understand those situations.

I have also worked in Mitsimatalik referred to in English as Pond Inlet conducting dialogue and engagement in the research of disability information and inclusion. I was able to meet locals and exchange some great conversations on proper accessibility guidelines that I can adopt for our own people. This type of exchange of knowledge such as this book will help in many ways and ultimately contribute to how we approach disability knowledge, services interaction, education, and accommodations. Yet, more is needed and through these relationships, we can achieve new understandings that will yield growth in many ways.

Impact of colonialism – Changing language, ideals, or concepts of disabilities

With the influence of colonialism, everything changes, even families break down because of drugs, alcohol, family violence, and even money. These can all have a direct and even an indirect impact because of colonialism. The actions of one can lead to the entire community or family structure being impacted in a negative way. The bigger problem is that the North is finally adapting to the new world of money, and everyone expects to get in on it. All these issues and more have contributed to the loss of the family, identity, ideals and values, and even traditional knowledge – all within 100 years after founding this new land.

Our language needed to change. We needed more education to work and pay for necessities, pay bills, and put money away for times of greater need. The rent is extremely expensive now in northern Canada. We were promised 2 dollars a month for life for rent, but now today it is 25 dollars out of $2,700 a month for a single unit. Food is extremely costly, a single bag of chips can cost as much as $16, and the youth rely on these types of junk food instead of living off the land, hunting, and using their natural senses to survive.

There are too many overpriced food products and equipment in the north. We need to adapt better, so together we can make a better change for us all.

Obesity is a major concern for us as this is considered as one of the major types of disabilities that effect the entire person, when they have diabetes that if left unchecked can result in multiple problems from mobile paralysis, blindness, and even death. As for alcoholism, many people have died from being frozen outside when they get lost under the influence, or when they go into crazed alcoholism moments, then remove their clothing and die. More is needed to educate our youth that colonialism is still a major contributor to our current and future challenges. These have changed the way we were to the way we are today. Through these changes, we see our people struggling the most with physical disabilities, learning problems, and invisible disabilities, so the time to act is now. Let's make connections with new members, partners, associations, and organizations to get the aid, so we can improve these health conditions so that no one else has to suffer. The protection of our children, youth, and the next generation is essential for the survival of our people.

The effects of colonialism as a method for change in disability knowledge

The effects of colonialism through the approaches of policies have impacted many people and led them down a bad path with labels, poor services, and the use of the residential school system. Yet, we must progress forward in our approach and attitude so that no one will be forgotten. We all have a right to learn in a safe place. This really speaks to me, very much so, and without the services, we cannot help one another as we are all in remote places – we need inclusion, support, money, and more to assist each other. We need better transparency with the territory and have leaders within the communities to help one another to achieve our goals. This process will take time and there have been great steps taken already, but more is needed. This is an ongoing approach to accessibility by providing accommodations through various types of services so that all Inuit and our brothers and sisters in other territories have the necessities not just to survive but to thrive.

Conclusion

Having reflected on that I should say I wanted to share from my heart, mind, spirit, and lips. In the spirit of International Day of Disabilities, we must learn that challenges are not barriers. The more we work together the better we become. Let us spread our arms around the world more and be inclusive. It is with this address that I have shared my thoughts, feelings, and spirit with all those who choose to read this chapter and perhaps take in some of the knowledge presented. We must understand that everyone learns in a different way for we all have our own gifts, talents, and abilities. The word 'disability' is rooted in colonialism and as such has caused so much pain and suffering, but as Indigenous peoples we must rise up and take back these negative words towards a 'reclaiming of disability' for now and forever.

18 From linguistic disability to linguistic diversity case studies of Taiwanese Indigenous peoples

I-Yun Cheng

Introduction

I-Yun Cheng conducts her PhD research at the University of Sydney and involves both museum studies and revitalizing Indigenous languages in Taiwan. She is examining whether Taiwanese museums can play a role as a mechanism to help Indigenous people conserve and retrieve their native languages. Although she does not have any legal status as a Taiwanese Indigenous person, she still identifies herself as an Indigenous Taiwanese because her mother's grandpa was Tsou, which is one of sixteen officially recognized Indigenous peoples in Taiwan. Therefore, she hopes her PhD research could contribute to the Taiwanese Indigenous peoples by honouring her Indigenous ancestors and the valuable linguistic diversity they left.

The purpose of the research project

Due to colonization and assimilation, most Indigenous languages have become endangered languages, including all Taiwanese Indigenous languages. With the loss of linguistic diversity, what the Taiwanese Indigenous peoples are experiencing is a linguistic disability. The United Nations General Assembly, thus, announced that 2022–2032 would be the period of the International Decade of Indigenous Languages (IDIL 2022–2032) after the International Year of Indigenous Languages 2019 (UNESCO, 2019). This period is a time for all global Indigenous people to highlight their linguistic diversity by conserving and revitalizing their native languages. Without revitalization, this type of disability will continue. This chapter will review, analyse, and discuss linguistic disability among Taiwanese Indigenous peoples by examining several case studies regarding Taiwanese Indigenous Elders.

What is linguistic disability?

Linguistic disability, including language disorders, is usually defined as difficulties or impairments in language-related disabilities. This might manifest in a variety of forms and even influence an individual's ability to understand, use, and process content of specific languages. Moreover, linguistic disabilities can affect both written and spoken languages as well (Radhakrishnan, ENT, Head and Neck Surgeon, n.d.). Linguistic disabilities usually stem from several types of disorders or symptoms regarding language including speech disorders, communication disorders, dyslexia, and writing disorders

DOI: 10.4324/9781032656519-22

(the dysgraphia). These disorders or disabilities are usually thought of as resulting from children's language development or they might be acquired due to illness or injuries (The Penn Medicine, n.d.).

Most of the modern linguistic disability studies focus on children. However, adults might also suffer from language disorders. As far as adults are concerned, they might also suffer from linguistic disabilities caused by a stroke or a traumatic brain injury (the TBI) – neurological conditions (Hach & Rose, n.d.). Furthermore, as they get older, Dementia and Parkinson's diseases might lead to the loss of language as well. Even though the main factors concerning linguistic disabilities among both children and adults come from medical issues, the reason Taiwanese Indigenous adults suffer from linguistic disabilities is more concerned with social and environmental barriers, especially for elderly grandparents. Their linguistic disabilities more likely resulted from a lack of stimulation and education along with structural violation, assimilation, discrimination, and marginalization.

Background information

The linguistic loss of Taiwanese Indigenous peoples dates back to at least 400 years ago. Taiwan was under various regimes including The Vereenigde Oostindische Compagnie (The VOC, 1602–1799), The Imperio Español (Spain Empire, 1492–1975), The Quing Dynasty (大清, 1636–1912), The Dainippon Teikoku (The Great Japan Empire, 1936–1947), and the Republic of China (The R.O.C., 1912–1949). Throughout these periods, diverse cultural and linguistic elements accumulated on the island (National Museum of Taiwan Literature, n.d.; Table 18.1).

Table 18.1 The summary of major languages and writing systems in different historical periods in Taiwan

Regimes	In Taiwan	Colonizer's language and writing system	Major Taiwanese languages and writing system
The Vereenigde Oostindische Compagnie (The VOC, 1602–1799)	1624–1662	Old Dutch (古荷蘭語); Latin alphabet,	Tâi-uân-uē (臺灣話); Hàn-jī (漢字)
The Imperio Español (Spain Empire, 1492–1975)	1626–1642	Español (Castellano); Latin alphabet,	Tâi-uân-uē (臺灣話); Hàn-jī (漢字)
The Ming- Zheng period (明鄭, 1628–1683)	1661–1683	Bân-lâm-gú (閩南); Hàn-jī (漢字)	Tâi-uân-uē (臺灣話)/ Hàn-jī (漢字)
The Quing Dynasty (大清, 1636–1912)	1683–1895	Manju-gisun (滿州語); Manju hergen (滿文),	Tâi-uân-uē (臺灣話), Hak-fa (客家話); Hàn-jī (漢字)
The Dainippon Teikoku (The Great Japan Empire, 1936–1947)	1895–1945	Nihongo (日本語)/Hàn-jī (漢字), Kana (仮名)	Tâi-uân-uē (臺灣話), Hak-fa (客家話); Hàn-jī (漢字)
Republic of China (The R.O.C.,1912–1949)	1945–	Mandarin/Traditional Chinese (繁體中文)	Mandarin/Traditional Chinese (繁體中文)

Source: Cheng, 2023

Disability imposed by colonial governments

Several derogatory titles were given to the Taiwanese Indigenous people by their colonizers. During the Qing Dynasty, Taiwanese Indigenous peoples were referred to as "Fān (番/蕃)," which denotes foreigners or ethnic minorities living in traditional Chinese society (Ministry of Education, R.O.C., 2021). The Indigenous people of Taiwan were then classified as either "Cooked Savage" (熟蕃) or "Raw Savage" (生蕃) (National Museum of Taiwan History, 2021). The category was based on the degree Taiwanese Indigenous peoples engaged with non-Indigenous peoples, especially the "Hàn-Jîn" (漢人, Chinese people) and their traditional territories. This was obviously discriminatory labelling Indigenous peoples as uncivilized peoples and belittling Indigenous culture, their traditional knowledge, and other customs (Nielsen & Robyn, 2019; Tuffin, 2008).

Since the majority of the "Cooked Savage" were plains dwellers, they were more prone to communicating and interacting with European and Chinese immigrants among other non-Indigenous peoples. As a result, the "Cooked Savage" are now referred to as the "Pinpu Peoples" (平埔族). (The CIP, n.d.b). In contrast, as more and more "Raw Savages" under the colonization of the Qing were forced to live in mountain areas, to keep them apart from non-Indigenous peoples, the colonial rulers even erected physical barriers known as "Thôo-gû" (土牛) in Tâi-gí (臺語,Taiwanese Hô-ló) (National Museum of Taiwan History, 2021). These movable barriers daily constricted the Indigenous territory so also contributed significantly to racial segregation (Feng-Nan Su et al., 2022). Furthermore, Qing authorities used the degree of assimilation as a yardstick to determine whether or not an Indigenous person was civilized enough or not. As time went by, more and more female "Cooked Savages" began to marry non-Indigenous men, particularly the Chinese, in order to avoid losing more of their land daily. They quickly assimilated into the new culture. Nearly all the Pinpu people's civilizations experienced a loss of culture and language as a result of this integration in the centuries that followed. In 1874 A.D., the Qing governors allowed Chinese immigrants to develop the Taiwanese mountains. In other words, the colonizers approved non-Indigenous peoples to claim the lands inhabited by the Raw Savage. This not only boosted the speed of assimilation but also increased the conflicts between Indigenous peoples and non-Indigenous peoples (Hou et al., 2022; Zhan, 2019; Figure 18.1).

The Japanese government took over the Qing government and became the new colonizer in Taiwan after "The War of Kah- Ngóo" in 1894 (Chou, 2020; Zhan, 2019). In order to separate Taiwanese Indigenous peoples, particularly those who had not fully assimilated as non-Indigenous peoples, the Japanese colonial rulers adopted the Qing dynasty's methods. For instance, Indigenous pupils were not permitted to attend the same primary schools as non-Indigenous Taiwanese students or Japanese children. The measure they took was the "Banjin kōgakkō" 番人公學校), which was known as "primary schools for the savage" in Japanese (Lee, 2003).

Thus, freedom to use the preferred native languages and writing systems was curtailed during the Kominka policy, which was recaptured by Japanese colonizers. Due to this extreme Japanese suppression, the Kominka policy was a major turning point in the usage of all original Taiwanese languages, including all Taiwanese Indigenous languages. Thus, Japanese ended up being Taiwan's sole legal language in addition to its national language. Although, Taiwanese writers were initially still allowed to publish in their original tongues, after 1935, numerous cultural institutions that primarily employed

Figure 18.1 The board of "I would speak national language (Mandarin) rather than dialect" 我要說國語不說方言) during the period of Martial Law, October 26, 2023.

Source: Photographer: By I-Yun Cheng in National Museum of Taiwan History

Hàn-jī publications and Tâi-uân-uē as a means of communication were outlawed. In addition, the "National Language Family (國語家庭)" scheme was put into effect by the Japanese Governors, to reward households for having fluent Japanese speakers. The goal of the Japanese administrators was to change Taiwanese culture and national identity from a relationship with China to one with Japan by encouraging the use of Japanese and suppressing other native languages (National Museum of Taiwan Literature, n.d.). Therefore, Taiwanese Indigenous peoples were forced to confront the terrible dilemma of linguistic loss since it was their first exposure to the experience of having their national language policy usurped by external colonizers (Cheng, 2023).

Following the end of the Second World War and the fall of the Great Japanese Empire, Taiwan, and the Korean Peninsula (조선반도, Chosŏn Pando) encountered profound political shifts and difficulties. A watershed in the history of the area was reached when the United Nations signed the Treaty of Peace with Japan, which gave the R.O.C. control over Taiwan. As a result, in 1945, the R.O.C. seized control of Taiwan (Wu, 2011).

In order to assert total control over Taiwanese society, the R.O.C. instituted a second national language policy in 1946, emphasizing Mandarin as the only legal and official language. The transition from Japanese to Mandarin as the primary language meant that many Taiwanese Indigenous peoples had to give up their mother tongue and were forced to adapt another external language again in a short period of time (Cheng, 2023).

During the Martial Law Era in Taiwan, which lasted until 1987, the R.O.C. governors maintained the national language policy with Mandarin. It had a far longer lifespan than the Japanese national language policy, which had had a greater overall impact on Taiwan's linguistic landscape and did more harm to Indigenous native languages. While the Japanese colonizers promoted the use of Japanese, Taiwanese pupils speaking native tongues in public were not penalized severely. In contrast, later on, people who used languages other than Mandarin under the Martial Law Era were fined, and the penalty was frequently as little as one Taiwanese dollar. Some were also made to stand in public, especially during morning meetings, and wear a board that said, "I do not speak my dialect (我不說方言)," which was a way of defilement (The Subcommittee on Languages of the Presidential Office Indigenous Historical Justice and Transitional Justice Committee, 2018, 2020). This oppressive measure was a reflection of the R.O.C.'s attempts to suppress linguistic diversity and enforce Mandarin as the sole language of communication.

This national Mandarin language policy had several terrible results on Taiwan's Indigenous linguistic diversity. It caused a negative impact on daily relationships as well as education and cultural preservation. Indigenous peoples valued their original languages and dialects highly, but they were suppressed, and younger generations were discouraged from learning and using them in favour of Mandarin. It even became a permanent post-traumatic stress disorder (Attwood, 2011; Sherwood, 2013) for some Indigenous elders who experienced both of the national language policies of Japan and the R.O.C. That's why there is a visible generation gap between Indigenous Taiwanese children and elders today. The linguistic barriers were ordered by colonial governors and kept growing so that the ongoing decline of Taiwanese Indigenous linguistic diversity continued.

The national language policies of Mandarin and Japanese were crucial instruments for reconstructing Indigenous Taiwanese national identity and facilitating integration. Both colonists followed the same policy, which first involved changing the registered full name. For some Indigenous peoples, they were forced to rename themselves more than twice throughout their lives. For instance, during the Kominka time, Balriwakes Raera (1910–1988), a well-known Indigenous musician from Pinuyumayan, changed his Indigenous name to Moriyasu Ichiro (森寶一郎). Then he had to rename himself to LIU,SEN-PAO (陸森寶)in Mandarin during the period of martial law. Due to their different naming systems and languages, it was clear that Taiwanese Indigenous peoples were negatively impacted by this strategy far more than non-Indigenous peoples. A large number of Indigenous peoples did not use a naming system in which the family name was added to the initial name. As a result, it was evident that many Indigenous peoples of Taiwan gave up their original names multiple times throughout the 20th century, in addition to giving up their native tongue twice (National Central Library, 2022; Table 18.2).

Naming is not just a representation of cultural identity, but it is also an interpretation of language. The current Taiwanese government rejects Indigenous peoples from

Table 18.2 Samples of 3 types of Taiwanese Indigenous peoples' names

Tribes	Indigenous name	Japanese name	Chinese name
Pinuyumayan	Balriwakes Raera (1910–1988)	森寶一郎(Moriyasu Ichiro)	陸森寶 (LIU,SEN-PAO)
Tsou (Cou)	Uyongu'e Yatauyungana (1908–1954)	矢多一大(Yata Kazuo)、 矢多一生(Yata I ssei)	高一生 (KAO,YI-SHENG)
Atayal	Losing Watan (1899–1954)	渡井三郎(Watarai Zaburō)、 日野三郎(Hino Zaburō)	林瑞昌 (LIN,JUI-CHANG)

Source: Cheng, 2023

indicating their traditional name with only the Roman alphabet spelling on their physical ID cards due to some technical excuses. However, it is ridiculous that non-Indigenous Taiwanese can present their names freely, no matter how silly it is, on their ID cards as long as they are using only Chinese characters. Due to the differences in languages, some Indigenous words cannot be spelled or presented with Chinese characters at all. The imposition of colonial policies aimed at assimilation and the promotion of national languages led to the erasure of Indigenous cultural identities. Indigenous peoples were coerced into adapting their names to conform to colonial formats. As an example, "Watan" was often transcribed in Chinese format as "瓦旦," which not only distorted its meaning but also carried potentially offensive connotations in Mandarin, as the character "旦" is typically associated with "daytime" or "actress" (NCCU, 2014). In other words, using Chinese characters to interpret Indigenous pronunciations is nothing but offensive. It is another structural discrimination on Taiwanese Indigenous peoples' culture and language. The linguistic disability is created by the non-Indigenous again (Valincinan, 2023).

Can school education be the treatment?

For the Indigenous peoples of Taiwan, linguistic impairment represents not just a disease that was acquired through colonial authority but also a profound loss of cultural diversity and traditional knowledge. As prominent linguist, David Crystal (1941–) said (Crystal, 2000) "language death would result in the loss of hereditary knowledge, values, and culture." All Indigenous peoples are dependent on their oral history to transmit culture, knowledge, and traditional values in the absence of literacy systems. Due to the linguistic impairment brought about by colonialism and assimilation, the Taiwanese have no choice but struggle to preserve their native tongues while maintaining their culture and knowledge. Even worse, Indigenous languages are hardly ever taught in schools because of the marginalized and absorbed educational policies. Despite the fact that the "National Languages Development Act" (2018) reclaims all of Taiwan's Indigenous languages as national languages, non-Indigenous people continue to denigrate them. Therefore, Indigenous children cannot communicate with their grandparents in Indigenous languages at all. Instead, they spoke Mandarin, which was the major language taught in Taiwanese schools, to their grandparents.

Many Indigenous grandparents have thus been deprived of their native languages twice since their birth. Whenever they speak with their grandchildren, they find themselves responding in their native tongue naturally. However, as their descendants hear languages they don't understand, it turns out that they feel wired. Even worse, some Indigenous grandchildren in Taiwan may feel that their grandparents are too old to talk to. Stated differently, the linguistic and generational divide between these Indigenous children and their grandparents is visible and getting wider.

Thankfully, Taiwan has seen a growth in the revival of Indigenous native languages over the past ten years or so. The 2000s witnessed Taiwanese experiencing and voting for the first time, which is when this trend began. After more than 50 years of assimilated national language policies that only focused on Mandarin, the ruling Democratic Progressive Party (the DPP, 民主進步黨,1986–) implemented new educational policies to teach Taiwanese native languages, including all Indigenous languages in primary schools (Li, 1996). Gaining support from the government, all non-Mandarin languages, however, remained vulnerable to extinction because of the lack of social consensus and the misconceptions about non-native speakers of Mandarin. Many people still discriminate against non-Mandarin speakers or those Indigenous students who cannot speak Mandarin fluently. From those racist viewpoints, one of the common excuses for their discrimination is that they only regard Mandarin as the official language of the country; languages other than that, such as all Indigenous languages, do not have the same legal standing. Therefore, they think it is not necessary to maintain the linguistic diversity of Taiwanese Indigenous languages (Yang, 2003).

The "National Languages Development Act" was officially promulgated in the Legislative Yuan (立法院), the highest legislative body in Taiwan, on December 25, 2018, following nearly two decades of waiting. The purpose of this act was to achieve linguistic diversity by ardently promoting and respecting each and every one of the native languages of Taiwan. This signalled the start of a new stage of Taiwan's revitalization of all native languages, including Indigenous languages. Furthermore, all Taiwanese native languages were given legal status as national languages; the same legal status as Mandarin in Taiwan now (Ministry of Culture, 2018).

For many years, Taiwanese Indigenous societies have shared a common language. However, the "National Languages Development Act" only marked the beginning of the treatment of Taiwan's Indigenous peoples' linguistic disabilities, which is an enduring disorder brought on by multiple colonial factors. Even though Taiwan now considers its Indigenous languages to be national languages, schools only teach them for 40 minutes a week. Mandarin, on the other hand, continues to occupy the title of national language and is allowed to be taught in schools for at least 40 minutes each day. Even more unbelievable is the fact that many educators teaching Mandarin frequently claim that non-Mandarin instructors are pilfering their jobs and creating a series of chaos in the educational system (Tsai, 2021). That is to say, despite the increasing awareness of Indigenous rights and cultural diversity, the structural violation is still found among Taiwanese Indigenous peoples.

It was not until 2021, that I started to learn Taiwanese Indigenous languages. To fulfil this goal, I visited an Indigenous tribe in March to teach English and exchange languages by learning their native Indigenous language. This tribe is situated in Taoyuan City, one of Taiwan's six special municipalities. The Atayal, who make up the third largest Indigenous group in Taiwan, is the majority of the Indigenous community residing here (The CIP, n.d.a). As per the latest statistics released by the Council of Indigenous Peoples (the CIP), there are 22,471 Atayal residents in Taoyuan City out of a total 95,364

Atayal population in Taiwan. Among these 22,471 Atayal people, 8,838 are living in Fuxing District, which is one of the residences of Indigenous Peoples in Taiwan (The CIP, 2023). Chang-Xhing Primary School (Pquwsan Biru'na Laqi Thokak; 長興國民小學) was located in the tribe I resided with. For any grade level, there was just one class. There were only six students enrolled in this tiny primary school overall (Chang-Xhing Primary School, n.d.).

Every Tuesday, I participated in the Atayal language class with the fifth and sixth graders. Ms. Ciwas Huang, the instructor, spent the majority of the class time helping pupils refresh the material they had learned over the previous few years due to the impending official exam in April. Additionally, the instructor utilized an iPad or Surface to help the pupils become accustomed to the assessment method used in class (Figure 18.2).

After studying Atayal for two months, I received a score of ten out of ten on the hearing portion of the exam, which I passed with 87 out of 100. Prior to the exam, like the majority of students, I was first really anxious. However, I still received a satisfying result in the end.

It was frequently contended by numerous non-Indigenous persons in Taiwan that learning and adapting an Indigenous language at their age was too late. For this reason, they do not think it necessary to show students or their children how to retrieve an endangered language on their own. The more of these adults living in our society, the more Indigenous languages are facing extinction. This crisis should not be found in educational systems anymore.

Figure 18.2 The certificate of passing Taiwanese Indigenous languages official examination with medium level, March 21, 2022.

Source: Photographer: By I-Yun Cheng

Apart from learning the Atayal language with the students, I was teaching third grade. This class consisted of just six students: two boys and four girls. Because of the small sample size, there was a discernible difference between these Indigenous kids. Michael frequently slept or became sidetracked in class and a relevant disability examination revealed that he had a learning disability. According to non-Indigenous educators, he had a very poor attitude for learning. Educating him was a source of some frustration. Compared to Michael, Susan was generally regarded as the class's best student. Not only did she consistently receive the best grades on all academic assessments, but she was also the first student to pass the official exam for Indigenous languages at the time. She was even granted $NTD 1,000 scholarship by the Taoyuan City Government because she passed the Indigenous language exam. Most of the time, she was eager to assist her schoolmates with a range of issues, including academic assignments; even if some moments, she was so ecstatic that she embarrassingly flaunted herself in front of her classmates. Therefore, teaching her brought me some sense of achievement.

Due to stigma from the media, Indigenous pupils are occasionally portrayed as being uncivilized or uneducated by nature. With the exception of physical education, they always struggle with learning problems in all other academic subjects. Although Susan's circumstance amply demonstrated that the media was merely fabricating false information about Taiwanese Indigenous students, it is undeniable that Michael's predicament matched these unfavourable stereotypes. Students, who are Indigenous, are not in the slightest disabled. Furthermore, Susan demonstrated that learning Indigenous languages in elementary school has little bearing on academic courses or language acquisition. Stated differently, there wouldn't be pandemonium if Indigenous languages were taught in schools. Taiwanese Indigenous students would only be discouraged from approaching their true native languages by adults, especially, the non-Indigenous justifications, or preconceptions of Indigenous peoples.

Tribal culture health stations

It seems that school education might not be the only guaranteed option to treat the linguistic disability of Taiwanese Indigenous people, at this moment, even with a number of political and legislative supports. To get over this acquired disorder, Indigenous Elders, especially those who are now grandparents, depend on themselves. Thus, to help Indigenous Elders maintain their native languages, and their physical and mental health at the same time, the CIP has launched a series of projects composed of the long-term care (the LTC) service and cultural, leisure activities. This facility is called a tribal culture health station (部落文化健康站, 文健站) in Taiwan (Huang, 2020). The original purpose of these stations was to keep Indigenous seniors from feeling alone or unsafe. However, as these brain-stimulating activities can help prevent dementia, they can also play a part in helping maintain and revive Indigenous languages, traditional knowledge, and culture (Chin-Ying Lai & Chun-Yen Kuo, 2021; Lin, 2022). The main idea of tribal cultural health stations is unquestionably suited to Indigenous populations. However, it is still unclear, if their services offered can truly meet the needs of the Indigenous Elders in local communities. The main problems involve several aspects: first of all and the most important concerns the budget. Most Taiwanese Indigenous communities are situated in mountainous areas, so transportation is always expensive and time-consuming. The second significant issue is of human resources as young Taiwanese Indigenous people need support in accepting their responsibility of passing down their native languages and customs from their tribal Elders. Thus, individuals with relevant nursing or health care degrees or certificates find it easier to find employment than others. However, by working as full-time care attendants in remote mountain Indigenous communities, these young people are unable to advance in their careers and continue to develop because of structural and systemic issues. The majority of young Indigenous carers choose to resign and relocate to cities in search of other employment opportunities because they lack ambition and a well-paying job. Such a consequence means that these tribal cultural health stations lack staff and become meaningless. Furthermore, they cannot be helpful in curing the linguistic disabilities among young Indigenous peoples in Taiwan. It is impossible to close any linguistic or generational gaps without the involvement of young Indigenous peoples. To make matters worse, the gap may continue to enlarge.

Intergenerational collaboration of saving Indigenous linguistic diversity

By coincidence, I participated in a few Atayal People's traditional rites while I was teaching students English at Chang-Xhing Primary School. The millet sowing ceremony in March, known as trakis in the Atayal language, was the most memorable. One of the most influential Atayal Elders in the tribe, Batu Watan, was invited to the school to perform this ceremony in order to impart traditional Atayal knowledge of trakis to young Atayal students (Figure 18.3).

In addition to imparting pertinent scientific knowledge, he also taught the historical and cultural significance of the word "trakis" along with a variety of Atayal terminology

Figure 18.3 The preparation for the Trakis ceremony: seeds of trakis, pork, wine made from trakis and sticky rice, September 2023.

Source: Photographer: By I-Yun Cheng in Chang-Xhing Primary School

(Yang, 2020). The Atayal kids at Chang-Xhing Primary School were able to comprehend the significance of trakis and its connection to their Atayal ancestors with their native languages through this meaningful and practical lesson imparted by Batu Watan. Furthermore, they were able to appropriately cultivate the trakis seeds after witnessing Batu Watan's demonstration. They were unquestionably not a group of Taiwanese Indigenous students experiencing any illnesses or impairments at that time. Instead, they were being taught something special that could only be imparted by knowledgeable Atayal Elders. If a non-Indigenous person took an Indigenous course, perhaps he or she would be the one who was thought of as disabled.

Actually, millet is common among almost all Taiwanese Indigenous peoples, not just the Atayal people. For example, the Bunun, usually living on both sides of the Central Mountain Range at an elevation of 500–1,500 m, also have a unique knowledge and culture of millet. In their native language, millet is called marooku. During the harvest season, they would also perform a festival celebration by singing. This song is called as Pasibutbut in the Bunun language (MING, 2022).

This diverse knowledge and culture about millet and Taiwanese Indigenous people is hardly taught in most Taiwanese schools or textbooks. It can only be taught by Indigenous Elders. In other words, apart from Indigenous native languages, Indigenous students are only seen as disabled due to the tough knowledge or techniques used by those, who are the non-Indigenous in Taiwan today. This structural violation keeps forcing Indigenous children to suffer unreasonably from the linguistic disorders and even other learning disabilities. What is worse, these racists do not consider that they could be wrong at all. They always claim it is all about equality and pragmatism, so Indigenous students should put much effort into learning other languages rather than their native language. Otherwise, they have to accept themselves as disabled or even inferior compared to non-Indigenous students.

Conclusion: none of us is an outsider

Since hundreds of years ago, it has been undeniable that linguistic disability is an ongoing issue among Taiwanese Indigenous societies. They are, especially the Elders, still said to be disabled due to the deprivation of their traditional knowledge, culture, and ideas that represent their native languages. Although the Taiwanese current government is trying its best to resolve this problem with all kinds of legislative and political measures such as the "National Languages Development Act," the tribal culture health stations, assimilation, discrimination, and marginalization are still unmovable. The non-Indigenous people in Taiwan are still considering that what the government does for Indigenous peoples makes them privileged. Therefore, they reject supporting the revitalizing of Indigenous languages. Moreover, they do not agree to invest more educational resources and social welfare to help Indigenous peoples cure their linguistic disabilities.

As human beings, every one of us will face the challenge of aging. Therefore, whether we are Taiwanese Indigenous peoples or not, we might suffer from linguistic disorders later as well. In other words, all Taiwanese are likely to face the problem of linguistic disabilities when we become someone's grandparents. As we understand it, linguistic diversity can be both a prevention and a treaty at this moment, so it is unreasonable to kill off Indigenous linguistic diversity with a number of racist and discriminatory excuses.

To sum up my experiences and viewpoints, none of us should be outsiders when it comes to the linguistic disability of Taiwanese Indigenous peoples. Even though I do not have the legal status of an Indigenous person in Taiwan, I have proved that a non-Indigenous person can also contribute to resolving the Indigenous linguistic disability by engaging with Indigenous societies and learning their native languages. Besides, the accusation that learning Indigenous languages is useless is totally ridiculous. At least, one Atayal girl is demonstrating that mastering her mother tongue has no negative effects on her scholastic achievement in any other subjects. Adult non-Indigenous people should know better than to make up stories or justifications to prevent their children from maintaining their linguistic diversity. They should fight against imposed linguistic disability by learning from either school courses or from Indigenous Elders themselves. It is health issue for all of us, not just the Indigenous Taiwanese.

References

Attwood, B. (2011). Aboriginal History, Minority Histories and Historical Wounds: The Postcolonial Condition, Historical Knowledge and the Public Life of History in Australia. *Postcolonial Studies*, 14(2), 171–186.

Center for Aboriginal Studies NCCU. (2014). 原住民族人名譜.

Chang-Xhing Primary School. (n.d.). *Chang-Xhing Primary School*. Retrieved 13/12/2023 from https://www.cses.tyc.edu.tw/index.php

Cheng, I.-Y. (2023). *Practices of The National Languages Development Act Case Studies of National Museum of Taiwan Literature*. Various Aspects of Literature: The 20th National Postgraduate Students Academic Conference of Taiwanese Literature, National Museum of Taiwan Literature.

Chin-Ying Lai, H.-C. L., and Chun-Yen Kuo (2021). Research on the Caring Practices and Service Difficulties in Tribal Culture and Health Service Stations: A Practitioner's Reflections. *Journal of Community Work and Community Studies*, 11(1), 1–44.

CHOU, W.-Y. (2020). *A New Illustrated History of Taiwan* (1st Ed.). Smcbook.

Crystal, D. (2000). What is language death? In D. Crystal (Ed.), *Language Death* (1st ed., pp. 1–26). Cambridge University Press.

Hach, A., and Rose, L. (n.d.). *Communication Disabilities Caused by Traumatic Brain Injuries*. Retrieved 04/12/2023 from https://www.unionlawfirm.com/new-york-injury- attorney/traumatic-brain-injuries/communication-disabilities-from-traumatic-brain-injuries/

Hou, Y.-L., Chen, Y.-H., Tsai, C.-H., Tung, W.-E., Li, T.-N., Lu, M.-F., Su, F.-N., Lee, W.-Y., & Shih, W.-C. (2022). *Object Stories of Taiwan's Indigenous People, the Han Taiwanese, and the Chinese Imperial Court and Officials: A NPM and NTM and NMTH Joint Exhibition Catalog* (W. Chia-Ni, Ming-Shan Chiang, Ed. 1st ed.). National Museum of Taiwan History.

HUANG, S. (2020). *The Analysis on the Accessibility for the Tribal Culture Health Station of Taiwanese Aborigine*. Tunghai University.

Lee, C.-L. (2003). 日治時期蕃童教育所之研究(1904–1937年) National Central University.

Li, C.-A. (1996). 語言政策及台灣獨立. 教授論壇專刊, 3, 113–134.

LIN, D.-R. (2022). 高齡藝術與預防失智症: 藝術課程活動設計 (1st ed.). Wu- Nan. National Palace Museum, National Taiwan Museum.

MING, L.-K. (2022). 布農族《祈禱小米豐收歌》（*pasibutbut*）的美學及其展演. Retrieved 22/10/2023 from https://www.kmfa.gov.tw/ArtAccrediting/ArtArticleDetail.aspx?Cond=62765 e91-7a9c-47d5-bb90-71cd680fc850

Culture, M. o. (2018, 25/12/2018). 立法院三讀通過《國家語言發展法》鄭麗君：讓每一個人都能以使用自己母語為榮! https://www.moc.gov.tw/information_250_95831.html

Ministry of Culture. (25/12/2018). 立法院三讀通過《國家語言發展法》鄭麗君：讓每一個人都能以使用自己母語為榮！ Retrieved 04/04/2024 from https://www.moc.gov.tw/information_250_95831.html

Ministry of Education, R. O. C. (2021). 番. In *Revised Mandarin Chinese Dictionary*.

National Central Library. (2022). *O ngangan no niyah*. Retrieved 21/09/2023 from https://www.ncl.edu.tw/information_237_13075.html

National Museum of Taiwan History. (2021). Struggling Indigenous People. In N.-Y. Chien & M.-H. Yu (Eds.), *Our Land, Our People: The Story of Taiwan Permanent Exhibition Guide* (pp. 46–47). National Museum of Taiwan History.

National Museum of Taiwan Literature. (n.d.). *Literary History*. Retrieved 08/08/2023 from https://www.tlvm.com.tw/en/History/HistoryList

Nielsen, M., & Robyn, L. M. (2019). Introduction: Crimes against Indigenous Peoples. In M. Nielsen & L. M. Robyn (Eds.), *Colonialism is Crime* (1st ed., pp. 1–25). Rutgers University Press.

Presidential Office. (2018). The Subcommittee on Languages of the Presidential Office Indigenous Historical Justice and Transitional Justice Committee. 從政府公文書初探 「推行 國語運動」對原住民族語言使用限制的歷史脈絡. 原住民族文獻, 36, 13–30.

Rohini Radhakrishnan, E., Head and Neck Surgeon. (n.d.). *What Are the Different Types of Language Disorders?* Retrieved 04/12/2023 from https://www.medicinenet.com/autism_pictures_slideshow/article.htm

Sherwood, J. (2013). Colonisation - It's Bad for Your Health: The Context of Aboriginal Health. *Contemporary Nurse: A Journal for the Australian Nursing Profession*, 46(1), 13.

Su, F.-N., Shih, W.-C., Chang, A.-L., Cheng, C.-S., Chen, Y.-H., Lee, W.-Y., Chuang, T.-H., Chun-Yachuang, Yan-Rong, H., Tseng, W. L., & Tseng, M.-T. (2022). 統治者的填充題 五十萬分一臺灣蕃地圖. In F.-N. SU (Ed.), 看得見的臺灣史. 空間篇: 30幅地圖裡的真實與想像 (pp. 182–189). National Museum of Taiwan History, Linking Books.

The Council of Indigenous Peoples. (2023). *Indigenous Population Statistical Data* (Updated in October, 2023). The Council of Indigenous Peoples.

The Council of Indigenous Peoples. (n.d.a). *Atayal*. Retrieved 13/12/2023 from https://www.cip.gov.tw/en/tribe/grid-list/A7F31083995F0E60D0636733C6861689/info.html?cumid=5DD9C4959C302B9FD0636733C6861689

The Council of Indigenous Peoples. (n.d.b). *The Tribes in Taiwan*. Council of Indigenous Peoples. Retrieved 20/08/2023 from https://www.cip.gov.tw/en/menu/data-list/87257EF55B9F062E/index.html?cumid=87257EF55B9F062E

The National Languages Development Act. (2018). Promulgated January 9, 2019 by Presidential Order Hua Zong Yi Yi Zi Di No. 10800003831.

The Penn Medicine. (n.d.). *Speech and Language Disorders*. Retrieved 04/12/2023 from https://www.pennmedicine.org/for-patients-and-visitors/patient-information/conditions-treated-a-to-z/speech-and-language-disorders#:~:text=Language%20disorders%20refer%20to%20someone, coming%20fr om%20others%20(receptive%20language)

The Subcommittee on Languages of the Presidential Office Indigenous Historical Justice and Transitional Justice Committee. (2020). sh' uka sa quit a thau a lalawa numa uqthawan puhubuq: kahiwan kunathathuinian a lalawa sa tandaduu a smuqum. In Presidential Office Indigenous Historical Justice and Transitional Justice Committee (Ed.), *pokavole tatopodhaolaeni, okavole'i takasokolro'o vaha* (pp. 107–117).

The UNESCO. (2019). *International Decade of Indigenous Languages 2022–2032*. Retrieved 04/12/2023 from https://www.unesco.org/en/decades/indigenous-languages

Tsai, H.-C. (2021). 國高中本土語文必修政策問題分析與建議. 臺灣教育評論月 刊, 10(11), 31–34.

Tuffin, K. (2008). Racist Discourse in New Zealand and Australia: Reviewing the Last 20 Years: Racism Review: New Zealand and Australia. *Social and Personality Psychology Compass*, 2(2), 17.

Valincinan, S. (20/11/2023). *原住民身分證單列族名議題懶人包* Facebook. Retrieved 06/12/2023 from https://www.facebook.com/savungaz2024/posts/pfbid0TbD3oAjxWMUfeoKh8gFucc7ge FwkTk9kjabRh9kpBePMRFqGt6e9s7LWKRxFgfkml

Wu, W.-H. (2011). 第二次世界大戰後的政治變遷. In *臺灣史*. Wunan.

Yang, C.-Y. (2003). *A Study of Homeland Language Curriculum in Elementary Schools: Comparison of Three Elementary Schools in Taiwan*. National Taiwan Normal University.

Yang, F.-Y. (2020). *泰雅生活誌：泰雅耆老口述歷史* (1st ed.). Morning Star.

Zhan, S.-J. (2019). *台灣原住民史*. 玉山社. (2019.4).

19 Mushi and Muhavu beliefs, understandings, teachings, and traditional knowledge of disabilities

Carine Sacerdoce Kananga

Introduction

I come from a small town called Goma in the Democratic Republic of Congo (DRC) born to a father of the Mushi tribe and a mother of the Muhavu tribe. The language spoken amongst the Bashi is Mashi and amongst the Havu is Kihavu. The Bashi and Havu people are hardworking.[1] They have their differences in sociocultural practices, but it is these differences that make each tribe unique in the DRC. My parents, part of the Bantu tribe in the province of South Kivu, lived off agriculture, gathering, fishing, hunting, and livestock; but agriculture is dominant. I worked as a psycho-social worker and music therapist with the *Renaître Grand Lacs Oganization*, which is in English (Reborn Big Lake) the area where I lived. There I mentored young people in livelihoods with the Education Development Center (EDC) in the Activités de l'Usaid pour le développement intégré des jeunes (ADIJ), a project of the international organization USAID for Actives for Integrated Youth Development', but I also worked at the Canadian Red Cross as an Emergency Responder.

This is who I am and where I come from, so the knowledge presented will come from the perspectives of the two tribes that are part of me.

Traditional knowledge influences dialogue

It is very important for any parent to see their children succeed, as there has always been this belief that parents are the best guides for their children and can, therefore, reframe them when the latter diverts from the right path. Everything the father suggests and plans is the best because he is the head of the family. For children with learning disabilities, teachers force them to learn at the same pace as others. They still use corporal punishment, intimidation, and humiliation, believing these will help the child learn and be able to improve. This approach to education originating from colonial practices might seem abusive but is the primary method of schooling in the Congo.

Parents felt humiliated by the demeaning image of the family that the child showed, the inability of their offspring to learn, and this challenge amongst the other school children resulted in a negative reflection by the parents, which often resulted in punishment. As with myself and my siblings, those who struggled in any compacity were wiped with

---

1 The name of the tribe is 'Shit' whose dialect is 'Mashi'. People belonging to this tribe are called the 'Bashi' when it's several and 'Mushi' when it's one. Same for the 'Havu' tribe, whose dialect is 'Kihavu'. The people belonging to this tribe are the 'Bahavu' when it's several and 'Muhavu' when it's one person.

DOI: 10.4324/9781032656519-23

a hand wipe that we had to bring to school. If this situation did not improve, the parents decided to direct them into careers, which they would have chosen for themselves, these would include but not be limited to mechanics, carpentry, agriculture, sewing, etc. as these professions were considered as low intelligence. However, these career paths would suit these children ideally as they could use their gifts to benefit themselves as these professions were ways of surviving and becoming self-sustaining.

Children with physical disabilities were considered useless by parents, so they did not pay their school fees. The children then ended up becoming beggars on the street or worse. It was not only Shi and Havu parents who had this belief about disabilities and learning disability, but all tribal parents combined from the DRC. This global response to all types of disabilities did not fit within the sociocultural perspectives of the tribal peoples of Congo, which was a colonial direction imposed on us by Belgium so has haunted the people who must struggle alone and feel abandoned with shame for being different.

The impact of colonialism on the Havu and Shi

Belgian colonization profoundly altered Congolese society and culture, as well as that of many other countries throughout Africa. Traditional governance structures were dismantled, dialects were marginalized in favour of French, and the Belgians resorted to various tricks to divide ethnic groups in order to be able to administer them and succeed in stifling our traditions. It was through this approach of dividing and conquering that the Belgian conquest of various tribes succeeded in assimilating them into a French collective that would embrace these new ideals. Plus, ruling a multilingual country under a single language would prove to be far easier for enforcing colonial authority when communication had to be in the official language. Individual tribal beliefs were replaced by Christian values and belief systems, which also included, but were not limited to the loss of human lives, deforestation, impoverishment, etc. As for the positive impact, I can share the construction of infrastructure, education, and various economic development was a way of pushing Congolese people to become diverse and able to reach higher with each passing year.

The impact on my own Havu and Shi perspective contributed to significant abuse, trauma, and murder due to this colonialism and this shakeup of the traditional tribe's ability to communicate. It led to a breakdown in culture. This occurred due to the gradual shift from tribal to French speakers that aimed to conquer not only the tribal mind and body but also the spirit, which is the pinnacle of the Congolese tribal essence.

Influence of Belgian colonialism: the act of altering Havu and Shi knowledge of disabilities and learning disabilities

Indeed, Belgian colonialism helped the Congolese society, in general, to be able to re-orient children living with disabilities and learning difficulties into professions, such as mechanics, sewing, carpentry, because before their arrival several of these trades did not exist. Yes, colonialism helped provide alternative living outcomes for people, who struggled with physical and mental disabilities, but the overall impact of colonialism was much worse than with other colonized countries in Africa. Today, thanks to awareness-raising on the rights of children and the person that the Congolese society in general has become aware and is learning how to go about it when a child has any disability. The introduction of Western education pushed Congolese people to view and understand disabilities differently, which would eventually lead to not only alternative occupations but also to ways to survive or at least give them a fighting chance to prepare for the outside world.

Understanding disabilities and learning disabilities from a community perspective

From a community perspective, disabilities and learning disabilities are very badly mis-understood, yet accepted. In the general ideology, such as with spirituality advocates, disabilities and disorders of learning are seen as a punishment, a condemnation, or a spell cast on the family of the person due to their interactions with others, acts of evilism, and disrespecting God. This person cannot be accepted and considered on an equal footing with others, by members of his family or the community in general. The parents of the latter will orient themselves more towards the church than towards science so that the child be delivered. The connection between tribalism and Christianity is intertwined as a missionary practice that gives an array of different reactions and responses to under-standing how disabilities and learning disabilities occur.

Alteration of language and information of disabilities in pre- and post-contact

Before colonization, there was already a tradition, well-established customs, standards to follow, and languages used to better understand each other. Information on disabilities was less known, one could only trust spirituality in case of any problems in order to get out of them. Everything was limited to agriculture, breeding animals, gathering, hunting, etc. After colonization, the integration of the new language was unfortunately not yet in place. New generations were favoured because French was inserted in all the dialects and some young people could not even communicate in these. This contributed to challenges in communicating with the new national language in conjunction with tribal languages. This created learning disabilities as in 'difficulties in reading, writing, and spelling', which reflected what people would refer to as dyslexia and whether this was a true learning dis-ability or just a challenge in learning a new second or third language, it caused significant difficulties to people learning this foreign language and the rules that governed it. It is thanks to colonization that we could assess and guide people with disabilities and learn-ing disabilities in the trades. Although this is a positive point, there are many negative attributes for people with disabilities that were underlined by traditional tribal informa-tion as it related to their Christian interpretation.

It is worth noting that the Swahili language is one way that Congolese people can communicate, and this language has replaced many of the tribal languages, especially, amongst the younger people   those who learn it with French. Here is a representation of meanings for 'disability' and/or expressions in Indigenous languages and even in Swa-hili translated into French. The word disability translates to '*Mulemavu*' in Swahili and can have several other distinct designations according to the types of disabilities. For example:

- A Deaf person translates to 'Kiziwi' in Swahili
- A Blind Man translates to 'Kipofu'
- A cripple translates into Swahili 'Kilema'

Here are some nicknames in Swahili that parents, teachers, and community members use generally when referring to people with learning disabilities, such as:

- 'Kiwerewere' refers to (careless or imprudent)
- 'Mpumbavu' refers to (fool or stupid)
- 'Mjinga' refers to (idiot)

These three nicknames are used when a person is unable to learn at the same pace as the others. They are used as insults, in mockery, and as ways of humiliating and discriminating people due to their physical appearances and how they communicate. This creates a barrier to learning, integration, and community growth as people who have disabilities or learning disabilities are shunned by their communities. These word associations impact the abused to the point that these nicknames affect their mental well-being and further contribute to a form of colonialism of the mind by limiting and rejecting people, even from one's own tribe; whereas the translations of different types of disability from a Shi and Havu perspective:

- Handicap means 'chirema'
- Blind means 'empumi erhabona'
- Deaf means 'echihurha' or 'bihuli'
- Mute means 'akaduma'

Unfortunately, until now, some Elders who have not had the chance to go to school are unaware of the existence of learning disabilities, so their knowledge changes depending on the location and schooling as community members and those who choose to follow a colonial education path. According to Elder Jeanine Rushongoka, she explains that people with learning disabilities have gifts, or talents, which can be used in many ways, depending on the situation, but are often looked upon in a negative way. This was due to Belgium colonialism, which altered the original understandings of learning and physical differences. These types of diversities should be celebrated and not condemned as with other colonial approaches to education. In sharing Elder Rushongoka knowledge she has given a photo as this will honour her and allow the reader to know who the person is (Figure 19.1).

Figure 19.1 Elder Jeanine Rushongoka, January 2024.

Source: Photographer: Carine Sacerdoce Kananga, Goma, Democratic Republic of the Congo

20 Language structure or a language-based disability (dyslexia) – how natural learning contributed to being disabled

John T. Ward

Introduction

This topic of language-based disability is a way to gain insight that has eluded researchers so is not well known. The knowledge within this chapter will be comprised of oral testimonies given by Elders that I have developed relationships with, and what I have researched as well as gathered along my path towards discovering – rediscovering myself through understanding my "disabilities." By diving into the realm of traditional Indigenous knowledge, how their education is conducted, and the natural learning abilities of Indigenous children and youth provide an insightful understanding that investigates this hidden aspect of Indigenous society. By looking more closely at Indigenous learning and their natural ways of development – a look into a pre-contact viewpoint will provide a clearer understanding of the current situations faced by many Indigenous peoples, especially, those who struggle within settler-colonial schooling on and off-reserve, and in community centres.

This realization of the current educational differences faced by many Indigenous peoples is not related to some sort of abuse in system(s), but in fact has a direct connection to colonialist-enabled tactics of education, social services, and foster care programs. This reflection and realization will enable a compacity of change that will influence generations to come. Hopefully, it will change the mindset, and attitude, as well, as how teaching Indigenous people has the potential to bring change as a result of looking differently at a situation, topic, and/or outcome. This would recondition the settler-colonial mindset to allow for "thinking outside the box" or "seeing the big picture" as either of these visual aids would provide the necessary approach to diversity in knowledge and adaptive learning. It would also affect how one society views a disability, whereas, in fact, it is that same society that is disabling the natural ways that another. Indigenous society has learned and must learn as it is their natural learning process. This process of (re)learning will follow the education-as-reconciliation approach, by allowing alternate ways to learn as strengths instead of learning for just examinations or tests. Knowledge must be taught to enrich the soul, mind, body, and spirit to move forward from this lifestyle onto the next evolutionary level.

Language structure

Many children in the Indian residential school (IRS) were labelled with learning disabilities. However, a big part of the cause for this was because Indigenous languages differ so greatly from English or French. Therefore, they would absolutely have had a hard time learning the language as they had never heard or lived with it before.

DOI: 10.4324/9781032656519-24

Zúñiga (2017) bases his knowledge on the work laid out by Boas (1917) that gives a solid understanding of the linguistical structure of Native American languages as a complex interwoven structure based on a morphosyntax of lexicons and syntaxes. Boas also states that the early information on Indigenous languages and their structure was based on "missionary grammars" (p. 1). Thus, this research was heavily influenced by Latin and Greek linguistical references, as the many varieties of Indigenous languages and the types of styles were challenging to learn. These early interactions with missionaries led to many linguistical incursions, such as replacing "w" with the letter "8" as seen within some Algonquin areas that spell k8e whereas, others spell as kwe, kwei, kwey, etc. This is the basis of the language structure, which is oral and phonetic.

Apart from the Western perspective of laying out and interpreting the language structure of the Indigenous people, a deeper look is necessitated into this structure, which brings into account the insight and knowledge of the Elders. Indigenous education is a culmination of multiple teaching and learning approaches all tied into their lifestyle focused on the family, which is based on orality. Oral traditions are learned at a young age, through all the senses, and are also referred to as simultaneous, multisensory, and holistic learning processes (Alberta Education, 2005; Duin & Duin, 2015; Loeb & Redbird, 2008).

Learning at a young age gives one the ability to learn a language from a traditional standpoint (McLeod et al., 2014). It is still possible today with specialized language classes, but Indigenous languages were never meant to be learned in a colonial academic fashion. When a society depends on survival as it was for Indigenous people at the time of first contact, this life necessity depended on action-based learning, which is the foundation of their languages (Fullerton, 2021, p. 44). This did not require colourful metaphors or language with a grammatical structure (Armstrong, 2013). This doesn't mean that Indigenous languages were simple, just that there was no need to crowd a sentence or statement with unnecessary words. Indigenous languages are based on a survival context with direct words (Elder Robert St-Georges, 2023). This can be understood by saying in the Indigenous language "*we need food*," so go and get it, as opposed to English "*I am hungry; therefore, I require a most delicious meal … yada yada it was marvellous.*" When communicating for food, lengthy wordy discussion is not necessary but will only prolong the wait to obtain nourishment. This type of difference in Indigenous languages was seen as barriers to civilization. so explains how Indigenous people were considered as disabled until they could demonstrate proficiency in either English or French.

The power of knowledge how oral history reshaped my perception of language-based disabilities: an alternate perspective of language structure

Elder Robert St-Georges (2023) explains that Algonquin children who did not know their language could still think and process knowledge in an Algonquian way. This could be perceived as a reversal of a thinking process or in other words as acting like a dyslexic. Elder Annie Smith St-Georges (2023) revealed that this contributed to intergenerational trauma. Indigenous children taught in English or French in a non-Indigenous school, in an education system that did not acknowledge their differences in learning styles, in fact, will disable the students as they will not be able to learn in their natural way. This is not to say that someone who is indifferent to learning a foreign language couldn't do it, yet with the proper method they could learn a new language. Like that of Elder Annie, who revealed to top university faculty, who were all non-Indigenous White professors that

Table 20.1 Algonquin language structure with Elders Annie and Robert Smith St-Georges

Subject	Verb	Complement/Consequence	English/French
Action	Reasoning for the action	Who did the action	Algonquin
Hunting	Food because of starving	Group of hunters	Algonquin

Source: Created by John T. Ward

after six months of learning Algonquin, they would have challenges in their language structure; thereby they would be labelled as having dyslexia. This powerful statement speaks truth to a simple interpretation by the colonial elite with their PhDs, yet who would not even be able to say kwe (hello) or make a successful sentence, so they would be labelled as disabled.

The Indigenous language structures of the Americas are comprised of three categories: roots, affixes, and residuals, which enables the structure of the languages (Dixon, 2014; Zúñiga, 2017). This is represented in the differences between English and Algonquin as an example (Table 20.1):

Whereas, in English, this would be seen as "We will go hunt because our families are hungry," while placing emphasis on who shot the animal and giving them praise. The main difference between Algonquin and English or French would be the fact that colonial languages place a heavy emphasis on the detail of language structure, which is engrained within the settler-colonial education. This is still seen in the French language (France) as being able to speak and write well is seen as a superior level but having any deficits in learning is viewed as disabled.

As Elder Robert St-Georges (2023) reveals that an

Algonquin student, who may not know their traditional language will still be able to process knowledge in the same way as their oral communication because of the structure differences from an Algonquin language to that of English or French. Their non-Indigenous teachers label them as dyslexic because of the reversal of language.

Therefore, Indigenous people do have dyslexia when it comes to oral communication and cognitive thinking; however, utilizing their superior visual-spatial 3D thinking as their normal cultural trait can be seen as an ability among settlers. Yet, these types of abilities are labelled as disabilities by colonial assessments. As Elder Peter Nakoochee (2022) revealed, he had dyslexia, then, at least, the negative part of spelling difficulties was removed. This suggests that the characteristic of dyslexia of a Cree Elder was a disability upon entering the IRS because he did not know the English language, which contributed to his language difference or a challenge that led to his dyslexia as a disability. This finally became an ability due to a divine spiritual experience that removed the "dis" from the ability.

From an Indigenous perspective, language must represent something or someone, as a visual image so, as the "non-image words" in English do not create an image; therefore, they do not exist. This explains the short alphabet structure and reveals an understanding that shows how someone can learn a language with a word that has no meaning or image. More importantly, it is like describing an image of something you have never needed, heard of, or felt, which is most difficult. Therefore, images are essential for Indigenous learners as part of their learning process (Lavoie et al., 2012). The fact remains that Indigenous language structure was greatly impacted by the influence of colonialism as it caused gaps in knowledge transfer from family and community members to the children. Post-Indian residential schools have revitalized language and culture in classes, but this process is still growing and developing by adding new words that a society slowly adopts. This renewal of Indigenous languages is one that is relational and requires the engagement of all the senses, body movement, and total physical response as it is a living language (Assembly of First Nations, 2019; McDonald, 2011).

This gives insight that the Indigenous language structure is not only a valuable method for learning a society's language, but it is also

> necessary for understanding what that language gives us -- an ontological perspective that goes beyond mere words. It takes on a strong spiritual connection, central to Indigenous identity, as well as the ability to communicate without 'non-image' words such as there, it, from, that, this etc

that Western society has. A good example of non-image English words "the dog is running," whereas in an Indigenous language, it would be "dog running." This confuses those who learn differently, such as dyslexics because they do not see these "non-image" words so read over them. They are, however, able to understand a large percentage of the text.

Visual-spatial learning

This process is defined by how in the "visual learning system, the learner recognizes objects, distinguishes sizes and shapes, perceives depth, notes colour, and uses visual-spatial awareness to estimate where" they are located in a place with their surroundings (Hindal, 2014, p. 557). He goes on to explain that

> visual-spatial learners are excellent visualizers and must visualise in order to learn. The visualisation is a key element in the mental processing of visual-spatial learners. Thus, they think primarily in images or pictures. Visual thinking is very fast, complex and not sequential.
>
> (p. 557)

It is this ability to utilize our mind's eye (Marshall & Masty, 2015; West, 2020) as a way of learning and navigating a colonial mindset that has historically limited the development of differences – not disabled.

Davidson and Klich (1980) revealed that

> aboriginal children of the Western Australia desert region of Central Australia were superior to children of European origin on visual spatial memory tasks involving location of both natural and artificial objects within a two-dimensional matrix. They regarded this superiority as an outcome of the enduring survival demands of a harsh desert environment on cultural adaptation of desert adults, and consequently on their children's development, and concluded that aboriginal children of desert origin are more imbued with ability for spatial memory than other white and black Australians.
>
> (p. 569)

McCarty et al. (2018) reflect on the ability that Indigenous languages contribute towards learning the language by utilizing "images [that] allow us to visualize and conceptualize the ontological perspectives of … our ancestors transported through time and language" (p. 166) as a way of conducting cybercartography – visualizing the landscape without using maps as William Commanda Morningstar did (Taylor et al., 2019). Hutchins (1983), as described in Matusov and Hayes (2000), says the "contextualized mediated actions (e.g., mapless navigation of Micronesian navigators in open sea" (p. 236) were able to move about without getting lost, while not utilizing any type of navigation aids. Gyarmathy and Plosz (2021) reveal that

> Australian Aborigine people demonstrate a cross-cultural difference in thought that is more than a matter of style or preference. Instead of words like 'right,' 'left,' 'forward,' and 'back,' 'which, define space relative to an observer … many other Aboriginal groups use cardinal-direction terms (north, south, east, west) to define space".
>
> (n.p.)

Therefore, instead of a learning style as this article suggests, perhaps Indigenous people, providing a distinctions-based approach could interpret these cognitive methods as part of their natural development.

Cultural differences in education

Many Indigenous children and youth seem uninterested or simply bored in school, which is referred to as 'cultural dislocation' due to non-Indigenous teachers not always connecting well with their students (Finlay & Akbar, 2016). The lack of cultural awareness gives the non-Indigenous teachers challenges when trying to connect with those from different social or cultural backgrounds. This becomes a deterrent to the children's learning (Landsman & Lewis, 2011). Indigenous teachers give accounts that non-Indigenous teachers do not know their students so that they cannot stimulate them or let them fully participate, as well as the lack of cultural practices in the school curriculum or activities.

Indigenous children have historically been labelled and blamed for their learning difficulties by those in authority. Many then drop out of school because of the labels and victimization by teachers. Who would want to participate in a classroom where one is subjected to a battery of insults, comparisons, and grievances that aim to limit one's ability to overcome their challenges? The average non-Indigenous Canadian with a disability does not live in a situation that resembles a Third World country, so they have more opportunities and greater accessibility to educational funding, economic development, and social services (Wingert, 2011) than an Indigenous child does. The average Canadian child has privileges that make daily living much easier with a great assortment of opportunities accessible to them. However, they still may have a few challenges with educational services; if they have learning disabilities as not all people can access the same level of choices.

Alexander (2010) stated that Indigenous children were often removed from their families, from their culture, or from their community because of a "diagnosis" that required remediation, which is often conducted off-community within larger cities. This separation process can result in two scenarios: (1) the child, from the enormous stress, develops anxiety that can lead to multiple factors that include alcoholism, doing drugs, or even suicide because of their loss of culture, community, language and their inability to fit back into the community or the family again or (2) they adapt to the new environment and never return home as they accept the off-community as their new home in the settler-colonial school, which results in a new lifestyle. Both scenarios have drastic end results: a new lifestyle path, deep depression, becoming a forgotten lost child, or even death. Uttjek (2016), who is a Sami disability scholar, focuses "primarily on the disability or a diagnosis" as a way to understand this cultural difference (p. 8) as well as why there is a need to choose either to understand a disability and to move forward in either a remediation method or a diagnosis that includes a cultural perspective. Indigenous people with disabilities should provide a significant compacity by contributing their knowledge of understanding who they are, and where they come from to allow them to take charge of where they will go (Ward, 2023a). It is traditional knowledge systems and a spiritual connection that guides all living beings (animals, insects, etc.) on their path of learning (Deerinwater, 2021).

Learning style or natural Indigenous learning

More (1984) commented on Kaulbach's previous research on "the performance of Indian students on visual, auditory, and kinesthetic perceptual tasks" (p. 5). Most of the samples included American Indians and Inuit and drew on the outcomes of the Draw-A-Man assessment with the Illinois Test of Psycholinguistic Abilities to enhance the speculation that

> Indian and Inuit children are most successful at processing visual information and have the most difficulty performing well on tasks saturated with verbal content … [However] it is too premature to imply from these results alone that Native children are deficit in the ability to conceptualize through language.
>
> (p. 30)

Vernon (1969) found that the most highly developed abilities for Inuit students were perceptual and spatial. Bowd (1974) also discovered that Indigenous boys had well-developed visual spatial and mechanical abilities. These results apply to a unique sociocultural learning style that begins with the method of communication – orality and strength through family connections, teachings and it lasts throughout their lifetime – learning without restrictions, limits, tests, and results have conditioned Indigenous expression. Navajo students explained that classmates failed specific subjects; even though, they demonstrated a superior visual-spatial intelligence (Gentry et al., 2014). DeVries and Golon (2021) discovered that these "students represent a significant portion of the identified gifted population … more than 80% of Native American students" (p. 54). DeVries and Golon (2021) further went on to illustrate the "understanding of the preferred learning style of most Native American students – visual-spatial. When teachers and their curricula address the needs of visual-spatial learners, those who think and learn in images, education becomes more meaningful" (p. 48). By utilizing superior visual-spatial processing, ideal for the natural learning development of Indigenous peoples, it contributes to hidden talents that would, if not followed, would go unnoticed. Parrish et al. (2012) provided insight into this need that the learning styles of Native Americans must include their own cultural values, which enables them to excel.

Analysing all these pertinent areas of Indigenous education versus a colonial learning style proves whether learning disabilities are truly a disability or merely a different learning style/ability, which is normal within an Indigenous holistic environment (DeVries & Shires-Golon, 2011). Perhaps, dyslexia should not be looked at as a disability, but as actually the natural way Indigenous people learn and process knowledge. As well, some Indigenous people voiced their opinions by contributing their knowledge towards the concept of disability without referring to normalcy (King et al., 2014; Kress, 2017). Thus, a so-called disability may be part of how Indigenous people traditionally learn, but it was considered a disability because of the colonial constructs and their inability to measure, see and truly understand how different cultures and societies may have their own systems of learning. This can explain the seeming similarities between a dyslexic and an Indigenous person as just two different perspectives. However, positive attributes have been associated with dyslexia such as imagination, storytelling, communication, visual-spatial abilities, and empathy (Aderin-Pocock, 2018), which are qualities seen among Indigenous peoples. Everyone, especially, Indigenous peoples have their own learning style, which shapes their individual development (Berghs et al., 2019; Peltier et al., 2020). This is not to say that all Native Americans have dyslexic characteristics, but it shows how Indigenous people have traditionally learned by processing information visually with oral tradition as their two main methods of communication, which could be mistaken as dyslexia.

Baber (2017) shared that "Indigenous Hawaiian students… are disempowered within the public school system as a result of settler colonialism" (p. 76) and explains that "the dyslexic population, like the Indigenous Hawaiian students, challenge the well-guarded traditions of the American academic system" (p. 14). Cramblit (2013) says too, that in California, "we need the development and use of a culturally and linguistically appropriate curriculum across the board" (p. 138) because the current approach of federal authorities in providing education to Native Americans "is just like a band-aid…. It gives them a little boost, but they can't read and write. Really, like, what are we? It's kind of like wasting our time" (p. 105). This can also be said for Canada. Lavoie et al. (2012) reflect that "as communities change, the teaching and learning process needs to be enriched by the multiplicity of cultures and linguistic backgrounds that learners bring into the classroom" (p. 196). This suggests that the colonial education system fails to adequately address the ways Indigenous children learn. This inability of non-Indigenous teachers and professionals to recognize that the Indigenous way of processing knowledge (learning) is different, may lead to the labelling of learning disabilities – disabled, which in fact may be the natural learning approach of Indigenous people (Stein et al., 2021).

By including an Indigenous curriculum, inclusive education would allow for the acceptance of certain cultural contexts that would benefit the student by accelerating their ability to learn and participate fully so they would feel and know their knowledge is accepted by honouring their natural learning abilities (Fillerup, 2011; Miles & Singal, 2010). This would also involve the behaviour of the teacher, who must assume respect for all students and not misinterpret a situation so judge a student's inability to respond, their being quiet or looking down as non-verbal communication or ignorance. In certain Indigenous cultures, this is a respectful gesture to authority, which can be easily misinterpreted (McCarthy et al., 2006). These cultural distinctions acknowledged would reflect a courteous interpersonal connection between teachers and students that must be understood to prevent miscommunication (Adams et al., 2014; Reo et al., 2017). Ford and Sassi (2014) explain that "race influenced classroom authority relationships would render cultural incongruence inconsequential, [and] invalidate the particular challenges that teachers and students face in classrooms characterized by racial difference" (p. 42). Any misperceptions such as these can lead to a deficit in talent development, which could result in isolation and even lead to distrust in settler-colonial education (Gentry et al., 2014).

Whereas, unfortunately, the ability to read quickly and effortlessly, with a good understanding is considered an indispensable asset today when performing independently, professionally, or academically as part of society (Conefrey, 2021). We have looked at a wide-ranging study of disabilities, learning disabilities as well as dyslexia from a two-eyed seeing approach – from both Indigenous and Western perspectives. Therefore, it can be ascertained that there is an ongoing divide between these two sets of knowledge regarding disability, with their many differences that do not seem able to meet. We further introduced Indigenous knowledge/beliefs, labelling disability, dyslexia, and other key factors to comprehend their impact on Indigenous children. We may, perhaps, begin to see that there is a greater percentage of dyslexia in society, but the methods of assessing it to determine actual numbers are not feasible. Thus, there may be many Indigenous people who do not have dyslexia, but struggle with reading or spelling, and may have some of the talents or abilities that are characteristic of dyslexia, or these might not be as visible to others as those who struggle with it fully.

Dyslexia connection to Indigenous peoples

This is why Indigenous children would best learn within a settler-colonial education by utilizing their strengths in the visual-spatial realm. Therefore, implanting a curriculum that is based on a multi-sensory, visual-spatial learning approach would strengthen the Indigenous students' natural learning style. Several educational programs exist that can stimulate a healthy cognitive development, when using settler-colonial written and readable text, which is not a method traditional to Indigenous peoples. Many of these programs were originally designed to help dyslexic people learn to read and write.

Dyslexia, a genetic and hereditary trait that can be passed on to offspring and among close-knit families, could become more prevalent among cultures that intermix or stay within close familiar connections (Kadry, 2019). Sachemspeaks (2012) explains that

> There are a good strong handful of ways of knowing that you have Native American Blood. One of them is the fact that we tend to be dyslexic, how dyslexic depends on the amount of native genes (Indigenous blood) we have.
>
> (para 1–2)

He goes on to say that "dyslexia in a native is the hard time our minds seem to [have] agreeing with the English language" (para 4). This realization could be more than what one person has released, as there can be cultural markers to indicate the possible similarities to dyslexia or at least the characteristics of dyslexia. How this came to be could be seen in two points: (1) the way Indigenous people process information, which was primarily and, in some places, entirely based on orality with a very limited usage of written text and (2) the cultural indoctrination during the IRS that aimed to reprogram how Indigenous children looked, acted, and learned in a foreign language with customs and beliefs that were entirely alien. It could even be an accumulation of both, if not more. This change in natural learning developed during the infamous IRS in which many teachers were poorly qualified (Barnes et al., 2006; Booth, 2009) but taught the Indigenous students to learn, think, process information, dress, act, and behave as White Christian people and not as "dirty, dumb savages."

Disability and labelling contribute to suicide

Suicide was a concept introduced by colonialism because natural societies value life and even value those who may be "labelled" and "deemed" as different (disabled) (Ross et al., 2015). Suicide stems from a series of untenable mental and physical abuses compounded by a systemic scale of attacks (Fuller-Thomson et al., 2012). Dionne (2008) explains how the outcomes of an abusive IRS educational environment provided the basis for traumas but could have been different. Dionne and Nixon (2014) share what has happened beyond the Residential School in the lives of the people, and how bullying continues within schools now. Further to this, are attitudes that are not natural that spawn children who take their own lives. The primary underlying cause is a child's having been labelled with a learning disability, unceasing teacher bullying, as well as physical or mental abuse, which all negatively impact the self-esteem of a child, who is already disadvantaged because of governmental policies, which limit Indigenous abilities.

Another common belief is that the infamous IRS had a significant negative impact on children, so it was a contributing factor to later Indigenous suicide (Elias et al., 2012). This is backed by the Canadian Council of Children and Youth Advocates (CCCYA, 2019). Elias and al state something similar:

> It has been theorized that suicide behaviours amongst Indigenous peoples may be an outcome of the mass trauma experienced as a result of colonization… qualitative evidence has suggested that the Indian Residential School System set in motion a cycle of trauma, with some survivors reporting subsequent abuse, suicide, and other related behaviours. It has been further postulated that the effects of trauma can also be passed intergenerationally. Today, there are First Nations residential school survivors, who may have transmitted the trauma they experienced to their own children and grandchildren.
>
> (Elias et al., 2012, p. 1560)

McBride and Siegel (1997) give compelling data on the spin-off of trauma suffered by Indigenous children labelled with learning disabilities. This can be linked to derogatory, social interactions, and stigmatization by teachers, who were entrusted with authority. All this can lead to later suicides. Angelakis et al. (2019) stated that "childhood abuse was associated with a particularly high risk for suicide attempts in adults" (p. 1057). This can explain the high disproportionate rate with those who struggle with disabilities, many of whom fall through the economic, social, and school cracks. Finlay and Nagy (2011) of the Pikangikum First Nation in Ontario reflected how suicide rates are five to seven times greater with Indigenous youth. As well, Imrie (2008) of the Office of Inuit Health for Health Canada and Harder et al. (2012) with the Indigenous Youth in Canada presented statistics on suicide that reflect that Indigenous suicide rates are roughly 3–36 times greater than non-Indigenous people, with the greatest occurrence among youth (Harder et al., 2012; Imrie, 2008). Anaya (2014b) indicates that suicide rates for First Nations youth who reside on reserves are five to six times greater than the national average.

High suicide rates have been considered as a major concern among Indigenous peoples (AFN, 2012), especially in northern Canada. Tjepkema et al. (2009) also stated that suicide is the primary cause of death among Indigenous peoples with disabilities in Canada. This depends on the area, community, and on the range of issues that change from one place to another (Pollock, 2016). First Nations, Inuit, and Métis have unequal rates of suicide compared to the rates of the national non-Indigenous (Canadian population) (Inuit Tapiriit Kanatami, 2016; Minh et al., 2013; Pollock et al., 2016). It has been argued that Indigenous people face a higher rate of disabilities and learning disabilities for several reasons such as an abundance of wide gaps in their basic living, education, and social, economic, health, and the judiciary systems not including racism and the impact of colonialism (Anaya, 2014a; NIEDB, 2019). Linda Siegel's research covered results from the effects of prolonged labelling and abusive language towards students with learning disabilities such as dyslexia. She referenced publications including McBride and Siegel (1997) and Siegel (2000) that analysed how traumatic events such as abusive language dehumanizes children and youth. She revealed that her research conducted on the streets of Toronto showed it was evident that there was a high representation of Indigenous homeless people, who were suspected of being a high risk (for suicide) probably due to the traumas of Residential Schools. Her research could set a precedent of how labels and abuse by teachers could be a factor for homelessness, incarceration, and possible suicide. Her insight and follow-up can provide possible answers and closure to families (Offet-Gartner, 2011; Radkowsky & Siegel, 1997). All this engenders kids with disabilities who fall through the cracks of the education system (Smylie et al., 2009).

Therefore, feelings of hopelessness can permeate their lives and may eventually lead to suicide if not addressed. The CCCYA (2019) explains that in "British Columbia, youth indicated the fear of stigma and labelling" (p. 17) as these have such a negative impact, which often plagued [already] troubled youth due to insecurities and past trauma (p. 21). Therefore, enhancing the well-being of Indigenous youth is of utmost importance to stop suicide (Ansloos, 2018). Therefore, a need exists for kids to participate in family and cultural activities – community engagement is critical among Indigenous worldviews to achieve a good quality of life and to sustain and nourish health stability (Cross et al., 2019; Fuentes & Lent, 2019). The parents must be involved.

Conclusion

Following the end of the IRS, and its settler-colonial education approach to learning, there was a push towards revitalizing the Indigenous language and culture within the post-colonial drive of decolonizing how Indigenous people "ought to" learn (Carlson, 2016; de Leeuw et al., 2013). These alternative curriculum with traditional teaching approaches provided the ideal learning environment that adapted for harvest, hunting, fishing, and sociocultural and spiritual practices of the Indigenous students, which was an essential aspect of their lifestyle as it was a strength.

It is a national and global shame that Indigenous peoples, as well as our knowledge and belief systems, are not utilized to contribute to areas such as education, environment, or climate change as we are the original stewards of the land and had we been part of the process for change, perhaps we would be living in a much better, cleaner, safer, and enjoyable planet. Just recently, Indigenous people have been asked and included in discussions in these areas and much can still be learned as a disability, which is often understood as abilities. By including different cultural perspectives, the knowledge systems of disabilities will be changed as a growing and transformative experience. Much of this forward thinking is needed in the 21st century the only difference is that the colonial mindset is stuck in the 20th century.

We all have our own abilities, talents, and superpowers – what are yours?

References

Adams, M., Carpenter, J., Housty, J. A., Neasloss, D., Paquet, P. C., Service, C. N., Walkus, J. and Darimont, C. T. (2014). Towards increased engagement between academic and Indigenous community partners in ecological research. *Ecology and Society*, 19(3), 5–15.

Aderin-Pocock, M. (2018). Doi: #MadeByDyslexia from Facebook. January 15, 2019.

Alberta Education. (2005). *Our words, our ways: Teaching First Nations, Métis and Inuit learners.* Edmonton, AB: Alberta Learning and Teaching Resources Branch (pp. 123–149).

Alexander, B. (2010). *The globalization of addiction: A study in poverty of the spirit.* USA: Oxford, UK: Oxford University Press.

Anaya, J. (2014a). *Report of the special rapporteur on the rights of Indigenous peoples.* New York City, NY: United Nations Press.

Anaya, J. (2014b). *The situation of Indigenous people in Canada* (pp. 1–22). New York, NY: United Nations Human Rights Council.

Angelakis, I., Gillespie, E. and Panagioti, M. (2019). Childhood maltreatment and adult suicidality: A comprehensive systematic review with meta-analysis. *Psychological Medicine*, 49(7), 1057–1078.

Ansloos, J. (2018). Rethinking Indigenous suicide. *International Journal of Indigenous Health*, 13(2), 8–28.

Armstrong, A. (2013). Star Trek: The original films. *The Objective Standard*, 8(3), 84–110.

Assembly of First Nations. (2012). *Assembly of First Nations education, jurisdiction, and governance: Cultural competency report, final report.* March 31, 2012.

Baber, C. (2017). *Unraveling dyslexia: The medicalization of learning differences as a form of structural violence in the American education system.* Master of Arts in the Department of Cultural and Social Studies. Omaha, NE: Creighton University.

Barnes, R., Josefowitz, N. and Cole, E. (2006). Residential schools: Impact on Aboriginal students' academic and cognitive development. *Canadian Journal of School Psychology*, 21(1–2), 18–32.

Berghs, M., Atkin, K., Hatton, C. and Thomas, C. (2019). Do disabled people need a stronger social model: A social model of human rights? *Disability & Society*, 34(7–8), 1034–1039.

Boas, F. (1917). Introductory. *International Journal of American Linguistics*, 1(1), 1–8.

Booth, T. T. (2009). *Cheaper than bullets: American Indian boarding schools and assimilation policy, 1890–1930.* In Images, Imaginations, and Beyond: Proceedings of the Eighth Native American Symposium, South-eastern Oklahoma State University (pp. 46–56).

Bowd, A. D. (1974). Practical abilities of Indians and Eskimos. *Canadian Psychologist*, 15(3), 281–290.

Canadian Council of Children and Youth Advocates. (2019). *Canadian council of child & youth advocates: A national paper on youth suicide.* Ottawa, ON: CCCYA Press.

Carlson, E. (2016). Anti-colonial methodologies and practices for settler colonial studies. *Settler Colonial Studies*. Doi: 10.1080/2201473X.2016.1241213.

Conefrey, T. (2021). Supporting first-generation students' adjustment to college with high- impact practices. *Journal of College Student Retention: Research, Theory & Practice*, 23(1), 139–160.

Cramblit, A. (2013). Overview of American Indian education in NW California. Karuk, Northern California Indian Development Council. In J. Silverman (Ed.), *U.S. Department of education tribal consultations and listening sessions.* Smith River, CA.

Cross, T. L., Pewewardy, C. and Smith, A. T. (2019). Restorative education, reconciliation, and healing: Indigenous perspectives on decolonizing leadership education. *New Directions for Student Leadership*, 2019(163), 101–115.

Davidson, G. R. and Klich, L. Z. (1980). Cultural factors in the development of temporal and spatial ordering. *Child Development*, 51(2), 569–571.

de Leeuw, S., Greenwood, M. and Lindsay, N. (2013). Troubling good intentions. *Settler Colonial Studies*, 3(3–4), 381–394.

Deerinwater, J. (2021). Colonial forces of environmental violence on Deaf, disabled, & ill Indigenous people. *Disability Studies Quarterly, 41*(4). Doi: https://dsq-sds.org/index.php/dsq/article/view/8479.

DeVries, M., & Golon, A. S. (2021). Making education relevant for gifted Native Americans: Teaching to their learning style. In J. A. Castellano & A. D. Frazier (Eds.), *Special Populations in Gifted Education* (pp. 47–72). Waco, TX: Prufrock.

DeVries, M. and Shires-Golon, A. (2011). Making education relevant for gifted Native Americans: Teaching to their learning style. In J. A. Castellano & A. Frazier (Eds.), *Special populations in gifted education: Understanding our most able students from diverse backgrounds* (pp. 47–72). Waco, TX: Prufrock Press.

Dionne, D. (2008). *Recovery in the residential school abuse aftermath: A new healing paradigm.* Lethbridge, AB: University of Lethbridge.

Dionne, D., & Nixon, G. (2014). Moving beyond residential school trauma abuse: A phenomenological hermeneutic analysis. *International Journal of Mental Health and Addiction, 12,* 335–350.

Dixon, R. M. W. (2014). *Making new words: Morphological derivation in English.* Oxford: Oxford University Press.

Duin, S. and Duin, R. S. (2015). The life Elixir of Amazonian societies in a multi-sensory museum exhibition. *Tipití: Journal of the Society for the Anthropology of Lowland South America, 13*(2), Article 12, 162–177.

Elias, B., Mignone, J., Hall, M., Hong, S. P. and Hart, L. (2012). Trauma and suicide behaviour histories among a Canadian Indigenous population: An empirical exploration of the potential role of Canada's residential school system. *Social Science & Medicine, 74,* 1560–1569.

Fillerup, M. (2011). Building a "bridge of beauty": A preliminary report on promising practices in Native language and culture teaching at Puente de Hózhǫ Trilingual Magnet School. In M. E. Romero-Little, S. J. Ortiz, T. L. McCarty, & R. Chen (Eds.). *Indigenous languages across the generations—Strengthening families and communities* (pp. 145–164). Tempe, AZ: Arizona State University Center for Indian Education.

Finlay, J., & Akbar, L. (2016). Caught between two worlds. *Canadian Journal of Children's Rights, 3*(1), 68–99.

Finlay, J. F. and Nagy, A. (2011). *Pikangikum: Root causes of suicide in a remote First Nation.* Toronto, ON: Office of the Chief Coroner.

Ford, A. C. and Sassi, K. (2014). Authority in cross-racial teaching and learning (re)considering the transferability of warm demander approaches. *Urban Education, 49*(1), 39–74.

Fuentes, M. and Lent, K. (2019). Culture, health, function, and participation among American Indian and Alaska native children and youth with disabilities: An exploratory qualitative analysis. *Archives of Physical Medicine and Rehabilitation, 100*(9), 1688–1694.

Fuller-Thomson, E., Baker, T. M. and Brennenstuhl, S. (2012). Evidence supporting an independent association between childhood physical abuse and lifetime suicidal ideation. *Suicide and Life-Threatening Behavior, 42,* 279–291.

Fullerton, S. (2021). Indigenous education: Land as text. *BU Journal of Graduate Studies in Education, 13*(2), 43–46.

Gentry, M., Fugate, M., Wu, J. and Castellano, J. A. (2014). Gifted Native American students: Literature, lessons, and future directions. *Gifted Child Quarterly, 58*(2), 98–110.

Gyarmathy, É. and Plosz, J. (2021). Atypical development spectra considering the hunter-breeder culture transition -Spectra of the atypical neural development. Doi: 10.31219/osf.io/k2tfx.

Harder, H., Rash, J., Holyk, T., Jovel, E. and Harder, K. (2012). Indigenous youth suicide: A systematic review of the literature. *Pimatisiwin: A Journal of Aboriginal and Indigenous Community Health, 10*(1), 125–142.

Hindal, H. S. (2014). Visual-spatial learning: A characteristic of gifted students. *European Scientific Journal, 10*(13), 557–574.

Hutchins, E. (1983). *Understanding Micronesian navigation.* In D. Gentner & A. Stevens (Eds.), *Mental models* (pp. 191–225). Hillsdale, NJ: Lawrence Erlbaum.

Inuit Tapiriit Kanatami. (2016). *National inuit suicide prevention strategy*. Doi: https://www.itk. ca/wp-content/uploads/2016/07/ITK-National-Inuit-Suicide-Prevention-Strategy-2016.pdf. Accessed on July 27, 2020.

Imrie, B. (2008). Letter to the editor. *Journal of Child and Adolescent Psychiatric Nursing, 21*(3), 125.

Kadry, O. (2019). The high degree of dyslexia amongst Indigenous people in Alexandrian. Personal communication. Alexandrian, Egypt.

Kaulbach, B. (1984). Styles of learning among Native children: Review of the research. *Canadian Journal of Native Education, 11*(3), 27–37.

King, J. A., Brough, M. and Knox, M. (2014). Negotiating disability and colonization: The lived experiences of Indigenous Australians with a disability. *Disability & Society, 29*(5), 738–750.

Kress, M. M. (2017). Reclaiming disability through Pimatisiwin: Indigenous ethics, spatial justice, and gentle teaching. *Ethics, Equity, and Inclusive Education (International Perspectives on Inclusive Education* (vol. 9, pp. 23–57). Emerald Publishing Limited. https://doi.org/10.1108/ S1479-363620170000009002.

Landsman, J. G. and Lewis, C. W. (2011). *White teachers, diverse classrooms: Creating inclusive schools, building on students' diversity, and providing true educational equity* (2nd Ed.). Sterling, VA: Stylus Pub.

Lavoie, C., Sarkar, M., Mark, M. and Jenniss, B. (2012). Multiliteracies pedagogy in language teaching: An example from an Innu community in Québec. *Canadian Journal of Native Education, 35*(1), 194–210.

Loeb, D. F., & Redbird, K. (2008). Fostering the literacy of Indigenous elementary school-age children. *Perspectives on Communication Disorders and Sciences in Culturally and Linguistically Diverse (CLD) Populations, 15*(1), 5–11.

Marshall, S. and Masty, E. (2015). *Mind's eye: Stories from Whapmagoostui*. Whapmagoostui, QC: Aanischaaukamikw Cree Cultural Institute.

Matusov, E. and Hayes, R. (2000). Sociocultural critique of Piaget and Vygotsky. *New Ideas in Psychology, 18*, 215–239.

McBride, H. E. A. and Siegel, L. S. (1997). Learning disabilities and adolescent suicide. *Journal of Learning Disabilities, 30*(6), 652–659.

McCarthy, A., Lee, K., Itakura, S. and Muir, D.W. (2006). Cultural display rules drive eye gaze during thinking. *Journal of Cross-Cultural Psychology, 37*(6), 717–722.

McCarty, T. L., Nicholas, S. E., Chew, K. A. B., Diaz, N. G., Leonard, W. Y. and White, L. (2018). Hear our languages, hear our voices: Storywork as theory and praxis in Indigenous-language reclamation. *American Academy of Arts & Sciences, 147*(2), 160–172.

McDonald, R.-A. J. (2011). *Assembly of First Nations: First Nations languages and culture impacts on literacy and student achievement outcomes review of literature*. Katenies Research and Management Services Akwesasne Mohawk Territory. April 5, 2011.

McLeod, S., Verdon, S. and Kneebone, L. B. (2014). Celebrating young Indigenous Australian children's speech and language competence. *Early Childhood Research Quarterly, 29*(2), 118–131.

Miles, S. and Singal, N. (2010) The education for all and inclusive education debate: Conflict, contradiction or opportunity? *International Journal of Inclusive Education, 14*(1), 1–15.

Minh, T. D., Fréchette, M., McFaull, S., Denning, B., Ruta, M. and Thompson, W. (2013). Injuries in the North – analysis of 20 years of surveillance data collected by the Canadian Hospitals Injury Reporting and Prevention Program. *International Journal of Circumpolar Health, 72*(1), 1–6.

More, A. J. (1984). Learning styles and Indian students: A review of research. Paper presented at the Mokakit Indian Education Research Conference. London, ON.

National Indigenous Economic Development Board. (2019). *The Indigenous economic progress report*. Gatineau, QC: The Queen's Press.

Offet-Gartner, K. (2011). Rewriting herstory: Aboriginal women reclaim education as a tool for personal and community, health and well-being. *Procedia - Social and Behavioral Sciences, 30*, 1499–1506.

Parrish, M. S., Klem, J. L. and Brown, D. R. (2012). Diversity in learning: A comparison of traditional learning theories with learning styles and cultural values of Native American students. *Ideas and Research You Can Use: VISTAS Article, 45,* 2–7.

Peltier, T. K., Heddy, B. C. and Peltier, C. (2020). Using conceptual change theory to help preservice teachers understand dyslexia. *Annuals of Dyslexia, 70*(1), 62–78.

Pollock, N. J., Mulay, S., Valcour, J. and Jong, M. (2016). Suicide rates in Aboriginal communities in Labrador, Canada. *American Journal of Public Health, 106*(7), 1309–1315.

Radkowsky, M. and Siegel, L. J. (1997). The gay adolescent: Stressors, adaptations, and psychosocial interventions. *Clinical Psychology Review, 17*(2), 191–216.

Reo, N. J., Whyte, K. P., McGregor, D., Smith, M. A. and Jenkins, J. F. (2017). Factors that support Indigenous involvement in multi-actor environmental stewardship. *AlterNative: An International Journal of Indigenous Peoples, 13*(2), 58–68.

Ross, A., Dion, J., Cantinotti, M., Collin-Vézina, D. and Paquette, L. (2015). Impact of residential schooling and of child abuse on substance use problem in Indigenous peoples. *Addiction Behaviour, 51,* 184–192.

Sachemspeaks. (2012). Dyslexia in Native Americans? Doi: https://sachemspeaks.wordpress.com/2012/12/08/dyslexia-in-native-americans/?blogsub=subscribed#subscribe-blog.

Siegel, L. S. (2000). Adolescent suicide and learning disabilities: A causal connection? *Lifenotes: A Suicide Prevention and Community Health Newsletter, 5*(2), 8–9.

Smylie, J., Kaplan-Myrth, N., McShane, K., Métis Nation of Ontario-Ottawa Council, Pikwakanagan First Nation and Tungasuvvingat Inuit Family Resource Centre. (2009). Indigenous knowledge translation: Baseline findings in a qualitative study of the pathways of health knowledge in three Indigenous communities in Canada. *Health Promotion Practice, 10*(3), 436–446.

Stein, S., Ahenakew, C., Jimmy, E., Andreotti, V., Valley, W., Amsler, S. and Calhoun, B. (2021). Developing stamina for decolonizing higher education: A workbook for non- Indigenous people. Version 2.2 – March 2021 (Working Draft).

Taylor, D. F., Anonby, E. and Murasugi, K. (2019). *Further developments in the theory and practice of cybercartography: International dimensions and language mapping* (3rd Ed.). Cambridge, MA: Elsevier.

Tjepkema, M., Wilkins, R., Senécal, S., Guimond, É. and Penney, C. (2009). Mortality of Métis and registered Indian adults in Canada: An 11-year follow-up study. *Health Reports, 20*(4), 1–21.

Uttjek, M. (2016). Living conditions among Sa´Mis with disabilities in Sweden. Project report. [Levnadsförhållanden bland samer med funktionsnedsättning i Sverige. Projektrapport.]. Stockholm: Nordens Välfärdscenter.

Vernon, P. E. (1969). *Intelligence and cultural environment.* London, UK: Methuen and Company.

Ward, J.T. (2023). Nòswàhanà-n Wìsakedjàk of Indigenous Elders' knowledge of disabilities, learning disabilities, and dyslexia through the lens of Indigenous disability methodologies. Ottawa, ON: University of Ottawa Press. (PhD).

West, T. G. (2020). *In the mind's eye: Creative visual thinkers, gifted dyslexics, and the rise of visual technologies.* (3rd Ed.). Guilford, CN: Prometheus Books.

Wingert, S. (2011). The social distribution of distress and well-being in the Canadian Aboriginal population living off reserve. *International Indigenous Policy Journal, 2*(1), 1–24.

Zúñiga, F. (2017). On the morphosyntax of Indigenous languages of the Americas. *International Journal of American Linguistics, 83*(1), 111–139.

Part IV

Challenging colonial authority – Infusing regional ideals and concepts

The chapters in Part IV provide an indebted approach towards understanding the complexity of colonialism and through various avenues illustrate this foreign influence and the consequences of changing the mindset of those who have been labelled as disabled. The authors represented here originate from the United States, Taiwan, Mexico, Indonesia, Pakistan, and Canada who have brought specific knowledge systems to reflect their own perspectives.

Barriers to learning

The knowledge presented by these authors in the area of educational barriers provides an insightful perspective that can shape many of the current situations faced by Indigenous peoples who struggle with their learning differences – learning styles or disabilities as depicted by settler-colonial educators. However, one must understand that there are alternative views to physical and cognitive differences beyond the settler-colonial model of deficit, by looking beyond the 'dis' we can see the 'abilities', which removes the barrier to learning. By breaking the barriers to learning, we can allow for the healing of those who have been most impacted by the segregation in schools because of policies and beliefs that separate students, many of whom are Indigenous children who learn and process information differently. These authors channel their efforts by revealing how students with disabilities are separated and often excluded from a communal approach to learning due to the colonial influence of educational practices and policies, which would have differed from their own Indigenous pre-contact experiences.

Colonial mindset

These chapters show in what the authors have shared a common thread of how colonialism has impacted their natural learning abilities to the point that it influenced their learning process, which could sum up the impact of the colonial mindset. The colonial mindset speaks heavily to the impact of labels, classifications, and the change of language from 'dis' to ability. Also, how one system of learning (traditional teachings) has been branded as backwards and in some places as savage, yet this form of education has endured since the dawn of time. There is particular application that can be learned from traditional education such as grassroots as seen in Part V as this accumulation can provide a positive outcome to learning that is meant to be a safe space unlike what the Elders in Part I revealed during their struggles in the forced residential school system.

DOI: 10.4324/9781032656519-25

There is a need to push aside this colonial mindset based on a European superiority complex as the only way to learn – through a White-settler approach, which has proven time again and again with the authors to be not the only way. We must seek out alternative methods of learning by infusing traditional knowledge and belief systems that can incorporate Indigenous ways of learning, but also by understanding that everyone learns in a different way. We are all unique and have special gifts and talents, even if not recognized by settler-colonial teachers or professors, they are there.

21 Disability support for Indigenous people
The Sweetgrass Method

Mark Standing Eagle Baez and Thomas Dirth

Disability is an essential expression of human diversity, and we should expect school communities to include and uplift those diverse experiences. According to the Individuals with Disabilities Educations Act, 45 C.F.R. Sec 300.8 (2018),

> A child with a disability means a child evaluated by §300.304 through 300.311 as having an intellectual disability, a hearing impairment (including deafness), a speech or language impairment, a visual impairment (including blindness), a serious emotional disturbance (referred to in this part as "emotional disturbance"), an orthopedic impairment, autism, traumatic brain injury, another health impairment, a specific learning disability, deaf-blindness, or multiple disabilities, and who, by reason thereof, needs special education and related services.

It is essential to know that bringing students (with/without disabilities) together to achieve optimal education outcomes to the greatest extent possible motivates efforts from multiple parties: students, parents and caregivers, school psychologists, teachers, administrators, and even the broader community. Of critical importance to support professionals in meeting disability education policy demands in a culturally informed matter is both a culturally responsive framework for working with Indigenous students and families and a conceptualization of disability that complements a culturally responsive framework. We propose The Sweetgrass Method (SGM) as an extant culturally responsive framework for practitioners working with Indigenous clients, as seen below (Baez, 2011, 2023; Baez et al., 2022). The SGM provides a framework by weaving three strands: (1) Introspection: A commitment to self-reflection (life-long practice to self-evaluation and self-critique on prevention/intervention supports), (2) Communication: A commitment to building relationships/partnerships with people and groups to address mental health concerns, and (3) Continuity: Ongoing supports/strategies towards power inequality and client support strategies towards a successful outcome (Baez, 2023).

To effectively bridge disability in the educational context to SGM we outline alternative conceptualizations of disability that push back against overly narrow medicalized definitions that pathologize and stigmatize (Dirth & Branscombe, 2017) and instead weave critical disability perspectives (Dirth & Adams, 2019) with Indigenous ways of knowing and evidence-based practices. For instance, we recommend integrating an affirmative orientation to disability (Swain & French, 2000) so that more consideration can be paid to the strengths and potential of a child with a disability rather than deficits needing fixing. By challenging "ableism" found in the Individualized Education Program (IEP) process, professionals can rethink taken-for-granted assumptions about learning

DOI: 10.4324/9781032656519-26

as an individualistic endeavor and reconnect the learning process to an interdependent community endeavor. In so doing, educational professionals will be better positioned to engage in introspection, communication, and continuity to benefit the students and families they serve.

Introduction

People with disabilities constitute one of the largest minority groups in the United States, comprising around 25% of the U.S. population (Centers for Disease Control, 2023). Disabled people also experience disparities across social domains ranging from health (Krahn et al., 2015) to socioeconomic status, employment (Friedman, 2020), and level of education (Erickson et al., 2015). Such ongoing disparities suggest there continue to be social, architectural, and policy barriers that people with disabilities face. In the case of education, these barriers can start at a very early age.

When children struggle in school or have identified disabilities, parents and caregivers often confront additional challenges to ensure their children receive the necessary support to meet their needs. One of these challenges is navigating the complicated world of special education. According to the Individuals with Disabilities Education Act (IDEA) of 2018, children with disabilities are entitled to a free appropriate public education (FAPE) to meet their unique needs. To accomplish this, every student who receives special education services in schools is entitled to an IEP. An IEP is a document that describes the programs, services, and goals tailored to the unique needs of each special-education student. All educators must adhere to the education program set forth by the IEP.

Unfortunately, students from racially and ethnically minoritized backgrounds, students who experience low-income and economic marginalization, and English language learners are all more likely to be inappropriately identified as having a disability (Sullivan, 2011; Sullivan & Bal, 2013) and less likely to be provided with the appropriate supports when they are diagnosed with a disability (Losen et al., 2015). Similarly, research indicates that *underdiagnosis* and *delayed* diagnoses in racial/ethnic minority students can be just as damaging in the educational trajectories of these students (Mandell et al., 2009). Therefore, equitable assessment of students from these backgrounds requires particular expertise. Professionals involved in eligibility determination must understand the implications of culture and language, demonstrate awareness of their biases and expertise regarding disability and culture, and seek consultation with more experienced colleagues when necessary.

American Indian/Alaska Native (AI/AN) people also face disability at a rate higher than other groups. The Centers for Disease Control (CDC) and Prevention found that AI/AN people are 50.3% more likely to have a disability than the national average (CDC, 2008). A large study of individual-level data on individuals 55 and older examined the prevalence rates of functional limitation, mobility disability, and self-care disability. It found that AI/AN people had the highest prevalence rates of functional limitations compared to African Americans or Whites and higher rates of all three disability types than Whites (Goins et al., 2007). However, the lens of health equity is impacted in significant ways for the AI/AN community due to the historical trauma experienced.

Additionally, health equity considerations must also include considerations of the support people many individuals with Intellectual Developmental Disability (IDD) have in their lives. AI/AN families consciously or unconsciously frame concerns related to disability through the cultural lens of their tribal society and the framework of the larger majority culture. Within this bicultural world, some values and norms of the Indian and White worlds are complementary, but others may conflict. Most conflicts, however, do not reach the stage where the family refuses outside help or resources for a child with disabilities. However, some can adversely affect a treatment plan because the family may still try to understand the disability within their cultural framework and seek help from tribal healers. Because the family's priority is to seek assistance within their own culture, this AI/AN family may appear to service providers as disinterested or not caring because they are not aggressively seeking modern remedies or resources as other families in similar situations might.

Disabilities and the context of disability for AI/AN youth

AI/AN students are narrowly over-represented in the special education population percentage (U.S. Department of Education, 2023; Figure 21.1). Most AI/AN children are educated through the public school systems in each state rather than schools run by the Federal Bureau of Indian Education (BIE). According to the National Association of State Directors of Special Education, 21% of AI/AN students in BIE-operated and funded schools are enrolled in special education compared to 13% of all U.S. public school students (Müller & Markowitz, 2004).

> Challenges related to disability are compounded by the fact that 58% of BIA (Bureau of Indian Affairs) educated students have limited English proficiency (LEP) as compared with 8% of public-school students. Approximately 80% of BIA-educated students can receive free or reduced-price lunches as compared with 40% of public-school students.
>
> (Müller & Markowitz, 2004, p. 4)

AI/AN students in special education programs have the highest dropout rate, the lowest academic achievement levels, and the lowest school attendance in the U.S. (Rampey et al., 2019). They are also at greater risk for mental health problems, suicide, drug and alcohol abuse, and involvement in the juvenile justice system (Gion et al., 2014). These outcomes are attributed to a variety of causes, such as lack of support from parents and family members, poor academic skills, poor student–teacher relationships, lack of a sense of belonging in schools, linguistic and cultural barriers, low expectations, and student transfer and mobility (Reyhner, 2010; Sarche & Spicer, 2008).

Figure 21.1 The Sweetgrass Method, 2023.

Source: Photographer: By Mark Standing Eagle Baez

The challenges for AI/AN students with disabilities are further complicated by culture and history, especially the legacy of colonial schools. Colonial schools became models for public education today, schools that center narratives that enable and even promote othering, oppression, and exploitation. Today's public education highlights individuality and competition over communal understandings, rationality and advancement over care, and separation from nature over networks of rooted relations (McCoy et al., 2020). Jointly, these methods teach children to view the land as a temporal and inactive set of sources constructed for human-entitled use and financial gain. These Western models have interrupted (but not destroyed) Indigenous practices of survival and knowledge transmission—our responsibilities to one another. Our embedded ways of learning, together with each other, continue to nourish and sustain us and, we believe, offer a more generative education model for all children.

As practitioners, we believe that to be in the right relationship, we must consider the services we offer our AI/AN clients. Recognizing cultural differences and incorporating cultural humility in service delivery is essential. Indigenous societies have long practiced indigenous ways of knowing, incorporating cultural-based, intergenerational, and applied learning strategies that have helped the next generation understand the meaning of living all living beings. These systems of education that have helped children learn the full spectrum of what it means to be human and take care of one another have been interrupted by colonial education models (McCoy et al., 2020; Table 21.1).

Table 21.1 Overview of IDEA school year 2021–2022

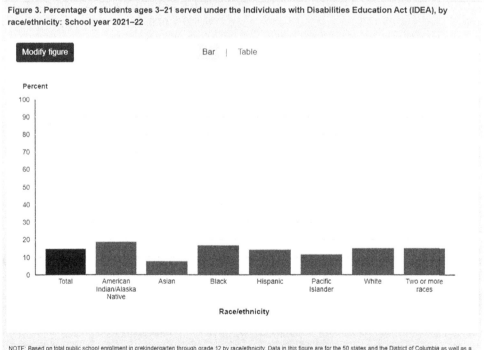

Figure 3. Percentage of students ages 3–21 served under the Individuals with Disabilities Education Act (IDEA), by race/ethnicity: School year 2021–22

NOTE: Based on total public school enrollment in prekindergarten through grade 12 by race/ethnicity. Data in this figure are for the 50 states and the District of Columbia as well as a small (but unknown) number of students from other jurisdictions. Race categories exclude persons of Hispanic ethnicity. Although rounded numbers are displayed, the figures are based on unrounded data.

SOURCE: U.S. Department of Education, Office of Special Education Programs, Individuals with Disabilities Education Act (IDEA) database, retrieved February 25, 2023, from https://data.ed.gov/dataset/idea-section-618-data-products; and National Center for Education Statistics, Common Core of Data (CCD), "State Nonfiscal Survey of Public Elementary/Secondary Education." 2021–22. See *Digest of Education Statistics 2022* table 204.50.

In the school year 2021–2022, the number of students served under IDEA as a percent of total enrollment for different racial/ethnic groups was:

- highest for AI/AN (19%) and Black (17%) students; and
- lowest for Pacific Islander (11%) and Asian (8%) students.

Today, increasing numbers of AI/AN parents of children with special needs understand that the values and laws of the modern world are superimposed on their world to improve the quality of life for their children. They, as parents (like non-Indian parents), can hold the institutions and agencies accountable due to these laws and their resources. There is no question that most Indian parents also know that mainstream society holds the economic resources to help them and their children with special needs. Mainstream society, therefore, has the power to determine what services or resources will be extended to Indian families and what resources will be made available to those with disabilities. When faced with a conflict regarding how this will be done and by whom, an Indian family may quietly refuse service or withdraw from interaction with the agencies. Providing culturally relevant services to Indian children with disabilities and their families in a bicultural world needs consideration of both the traditional tribal world and the modern world (Joe, 1997). The extent to which an Indian family quickly accepts diagnostic or intervention plans for their child with a disability is greatly influenced by the family's level of acculturation. The more they adhere to traditional tribal practices, the more likely they will require additional time to come to terms with modern beliefs about the etiology and treatment of disabilities.

Although most tribal groups had experiences with disabilities, most languages do not contain single words for various disabilities. No negative terminology or slang refers to disability (Caldwell et al., 2005). For example, among the Navajos, there is no word for mental disorder; rather, one might say that this child "lags or falls behind [others]." Suppose this Navajo child is diagnosed with Downs' Syndrome and is from a more traditional Navajo family. In that case, the family may disagree with school officials when their child is said to have a disability. They may welcome the child's placement in special education. However, from the family's perspective, they feel that their child functions well at home and exhibits no physical evidence of a disability. In other words, all the body parts are in their appropriate places. The child walks, eats, and helps others at home. As the culture of Native American families changes, the families' attitudes and perceptions of disabilities also change. For example, a more acculturated Navajo family, whose modern values emphasize academic achievements, will be devastated when they have a child diagnosed with Downs' Syndrome. Their response is different because it is essential to them that their children excel in school.

Reframing disability for culturally responsive practice

Discussions of disability are often burdened by taken-for-granted assumptions about what disability is, how it affects a person, and whose responsibility it is to manage the effects of a condition. These beliefs about the nature of disability can vary according to the *model* of disability that one is deploying. Broadening the possibilities for culturally responsive approaches to disability is necessarily dependent on greater awareness and appreciation for various disability models and how they affect beliefs of and behaviors toward people with disabilities.

Disability models significantly predict various perceptual, attitudinal, and behavioral responses to people with disabilities (Dirth & Branscombe, 2017). According to Olkin (2002), there have traditionally been three significant categories of disability models that vary according to the ultimate causality of the disability difference. The *moral model* positions disability as an ethical lapse, the consequence of evil, or some test of faith. The *medical model* emphasizes the biological/physiological processes that cause disability differences. Finally, the *social model* emphasizes the socially constructed nature of disability and suggests that environmental and social barriers cause most of the disability-related limitations. While the moral model is the oldest and most widely used in human history, the medical model has dominated approaches to disability in the West since the mid-19th century, primarily as more societal emphasis was directed toward eugenicist and social Darwinist ideologies (Olkin, 2002). The advent of the social model coincided with the era of U.S. civil rights movements in the 1960s and 1970s and marked a distinct contrast to the oppressive components of the medical and moral models (Fleischer et al., 2012). The social model aligned with efforts to deinstitutionalize/ depathologize disability, promote disability integration into communities, and cultivate self-determination and pride for the disability community (Linton, 1998). The social model served as a significant catalyst for the disability activism that produced the Rehabilitation Act (1979), the Americans with Disabilities Act (ADA, 1990), and the Individuals with Disabilities in Education Act (IDEA, 2018).

As more doors have been opened to people with disabilities, especially, in educational domains, so too did scholarship by and for people with disabilities see incredible generativity over the last 30 years. *Disability Studies* is a cross-disciplinary approach centered on disability experience and perspectives. It is particularly generative in refining and expanding upon the social model to appreciate the multitude of disability experiences fully. For example, the *sociopolitical model* amplifies the minority group nature of disability and the political legitimacy of being the largest minority group in the country and around the world (Hahn, 1988). Likewise, the *affirmative model* amplifies the innovativeness, creativity, and generative qualities of disability experiences, which should be leveraged to better understand the diversity of human experience (Swain & French, 2000). Finally, there is a constellation of *critical disability models* (e.g., Annamma, Connor, & Ferri, 2013; Campbell, 2009; Grech, 2012) that calls into question the "just-so" nature of ability. In short, these models' priorities are to reveal how structural affordances of ability are ultimately disabled through resource extraction, exploitation, and displacement (see Dirth & Adams, 2019).

Broadening awareness and appreciation of disability models is essential to moving forward with culturally responsive approaches because models can generate alternative points of emphasis, intervention trajectories, and possibilities for meaning-making in the context of disability experience that can often be fraught.

No single model can gather the full complexity of disability experience, and disability models often contain tradeoffs in terms of how a disabled person might make sense of and accommodate their experience of difference. Appreciating that disability is an experience that must be understood in context, so too is the meaningfulness of disability models largely dictated within cultural context. Towards setting a solid foundation for a SGM approach to working with AI/AN students with disabilities and their families in the context of IEP meetings, the breadth of disability models can allow for more attentiveness to the unique cultural context of students and their families rather than forcing them into a limited disability paradigm.

A mile in someone's moccasins

Identifying the student's ethnic background, cultural identification, languages spoken and preferred, spirituality, and ties to the community is essential. Implementing cultural methodologies, partitioners, and educators working with AI/AN students identified with disabilities can assist with early cultural discussions in developing cultural understandings and knowledge upon the initial dialog. Baez et al. (2022) suggest that educators/counselors facilitate the learning for AI/AN youth on academics, behaviors, and emotional knowledge by weaving culturally relevant pedagogy and culturally sustaining pedagogy, which may provide the best approach to understanding cultural dynamics and experiences. The first step in the relationship with AI/AN students/parents is honoring the people's experiences. This step suggests honoring the gifts they come with and addressing areas of need. It is not easy to understand if we do not truly understand the culture or perceptions. "A mile in someone's moccasins" could be a reminder to practice empathy and humility. For example, do practitioners ever think holding annual IEP meetings or initial evaluation of a student with a possible disability is a positive meeting for AI/AN families? AI/AN parents are asked to attend an initial meeting or an annual IEP to address their child's disability or areas of concern in their academics or behaviors. For some families, inviting them to discuss the problems (disabilities) can be culturally inappropriate or culturally insensitive if the meeting is only focused on a problem with the child/student. Indigenous people embrace the whole person, which means honoring ALL of the person, their gifts, strengths, and areas of being different. How does someone continue to be connected in a healthy relationship if one side of the relationship only addresses the problems/disability of the other person? For Indigenous people, this would not honor the relationship of honoring one another. The relationship between non-Native practitioners and AI/AN families will continue to struggle if the special education team only addresses the negative strategies of the particular disability. Suppose the special education team, working with AI/AN families and students, fails to incorporate spiritual/cultural intelligence into the initial dialogue and service plan. In that case, the struggle for a successful outcome will continue (Baez & Baez, 2023). A more spiritual/cultural intelligence approach of honoring the person (talents and spiritual gifts) will result in a better outcome for the IEP meeting (Figure 21.2).

There is a gap in the literature on disability in rural AI/AN communities. This gap is significant as AI/AN identified experience some of the highest prevalence rates of disability (Mashinchi et al., 2022). Some reason could be that the practitioners providing the services do not factor in the cultural component. Practitioners may need to help working with AI/AN students for several reasons. Among the possibilities are the following:

• The practitioner may lack basic knowledge about the student's ethnic and historical backgrounds.
• The school psychologist's style may drive away the student.
• The student may sense that their worldview needs to be valued.
• The student may feel uncomfortable talking openly with a stranger.
• The ethnic background of the school psychologist may create student apprehension.

Incorporating culturally responsive research and evaluation can help alter narratives to address current community conditions and highlight assets that contextualize disability (Wesner et al., 2022). Doing so requires reframing disability according to alternative disability models and reframing the IEP context according to the SGM.

Figure 21.2 Dr. Mark Standing Eagle Baez Moccasins.
Source: Photographer: By Dr. C. Alllison Baez

The Sweetgrass Method

American Indians/First Nations people have held sweetgrass (Óhonte Wenserákon) sacred for a long time. Sweetgrass is used to purify oneself—mentally, emotionally, physically, and spiritually—in hopes of grounding the person in healing. Grounded in this tradition, the S.G.M. is a culturally responsive framework for working with Indigenous clients (Baez et al., 2022). It is a community-based participatory practice approach incorporating practice-based evidence (PBE), which looks at what works for the community setting. PBE includes a range of behavior approaches and supports derived from and supportive of the positive culture of the local society and traditions (Bartgis & Bigfoot, 2010) and is an effective practice for AI/AN school communities.

The SGM weaves together Western and Traditional approaches to serve Indigenous clients best. It incorporates three strands: Introspection, a life-long commitment to self-reflection, and cultural humility. Communication is a commitment to building relationships and partnerships with people and groups to address mental health concerns. Continuity, ongoing support, and strategies for students and their communities that foster long-term success.

First strand: introspection

Recognizing one's culture and how it influences behavior is necessary, but insufficient for working effectively in a multicultural society (Baez et al., 2022). Such awareness is particularly successful for professionals providing services to Indigenous populations, as they must be respectful and nonjudgmental and avoid assumptions and expectations to serve their students best (Baez & Isaac, 2013). This cannot happen if we are not grounded introspectively. Introspection includes reflecting on professional competencies and practicing self-care to promote spiritual, emotional, physical, and mental wellness to bring understanding, clarity, and preparedness to prevention strategies and support. The Introspection strand of the SGM braid also allows educators to be examples of healthy leaders for the AI/AN and Indigenous individuals to whom they provide services.

Introspection also incorporates cultural humility. Cultural humility starts with a commitment to exploring one's cultural beliefs and values because responding effectively to others is more accessible than understanding yourself (Baez, 2023). When practitioners apply cultural humility, they ask sincere and curious questions about, for example, the client's ethnicity, gender, sexual identity, sexual orientation, social needs, and language. Practitioners can also take the opportunity to think about their assumptions concerning disability itself. Because of the dominance of the medical model of disability in education settings, practitioners may take for granted the "objectivity" of disability and not consider how they could expand and complicate their understanding of the disability context.

Counselors knowledgeable of AI/AN perspectives of mental health also understand that the primary goal of psychological helping to address special education needs is to explore issues related to a student's reason to act out and help them find healing (Baez et al., 2022). Through introspection, we can assist our students in finding healing and provide support for their academic and social-emotional growth.

In this strand, the practitioner/educator becomes aware of their biases, strengths, and limitations. This strand also begins to look at the contemporary challenges of AI/AN historical injustices and several systemic issues that hinder Indigenous children and youth's access to high-quality education. In addition to possible strategies, one could use them to provide for the student's successful outcome.

Second strand: communication

The second strand of the braid, Communication, refers to how the work becomes action with those you work alongside. Family partnerships and communities are critical when supporting AI/AN students. In particular, the community is essential to supporting the growth and success of students with disabilities in schools and the local society. This second strand in the SGM braid is an evolving approach that calls for active participation from practitioners, families, community, and students, all of whom work together in shared problem-solving to achieve a common goal (Baez & Isaac, 2013; Baez et al., 2022). All these different groups must communicate well to work together effectively. However, this can be challenging when the partnerships include AI/AN and non-AI/AN members. In this strand, the practitioner/educator would look at ways to develop a dialogue/relationship with the student/family and ways of disseminating culturally responsive support.

As a community, providing a safe place to honoring our people's experience (HOPE) or *honor our people's experiences* without judgment (Baez et al., 2016) is essential. Non-AI/AN providers can communicate respect for their AI/AN clients' stories, feelings, and understanding of what they are experiencing through HOPE. For example, most AI/ANs understand the purpose and use of Sweetgrass, used to cleanse the mind, spirit, and body. According to C. A. Baez, "the culturally responsive technique of the S.G.M.

discusses how practitioners would approach with openness to honoring our people's experiences" (personal Communication; April 2015). This approach means embracing the experiences that AI/AN students and parents may factor into choices. It is necessary to communicate the support strategies available to parents or guardians in a culturally responsive and appropriate manner, mainly when working with the family of a child who meets the eligibility criteria for a student with disabilities. For AI/AN parents, trust is essential in any conversation, mainly when working with non-AI/AN providers. Based on historical trauma, AI/AN caregivers have many reasons not to trust school personnel. They may not feel comfortable or be receptive to discussions about their child's behavior when they do not know, let alone trust, the person sharing such information.

To further this second strand as it relates to a culturally centered disability context, practitioners can leverage alternative models of disability that reorient the critical factors from the bodies and minds of disabled individuals to the cultural context of ability that exists between the education institution and the family/support network of the child. For instance, by taking a social and/or affirmative model approach to disability, a practitioner is better prepared to contextualize the disability as a distinct strength, not pathology, of a child. Moreover, a practitioner is better able to honor the experience of a family and their child by situating disability in context rather than an objective property of an individual child.

Third strand: continuation

The third strand in the SGM braid involves maintaining a continuum of culturally responsive services that are delivered with consistency. This includes support for youth, parents/guardians, community, and staff development. Providing ongoing culturally responsive approaches is vital to improving social-emotional and academic outcomes for AI/AN and Indigenous youth (Baez et al., 2022). This strand also focuses on continued research on new prevention strategies and ongoing social support services that weave together Western approaches and AI/AN traditional methodologies for students with disabilities. Although consistently continuing services may sound intuitive as best practice, it only sometimes happens. Moreover, when systems break down, Indigenous families may feel abandoned by providers who fail to continue to show up for them.

By leveraging alternative models of disability, especially critical models that challenge ableist values of autonomy and competition, practitioners can position continuity as a counterpoint to these unsuccessful and unsustainable arrangements. Centering interdependence as the normative value and ideal arrangement has proven its transformative potential within the disability community (Fleischer et al., 2012). Therefore, as practitioners reach out to a family and be honest and transparent about their current state in the services that must be provided, it is critically important to see this relationship as bidirectional support. For example, practitioners should communicate effectively with parents about what will be helpful for the student's progress and success, and then empower families to make suggestions, articulate what would be beneficial resources coming from the practitioner, and define what family support will look like. Because continuity can be challenging, especially where a provider needs staffing help to follow through with too large a caseload or too many mandated special education evaluations to complete, structuring this arrangement through interdependent values can help maximize support delivery across the different parties.

3-step process to the Sweetgrass Method for students with disabilities

The first step in the SGM process is the *initial consultation and needs identification*. When practitioners work with students with disabilities, beginning with a communication process that builds relationships and promotes information sharing is essential. Practitioners begin this initial consultation with cultural humility. This is essential when working with Indigenous students with disabilities because it is grounded in embedding traditional cultural methods and authentic content into practitioners' approaches (Baez et al., 2022; Baez & Baez, 2023). Next, the practitioner identifies and prioritizes the client's needs, asking for examples of disability needs and focusing on specific target areas. Practitioners set goals and develop strategies for the classroom and home. Identifying the needs during the initial assessment helps practitioners determine what must be accomplished to reach expected IEP goals. This needs identification to inform an overall plan and approaches. For example, the initial consultation and requires identification regarding disabilities may determine the forms of the disability, if the behavior warrants intervention, and how often the student's needs continue after repeated teacher intervention (Baez et al., 2022; Baez & Baez, 2023).

The second step is a *needs analysis* to identify the reasons for the problem and how to overcome the gap between what is and should be. As practitioners, we are trained in this area to provide a functional behavioral assessment (FBA), but the question is, how should one administer an FBA to AI/AN students? In facilitating this assessment among AI/AN students, the practitioner should have an approach incorporating cultural relevancy and cultural sustainability. The initial cultural dialog with the student is essential in developing cultural understandings and knowledge when identifying behavioral, healthy social, and emotional needs. The SGM intentionally has the practitioner focus on cultural humility as a strand for successful approaches. developing the

The last step is the *needs evaluation*. This step is when collaborators review the data collected by the team of professionals. This data gathering allows the practitioner to determine the child's progress regarding the intervention and the services' overall success. The practitioner and consultees share feedback throughout the consultation to enable immediate modifications to the treatment plan when needed. The data from a needs assessment assists practitioners in determining why students are failing, some of the barriers they face, and their strengths. This last step can assist practitioners in identifying student needs, informing behavioral strategies to address those needs, and pinpointing the high-need areas for small groups. A suggested meeting or consultation time with the clients/students is up to three or four meetings that would need to occur for support and direction for the client/student. A suggested time would be 45–60 minutes per meeting. These steps will weave in the SGM to incorporate a culturally responsive approach to service delivery for the indigenous clients that are being serviced.

Case example: an SGM approach to an IDEA MET

Johnny White Horse is an AI/AN 7th grader sent to meet with Mike, the school psychologist, due to the student falling behind and failing his English and Math classes. Applying the SGM (see Figure 21.3), Mike would begin with introspection. Applying this approach would include thinking through what he knows and does not know about Johnny's' culture and reflecting on where there may be similarities and differences between Johnny's

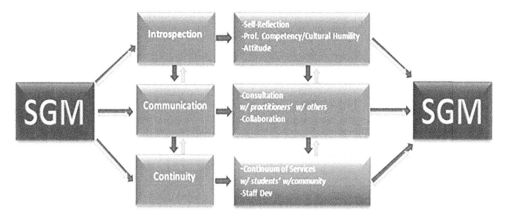

Figure 21.3 Overview of SGM model.

traditions and his own. It would also mean assessing self-care and how calm and equipped he felt to handle Johnny's case.

Communication with Johnny would begin from a place of cultural humility and curiosity to build trust. Mike might thank Johnny for coming to the meeting and explaining that she cares about him and where he comes from, so they must discuss what happened. Gazing around the room without staring directly at Johnny, Mike could start by sincerely wanting to learn about Johnny and asking him about any preferred terms or his Tribal name. Like most discussions with students about complex issues, the conversation would likely carefully and patiently explore Mike's perspective about the difficulties with Johnny's academics or social-emotional needs, with Mike checking for understanding.

It would be necessary for a practitioner applying SGM to communicate to Johnny that addressing academic deficiencies requires ongoing collaboration with his caregivers. Thus, Mike would want to be clear with Johnny about all plans to speak with his parent(s) or guardian(s) before connecting with his family. Applying the fundamentals of the SGM Communication braid, Mike would invite Johnny's caregiver(s) for a meeting to discuss the special education issue and ensure they know they have a voice and a valued perspective. Mike would aim to establish an equal partnership with Johnny's family and avoid any implication that, as a school staff member, he was more of an expert or held more power than the caregivers. Instead, Johnny's family members are experts on Johnny, and by hearing their stories and honoring their experiences, Mike will be better equipped to support him.

Addressing Johnny's special education needs would be ongoing and collaborative. Mike would need to "show up" consistently and work patiently to establish and maintain the trust required to work with Johnny to change his behavior. Consistent communication with Johnny's family would also be essential. For example, Mike might call home periodically to check in for updates or to share successes when Johnny has made progress toward his behavioral goals. The three strands of the SGM braid would remain woven throughout the process, and through reflection, Mike would continue to learn and strengthen her skills for working with the AI/AN community.

Conclusions

America's classrooms are increasingly diverse, and many new teachers have few opportunities to develop multicultural competency prior to on-the-job experiences. Unfortunately, it is students of color who are disproportionately affected. What is most disturbing is that these circumstances are not new for minority students, and efforts to change the adverse outcomes have been largely unsuccessful.

Although federal and state laws dictate that AI/AN children must receive an education that recognizes their heritage and culture, many families of AI/AN students do not believe that their cultures and histories are adequately represented in their children's daily school experience. By incorporating cultural methods into the initial supports/strategies for the individual, we are more likely to see better outcomes. As mentioned, the SGM applies community-based participatory practices in a partnership approach that involves Indigenous community members, Indigenous and other organizational representatives, and academic professionals in all aspects of the process.

As we have argued, now is the time for dialogue between Indigenous and non-Indigenous peoples about their understanding of special education and specific disabilities. The emerging literature reveals that disability scholars from the global north and south need to reflect further on the language and concepts concerning disability. Such reflections must address how colonialism and the resulting social disadvantages have led to dislocation, the loss of land rights, and disruption to traditional livelihoods, resulting in violence, substance abuse, and mental health issues. These factors are recognized as correlated to high impairment rates, and meaningful dialogue about the experiences of impairment and disability amongst indigenous peoples cannot occur in a historical vacuum.

As practitioners and educators, we can make positive school changes by building relationships and partnerships with our AI/AN parents and communities (Baez, 2023). Understanding AI/AN youth is crucial to begin a healthy dialogue between the student, the practitioner, and the educator. This also allows the opportunities to develop approaches to special education and mental health that are culturally responsive for AI/AN youth. With an understanding of the SGM, the school psychologist can form cross-cultural connections in a mutual relationship with the student, the family, and the community. Indigenous communities are eager to advance effective solutions for academic and behavioral strategies.

References

Americans With Disabilities Act of 1990, 42 U.S.C. § 12101 *et seq.* (1990).

Annamma, S. A., Connor, D., & Ferri, B. (2013). Dis/ability critical race studies (DisCrit): Theorizing at the intersections of race and dis/ability. *Race ethnicity and education*, 16(1), 1-31.

Baez, M. S. E. (2011, March/April). Significant partnerships with Native American Students, parents, and schools: A Sweetgrass Method. *National Association of School Psychologists (NASP) communiqué*.

Baez, M. S. E. (2023, November). Applying the Sweetgrass Method to address bullying for Indigenous. *National Association of School Psychologists (NASP) communiqué*. https://www.nasponline.org/resources-and-publications/periodicals/communiqu%C3%A9-volume-52-number-3-(November-2023)/applying-the-sweetgrass-method-to-address-bullying-for-indigenous-youth

Baez, M. S. E. and Baez, C. A. (2023). Cultural-emotional learning among American Indian/Alaska native students. *Journal of Indigenous Research*. https://digitalcommons.usu.edu/kicjir/vol11/iss1/1/

Baez, M. S. E., Baez, C. A., Lavallie, B. and Spears, W. (2022). Sweetgrass Method: A culturally responsive approach to mental health. *Journal of Indigenous Research*. https://digitalcommons.usu.edu/cgi/viewcontent.cgi?article=1174&context=kicjir

Baez, M. S. E. and Isaac, P. (2013). A sweetgrass method of bullying prevention for Native American youth. *Journal of Indigenous Research*, 3(1), 1.

Baez, M. S. E., Isaac, P. and Baez, C. A. (2016). HOPE for Indigenous people battling intergenerational trauma: The Sweetgrass Method. *Journal of Indigenous Research*. https://digitalcommons.usu.edu/kicjir/vol5/iss2/2/

Bartgis, J. and Bigfoot, D. (2010). Evidence-based practices + Practice-based evidence. *National Council of Urban Indian Health*. https://ncuih.org/ebp-pbe/

Caldwell, J. Y., Davis, J. D., Du Bois, B., Echo-Hawk, H., Erickson, J. S., Goins R. T., et al. (2005). Culturally competent research with American Indians and Alaska Natives: Findings and recommendations of the first symposium of the workgroup on American Indian Research and Program Evaluation Methodology. *American Indian Alaska Native Mental Health Research*, 12(1), 1–21.

Campbell, F. K. (2009). *Contours of ableism*. Basingstoke: Palgrave Macmillan.

Centers for Disease Control and Prevention (2008). Racial/ethnic disparities in self-rated health status among adults with and without disabilities—United States, 2004–2006. *Morbidity and Mortality Weekly Report*, 57(39), 1069–1073. http://www.cdc.gov/mmwr/preview/mmwrhtml/mm5739a1.htm

Centers for Disease Control and Prevention (2023). *Disability and Health Data System* (DHDS) [Internet]. [updated 2023 May; cited 2023 May 15]. http://dhds.cdc.gov

Dirth, T. P. and Adams, G. A. (2019). Decolonial theory and disability studies: On the modernity/coloniality of ability. *Journal of Social and Political Psychology*, 7(1), 260–289.

Dirth, T. P. and Branscombe, N. R. (2017). Disability models affect disability policy support through awareness of structural discrimination. *Journal of Social Issues*, 73(2), 413–442.

Erickson, W., Lee, C. and Von Schrader, S. (2015). Disability Statistics from the 2013 American Community Survey (ACS). Ithaca, NY: Cornell University Employment and Disability Institute (EDI). Retrieved September 25, 2023 from www.disabilitystatistics.org

Fleischer, D. Z., Zames, F. D. and Zames, F. (2012). *The disability rights movement: From charity to confrontation*. Philadelphia, PA: Temple University Press.

Friedman, C. (2020). The relationship between disability prejudice and disability employment rates. *Work*, 65(3), 591–598.

Gion, C., McIntosh, K. and Horner, R. (2014). *Patterns of minor office discipline referrals in schools using SWIS PBIS Evaluation Brief*. OSEP National Technical Assistance Center on Positive Behavioral Interventions and Supports. Eugene, OR.

Goins, R. T., Moss, M., Buchwald, D. and Guralnik, J. M. (2007). Disability among older American Indians and Alaska Natives: An analysis of the 2000 Census public use microdata sample. *The Gerontologist*, 47(5), 690–696.

Grech, S. (2012). Disability and the majority world: A neo-colonial approach. In D. Goodley, B. Hughes & L. Davis (Eds.) *Disability and social theory: New developments and directions*. (pp. 52–69). London, UK: Palgrave MacMillan.

Hahn, H. (1988). The politics of physical differences: Disability and discrimination. *Journal of social issues*, 44(1), 39–47.

Individuals with Disabilities Education Act, 45 C.F.R. § 300.8 (2018). https://sites.ed.gov/idea/regs/b/a/300.8

Joe, J. R. (1997). American Indian children with disabilities: The impact of culture on health and education services. *Families, Systems, & Health*, 15(3), 251–261.

Krahn, G. L., Walker, D. K. and Correa-De-Araujo, R. (2015). Persons with disabilities as an unrecognized health disparity population. *American Journal of Public Health*, 105(Suppl 2), S198–S206.

Linton, S. (1998). *Claiming disability: Knowledge and identity*. New York, NY: NYU Press.

Losen, D., Hodson, C., Keith, M. A., Morrison, K. and Belway, S. (2015). "Are We Closing the School Discipline Gap?" Los Angeles: The Civil Rights Project.

Mandell, D. S., Wiggins, L. D., Carpenter, L. A., Daniels, J., DiGuiseppi, C., Durkin, M. S., ... Kirby, R. S. (2009). Racial/ethnic disparities in the identification of children with autism spectrum disorders. *American Journal of Public Health*, 99(3), 493–498.

Mashinchi, G. M., Hicks, E. C., Leopold, A. J., Greiman, L. and Ipsen, C. (2022). The intersection of disability status and rurality in American Indian/Alaskan Native communities. *Frontiers Rehabilitation Sciences*, 3, 875979. Doi: 10.3389/fresc.2022.875979

McCoy, M. L., Elliott-Groves, E., Sabzalian, L. and Bang, M. (2020). Restoring Indigenous systems of relationality. Testimony. Center for Humans and Nature.

Müller, E. and Markowitz, J. (2004). Disability categories: State terminology, definitions, and eligibility criteria. Alexandria, VA: Project Forum at the National Association of State Directors of Special Education.

Olkin, R. (2002). Could you hold the door for me? Including disability in diversity. *Cultural Diversity and Ethnic Minority Psychology*, 8(2), 130–139.

Rampey, B. D., Faircloth, S. C., Whorton, R. P. and Deaton, J. (2019). *National Indian Education Study 2015: A closer look* (NCES 2019–048). National Center for Education Statistics. https://eric.ed.gov/?id=ED594657

Reyhner, J. (2010). Indigenous language immersion schools for strong indigenous identities. *Heritage Language Journal*, 7(2), 299–313.

Sarche, M. and Spicer, P. (2008). Poverty and health disparities for American Indian and Alaska Native children: Current knowledge and future prospects. *Annals of the New York Academy of Sciences*, 1136, 126–136.

Sullivan, A. L. (2011). Disproportionality in special education identification and placement of English language learners. *Exceptional children*, 77(3), 317–334.

Sullivan, A. L. and Bal, A. (2013). Disproportionality in special education: Effects of individual and school variables on disability risk. *Exceptional Children*, 79(4), 475–494.

Swain, J. and French, S. (2000). Towards an affirmation model of disability. *Disability & Society*, 15(4), 569–582.

United States Department of Education. (2023, March). Guiding principles for creating safe, inclusive, supportive, and fair schools. *United States Department of Education*. https://www2.ed.gov/policy/gen/guid/school-discipline/guiding-principles.pdf

Wesner, C., Around Him, D. and Sarche, M. (2022). Child development in Indigenous communities: Promoting equity and resilience across a continuum of Tribal early childhood programs and services. Tribal Early Childhood Research Center (TRC) Brief, November 2022. https://coloradosph.cuanschutz.edu/docs/librariesprovider205/trc/trc-brief-indigenous-child-development-nov-2022.pdf

22 Indigenous peoples with disabilities in Taiwan

The experiences of Paiwan people

Kui Kasirisir (Hsu, Chun-Tsai)

Introduction

The development trajectory of Taiwan's Indigenous peoples mirrors similar experiences in other nations. They have endured political conquest, governmental neglect, discrimination, prejudice, segregation policies, assimilation, then cultural preservation, and a resurgence in political and cultural rights. In a proactive move to safeguard the rights of Indigenous peoples, the United Nations adopted the United Nations Declaration on the Rights of Indigenous Peoples in September 2007. On August 1, 2016, Taiwan's Indigenous Peoples' Day, President Tsai representing the government, formally apologized to the Indigenous peoples of Taiwan. In the same year, the "Presidential Office Indigenous Historical Justice and Transitional Justice Committee" was established. These developments symbolize a growing domestic and international recognition of past injustices and unfair practices against Indigenous peoples, prompting a reconsideration of concepts like 'affirmative action,' 'compensatory justice,' and 'transitional justice.' However, the full civic rights of Indigenous peoples, especially their social rights, are often denied by mainstream society, leaving them in positions of vulnerability, poverty, and limited choices. This disadvantaged status has been ingrained in societal structures from the outset and perpetuated across generations, making it challenging for them to receive adequate care within the systems established by the mainstream society (Hill, 1996, pp. 276–281) (Figure 22.1).

The experiences of the Paiwan people with disabilities and Policies

Indigenous persons with disabilities often face a form of double discrimination due to their Indigenous identity and their disability. This discrimination largely stems from an inadequate understanding and recognition of both Indigenous issues and disabilities, leading to persistently unfair treatment in society. In Taiwan, the "Indigenous Peoples Basic Law" enacted in 2005, particularly Article 26, emphasizes the need to specially safeguard the rights of Indigenous children, the elderly, women, and people with disabilities. The Convention on the Rights of Persons with Disabilities (UNCRPD) acknowledges the dual discrimination faced by Indigenous persons with disabilities, implying that Articles 4 and 5, which deal with general obligations, equality, and non-discrimination, encompass the protection of the rights of Indigenous peoples. However, the Act to Implement the UNCRPD, passed domestically in Taiwan on August 20, 2014, does not specifically mention Indigenous peoples, seemingly contravening the spirit of the UNCRPD.

DOI: 10.4324/9781032656519-27

Figure 22.1 Photograph of Kui's daughter and niece, the connection between family, July 2023.

Source: Photographer: Kui Kasirisir at Paiwan community gathering

Furthermore, when considering the legal framework and conventions related to the rights of persons with disabilities, the current People with Disabilities Rights Protection Act in Taiwan does not mention Indigenous peoples or ethnic issues. This omission reveals a form of 'cultural blindness' in the Taiwanese legislation towards Indigenous persons with disabilities. It fails to 'see' the unique challenges and difficulties they may face in terms of cultural discrimination, unequal resource allocation, and geographical limitations in policy and service measures.

I grew up in a tribal community, so my Indigenous name is Hsu, Chun-Tsai. I frequently encountered individuals with disabilities, many of whom were relatives with disabilities acquired in middle age due to illness or occupational hazards. The primary caregivers were typically family members, who not only tended to their needs, but also strove for self-care. There were times when the disabilities seemed 'invisible' or 'unfelt,' but this did not mean that these individuals did not require assistance and support. Their inability to engage in activities as they did before often led to feelings of helplessness and resignation. This was particularly evident in conversations with my grandmother and great-grandmother, whose expressions and words vividly conveyed the sense of being imprisoned by their disabled bodies. As a result, they became less inclined to leave their homes or interact with other elders in the tribe, highlighting the increased importance of familial care, support, and understanding during such times. This is also why I studied at the National Pingtung University of Science and Technology, so I could help my people.

The research

I hold a Ph.D. from the University of Brighton, and I am a professor in the Department of Social Work at the National Pingtung University of Science and Technology in Taiwan. I have participated in the Taiwan Association of Indigenous Social Work and the Taiwan Indigenous Professors Association. My specialties include Indigenous social work, Indigenous social welfare, health and social care with Indigenous peoples, and Indigenous community development. I received research funding from the National Science and Technology Council of Taiwan for a project conducted from August 2021 to July 2023 titled "Hearing Their Voices and Stories: A Study on the Paiwan People (Indigenous) with Disabilities and Their Families in Pingtung County." This research primarily focused on the Paiwan community residing in Pingtung County, and employed methods such as literature review, fieldwork, in-depth individual interviews, focus groups, and surveys. The primary objective was to explore and understand the cultural perspectives of the Paiwan ethnic group in Pingtung County towards physical and mental disabilities, compiling the voices, stories, and needs of the Paiwan people with disabilities and their families. This involved analyzing the community's perception, attitudes, and acceptance levels towards individuals with disabilities. The study successfully conducted 20 individual interviews and 4 focus groups, involving participants such as Paiwan individuals with disabilities, primary caregivers, and academic experts. Regarding the survey, it targeted the Paiwan population of Pingtung County aged 18 and above, focusing on their awareness, attitudes, and acceptance of physical and mental disabilities. A total of 505 questionnaires were completed (Kasirisir, 2023).

According to the research data collected in this study, it was found that 37.4% of the respondents had family members with physical or mental disabilities, most of which were due to illnesses or work-related accidents. Additionally, 40.5% of the respondents perceived only minor differences between individuals with disabilities and other members of their tribe. Notably, 40.2% of the respondents believed there was no difference at all, as they considered individuals with disabilities as integral family members of the tribe (Kasirisir, 2023). However, the Paiwan people's traditional cultural perspectives intertwined with modern medical views have shaped stereotypical impressions of the Paiwan with disabilities across different generations. In the Indigenous communities, particularly among teachers, parents of young children, and elders, there is a limited understanding of physical and mental disabilities, including related assessments and welfare rights. This lack of awareness often leads to missed opportunities for early therapeutic interventions for children and adolescents.

Furthermore, discrimination against Indigenous identities and individuals with disabilities is pervasive, both in Indigenous areas and urban districts. This discrimination spans various living environments, age groups, and occupational types. Additionally, resources for individuals with disabilities in Indigenous regions are significantly lacking in terms of accessibility, availability, and information. This insufficiency not only imposes a multifaceted burden on caregivers (including financial, physical, psychological, and tribal relational aspects) but also complicates care due to the diversity of disability types and the corresponding range of needs, which are often challenging to meet or accommodate. Moreover, the dispersed living patterns of individuals with disabilities in Indigenous areas, coupled with a scarcity of idle space in these regions, further complicate the establishment of necessary resources for them. These various factors collectively exacerbate

Figure 22.2 Photograph of Paiwan Elders and grandchildren, intergenerational support has no
limits, July 2023.

Source: Photographer: Kui Kasirisir at Paiwan community gathering

the challenging environment and circumstances faced by the Paiwan people with disabilities. Their situation is rendered more severe due to the compounded difficulties of limited
resources and widespread discrimination (Figure 22.2).

Development of policies and research on Indigenous Taiwanese with disabilities

The development of policies for persons with disabilities in Taiwan began to gain clarity
and structure with the passage of the Welfare Law for Handicapped Persons in 1980.
Subsequent amendments have led to a more comprehensive framework for disability
policies and services. The motivation behind each amendment was to reduce or alleviate the 'disability' challenges, aimed to ensure that persons with disabilities enjoy the
same rights to life and quality of life as the general population. The 1980 "Welfare Law
for Handicapped Persons" focused on providing compensatory welfare measures to assist persons with disabilities towards self-reliance. The Physically and Mentally Disabled
Citizens Protection Act of 1997 aimed to promote and safeguard equal opportunities for
persons with disabilities in social participation. In 2007, the Persons with Disabilities
Rights Protection Act was influenced by the 2006 UNCRPD. This act marked a significant shift in perspective, aligning policies and legal standards with human rights principles. It represented a paradigm shift from a medically oriented and individual model of
disability to a rights-oriented and social model (Wang, 2013, 2017).

In 2007, alongside the amendment of the People with Disabilities Rights Protection Act, Taiwan introduced the "International Classification of Functioning, Disability and Health" (ICF) as the basis for domestic disability assessment and needs evaluation. This system leans more towards a social model in its operational concept (Chien et al., 2019). Following the revision of the Act and the introduction of the ICF system, the Ministry of the Interior in 2009 announced the White Paper on the Rights and Interests Protection of Persons with Disabilities. This document outlined objectives for various stages of implementation, addressing seven key needs: welfare services, medical care, education, employment, accessible environments, economic security, and comprehensive issues. The White Paper adopted an ethos of universalism and a life course perspective as the basis for its planning. This approach aimed to ensure that persons with disabilities could have opportunities to meet their life needs at different stages, similar to the rest of the population. This initiative represented a significant step in integrating the needs and rights of persons with disabilities into broader societal and policy frameworks (Ministry of the Interior, 2009).

Although the ICF requires further refinement and improvement, its fundamental concepts are still worth persistent efforts for implementation. For instance, the ICF framework emphasizes the importance of environmental factors, understanding the barriers that hinder persons with disabilities from participating fairly in social life. This concept parallels the 'Person in Environment' (PIE) approach used in the field of social work (Chou et al., 2015). This emphasis on environmental factors is particularly relevant for Indigenous persons with disabilities. They face the usual challenges encountered by persons with disabilities in various life environments, plus the often-overlooked colonial societal and cultural contexts (Gilroy et al., 2013). These aspects align with Gail Baikie's (2009) Indigenous version of the PIE model. Mainstream society often fails to recognize the impact of these two environments (colonial societal environment and cultural context) on Indigenous peoples. These environments are challenging to measure or perceive because they are ingrained in everyday life, invisible and intangible. This is why the preamble of the UNCRPD specifically mentions the plight of persons with disabilities who face multiple or aggravated forms of discrimination based on race, colour, sex, language, religion, political or other opinions, national or social origin, property, birth, age, or other status. It acknowledges the complex layers of challenges faced by individuals at the intersection of various identities, including Indigenous persons with disabilities.

The research conducted by various scholars highlights the unique challenges faced by Indigenous persons with disabilities, especially in remote areas. Pan et al. (2018) noted that individuals with disabilities living in remote areas are limited by geographical constraints, which affect their willingness to use services due to poor transportation and economic inefficiency. Huang et al. (2016) found that in the eastern Indigenous communities, the non-use of assistive devices is deeply influenced by socio-cultural factors, including economic disparities, lack of medical resources, and cultural communication barriers. They even suggested that the assistive device design should incorporate cultural and local relevance to meet the needs of these communities. Moreover, Shu-Hui Wang (2014) emphasized the need to consider the cultural uniqueness of Indigenous students when assessing disabilities, as their learning outcomes can be adversely affected by cultural and familial environments. Wu and Chang (2015) argue that the assessment of learning and intellectual disabilities, educational content, and learning evaluations for

Indigenous students should take into account the impact of ethnic cultural factors to reduce 'false positives' caused by cultural factors (Liu & Juan, 2019).

In addition to the service and policy considerations for Indigenous persons with disabilities, the advocacy and promotion of measures for their rights must also consider the cultural characteristics and geographical limitations of Indigenous communities (Chien et al., 2019). Failure to do so may lead to 'cultural gaps' in service implementation and information dissemination. Wang, Yu-Yu (2013) conducted a comprehensive study on Indigenous persons with disabilities in central Taiwan. As discussed, these individuals and their families, due to factors like economic income, language communication, cultural environment, and geographical and resource limitations, prefer to stay in their familiar homes. This preference indirectly affects the planning and flexibility of care arrangements. For instance, the primary caregivers are often spouses, and the caregiving relationship and perspective are influenced by life course, autonomy, and economic conditions. Therefore, Wang, Yu-Yu (2013) emphasizes that policies for Indigenous persons with disabilities should not only focus on 'care,' but also on providing adequate support to enable them to live independently in an environment rich in tribal culture.

Summary: understanding the challenges faced by Paiwan people with disabilities

This comprehensive study delved into the unique experiences and challenges encountered by the Paiwan Indigenous community in Taiwan, particularly focusing on individuals with disabilities. The research sheds light on the dual discrimination faced by these individuals, stemming not only from their disabilities but also from their Indigenous identity. The study emphasizes the interplay between traditional cultural perceptions and modern medical understandings, shaping the community's stereotypes about disabilities across different generations. Limited awareness and knowledge about disabilities, including identification and welfare rights, is evident among community members, especially, teachers, parents of young children, and Elders. This knowledge gap often results in missed opportunities for early interventions and therapeutic support for affected children. Discrimination against Indigenous identity and disabilities pervades both native villages and urban areas, affecting various age groups and professional sectors. Additionally, the inadequate accessibility, availability, and information regarding disability resources in native villages impose multifaceted burdens on caregivers and hinder effective responses to diverse disability needs. The study underscores the need for tailored policies and services that respect the cultural and environmental contexts of Indigenous communities. Recommendations include comprehensive disability awareness initiatives, efficient information dissemination, professional workforce development, and the establishment of an integrated service system specifically designed for Indigenous individuals with disabilities. In conclusion, this research underscores the urgency of addressing the challenges faced by Indigenous Paiwan people with disabilities in Taiwan. It advocates for inclusive policies and support systems that not only recognize the diversity of disabilities but also acknowledge the cultural heritage and geographical circumstances of these communities. Such efforts will contribute to a more equitable and inclusive society for all individuals, regardless of their disability status or Indigenous background (Figure 22.3).

Figure 22.3 Photograph of traditional songs of the Gapedang, power of Indigenous resilience July 2023.

Source: Photographer: Kui Kasirisir at Paiwan community gathering

References

Baikie, G. (2009). Indigenous-centred social work: Theorizing a social work way-of-being. In R. Sinclair, M. A. Hart, & G. Bruyere (Eds.), *Wicihitowin: Aboriginal social work in Canada* (pp. 42–64). Halifax: Fernwood Publishing.

Chien, H.-J., You, Y.-J. and Wu, Y.-S. (2019). A decade in review and outlook: Disability welfare services. *Community Development Journal, 168*, 5–19. (In Chinese).

Chou, Y.-H., Lee, S.-J., Hsieh, T.-J. and Chang, Y.-C. (2015). Current status and challenges of disability needs assessment systems under the ICF framework. *Community Development Journal, 150*, 40–57. (In Chinese).

Gilroy, J., Donelly, M., Colmar, S. and Parmenter, T. (2013). Conceptual framework for policy and research development with Indigenous people with disabilities. *Australian Aboriginal Studies, 2*, 42–58.

Hill, M. (1996). *Social policy: A comparative analysis*. Hemel Hempstead, Hertfordshire: Prentice-Hall/Harvester Wheatsheaf.

Huang, H.-C., Subeq, Y.-M. and Wang, Y.-C. (2016). An initial exploration of assistive device utilization among Indigenous peoples: A cultural care perspective. *Taiwan Indigenous Studies Review, 19*, 153–178. (In Chinese).

Kasirisir, K. (2023). *Hearing their voices and stories: A Study on the Paiwan people (Indigenous) with disabilities and their families in Pingtung county.* (MOST 110–2410-H- 020-014-SS2). Taipei, Taiwan: National Science and Technology Council. (In Chinese).

Liu, C.-L. and Juan, H.-C. (2019). *Prevalence analysis of indigenous students with disabilities in Taiwan's National Education System.* (NAER-107–12-H-2-04-00–1–04). Taipei, Taiwan: National Academy for Educational Research. (In Chinese)

Ministry of the Interior (2009). *White paper on the rights and protection of persons with disabilities*. Taipei, Taiwan: Ministry of the Interior. (In Chinese),

Pan, P.-C., Chen, F.-C. and Ye, Y.-H. (2018). Implementation models and challenges of the independent living support program for persons with disabilities in Pingtung county. *Community Development Journal, 164*, 85–91. (In Chinese).

Wang, K.-Y. (2017). Governance of disability and uncontrolled policies: A review of Taiwan's disability policy. *Taiwanese Sociological Association Communication, 87*, 5–10. (In Chinese).

Wang, S.-H. (2014). A brief discussion on the identification of learning and intellectual disabilities among Indigenous elementary and junior high school students: A case study of Hualien county. *The Journal of Yun-Chia Special Education, 19*, 20–28. (In Chinese).

Wang, Y.-Y. (2013). *Exploring the care needs of tribal Indigenous persons with disabilities and the future direction of long-term care service development.* (NSC 100–2420-H-260–004-). Taipei, Taiwan: National Science and Technology Council. (In Chinese).

Wu, C.-C. and Chen, C.-S. (2015). Critical race theory: Examining the prevalence of special education needs among Indigenous students in Taiwan. *Special Education Forum, 18*, 57–65. (In Chinese).

23 Difference wisdom
Reimagining disability dialogue

Lavonna L. Lovern

Introduction

As with many of the articles I have worked on regarding disability, the issues seem trapped in a continuing and often unchanging dialogue. Many of the dialogues, articles, and conference panels continue to cover the same phenomenal experiences and concerns voiced 30 years ago. It is not that adjustments and changes, even advancements, have not occurred. However, there is a similarity of conversation that has led me to examine the epistemological base assumptions in order to explore why some of my colleagues and I feel we are having the same discussions over all these years. For many of us, there has been unsatisfactory advancement involving social and political equality of opportunity and respect because of limiting Western dichotomous labels such as ability and disability, or persons with disabilities and those without disabilities.

This paper is offered as a critique of Western dialogues on disability studies. It follows Bell's lead in advancing inclusion into diversity discussions. This was originally written during the COVID pandemic, which offered unique insight into the phenomenological and lived experiences of individuals with differences, what Western culture terms as "disabilities". We begin with an analysis of Western concepts of the binary hierarchy and how that relates to the concept of disability and ability. It is followed by an examination of the paradox of the binary; after this, a brief introduction to some Indigenous epistemology on difference. Finally, it concludes with three short case studies to illustrate wisdom found in difference and how this knowledge can be used to restructure and advance disability discussion in academia as well as the broader American culture. Acknowledging that differences, or disabilities, are culturally constructed can allow for advancements in dialogue and in political and social equality. While this work involves a discussion of Indigenous cultures, it is understood that each Indigenous community has differences in language, history, knowledge, and wisdom as well as social and political institutions. The final claim is that many global Indigenous groups (and the premise of this book) share a similar idea of difference that offers alternate knowledge to that expressed in Western cultures.

With the goal of exploring the phenomena of experiential sameness over the past 30 years of dialogue, I continue to invoke and begin with human rights dialogues and their impact on issues of difference. The concept of equality enshrined in human rights discussions are foundational assumptions in both Western and Indigenous communities. While the specifics are unique to each community, these discussions tend to align with the understanding

DOI: 10.4324/9781032656519-28

that all humans are unique, necessary, and adaptable.[1] This understanding implies, if not establishes, an equality of engagement involving persons regardless of physical or mental differences. No clause eliminates individuals specified as being "different" based either on universal standards or standards of social construct. However, Western models of individuals, self, and community involving designations such as "normal", "disabled", and "valued" continue to embrace dualistic hierarchies that reduce persons with culturally recognized designations of difference to the position of inferior "Other". By continuing to use Western models that structure disability dialogues according to competitive and individualistic binary hierarchies, disability dialogues continue to devalue the abilities an individual may have and, instead, emphasize the abilities they lack. Defining the "self" is then an outsider designation hindering individual liberty and self-definition as well as the ability to obtain equality in terms of social and political positioning.[2] To promote social and political equality, it is recognized that continuing discussions that establish a hierarchically superior, competitive, and individualistically designated position must be altered.

Much as discussions of disadvantage and race require the examination of advantage and whiteness, disability must examine "ableness". This paper endeavors to complicate and change the dialogue by exploring the impact of hierarchical binaries and Western constructs of individualism involving disability/ability discussions, which leads to a paradox of binaries and continues to stall the discussions. So, we must look at Indigenous constructs of difference that focus on interdependence, reciprocity, and wellness. While there are no essentialist or universal constructs regarding Indigenous approaches to disability, wellness, or community, these unique communities do share similarities involving differences that offer opportunities to advance Western dialogues and provide alternatives to traditional binary thinking. This is not to say that such discussions should encourage an individual to leave one system to take up another, but rather that disability discussions should be more inclusive in the discussion and allow different perspectives on these issues with the possibility of rethinking how we structure conversations involving differences.

Western "disability" dialogue

As expressed by Davis and Barnes, in separate works, conversation regarding "disability" is primarily Western (Barnes, 2010; Davis, 2010). The designation began and largely remains within Western academic and activist language classifications; and, while appropriate for Western communities, should not be universalized or essentialized. Additionally, Western classifications continue to focus on Western reductionist medical models and ignore individual lived or phenomenological experiences. As a result, discussions concentrate on "solving or overcoming" the issue(s) (Clare, 2017). Additionally, Western constructs assert independence as the primary means of "solving or overcoming" the

---

1 It should be noted that Indigenous communities, while each being unique in epistemology, ontology, and phenomenology, tend to extend rights beyond humans to non-human persons including those that have come before and will come after and those involving the spiritual.

2 It must be noted that the term "equality" requires a referent in order to ensure meaning. Often when "equality" is left without referent, the terms become a product of equivocation. While being left somewhat ambiguous here, the claim is that there is a lack of social and political equity within Western cultures that cannot be eliminated using the hierarchical binary of abled/disabled.

"problem", which establishes the lived experience as individual rather than communal and often uses competition as the essential motivator. Praise is then often extended to individuals, who have "overcome" their disabilities without the assistance of the government or other community members. Similar praise is withheld from those who continue to struggle, which is an issue as many disabilities are chronic and cannot be "overcome" either by sheer will, a "can do" attitude, or current medical practices. Failure to "solve" the problem or to make it disappear from the public eye, places the individual in the "failed", "broken", "inferior", or "weak" position. Such designations involve outsider rather than insider phenomenological knowledge of disability, giving control of the conversation to parties including academics, governments, and those culturally defined as abled. It is, however, Wendell (2008) who challenges these ideas by reminding us that should we live long enough, disability will be everyone's lived experience.

While there is no possibility to clearly establish why Western dialogues continue to dichotomize terms such as "abled" and "disabled", several logical components exist that help support, require, and maintain this status quo. To examine these issues, it is important to begin with a brief discussion of some of the problems in Western constructions involving dichotomy.[3] Waters (2004) states that Western ontology rests on "conceptual categories…[that] signify a discrete (limited and bounded) binary dualist worldview". She further asserts that "the Euro-American binary…empowered and facilitated the misinterpretations of the Indigenous nondiscrete (nonlimited, nonbounded) binary dualist worldview" (2004, p. 98).[4] The discrete binary embeddedness reinforces categorizations such as "White/Black", "developed/underdeveloped", "advantaged/disadvantaged", "normal/abnormal", or "abled/disabled". While often understanding at some level that such designations actually represent continuums rather than a strict binary. Discussions continue to envelope the discrete binary in a way that establishes obstacles involving definitions and the pursuit of social and political equality.

Here, I present the example I often used in classes to help students think about these issues. While it is recognized that there is a difference between someone needing glasses and someone with no vision, it remains unclear when limited eyesight becomes a disability. Some researchers and advocates argue that a designation of "disability" should be determined by the individual experiencing a "significant impairment". However, this simply exacerbates Western definition problems. For example, I have an aunt who finds wearing reading glasses a significant impairment. She claims it is a serious detriment to her ability to function and so they create serious difficulties in her lived experience. Should she be allowed to designate herself as disabled? It may be reasonable for her to do so, but does it qualify her for government and social programs? The differences in one claiming a disability and one claiming social and governmental resources is an example of insider versus outsider definitions of "self" and one's ability to function equally. Indeed, these definition difficulties are the primary reason for the continued use of discrete binaries, which support political and social biases based on preferential positioning and outsider categorization.

Binaries do not necessarily entail hierarchical positioning. However, when formulated within Western normative language patterns, such designations reinforce the idea that gives

---

3 It is true that Western logic does not entirely embrace the binary and allows for differing empirical and modal options. However, less logically familiar academic areas, along with general Western communities, often fall prey to the less complex logical binary.

4 For more detail on her argument, one should read her entire work. For this paper, it is enough to note that Euro-American and Indigenous ontologies are significantly different.

one term the position of superior and the other, the position of inferior, allowing biases and prejudices to infiltrate these dialogues. In establishing such valuing, Western hierarchical positioning involving White, developed, advantaged, normal, and abled represents the preferential position while of-color, underdeveloped, disadvantaged, abnormal, and disabled represent the inferior position. This positioning is further supported in Western communities to involve cultural constructs of individualism and competition. Given that someone must win, and someone must lose, equality is a virtual impossibility both in dialogue and in lived experience. To establish an equality of social and political positioning, Western constructs would need to both recognize differences and give them a superior/inferior label while also attempting to place the superior/inferior labels/individuals as equal so that both are "winners" or equal. Such attempts result in the paradox of the binary to be discussed later.

Tension between foundational concepts of hierarchical binaries and other aspects of Western epistemology, involving issues of empirical "certainty", create problems in determining the accuracy of preferential positions.[5] This means that disability designations cannot be approached, as is often implied in discrete binaries, as indicating an absolute or certainty of preferential positioning. Preferential positioning is rather a matter of probability stemming from perspective or cultural biases. As pointed out earlier, there is no universal construction of disability. Accordingly, there is no basis for attempts to extrapolate either Western designations or positional preferences to non-Western paradigms. Additionally, there is no way to logically assert a paradigm dominance that justifies an infringement on or an objective superiority over another paradigm.[6] For this, and other logical reasons, Western orientations involving mental and physical disabilities should be considered only within Western paradigms that embrace discrete hierarchical binaries, which themselves require further examination to deal with both logical tensions and systemic bias (Corker and Shakespeare, 2002).

Given the inequality supported by hierarchical binaries, dialogues involving "disadvantaged" and "disabled" need to be reinvented to eliminate biased negative associations. However, it is unclear that such a possibility can occur in Western cultures that use hierarchical binaries as a foundational epistemological orientation. Bell (2010) has noted that Western disability dialogues adhere to Western constructs and Western authorities creating what he calls "incestuous" discussions (1997). He further notes that even within Western communities, current dialogues of disability do not move beyond White historical constructs. Therefore, the embeddedness of the hierarchical binary itself works against inclusion and diversity as can be seen in the Western/White assumptions that Western/White epistemology is preferable, has won, and "Other" epistemologies are inferior, have lost.[7]

Paradox of the binary[8]

The embeddedness of the binary paradox became more obvious recently as I met with a group of academics, activists, and professionals dealing with educational recognition

5 Philosophical tensions beginning with Hume (1961) and moving through the verifiability principle, and into late-modern philosophy and issues of epistemological certainty should be consulted for more information, including Wittgenstein (1969).

6 For more advanced discussions Husserl (1970), Habermas (1996), and Bourdieu (1999) are useful resources. Coherence theories offer greater understanding of why binaries should not be universalized.

7 Willinsky (1998) offers a provocative discussion on how differencing occurs.

8 The meeting in this section will not be specifically identified as neither the meeting organizers nor the individuals need to be identified to protect the openness and candid discussions that were involved in the event.

and service to people with disabilities or disabled populations. As noted earlier, one of the primary issues involved in disability discussions is government and social assistance. Given that communities have a limited amount of capital, social or monetary, providing assistance to all of those deemed disabled can be problematic or impossible. If people are allowed to self-identify, resources may be over-taxed and some individuals might attempt to gain resources without "qualifying". However, the establishment of requirements, guidelines, and definitions defines the individual from an "outsider" perspective. The use of medical and psychological designations is equally vague as can be easily noted by designations of "on the spectrum". Questions as to who deserves or qualifies for resources represent a significant challenge not only to government and social structures, but also to individual liberty, identity, and autonomy.

As the two-day meeting progressed, individuals expressed an interest and even an appreciation of Indigenous constructs of difference, which will be discussed later. They noted that this new perspective caused them to think of the students they served in a different light. One individual noted that even thinking about which "system" was "better" caused her to stop and think "Why am I putting that in the binary". "Why do I think that one has to be *the answer*, the winner?" From my experience, the discussions that followed were some of the best that I have been involved in over the 30 years I have worked in this area.

Another woman noted that her entire job was to classify and designate students as disabled in order to obtain the proper resources. She wanted to know if any of us thought there was a way around the outsider designation and the impact classifications can have on students as they go through school. It was decided that a great deal more thought, and discussion would need to occur, but that looking at these issues from alternative cultural perspectives could potentially provide opportunities and ways to eliminate the binary hierarchy that places the labeled "disabled" in the inferior "Other" position. When asked, my answer was that I did not know if Western/White cultures could give up such embedded foundational assumptions. Indeed, is unclear to me whether a community can alter foundational epistemological or phenomenological assumptions.

While the above discussion of the binary paradox establishes one of the paradoxical aspects, there are other aspects that should be acknowledged and studied. Indeed, a discussion as to whether the binary paradox is a single paradox with multiple aspects or separate paradoxes is something to be discussed in other settings. Other issues involved with this paradox include individual definitions of "self" given internal and external phenomenological experiences, perceptions of lived experiences, and social and political positioning.

Another aspect of the paradox involves the historical designations of "normal" as noted by Davis (2010) Barnes, and others in the academic and activist field of disability studies. Historically, Western/White orientations supporting disability can be seen to encode concepts such as Plato's "ideal human" which later, with the use of the mathematical mean, became the "average human" as often used in both medicine and psychology. However, in attempting to "pin down" what counts as the "ideal", "perfect", or even "average" human, fails. There is no universal agreement, even within the medical or psychological fields, as to how one can define, let alone identify such beings. Given the inability to identify the "normal" individual, it is equally impossible to establish the abnormal unless one goes to extremes. For example, it is easy enough to phenomenologically experience the difference between the freezing and the boiling of water, although superiority and inferiority seem only situationally determined. Neither extreme can be established as the "normal" positioning of water and in fact it appears absurd to even have the discussion. The designations on the continuum between the extremes of water temperatures create an even more complex and difficult designation when one attempts to "pin point" the "normal" for water.

Given the difficulty of determining human levels, types, and characteristics of disability involving the continuum of lived experience as well as the phenomenological experience of others, strategies for minimizing or eliminating paradoxical aspects of the binary appear to be impossible. In other words, is there a possible game theory strategy in Western/White designation that allows for a recognition of disabilities, even significant disabilities, without the designation of superior and inferior or no winner/loser designations? Would it be possible for both positions to equally win or equally lose in social and governmental capacities?

In delving into the depths of paradoxes, one does need to be cautious as to how paradoxes are approached. We again reference the Western/White orientation to paradox and reason, where paradoxes are thought of as puzzles to be solved or as riddles that reason can resolve. For other cultures, reason is not the means for dealing with paradoxes. Instead, individuals should approach, as Huston Smith claimed, as windows to a higher or different type of knowledge. Moving "through" a paradox would then be not so much of a metalanguage to discuss the language problem, but the potential of a new and/or unique way to understand the issue at hand. Reason would then be the wrong approach to paradoxes and understanding their unique knowledge/wisdom, which brings us to the next aspect for consideration. I am not claiming that one must choose between Western and non-Western perspectives, nor am I claiming that there is an "ideal" or "necessary" answer to the binary paradox or, for that matter, how to define and enact approaches to differences culturally or individually. Instead, the following is offered as a difference in culture, lived experience, and a reorientation involving differences, knowledge, and wisdom. The recent COVID pandemic highlighted some interesting phenomenological experiences and some lived experiences that could have benefited from an acknowledgment of difference wisdom. Indeed, by repositioning epistemological and axiological[9] understandings of difference, opportunities for advancing disability discussions beyond the perceived circular discussion may be possible; thus, achieving Bell's call for inclusion.

Indigenous constructs influencing "difference" dialogue

In response to Bell (2010) call for inclusion and diversity, we will focus on Indigenous perspectives regarding difference and wellness.[10] As documented in academic research, Indigenous epistemologies are equal to, while differing from, Western epistemologies in terms of coherence, applicability, epistemology, complexity, and logic.[11] For example, understanding the difference between Indigenous natural geometries and Western Euclidian geometry illustrates a difference in voice and phenomenological orientation. While Euclidian geometry focuses primarily on abstract mathematics as its foundation, Natural geometries find foundation in Spirit (Eglash, 2005; Urton, 1997). Additionally,

---

9 Axiology can be thought of as ethical or moral determinations within a society. These designate normative evaluations, or the designations of superior and inferior actions.

10 Readers are reminded that no single element is agreed on by all Indigenous people. Each community is unique and complex.

11 While Western theories often claim that all human knowledge at its foundation follows the same logic, Indigenous scholars tend to deny any such logical supervenience.

Indigenous recognitions of various theories, including various natural geometries, do not involve a hierarchical valuation. In other words, "different from" means "different from", not "better than" or "worse than".[12]

In general, Indigenous cultures accept the lived experience of spirit as the foundation of phenomenology. In addition, phenomenological experience tends to be understood as being in flux which entails that existence continually changes. It follows then that preferential positioning is excluded as a foundational element in Indigenous knowledge (Talamantez, 2006). Moreover, as the experience of reality is unique to each individual, both knowledge and positioning require significant consideration of the subjective component of one's lived experience. Positioning preference becomes variable, or situationally dependent, and allows for differences in the understanding of what counts for knowledge or wisdom. Wisdom rather than "truth" becomes the object of lived experience and binds communities through reciprocity. Reciprocity, in turn, recognizes that beings possess various types of wisdom that, when brought together, create a balanced community. It follows then that Indigenous epistemologies tend to embrace interdependence and reciprocity combined with spirit to inform understandings of difference (Denzin et al., 2008; Lovern & Locust, 2013).

Spirit at its ultimate level is understood to be whole,[13] and the parts represented by individual beings, both human and other-than-human, retain an interconnectivity at the spiritual level. Using Cajete's discussion of Indigenous multileveled epistemology, one begins to understand the phenomenological complexity involved with differences (Cajete, 2008, pp. 28–31). Being able to inhabit or engage multiple spheres denies hierarchical or preferential positioning as each sphere holds unique wisdom. Like natural geometries, Indigenous communities involve both complex and subjective phenomenological realities. Varying experiences require varying skills emanating from wisdom differences, which, in turn, allow communities to balance. It is the reciprocity involving communal/individual balancing that promotes wellness as well as social and political equality.

Indigenous claims of subjectivity, as is often argued in Western conversations, necessitate neither relativism nor anarchy. Indigenous knowledge embraces difference as necessary to advance individual and communal wellness, as the two are interdependent. An individual or group may hold that their way is preferable for them, but that does not mean that the preference should or could be extrapolated or universalized beyond them. Ways of being are neither universal, nor essential, and often do not translate beyond the specific individual or group.[14] The value of differences is that they allow for learning and teaching so as to promote spiritual understanding (Lovern & Locust, 2013). Learning and teaching are not independent activities but are also interdependent and include communal, human,

---

12 This is an idea recognized in Western logic, but not employed in Western hierarchical dichotomies, creating logical tensions.
13 It should be noted that while individual spirits are generally considered whole, they can be damaged by certain experiences or events. However, one should not assume that an individual with a different, even a severely differenced body, has a damaged spirit. The individual's spirit may be completely whole and undamaged regardless of the body's condition. The reverse can similarly be stated. A person with a seemingly whole body may have a damaged spirit.
14 For example, there are various Indigenous understandings as to why body and mind differences occur including individually caused, other caused, Creator made, and chosen by the individual before birth. Often the reason for the difference is considered important only insofar as it helps one to come to balance with the situation, not as a means of instilling guilt.

and nonhuman, reciprocity. Establishing wellness in both individuals and communities requires learning and teaching amid complex levels of lived experiences (Linklater, 2014).

Indigenous understandings of difference may be more understandable to the non-Indigenous when thought of in terms of talents. Someone may not have a talent for seeing while another may not have a talent for walking. Together the two have what the other lacks and so, as an intertwined whole, create balance. Furthermore, as no being is complete without talents, even if experiencing an extremely different lived experience, all talents are valued for the wisdom they represent.[15] Additionally, since no individual possesses all talents, there is no "ideal" human. In the same way, there are so many differences between any two given individuals that identifying which should be considered "important" and which is not is often considered an unanswerable question. For example, why consider one skin color preferable as a differing construct? Why not differentiate according to attached or unattached earlobes? Finally, individual talents change, and differing circumstances require different talents. These circumstances are in flux, meaning that a talent that is important at this moment will likely not be important in future moments as circumstances change.

Understanding wellness is then not a matter of overcoming or eliminating differences; wellness involves balance, interdependence, and reciprocity within the community, both human and other-than-human. Furthermore, as Indigenous communities do not embrace an idea of a "fixed", "able-bodied", "normal", "average", or "ideal human", all beings both have and lack talents, allowing for the understanding that one can learn from areas where one lacks talent and teach from areas of talent. As talents and situations constantly shift, balance is not a position achieved and kept. It is a journey, not a destination. Indigenous understandings of difference fundamentally reflect positive rather than negative understandings associated with difference designations, making Indigenous positions a missing and much-needed dialogue partner.[16] The Indigenous voice can expand Western discussions with knowledge and wisdom that challenge hierarchical binaries while recognizing that differences in paradigms are neither better than nor worse than others; thus, emphasizing both variation and equality. This type of game theory strategy allows for the possibility of acknowledging differences, while also allowing all players to win or all players to lose as well as the possibility of a win-lose scenario. In this strategy, it is the element of hierarchical preference that has been eliminated.

Difference wisdom

Here, is briefly illustrated some Indigenous difference wisdom gleaned from the recent COVID pandemic that could have assisted many had people of difference been given the knowledge and respect that those deemed non-different experienced. As a result of the

---

15 There is an understanding that, while bodies may be different, spirit is always whole. That does not mean spiritual illnesses do not exist, only that such tend to be considered in a different category of unwellness. An individual with a severely different body may experience no spiritual illness and so remains spiritually whole and equally interconnected with all beings.

16 It should be noted that often in Indigenous communities, differences are recognized. However, many may not accept designation of "disabled" or allow their children to be so identified because of issues of labeling. This was another topic of the above-mentioned meeting that pointed to a dilemma. Labeling can indeed have negative impacts and limit an individual's options, but without labeling, resources may not be allotted. It is the case that some Indigenous people will not accept the labeling even if it comes with resources as it denies the wisdom of the difference in one's lived experience. They note the value in difference.

pandemic, issues of isolation, anxiety, and distancing led to reports of increased mental and physical stress, so the phrase "the new normal" has become popular in the U.S. Interestingly, the "new normal" for some people shares similarities with the "old normal" for many people of difference. Here, I assert anecdotal evidence regarding Indigenous ways of viewing difference and how this understanding can advance Western dialogues of disability in a way that benefits both "disabled" and "abled" persons. The embeddedness of interdependence and reciprocity recognizes the equality and importance of difference and the value it plays in wisdom and the advancement of individual/community wellness. Currently, both national and international reports evidence that COVID disproportionally impacted global Indigenous communities for reasons that include lack of access to healthcare, poverty, lack of government support, and racism (Nuorgam, 2020–2021; Wade, 2020). While these must be addressed, that discussion must be left for another paper. Here, we focus on Indigenous constructs of wellness during the pandemic. Using three brief case studies, one can begin to engage with the wisdom gained by those, who have experiences regarding differences. These cases, and those not written here, often involve the teaching of resiliency, leadership, and perseverance involving traditional concepts of reciprocity. There is a great deal that can be learned from those designated as "disabled" in Western dialogues.[17] Here I offer only three examples regarding the value of difference wisdom. However, it is hoped that the study of difference wisdom becomes a standard in disability studies.

COVID created the need to reassess much of our daily lives such as the most important isolation. Attempting to leave the house to obtain daily necessities such as toilet paper or medicine created new and anxiety-ridden challenges for many people. Identifying how to deal with these lived experiences for many created mental and physical unwellness. The U.S. experienced a rise in the use of depression and anxiety treatments and medication. In the first case study, an individual diagnosed with panic disorder and agoraphobia[18] shared difference wisdom gained from years of navigating such challenges. For this individual, the chaos of the pandemic seemed familiar and almost "normal", as the stress of socially engaging or traveling had challenged her to balance and gain skills to which she may not have otherwise had access. Her difference wisdom assisted others within her community to create or embrace solutions for shopping, obtaining daily necessities, and assisting in distance care of family and friends. Her ability to translate chaos into workable structure proved helpful to her community as they worked together to protect the vulnerable as well as to understand and cope with the "new normal" of isolation and germ fears.

In a second case study, COVID isolation and distancing required many to rethink and adjust social support roles such as caretaking and obtaining medical treatment for themselves and family members. Even receiving non-COVID medical treatment became threatening for many and required adaptation in order to ensure safety. Family and friend support systems, child care that allowed one to work effectively, and accessing education represented significant obstacles and disrupted familiar and comfortable routines.

---

17 This is not to say that similar events did not happen in Western communities. It is only to note that these are enshrined Indigenous community components involving interconnection and responsibilities whereas Western communities continue to struggle with enshrined issues of individuality and rights.

18 It should be noted that all "diagnoses" have variants, and none should be considered universal or essential.

To assist those new to these experiences, one individual, diagnosed as having recurring "clinical post-partum depression", worked to establish a community for new mothers during the pandemic as these women were reporting increased depression and post-partum problems. The diagnosed individual's skills in relaxation and self-care, along with her experiences dealing with mental and physiological post-birth changes, allowed her to help other mothers as they faced the difficulties of infant care in isolation. For many of these women, they did not suffer from post-partum issues but lacked the support of family and friends. One individual even talked to the woman with difference wisdom about how she was unable to share the first-year events with anyone so that her daughter could remain healthy, which increased her sadness and grief over lost opportunities and lost memories. The woman's wisdom with isolation, fear, and doubt during the post-birth experiences in isolation and the worry and doubt that followed allowed her to create a community of new mothers. For many of these women, experiencing new babies while in isolation turned from overwhelming to a community of support in dealing with colic to dealing with online and in-person physician visits. This "new normal" was new not just to these mothers, but to family and friends, who had no experience or advice on how to approach these unique situations. The woman of wisdom difference said she emphasized the need for interdependence and reciprocity as they all worked together to navigate these lived experiences. This community offered many a way to openly and honestly deal with their doubts, fears, and emotional experiences with people who better understood what they were experiencing. From these discussions grew support and solutions while maintaining safety protocols in a nonjudgmental atmosphere.

As the daily obstacles increased and continued over months, many people expressed feelings of being "overwhelmed" and "out of control". The cry for "normalcy" even turned into movements to eliminate masking and distancing procedures and to claim that the pandemic was no worse than other influenzas. So, while some attempted to achieve normalcy by ignoring precautions, others sought alternative ways, based on precautions, to deal with daily life in a global pandemic. In some cases, the different approaches led to breaks with family and friends making support even more difficult and causing additional levels of insecurity, anxiety, and anger. Family and friend relationships felt volatile and for many permanently damaged.

The third case study involves a couple, whose muscular dystrophy diagnoses included different levels of mobility and the use of a feeding tube, their years of difference wisdom advanced many unique solutions for avoiding infections and dealing with the need for a more isolated lived experience. This couple had long dealt with germ and infection avoidance, accessing food and government assistance, and the need to work from home, while staying emotionally and physically balanced. Their wisdom as well as their prior established community readily illustrates how the knowledge of interdependence and reciprocity can benefit. This couple was able to help teach many how to promote happiness, satisfaction, and fulfillment while incorporating the precautions necessary for health and safety. In addition, they were able to assist in terms of maintaining distance relationships using technology as these were skills they had advanced in their own lives. Their ability to help others talk openly and honestly about their experiences, challenges, and emotions contributed to the wellness and balance of many during the pandemic. For many impacted by their teachings, it was the couple's ability to focus on what was most important and what could be controlled that inspired others to consider similar assessments.

The above three examples represent the plethora of untapped difference wisdom. Their wisdom taught skills including adaptation, balance, gratitude, and creativity. Additionally, the abilities they shared instilled hope and even humor in extreme circumstances and encouraged an atmosphere of wellness. I do not claim that individuals classified according to Western disability categories access information that those classified as abled do not, I only note that for Indigenous communities different experiences are valuable in the balancing of community and individuals, especially in times such as the recent pandemic. As many were challenged, physically and mentally during COVID in ways that were new to them, the skills, and unique solutions of those who had had experience with these differences became even more valuable. Their talents and experiences offered valuable insight on how to not only survive mental, physical, and emotional challenges during the pandemic; but, when understood as equal community partners, their wisdom could assist in improving a multitude of outcomes. Indigenous epistemologies tend to recognize that the concept of equality is indeed enshrined in human rights and requires all voices to be equally represented and valued as dialogue partners. Government and community cannot be excluded from the conversation as these institutions often offer practical, albeit limited resources. However, individuals of difference should not be excluded from any aspect of existence because it is their wisdom that gives insight into lived experiences of difference and offers unique solutions for both individuals and communities. Critics may claim that the difference wisdoms illustrated above are not especially profound as they involve "ordinary" activities such as shopping and childcare. However, most of our daily activities rarely qualify as profound until they are impaired as was evidenced in the pandemic.

References

Barnes, C. (2010). A brief history of discrimination and disabled people. *The disability reader.* Davis, L. J. (Ed). Routledge: New York. 21–32.

Bell, C. (2010). Is disability studies actually white disability studies? *The disability reader.* Davis, L. J. (Ed). Routledge: New York. 374–382.

Bourdieu, P. (1999). *Language and symbolic power.* Thompson, J. B. (Ed). Raymond, G. and Adamson Trans. Harvard University Press: Cambridge.

Cajete, G. (2008). Seven orientations for the development of indigenous science education. In *Handbook of Critical and Indigenous Methodologies.* In N. K. Denzin., Y. S. Lincoln & L. T. Smith. (Eds), (pp. 487–496). SAGE Publications.

Clare, E. (2017). *Brilliant imperfection: Grappling with cure.* Duke University Press: Durham.

Corker, M. and Shakespeare, T. (2002). *Disability/postmodernity: Embodying disability theory.* Continuum: London.

Davis, L. J. (2010). Constructing normalcy. *The disability reader.* Davis, L. J. (Ed). Routledge: New York. 3–19.

Denzin, N. K., Lincoln, Y. S. and Smith, L. T. (2008). *Handbook of critical and Indigenous methodologies.* Los Angeles: Sage. 217–232.

Eglash, R. (2005). *African fractals: Modern computing and Indigenous design.* Rutgers University Press: New Brunswick.

Habermas, J. (1996). *Between facts and norms.* Rehg, W. Trans. The MIT Press: Cambridge.

Hume, D. (1961). *A treatise of human nature.* Doubleday and Company, Inc.: New York.

Husserl, E. (1970). *The crisis of European sciences and transcendental phenomenology.* Northwestern University Press: Evanston.

Linklater, R. (2014). *Decolonizing trauma work: Indigenous stories and strategies.* Fernwood Publishing: Halifax.

Lovern, L. and Locust, C. (2013). *Native American communities on health and disability*. Palgrave Macmillan: New York.

Nuorgam, A. (2020–2021). COVID-19 and Indigenous people. UN. Department of Economic and Social Affairs: Indigenous People. www.un.org/development/desa/indigenouspeoples/covid-19.html

Talamantez, I. M. (2006). Teaching native American religious traditions and healing. *Teaching religion and healing*. Barnes, L. L. and Talamantez, I. (Ed). Oxford University Press: New York. 114–126.

Urton, G. (1997). *The social life of numbers: A Quechua Ontology of numbers and philosophy of arithmetic*. University of Texas Press: Austin.

Wade, L. (2020). COVID-19 data on Native Americans is 'a national disgrace.' This scientist is fighting to be counted. *Science*. www.sciencemag.org/news/2020/09/covid-19-data- native-americans-national-disgrace-

Waters, A. (2004). Language matters: Nondiscrete nonbinary dualism. *American Indian Thought* (pp. 97–115). Waters, A. (Ed). Blackwell Publishing: Malden.

Wendell, S. (2008). Toward a feminsit theory of disability. *The Feminist Philosophy Reader* (pp. 104–124). Bailey, A. and Cuomo, C. (Ed). McGraw Hill: Boston.

Willinsky, J. (1998). *Learning to divide the world: Education at empire's end*. University of Minnesota Press: Minneapolis.

Wittgenstein, L. (1969). *On certainty*. Anscombe, G. E. M. and von Wright, G. H. (Ed). Paul, D. and Anscombe, G. E. M. Trans. Harper and Row: New York.

24 The birth and care of Määt Jääy in a context of structural violence, "disability" in a Mixe town in Oaxaca

Zoila Romualdo Pérez

Introduction

Indigenous peoples in the world constitute a social group with a history and cultural identity built from the thought formed by the nature/territory/community triad, which has generated a particular form of struggles and resistance, forms of organization of community life, and various care practices for the physical and spiritual being.

However, the trajectory of Indigenous peoples has been marked by a painful reality of exclusion and social marginalization, generated by injustice rooted in social structures. This situation subjects them to persistent forms of exploitation, oppression, exclusion, and a constant condition of poverty (Rilko-Bauer & Farmer, 2017; Taylor, 2006) that gives rise to high rates of mortality, injuries, stigmatization, and psychological damage (Farmer, 2004).

Unfortunately, this reality becomes even more challenging for Indigenous people with disabilities, since violence is entrenched, normalized, and accepted as part of the social fabric, which has given rise to living conditions characterized by inaccessibility to health services, discrimination, stigmatization, and other forms of exclusion that constitute serious violations of human rights.

In this context, I address the situation of birth and care of Indigenous girls and boys with "disabilities[1]" whose mothers were victims of structural violence, situations that triggered cases of maternal death, and the current condition of "disability." This chapter is the product of a qualitative research with an ethnographic approach, carried out in the master's program in nursing of the National Autonomous University of Mexico (UNAM), entitled Care practices for girls and boys with disabilities in Mixes families, and their configuration by the social and cultural context (Romualdo, 2019).

Between diversities and inequalities: The case of "disability" in the Mixe people

The term "disability" encompasses various interpretations, the most predominant being the biomedical view, which defines and classifies it according to deficiencies, limitations, and restrictions in participation. This perspective is not shared by Indigenous peoples, whose history, knowledge, and relationships are based on a cultural heritage marked by a spiritual connection with nature, in which the relationship between human beings and nature is fundamental for existence, promoting a reciprocity and mutual respect.

---

1 The term disability is placed in quotes because the chapter relates the worldview of a Mixe indigenous people, whose knowledge, and forms of organization in life, health and illness are not compatible with the knowledge of the biomedical model of health.

DOI: 10.4324/9781032656519-29

The above allows people from Indigenous peoples to share a community life influenced by a shared cultural worldview, where interaction with Mother Nature fosters the acceptance of diversities without prejudice or exclusion. According to this vision, people exist in their territories as they were created by Mother Nature, giving rise to a way of living in a relationship of acceptance, understanding, help, and care, where each living being needs and deserves to be provided for. This is how in the Ayuujk Jääy region, the term "disability" does not make any sense, since the existence of each Mixe life is a product of the relationship maintained with nature, specifically, the life of each Tu'uk Nëëm Jääy, a supreme spiritual being is requested who inhabits one of the sacred places of the community, known as the Ancient Mother (Romualdo, 2023).

In the Mixe people, diversity promotes respect, compassion, care, and teaching to cope with life in the community, as well as the Määt Jääy, people who cannot walk, speak, be independent, and with some physical deformation in the body; the Úum, those who do not articulate words with their mouths; Nät, those who do not perceive sounds with their ears; Jëntëny, those who totally lack vision and Ëjjy Jääy, apparently physically healthy people. They are all creations of nature that need physical and spiritual care, in addition to life teachings so that they can develop a life according to their own needs.

Thus, while in biomedicine the functional classification of the anatomical structures of the body predominates to name the various types of disabilities according to limitations and deficiencies, among the Tu´uk Nëëm Jääy a relationship of respect is maintained towards the diversities, sent, and created by nature, where the role of families and communities is to ensure the well-being of all through rituals that are offered to the spiritual beings that inhabit the main sacred caves of the community.

The Määt Jaääy, Úum, Nät, Jëntëny, like the other members of the community, must learn to live in coexistence with nature; therefore, they learn to work the land, to harvest the riches that nature provides, to perform worship rituals, to help care for others, to provide food, and what is necessary for family subsistence.

Although diversity is accepted and Indigenous communities strive to maintain collective well-being through harmonious coexistence with nature, social, economic conditions and geographical locations are the main causes of high rates of morbidity and mortality, precarious living conditions, experiences of discrimination, premature death, disability, etc. This is the case of most countries that have lower human and economic development; in Bolivia alone, 68% of maternal deaths occur in Indigenous women; in Colombia, the risk of mortality from obstetric causes among Indigenous women is between two and six times higher than that of non-Indigenous women (Márquez et al., 2017); in Mexico, problems during childbirth represent one of the main factors of childhood disability, with 6.5% of children affected, with Oaxaca being the state with the highest percentage (6.6%), followed by Guerrero, Tabasco, Zacatecas, and Veracruz (Instituto National Statistics and Geography, 2020, 2021). Areas within Oaxaca which concentrate half of the Indigenous population with disabilities between 3 and 17 years old have a higher percentage of disability than other parts of the country (National Institute of Statistics and Geography, 2020).

The situation of perinatal mortality is a persistent issue in Indigenous communities due to various factors such as those related to inequalities in social structures, gender relations (García et al., 2006), inaccessibility to health care services, barriers of language, and cultural misunderstanding. Despite the important efforts made through strategies, public policies, and the contribution of midwives in childbirth and puerperium care (Dias-Scopel & Scopel, 2018; Icó & Daniels, 2020; Manrique, 2022; Maternal Mortality Observatory, 2022), Indigenous populations remain in the red in terms of mortality and disability associated with maternal-perinatal complications (UN Permanent Forum on Indigenous Issues, 2016).

What has been explained so far leads to the next section, where the situation of the birth of Mixe girls and boys will be addressed as an important factor for the appearance of "disability" in a context of structural violence. The Mixes call themselves "The Never Conquered" because, during the Spanish conquest, their location protected by imposing mountains prevented invaders from reaching their territories. This circumstance has allowed them to preserve their own form of social and cultural organization to this day.

The birth of Määt Jääy[2] in a Mixe village in Oaxaca[3]

Indigenous women face complex life situations within their community's social context, labor and birth of a baby are some of them. Especially when the knowledge of childbirth does not coincide with the standards considered normal by biomedicine (Andina, 2002; Mexican Institute of Social Security, 2019), this has happened with pain, one of the main symptoms indicative of labor in knowledge. Medically, pain is presented as a constant experience (García et al., 2016), a sensation that one takes care of to avoid experiencing (Bula et al., 2019; Dias-Scopel & Scopel, 2018).

However, the experience and perception of pain vary in different cultures. For example, among the Bororo in Brazil, pain during childbirth is considered a normal physiological process and is experienced without interventions. For these women, childbirth represents a moment to demonstrate their strength and courage, shown through silence and resignation, an attitude learned since childhood due to cultural practices that value pain as part of belonging to the social group (Knupp & Saléte, 2016). On the other hand, Guna women give birth without pain thanks to the consumption of a plant called Tuleina, which facilitates dilation and in many cases allows a pain-free birth (Martin & Grigera, 2017).

In contrast to Bororo women who feel pain but do not express it, Mixe women do not experience pain during childbirth, which has baffled health personnel (Knupp & Saléte, 2016) and the women themselves. This is the case of Tu:h, mother of Tsëpajkxn, while working in the field, she felt the need to go to the bathroom and, at that moment, her baby was born and fell to the ground. She immediately cleaned and wrapped her, moved her to her bed, and He lay down next to her. Tu:h was not expecting delivery because there was no pain, and she was also unsure of her due date since she had not been able to receive prenatal medical attention. Tell Your:

> So, when she was born in the cornfield (I was working in the cornfield) … she fell to the ground, she fell among the dry corn, she was born in the month of December, when the party was in Cerro de Guadalupe… your grandparents were there celebrating… I had her alone …I just cleaned it with clothes and rolled it up… I was fine, I didn't feel anything.

---

2 Määt Jääy, in the Mixes, is the name given to people with disabilities.
3 In this chapter, Mixe pseudonyms are mentioned, which represent the most traditional symbols of Mixe community life, which were used in the research process to maintain the anonymity of the female caregivers and their children with disabilities. In the case of the informants, the following pseudonyms were used: Tu:h (rain), Mo:hk (corn), Dzuk (lightning), Pew (wind), Koots (night) and Nëë (water), for the girls and children: Tsëpajkxn (peach), Timte (seed), Ma′kx (forgiveness), Tiksj (clear), Tyëjk (house), Tep (cold), Mëjk (strong).

Over time, Tsëpajkxn received medical attention and was diagnosed with cerebral palsy, from the family's knowledge she is Määt Jääy.

In another case, the mother of Mëjk (8 years old) and Tep (16 years old) experienced this situation. According to Nëë, the children's father, a few weeks before Mëjk's birth, they went to the regional community hospital due to incipient discomfort that did not become painful. There was still time left before the estimated delivery date, so the health personnel determined that she was not in labor and suggested they return at another time. The couple returned to their home, located between high and lush mountains.

On the day of birth, the mother was busy with housework and did not feel pain until she started bleeding. The baby would not descend and Nëë desperately searched for help to take the mother to the hospital. Coincidentally, the municipal authorities were holding a party nearby, which seemed like a fortuitous opportunity. However, when he approached them, he received no response. It took a long time until one of them agreed to take her to the center of town to seek medical assistance. During the long hours of waiting and the trip along a rarely traveled road, Nëë returned too late and Mëjk's mother had died.

Upon arrival, the grandfather tried to resuscitate the baby, who was finally born. At first, the baby showed signs of cyanosis, but with time and the grandfather's efforts, he began to cry and regain his natural tone. Faced with this tragic situation, the person accompanying Nëë offered to take the father and baby to seek medical attention. This time, they would undertake a trip to the state capital, a journey that would last four hours. Over time Mëjk was diagnosed with tetralogy of Fallot, although from the knowledge of the Mëjk family he is a Määt Jääy.

For her part, Dzuk, Ma'kx's mother, went to a midwife after her doctor conditioned her care with a considerable sum of money, impossible for the family to pay at that time and even though the ultrasound had revealed oligohydramnios (under amniotic fluid level), the woman did not receive the care she needed. Dzuk notes:

> When I suddenly stopped, I was already all wet, I already went to the same doctor and he said, no, your son is going to be born, but he is going to be born by cesarean section, we need 10 thousand pesos for him to be born. But since then for me it was 50 thousand, 12 years ago, but you didn't tell us that, I told you, never… but I'm very busy, I can't attend to you and he came in.

Thus, she goes to the midwife, who, in the attempt to induce pain, administered a medication, whose name and/or component is unknown to Dzuk, an act that ended in hemorrhage and without labor pain, subsequently diagnosed with cerebral palsy.

In other cases, Tïmte's mothers, Ma'kx and Tyëjk, attended their follow-up appointments to review and monitor the pregnancy, without feeling any discomfort or signs of pain that would indicate an imminent birth. However, ultrasounds revealed a decrease in amniotic fluid, indicating the need to proceed with delivery, emergency cesarean sections were scheduled, but not all were performed in a timely manner. In Tïmte's case, the caesarean section was carried out immediately, while Tyëjk remained in his mother's womb for one night and most of the next day, being attended to at birth only when bleeding began. Koots notes:

> No, it didn't hurt, when the liquid ran out it started to hurt, but it wasn't even possible, I think it was at 5 o'clock when they passed it, it had already started to hurt and it didn't hurt much either, it just started to bleed, we went Let's see and she was only bleeding and then they operated on her, the baby was already very strange when they took her out, she was already green, she almost died.

At almost two years old, Tyëjk was diagnosed with probable cerebral palsy. The diagnosis has not been confirmed because he has not received further medical attention, but the family cares for him like Määt Jääy.

Of the seven boys and girls, whose stories were part of this research, two were born at term (Tijks and Tep) and without complications, but gradually they presented limitations in mobilization and ambulation, two of the births were attended at the regional hospital of the community and one was born in the countryside. In these women, the absence of pain was so distinctive that only the presence of hemorrhage was the key indicator for urgent delivery, which later led to a life with disability.

This is how the Mixes women experienced the situation of labor and birth of the current Määt Jääy boys and girls, and there were various circumstances that favored the suffering from pregnancy, birth, and certainly in the puerperium (although it was not the subject of research on this occasion) and continues like this in daily life. The conditions of labor and birth were decisive in shaping a life with disabilities crossed by various forms of violence in its multiple forms of expression.

The structural conditions that surrounded the lives of these families, characterized by geographical difficulties, scarcity of means of transportation, and lack of access to health services, led to tragic events such as preventable maternal death and disabilities in girls and boys.

In the next section, I will describe how female caregivers begin a trajectory of care for Määt Jääy people that must last the rest of the life of some of them, care that is crossed and marked by the structural and cultural conditions of family life.

Caring for the newborn Määt Jääy: Between encounters and disagreements

Despite the experiences and circumstances in which a baby is born, this new member of the family is welcomed with rituals to establish their relationship of community life in interaction with Mother Nature. Thus, under the guidance of the village shaman, the care of every newborn begins with gratitude to the Ancient Mother, who is also asked for the well-being of that new being, before, during, and after birth.[4] Every newborn Mixe boy or girl is welcomed through family coexistence, accompanied by a typical food called machucado. This typical dish is a symbol of famine and is consumed twice a year, on the third day of a baby's birth, and at the beginning of the harvest. A ritual is performed to Mother Nature, where one blesses and gives thanks for life, health, well-being, and asks that food not be lacking in this new beginning. After this welcoming ritual, the family begins the Mixe cultural care known as making a custom, which has two variants. In the context of newborn care:

- Make a habit as a thank you to Mother Nature. Mothers express their love for the baby by visiting sacred caves, with prior guidance from the fortune teller (shaman) to ask for the health, well-being, and healthy growth of the baby, always seeking the Mëjkt ät, which refers to the optimal state of well-being, even when there is illness and/or precarious living conditions.
- Make a habit to heal an illness and ask for well-being. Through the guidance of the fortune teller (shaman), the family performs rituals in sacred caves. During this ritual,

4 To delve deeper into the topic of gratitude to the magical being known as Ancient Mother, we invite you to read the following chapter. Chapter 10: Indigenous philosophical thought and biomedicine in disability, pages 237–239, from the book Disability in the indigenous and native peoples of Abya Yala A decolonial, intercultural and critical turn. Available at: https://libreria.clacso.org/publicacion.php?p=2927&c=0.

prayers are performed, and chicken sacrifices are made, with the intention of leaving the disease in the sacred places specified for this purpose and asking for well-being from the mystical beings of nature, who care for and protect the people.

Caring for a newborn is a joy shared among the women of the family, who care for it through physical contact, hugs, and cuddles in their arms. The first days are of celebration and frequent visits. There are those who bring food and drinks as a sign of respect and affection. But as the days go by, the environment becomes lonely, especially when the baby begins to show signs that suggest possible problems in its growth and development. Then, the journey begins in search of help, explanations, and solutions from the mother and close family.

In most families, the first step is to visit the community's fortune teller or shaman, who offers guidance on the newborn's situation, which begins with rituals in sacred places to "cure" the baby and ends with acceptance rituals, and gratitude to nature for the life of the person. Families that have economic resources seek medical assistance to explain the person's developmental conditions and this is where they receive the diagnosis of disability, but the diagnostic labels are not adopted by the majority of mothers, but rather by them from their own knowledge and notions of the body establish a form of care according to the cultural context, although I must mention that some try to follow the care recommended by health personnel, but in the long run it does not make any sense since it involves constant travel, expenses transportation, search for medical equipment, etc., which result in emotional and economic wear on the family (Pérez, 2016).

Thus, families in this journey of searching for answers, attention, and care between health personnel, fortune tellers (shamans) and religion[5] tend to get confused, generally at first they think that the babies are going through a disease process (understanding the disease as pain or physical discomfort, which is cured with medication or rituals to sacred places) (Romualdo, 2019), little by little they realize that it is not an illness, that it is a condition granted by the Ancient Mother, and this is corroborated by the fortune tellers, that is when he acquires the identity of Määt Jääy.[6]

When families understand, identify, and accept that their son or daughter is Määt Jääy, they understand that they must take care of their life and well-being, although the process is accompanied by uncertainty, fears, and social criticism. There are community and cultural constructions that try to explain the origin of disability, such as those related to violations of social and religious norms (Fontes, 2014). For Tu'uk Nëëm Jääy mothers, it is clear that the situation of labor and birth was a predisposing factor.

"Disability" entails challenges that subject the mother to situations of violence, rejection, and discrimination, by the family and the community. This was experienced by Tu:h, mother of Tsëpajkx, who faced rejection and violence from her father and the community, receiving hurtful words related to her status as a single mother. In an attempt to protect and care for her daughter, she decided to move away from her community and seek employment in Mexico City, leaving her other children in the care of her mother. However, the situation did not improve because her daughter began to show

5 Religious syncretism predominates in the Mixes.
6 If the reader wishes to delve deeper into this cultural concept, Määt Jääy, we invite you to review Chapter V. "Disability" from and in indigenous peoples in Abya Yala/Afro/Latin/America: approaches from Colombia (Êbêra Eyábida world) and Mexico (Ayüük Jääy world, from the book Who is the subject of disability? Explorations, configurations, and potentialities. Available at: https://www.clacso.org/wp-content/uploads/2021/05/Quien-es-el-subject-of-disability.pdf.

developmental problems, so she decided to return, exposing herself to social criticism and judgment.

Most female caregivers have established a care routine, in which each member of the family has a role and an assigned task, although the greatest workload and responsibility usually falls on them. In her eagerness to guarantee the continuity of life, one of these women, dedicated to agricultural work, took her daughter with her while she worked in the field. To protect her from the sun, he placed her in a narrow wooden box next to a tree or plant that provided shade, while she, under the sun's rays and with her hands in the ground, continued cultivating the land.

In the Mixe region, women and their families provide care according to their own knowledge and resources, which consist of physical rehabilitation therapies under bio-medical guidance, spiritual practices such as baptism, and worship of Mother Nature through rituals led by shamans. This diversity of care seeks to maintain the continuity of life despite adverse circumstances.

As a conclusion and reflection for health personnel

Health care for Indigenous people has been strongly influenced by the hegemony of bio-medicine, which does not always adjust to the comprehensive needs of these communities. Generally, biomedicine establishes care and treatment routes based on diagnostic labels, anatomically and physiologically evaluating the sick body, without much consideration of the social, cultural, and economic context of the people.

The lack of social and cultural sensitivity has generated experiences of pain and suffering, causing premature deaths, disabilities, and other complications that could be avoided if other perspectives on health care and illness were taken into account.

The perinatal contexts presented here illustrate the need for healthcare personnel to question their own knowledge, recognizing that the biomedical approach is not the only explanation for the ills and pains that affect society. The life circumstances documented in this chapter demand health professionals sensitive to cultural and social diversity, aware of gender and human rights issues, capable of implementing intercultural care strategies to prevent premature deaths, reduce maternal and neonatal morbidity and mortality, as well as how to avoid disabilities caused by negligence.

The social and cultural context in which these Indigenous women have brought life and cared for their children has been marked by situations of suffering, precariousness, rejection, abandonment, and death. These circumstances require being understood from multiple disciplines, especially by health professionals, since cultural worldviews guide practices and forms of care in the search for well-being and health in everyday life. Understanding the socioeconomic characteristics and living conditions of Indigenous peoples implies recognizing the existence of social determinants of health and disability.

References

Andina, E. (2002). Trabajo de parto y parto normal. Guías de prácticas y procedimientos. *Revista del Hospital Materno Infantil Ramón Sardá, 21*(2), 63–74.

Bula, J., Maza, L. and Orozco, M. (2019). Prácticas de cuidado cultural en el continuo reproductivo de la mujer Embera Katio del Alto Sinú. *Enfermería: Cuidados Humanizados, 8*, 102–138.

Dias-Scopel, R. and Scopel, D. (2018). ¿Quiénes son las parteras munduruku? Pluralismo médico y autoatención en el parto domiciliario entre indígenas en Amazonas. *Brasil. Desacatos, 58*, 16–33.

Farmer, P. (2004). An anthropology of structural violence. *Current Anthropology, 45*(3), 305–325.

Fontes, C. (2014). Discapacidades en niños y jóvenes Tapietes y Guaraníes: Análisis de las prácticas y saberes comunitarios. *Rev. argent. salud pública*, 5(19), 26–32.

Foro Permanente para las Cuestiones Indígenas de la ONU. (2016). Salud y Mortalidad Materna de las Mujeres Indígenas. https://www.unfpa.org/sites/default/files/resource-pdf/factsheet_v20_Spanish.pdf

García, L., Jácome, T., García, J., Hernández, L., Loggia, S., Acevedo, E., González, G., Rodríguez, C., Arteaga, E. and Reyes, E. (2006). Las mujeres indígenas de México: Su contexto socioeconómico, demográfico y de salud. http://cedoc.inmujeres.gob.mx/documentos_download/100833.pdf

García Rodríguez, Y., Anaya González, J. L., Acosta Limaico, M. B., Álvarez Moreno, M., López Aguilar, E. and Vasquez Figueroa, T. I. (2016). Satisfaction of women attended with culturally appropriate birth in Loreto, Orellana (2016). *Cuban Journal of Obstetrics and Gynecology*, 42(4), 485–492.

Icó, M. and Daniels, S. (2020). Parteras mayas tradicionales cuidando la salud de las mujeres. Cultural Survival. https://www.culturalsurvival.org/news/parteras-mayas-tradicionales-cuidando-la-salud-de-las-mujeres

Mexican Social Security Institute. (2019). Surveillance and friendly attention in labor in low-risk pregnancy. Mexican Institute of Social Security. https://www.imss.gob.mx/sites/all/statics/guiasclinicas/052GRR.pdf

Instituto Nacional de Estadística y Geografía. (2020). Principales resultados del Censo de Población y Vivienda 2020 Estados Unidos Mexicanos. https://www.inegi.org.mx/contenidos/productos/prod_serv/contenidos/espanol/bvinegi/productos/nueva_estruc/702825198060.pdf

Instituto Nacional de Estadística y Geografía. (2021). Estadísticas a propósito del Día del Niño (30 de abril). https://www.inegi.org.mx/app/saladeprensa/noticia.html?id=6473

Knupp, R. and Saléte, B. (2016). Análise do nascimento Bororo: Aspectos culturais da dor de parto. *Mundo da Saúde, São Paulo*, 40(2), 160–168.

Manrique, D. (2022). Curanderas y parteras: Saberes que reivindican y tensionan. *Sociologías*, 24(59), 84–107.

Márquez, L., Plana, A. and Villarroel, M. (2017). Mortalidad materna en pueblos indígenas y fuentes de datos. Alcances y desafíos para su medición en países de América Latina. Naciones Unidas. https://repositorio.cepal.org/server/api/core/bitstreams/48b6b5ba-65db-4098-bfa4-e1f8993a6efe/content

Martin, C. and Grigera, A. (08 de agosto de 2017). ¿Por qué las mujeres Guna paren sin dolor? Inter-American Development Bank. Recuperado el 28 de octubre 2023 de. https://blogs.iadb.org/igualdad/es/4122/

Observatorio de Mortalidad Materna. (2022). Situación actual de la partería en México. Informe final. Chiapas, Guerrero, Oaxaca. https://omm.org.mx/wp-content/uploads/2022/02/Situacio%CC%81n-actual-de-la-parteri%CC%81a-indi%CC%81gena-en-Me%CC%81xico.-Informe-final.-Chiapas-Guerrero-Oaxaca.pdf

Pérez, I. (2016). Análisis del entorno de Malawi como guía del cuidado de un niño con discapacidad. *Index Enferm*, 25(3), 136–140.

Rilko-Bauer, B. and Farmer, P. (2017). Structural violence, poverty, and social suffering. In D. Brady and L. M. Burton (Eds.), *The Oxford handbook of the social science of poverty* (pp. 47–74). Oxford University Press.

Romualdo, Z. (2019). Las prácticas de cuidado al niño con discapacidad y su configuración por el contexto social y cultural [Tesis de maestría]. Universidad Nacional Autónoma de México.

Romualdo, Z. (2023). El pensamiento filosófico indígena y la biomedicina en la discapacidad. Avanzando hacia la interculturalización de los sistemas de salud. En: Z. Romualdo, M. Lapierre, A. Moctezuma, X. Escobedo & A. Yarza, Discapacidad en los pueblos indígenas y originarios de Abya Yala Un giro decolonial, intercultural y crítico (pp. 227–275). CLACSO.

Taylor, J. (2006). Explaining difference: "Culture," "structural violence," and medical anthropology. University of Washington Office of Minority Affairs & Diversity.

25 We belong to you, but you don't represent us a Javanese (Indonesian) experience of disabilities

Umar

Introduction

Umar's lived experiences as a person with a physical disability serve as the starting point for this chapter. This topic is related to his PhD research on digital disability activism, which is his heartfelt effort to foster disability self-representation in his country, Indonesia. Living as a person with a physical disability in Indonesia was challenging as he was bullied, stigmatized, and discriminated. When he was six years old, he was rejected by schools due to his physical disability. His parents did everything they could, so he could study at a general school rather than a specialized one. Despite the physical difficulties and the bullying that he suffered over the years, he was a good student and proved that he deserved to study just like what they called "normalized" students. He was one of the very fortunate people with disabilities to receive full scholarships for both of his graduate studies, and he was thrilled to study at the University of Sydney to deepen his insight into inclusion.

Societies in developing countries like Indonesia still consider people with disabilities as invisible. They are labelled as unproductive, and their rights are unfulfilled. The emerging stigma impacted those with disabilities. These problems became even more complicated because the people with disabilities are represented as to be pitied in the Indonesian mass media, which then emphasizes the need for disability self-representation. Together with Rumah Disabilitas, my disabled friends and I are working on raising disability awareness through digital platforms. Our aim is to build a positive representation regarding Indonesian people with disabilities.

For many years, Indonesian people with disabilities became anxious to present their real self. Disability-based organizations have a crucial role in managing disability representation. Thus, in this chapter, I address disability narratives based on lived experiences. To avoid bias, I try not to only share my story, but that of my friends as well, with diverse types of disabilities. Therefore, this chapter discusses different disability experiences from an Indonesian perspective. I am also interested in examining the role of disability organizations and social media in forming disability self-representation.

People with disabilities and self-representation

Some societies have pervasively stigmatized those with disabilities (Madyaningrum et al., 2022; Suharto et al., 2016), rejected their existence (Nurhayati, 2020), and some even restricted their participation in society (Lusli et al., 2016; Septian & Hadi, 2021). These issues led to disparities in the realization of persons with disabilities' human rights

DOI: 10.4324/9781032656519-30

(Widinarsih, 2017). As a result, people with disabilities frequently experience emotions of anxiety and helplessness (Madyaningrum et al., 2022).

Disability is presented in either an empathic (Nurhaqiqi, 2019) or pitiful way (Halim, 2021). The media representations of disability are biased and portrayed in a negative way (Setyowati et al., 2020) so have disregarded people with disabilities (Widinarsih, 2017) and drive the disability inclusion movements (Ellis & Kent, 2011), including the disability organizations (Craig & Bigby, 2015a). These individuals and organizations do not only pave the way to disability representation (Madyaningrum et al., 2022) but also raise awareness (Mineur et al., 2017).

In line with the title of this chapter, discussions of disability representation cannot be separated from debates regarding "who represents who" (Rice et al., 2015). Hence, disability representation is related to the concept of self-representation, which is a notion that is recognized as a representational approach that engages the subject in articulating their own sense of agency (Seubert, 2022). The concept behind this self-representation can be applied to activism to comprehend and present oneself (Hunt et al., 2020). For people with disabilities, self-representation is an integral part of disability inclusion movements (Cocq & Ljuslinder, 2020).

Self-representation is also connected to Erfing Goffman's concept of self, where individuals present their two-sided self depending on social interactions (Humphreys et al., 2019). This concept is in line with disability representation in which people with disabilities shape their identity and present themselves based on different social settings, which might impact their view of self and others (Nario-Redmond et al., 2013). This kind of representation allows them to be acknowledged and respected with a disability, which is crucial to evolve for disability inclusion (Mineur et al., 2017).

Disability living as third culture kid

I am a proud Indonesian, who has lived in two other cities besides my hometown, Surabaya. However, this is not as beautiful as imagined. A study by Sloper (1999) showed that compared to other families, families who raised children with disabilities had lower incomes. Thus, poverty forced both of my parents to be migrant workers in Jeddah, Saudi Arabia, the city where I was born and raised. This condition worsened my social life as a person with a physical disability, as I grew up with bullying and discrimination.

A five-year-old, Umar, was not brave enough to go out of the house to play along with their neighbours. When my whole family went to Mecca for a pilgrimage, Mama put the hijab on me to cover my hands (Figure 25.1). This was the only way to self-represent myself among the crowd. After all the school rejections, my self-representation was positive as I poured my love into public speaking by joining speech competitions. Yet, it did not always end as beautifully as imagined. Stigma and discrimination were part of my self-representation journey.

Living there for 19 years was sufficient time to witness how Jeddah is a livable city. The people are welcoming and respectful as they have a high-context culture, not to mention are influenced by the Islamic values of brotherhood. With a disability, I felt safe in the city, although some children teased me or were afraid of my hands. In 2015, when I graduated from high school, I left Jeddah with the hope that Indonesia would be as inclusive as that city.

I was lucky to have returned to Indonesia when I had the resilience to cope with such rejection from society. Pitiful gazes from adults and the children's fear of my disabled hands

Figure 25.1 Umar's public appearance, 2000.

Source: Photographer: By Umar mother 'Personal Documentation of Umar'

were a part of my three-month adaptation in my neighbourhood. This limited me when I presented my "disability self" among them as my confidence declined. It has always been my Mama who represented me at several events. I was too shy or even just avoided.

Some people told me not to pursue college, arguing that a person with physical disability had no future. I realized that this would leave me even more behind, so I refused to believe the people who dismissed me. I attended college and proved all my abilities and amidst all the accessibility challenges and ended up as the best graduate. It was life-changing as I was then confident to self-represent myself as an empowered person with a physical disability. I am grateful to be able to have a professional career afterwards.

My lived experiences drove me to take part in advocating disability rights and inclusion on several occasions. I am one of the very fortunate people with disabilities to receive full scholarships for both of my graduate studies, and I am thrilled to study at the University of Sydney to deepen my insight into inclusion. This university practices disability inclusion, which is stated in its policy. Three months before I left for Sydney in April 2023, I registered with the university's Inclusion and Disability Services.

I arrived in Australia like an empty glass until I finally poured in an insight on how this country applies disability inclusion not only in its policy but also into practice. Surprisingly, I live like other normal people, something I never did in Jeddah or Surabaya. There are no negative views and no children who are frightened of my hands. During the International Student Welcome Day, the University of Sydney's board also emphasized the representation of disability as part of its diversity, advocating that every student has equal rights.

After a week in Sydney, I was thinking that Indonesia was left far behind in terms of disability inclusion, but both of my supervisors, Professor Gerard Goggin and Professor Jennifer Smith-Merry, ignited my passion to contribute to accelerating Indonesia's disability research plan by conducting research on digital disability activism. As a third culture kid, there is much to discuss, but for the sake of this chapter, I will highlight an Indonesian perspective with diverse narratives on disability self-representation.

Disability lived experience: an Indonesian perspective

Disability is a complex issue in Indonesia, especially, relating to socio-cultural relations (Thohari, 2019). I experienced innumerable bullying and discrimination, so I involved five friends with different disabilities to gather diverse disability lived experiences. First, is Aida Mujtahidah (Aida) who was born with hemiparesis which limits her physical mobility. Physical boundary is also faced by Muhammad Karim (Karim) with his wrist deformity and scoliosis. While Hani Rahmayanti (Hani) has hearing and speech limitations. In contrast, Ana Fransiska (Ana) and Sri Melati (Imel) experienced disability when they reached maturity with Hip Dysplasia and Blindness, respectively.

In Indonesia, having a disability is considered bad karma (Ellis & Kent, 2020) and could cause disgrace to the family (Kusumastuti et al., 2014). When I was one month old, someone told Mama to drown me, thinking that I would be a burden to my parents. Karim has a similar story, in which his parents were blamed and forced to confess their past sins. This has prompted Karim and I to prove them wrong and we are thankful to be pursuing doctorate degrees and empowering our fellow disabled friends.

The most common problem that all of us have encountered is stigmatization (Septian & Hadi, 2021). Individuals with disabilities are considered invisible which impacts the fulfilment of rights (Widinarsih, 2017), including access to the workplace (Damayanti & Sabiq, 2018). My hands with different lengths limit me in having many career options. This also happens to Karim, who was discriminated against on employment.

The continuing stigma (Madyaningrum, 2017; Suharto et al., 2016) and marginalization of people with disabilities have disadvantaged them in a way so that they are not accepted (Widinarsih, 2017), often hidden (Triwahyudi & Setiawan, 2014) and isolated (Nurhayati, 2020). Imel deplores society's level of ignorance towards people with disabilities. Not only towards blind people, but Hani mentions society's ignorance also to deaf people like her. This ignorance reflects the invisibility of people with disabilities in everyday life.

Aside from limited access to participation (Septian & Hadi, 2021), some people with disabilities are rejected in some elements of life (Widinarsih, 2017). Not much different from my experience, Aida has had a couple of rejections in her life. She failed to study at her dream boarding school not because she was not qualified, but due to the lack of accessibility. Among all the pathetic experiences, the worst was when a family refused to marry their son to a lady like her.

Those problems are significant factors for disability self-representation, which is also dependent on self-acceptance. Individuals with congenital disabilities tend to have a higher self-acceptance (Agustina & Valentina, 2023; Sari, 2022), which Aida, Hani, Karim, and I all agree on. The only thing that makes us anxious is the amount of bullying we receive. My school years were sad I was bullied and excluded from friendships. In contrast, Karim was feeling accepted until one of his friends told him that he was implicitly bullied.

While for Ana and Imel, they needed to adapt. This is in line with Agustina & Valentina's study in 2023, which indicated that people, who experienced disability in adulthood, might require a longer time for self-acceptance. 22-year-old Ana felt confused about being diagnosed with Hip Dysplasia and needed a year to overcome her insecurity when it comes to mobility. In some moments, her hip hurts and limits her from doing physical activities like sports. Physically, she seems to be fine like other women. Thus, her condition can be considered as an invisible disability (Mantilla, 2022).

On the other hand, Imel's life was changed back in 2011, when she became blind after a three-week coma, suffering from meningitis and tuberculosis, which caused her brain to swell. Her eyesight suddenly darkened with only limited sight in her right eye. Her life drastically changed, and she gave up on her career as a doctor. Erviana (2019) specifically mentioned that people who experienced non-congenital blindness require a longer time to adapt and accept themselves. Imel took five years to cope with her condition and discover a "new" self. After all the struggles, she committed to becoming an independent and self-centred person as she was thankful that blindness let her focus on herself by not comparing herself to how others looked.

Presenting the real self: the anxiety

Stigma has limited people with disabilities participating in society (Lusli et al., 2016). This social exclusion leads to their anxiety (Craig & Bigby, 2015b). Hani and I share the same experience about social anxiety. With her limited hearing and speech abilities, miscommunication has been part of Hani's everyday life, and she is often perceived as arrogant for being unable to listen and respond to new people. We were both excluded from some opportunities. Being the only student with a disability at school, I have no option, but to isolate myself as some students are afraid of my hands.

Disability is often associated with gender expression in which those with disabilities are perceived as less masculine (Lee, 2020). Disability's vulnerability is seen as weak and connected with the feminine (Rice et al., 2015). Prior to the COVID-19 pandemic, I was thinking of pursuing a master's abroad, but then I was prohibited by both my parents. They always thought that I would not survive. It was the same for Imel. Upon the sudden disability, she was forced to stay home. Until she made her biggest decision to study in the United Kingdom, which was opposed by her whole family. Both of us are lucky to have proved that we can endure being independent studying overseas (Figure 25.2).

Connecting with other humans is part of disabled people's interpersonal needs (Muhamad et al., 2019; Rajabi, 2020). By getting involved in society both physically and virtually, I could satisfy this need. This self-representation effort requires adjustment as it is related to impression management (Humphreys et al., 2024). Considering this factor, my frontstage is a resilient disability as shown on my social media that is visual (Cocq & Ljuslinder, 2020). This visuality allows for an idealized self-representation online (Humphreys et al., 2024), which is also done by Karim and Aida.

From a disabled person's perspective, they always want to be independent in socio-economic life (Damayanti & Sabiq, 2018). Sadly, society views disability as vulnerable members (Rice et al., 2015), who are socio-economically dependent (Nurhayati, 2020). Imel emphasized that disability does not make someone crippled and for her, blindness only limits her mobility not independence. She criticized the disability stigma that views individuals with disabilities are dependent on others. Ana and Hani agree

Figure 25.2 Umar's self-representation by showing hands, 2023.

Source: Photographer: @umarsyaroni Instagram (https://instagram.com/umarsyaroni)

with Imel, and both have anxiety to present their disabled self as they want to avoid being perceived as complicating others.

Indonesian disability: from media to self-representation

Even though there are a huge number of disabled persons in Indonesia, most disability-related topics are still not adequately covered by the media (Halim, 2021). Disability is usually only represented during the International Day of People with Disabilities (Tsaputra, 2016). Even worse, disability is not perceived equally by the Indonesian media but as empathic and submarginal (Nurhaqiqi, 2019).

Disabled persons' reality is being woven by media industries with pitiful and inspirational narratives (Södergren & Vallström, 2022). I have been included in several media coverages, but most included my story on bullying and discrimination, which I wish to forget, or instead of focusing on disability inclusion in the workplace and education. Imel hates it when she is called "inspiring", not because she does not want to inspire others, but rather because her so-called "inspiring story" always begins with a pitiful perspective.

> I am grateful to be referred to as an inspiration. However, it left me confused that all my stories started with "Imel's fate is unfortunate or who wouldn't be sad if they lost their eyesight like Imel?" and many more. I need time to accept all these stories and reflect. Is my life that sad?
>
> (Imel, October 8, 2023)

With its vulnerability, disability exploitation often happens (Satriana et al., 2021). It is seen as a unique selling point, so its representation is biased (Setyowati et al., 2020) and prejudiced (Tsaputra, 2016). Aside from being considered as an inspiring disability, Imel is triggered to be exploited by the media. She is tired of getting asked the same questions for the same disability narratives, rising out of darkness in life.

Disability is represented inspirationally when it is related to a commercial agenda (Setyowati et al., 2020). Aida has a similar story with Imel and me, in which she was used as an object for selling. Both Aida and I refused to be included in promotional content that highlighted disability as the centre of attention and seen as "different" or as stated by Goethals et al. (2022) that mass media covers people with disabilities as "Other".

People with disabilities are not depicted in the media in a proper way as most are negative portrayals, although it is their right to have media representation (Halim, 2021). Disability is a normal human experience that should be normalized (Suharto et al., 2016) and seen the same way as those without a disability (Cocq & Ljuslinder, 2020). All of us in this chapter agree that disabled people should be seen as normal human beings. Karim hopes that disability is represented equally as any other diversity. For Aida, understanding that everyone has a similar nature should be common (Figure 25.3).

Indonesian people with disabilities are viewed as an obstacle and objects of pity (Dibley & Tsaputra, 2019) which contrasts with the desired representation of the disabled people themselves (Damayanti & Sabiq, 2018). Hani always wanted to be seen as an independent person, especially when communicating with other people. It needs courage and confidence for her to use "deaf" as her identity and she finally has reached the level

Figure 25.3 Karim's self-representation on mass media, 2023.

Source: Photographer: @karim.muhamr Instagram (https://instagram.com/karim.muhamr)

of resilience she expected to present herself. While for Aida and Karim self-representation is not an option as they have physically visible disability. Hence, they always present their real disability selves.

Community involvement for a broader self-representation

Amidst the social challenges they face, people with disabilities require collective action that empowers them (Nario-Redmond et al., 2013). Therefore, local disability organizations have formed (Fuad, 2011; Yulianto, 2011) to promote disability rights and awareness because of the increasing recognition of the unique characteristics of disability (Kulick & Rydström, 2015). Even though PWD exists, disability concerns are rarely discussed in social movement discourse, especially, in developing nations like Indonesia (Friedman & Owen, 2017).

Interpersonal needs have motivated people to join organizations that share similar attributes to their needs (Muhamad et al., 2019). These support groups are believed to shift the members' self-efficacy (Nario-Redmond et al., 2013). All embroiled participants and I agree that disability organizations serve as support groups that foster higher self-esteem. It is not surprising that people with disabilities have social anxiety (Craig & Bigby, 2015a) but together with organization, they can develop themselves (Madyaningrum et al., 2022). After joining her disability group, Ana portrayed herself as a strong woman and hoped to be a light for others.

Disability organizations have shown themselves to be effective in empowering members (Seubert, 2022). This sense of empowerment has been felt by all this chapter's participants. I personally joined Rumah Disabilities in 2021, a non-governmental organization that raises disability awareness. I can empower and feel empowered at the same time. For people with disabilities, organizations are used to get out of social isolation and fight the disability stigma collectively (Madyaningrum et al., 2022), as we do not feel alone, but rather feel accepted.

By sharing similar experiences, disability organizations can enhance social bonds, attachment, and connections among members (Hebron, 2018). Aida and Imel mention a sense of belonging between people with disabilities, who are connected through the same platform so that disability organizations can build a circle of friendship. Disability organizations also enable members to build positive representation (Mineur et al., 2017). For Hani, she could confidently present her deaf self after finding a disability community that shares the same experience as her.

With its diverse members, disability organizations are effective tools for activism (Madyaningrum et al., 2022), including information activism (Ellis & Kent, 2020). Hani and Karim use their disability community to exchange their experiences and delve more into diverse types of disabilities. This social interaction resulted in personal and collective development (Madyaningrum, 2017). Hani added that disability organizations help to develop her critical thinking in viewing challenges.

For a bigger impact, activism is also involved in the disability organizations' social interactions (Madyaningrum, 2017), advocating disability rights and raising disability awareness (Dibley & Tsaputra, 2019). For Ana and Hani, disability groups do not only serve as platforms for mutual sharing but also collective activism in raising disability awareness on a broader scale. Karim and I are in favour of them, and our inclusive communities conduct empowerment events. We do believe that disability organizations have multidimensional impacts both for members' personal and collective settings.

In this digital age, social media can be used to connect people with disabilities through virtual communities. There is space between experience and the representation of experience of disabled people, which emphasizes the importance of lived experiences (Rajabi, 2020). Rumah Disabilities in which I am involved, for instance, empowers people with disabilities across Indonesia virtually. This virtual community allows for self-representation online (Mineur et al., 2017). For Aida, Hani, and I, having diverse disability friends allows us to accept our disability self and finally self-represent ourselves.

Social media: an emerging disability self-representation

The digital age has made it easier for people with disabilities to participate virtually in online forums and chats (Bexley, 2015), use online platforms (Ellis & Kent, 2016), and become part of the social inclusion movement (Ellis & Kent, 2011). According to numerous studies, the Internet can serve as a virtual public sphere or venue where marginalized groups can express their opinions and create public opinion that effectively influences public policy (Hersinta, 2019).

As technology has advanced, social media is commonly used by people with disabilities to present themselves online (Cocq & Ljuslinder, 2020). As for myself, I use my social media accounts to share my positive achievements. By doing so, I can raise awareness of disability inclusion. Starting from my close environments, I constantly present my lived experiences as a disability. Aida, Hani, and Karim also use social media to self-represent themselves the way they want.

Over the past ten years, more disability activists in Indonesia have started to use social media to advocate for disability rights (Ellis & Kent, 2020). As an empowered disabled person, I functionalized social media as a tool for disability awareness. Social media gives voice to disability thoughts and stories (Hersinta, 2019). By simply self-representing my disability self, I can bring disability topics online. Aida and Karim also consider themselves disability activists and like me, they raise disability awareness on various social media platforms.

Among all social media platforms, Instagram has been shown to be useful for self-representation (Leaver et al., 2020) as I proudly displayed "Disability Activist" on my profile (Figure 25.4). With that, people can recognize me both as a disabled person and activist. Instagram is also a useful tool for advocacy on issues like inclusion and disabilities

Figure 25.4 Umar's self-representation through Instagram profile, 2023.

Source: Photographer: Umar @umarsyaroni Instagram (https://instagram.com/umarsyaroni)

(Cahyadi & Setiawan, 2020). Since 2016, Instagram has been my top platform to raise disability awareness and inclusion by sharing lots of disability-related content there.

Instagram allows its users to meet their interpersonal needs through human connection (Leaver et al., 2020). This platform enables me to connect with my friends with disabilities across Indonesia who have similar lived experiences. Instagram use should not be motivated by gaining followers but for influence as well (Kim et al., 2017). With my self-representation on this platform, I could be invited to many events where I address disability inclusion messages.

Social media are always connected to empowerment (Södergren & Vallström, 2022) and Instagram with its broad content tends to serve as an empowering tool (Leaver et al., 2020). I am grateful that my shared content on my social media platforms including Instagram can empower my disabled friends to then have the courage to leave their comfort zones by self-representing their disability selves. Some are getting inspired by my stories of struggle, and they follow my steppingstone to pursue higher education and get access to the workplace.

Engagement is offered by social media, in which disability activists can connect with other advocates for disability rights (Ellis & Kent, 2016). Aida and Karim have similar preferences as I do by using Instagram not only for personal use but for disability awareness. They can relate to fellow activists and join the crowd to foster an inclusive society. Instagram is effectively visualizing diversity, and for people with disabilities, it is a practical tool to self-represent themselves visually (Cocq & Ljuslinder, 2020). Karim and I are proud to display our disability hands in most of Instagram content. While Aida shares her accessibility struggles in education and visualizes her disability by including her walking stick and wheelchair in some of her content. Therefore, our digital self-representation relies on visuality (Figure 25.5).

Figure 25.5 Wheelchair as Aida's visual self-representation, 2023.

Source: Photographer: Umar @aidamudjib Instagram (https://instagram.com/aidamudjib)

Disability can also be represented by Instagram hashtags as they have specific meanings and function patterns (Baym, 2015; Sloan & Quan-Haase, 2017). In raising disability awareness, Karim's activism on Instagram is completed with hashtags. In a broader discussion, social media can be used to criticize current conditions (Humphreys et al., 2024), which is also covered by Instagram (Cahyadi & Setiawan, 2020). Aside from sharing inspirational stories about receiving a full-ride scholarship for a master's in international relations, Aida is vocal in criticizing the lack of accessibility she experienced.

Rajabi (2020) highlights the virtually connected disability community through social media which satisfies their interpersonal needs. Hani and Ana do not self-present themselves online but only used Instagram for personal use as viewers. They mostly rely on shared content, including disability information, opportunities, and empowerment programs. This is in line with the informational activism that social media offers to its users' demands (Hersinta, 2019).

Towards inclusive Indonesia in 2045

All five participants and I come into line that self-representation is our collective effort not only to present the disability narratives but also as part of fighting the disability rights fulfilment. After all the disability activism, Aida and I believe that inclusion should be built from the closest environment. This serves as a deep responsibility to me because when I was born, not all my family members accepted me. My parents' faith has brought me to who I am today.

Researching social media, it is extremely upsetting to witness how Indonesian social media lack a positive disability representation. All five participants and I emphasize the need for disability representation in digital space. However, above all, providing a safe digital space for everyone is essential. As an empowered person with a disability, I am committed to passing on my burning torch. Therefore, through my lived experiences, I want to encourage my fellow readers with disabilities, especially, in Indonesia, to foster our self-representation.

The global inclusion tagline is "Nothing about us without us" and it would never be possible without including those with disabilities – even through digital spaces. Let us embrace our social media as we are the actors who can create a collective frontstage disability representation. Imagine an amazing world where discrimination could not grow and foster, and everyone would have a smile on their face without anyone left behind. The future is in our hands and together we foster our idealized self-representation. To represent our disability selves and those with disabilities, who are underrepresented. Yes, for us.

References

Agustina, E. and Valentina, D. T. (2023). Penerimaan Diri Penyandang disabilitas Fisik Pascalahir. *Psychopreneur Journal, 7*(1), 29–45.

Baym, N. K. (2015). *Personal connections in the digital age* (2nd Edition). Polity Press.

Bexley, A. (2015). Social media ignites disability movement in Indonesia. Asia Foundation. https://asiafoundation.org/2015/12/09/social-media-ignitesdisability-movement-in- indonesia/

Cahyadi, A. and Setiawan, A. (2020). Disability and social media: Exploring utilization of Instragram platform as a tool for disability advocacy. *Al-Balagh: Jurnal Dakwah Dan Komunikasi, 5*(2), 223–250.

Cocq, C. and Ljuslinder, K. (2020). Self-representations on social media. Reproducing and challenging discourses on disability. *Alter, 14*(2), 71–84.

Craig, D. and Bigby, C. (2015a). "She's been involved in everything as far as I can see": Supporting the active participation of people with intellectual disability in community groups. *Journal of Intellectual and Developmental Disability*, 40(1), 12–25.

Craig, D. and Bigby, C. (2015b). "She's been involved in everything as far as I can see": Supporting the active participation of people with intellectual disability in community groups. *Journal of Intellectual and Developmental Disability*, 40(1), 12–25.

Damayanti, M. and Sabiq, F. (2018). Implementation of public facilities and disability treatments: A comparison between Indonesia and Malaysia. *Proceedings of the International Conference on Diversity and Disability Inclusion in Muslim Societies (ICDDIMS 2017)*. https://doi.org/10.2991/icddims-17.2018.3

Dibley, T. and Tsaputra, A. (2019). Changing laws, changing attitudes: The place of people with disability in Indonesia. In G. Fealy & R. Ricci (Eds.), *Contentious belonging* (pp. 77–94). ISEAS Publishing.

Ellis, K. and Kent, M. (2011). *Disability and new media*. Routledge.

Ellis, K. and Kent, M. (2016). *Disability and social media*. Routledge.

Ellis, K. and Kent, M. (2020). Communicating autism on the internet the emerging of neurodiversity movement in Indonesia (Doctoral dissertation, Curtin University).

Erviana, T. (2019). Perbedaan Penerimaan Diri Penyandang Disabilitas Netra Sejak Lahir dan Setelah Lahir di UPT PPSDN Penganthi Temanggung. Universitas Negeri Semarang.

Friedman, C. and Owen, A. L. (2017). Defining disability: Understandings of and attitudes towards ableism and disability. *Disability Studies Quarterly*, 37(1), 2–30.

Fuad, B. (2011). Revitalisasi Gerakan Difabel di Indonesia (the Revitalisation of Difabel Movement in Indonesia). *Jurnal Perempuan*, 69, 25–36.

Goethals, T., Mortelmans, D., Van den Bulck, H., Van den Heurck, W. and Van Hove, G. (2022). I am not your metaphor: Frames and counter-frames in the representation of disability. *Disability and Society*, 37(5), 746–764.

Halim, R. (2021). People with disabilities as motivational objects in the kick Andy Talkshow program. *The Social Construction Approach of Reality Theory*, 15(2), 2548–9496.

Hebron, J. S. (2018). School connectedness and the primary to secondary school transition for young people with autism spectrum conditions. *British Journal of Educational Psychology*, 88(3), 396–409.

Hersinta. (2019). Tweeting autism - a framing analysis of Twitter conversations on autism in Indonesia. Proceedings of the 4th International Conference on Contemporary Social and Political Affairs (ICoCSPA 2018), August 2018, 142–152.

Humphreys, L., Paley, A. and Rinaldi, S. (2024). *Digital media: Identity management* (W. S. Lehmann, Ed., pp. 213–222). Routledge.

Hunt, X., Swartz, L., Braathen, S. H., Jordan, C., & Rohleder, P. (2020). (Re)presenting the self: Questions raised by a photovoice project with people with physical disabilities in South Africa. *Disability and Society*, 35(6), 876–901.

Kim, S., Han, J., Yoo, S. and Gerla, M. (2017). How are social influencers connected in Instagram? In G.L. Ciampaglia et al. (Eds.), *Social Informatics Conference 2017* (pp. 257–264).

Kulick, D. and Rydström, J. (2015). *Loneliness and its opposite*. Duke University Press.

Kusumastuti, P., Pradanasari, R. and Ratnawati, A. (2014). The problems of people with disability in Indonesia and what is being learned from the world report on disability. *American Journal of Physical Medicine & Rehabilitation*, 93(1), S63–S67.

Leaver, T., Highfield, T. and Abidin, C. (2020). *Instagram: Visual social media cultures*. Polity.

Lee, M. (2020). Knowing North Korea through photographs of abled/disabled bodies in western news. In J. Johanssen & D. Garrisi (Eds.), *Disability, media, and representations; Other bodies* (pp. 94–113). Routledge.

Lusli, M., Peters, R., van Brakel, W., Zweekhorst, M., Iancu, S., Bunders, J., Irwanto and Regeer, B. (2016). The impact of a rights-based counselling intervention to reduce stigma in people affected by leprosy in Indonesia. *PLOS Neglected Tropical Diseases*, 10(12), e0005088.

Madyaningrum, M. E. (2017). Disability organisations as empowering settings: The case of a local disability organisation in Yogyakarta Province, Indonesia. Victoria University.

Madyaningrum, M. E., Sonn, C. C. and Fisher, A. T. (2022). Disability organizations as empowering settings: Challenging stigmatization, promoting emancipation. *American Journal of Community Psychology, 69*(3–4), 474–483.

Mantilla, S. (2022). Invisible disability, public health, and visual social media communication. The University of Sydney.

Mineur, T., Tideman, M. and Mallander, O. (2017). Self-advocacy in Sweden—An analysis of impact on daily life and identity of self-advocates with intellectual disability. *Cogent Social Sciences, 3*(1), 1–16.

Muhamad, J. W., Harrison, T. R. and Yang, F. (2019). Organizational communication: Theory and practice. In Stacks et al. (Eds). *An integrated approach to communication theory and research* (pp. 359–374). Routledge.

Nario-Redmond, M. R., Noel, J. G. and Fern, E. (2013). Redefining Disability, re-imagining the self: Disability identification predicts self-esteem and strategic responses to stigma. *Self and Identity, 12*(5), 468–488.

Nurhaqiqi, H. (2019, October 7). Difable literacy: Analysis of difable representation in Indonesian media. https://doi.org/10.4108/eai.30-7-2019.2287625

Nurhayati, S. (2020). Social inclusion for persons with disabilities through access to employment in Indonesia. *Prophetic Law Review, 2*(1), 1–21.

Rajabi, S. (2020). Losing someone like us: Memetic logics and coping with brain tumours on social media. In J. Johanssen & D. Garrisi (Eds.), *Disability, media, and representations: Other bodies* (pp. 51–74). Routledge.

Rice, C., Chandler, E., Harrison, E., Liddiard, K. and Ferrari, M. (2015). Project ReVision: Disability at the edges of representation. *Disability and Society, 30*(4), 513–527.

Sari, Y. P. (2022). Penerimaan Diri Penyandang Tuna Daksa di Kota Bengkulu. Universitas Islam Negeri Fatmawati Sukarno Bengkulu.

Satriana, S., Huda, K., Saadah, N., Hidayati, D. and Zulkarnaen, A. (2021). Covid-19 impacts on people with disabilities in Indonesia: An indepth look. https://kompak.or.id/id/download/519/2021_ COVID-19 Impacts on People with Disabilities in Indonesia_Bappenas_MAHKOTA-KOMPAK.pdf

Septian, E. R. and Hadi, E. N. (2021). Reducing stigma of people with disabilities: A systematic review. *Journal of Medical and Health Studies, 2*(2), 31–37.

Setyowati, R. M., Setya Watie, E. D. and Saptiyono, A. (2020). Representation of disability achievements in television talk show programs. *Journal The Messenger, 12*(1), 40–51.

Seubert, F. J. (2022). 'Sanitise your hands with rainbows!' Encouraging self-representation in times of crisis: Inclusive reflections on Covid-19, together with women with learning disabilities from East London. *Research in Drama Education, 27*(4), 443–457.

Sloan, L. and Quan-Haase, A. (2017). The SAGE handbook of social media research methods. In L. Laestadius (Ed.) The *SAGE handbook of social media research methods* (pp. 1–31). SAGE Publications Ltd.

Sloper, P. (1999). Models of service support for parents of disabled children. What do we know? What do we need to know? *Child: Care, Health and Development, 25*(2), 85–99.

Södergren, J. and Vallström, N. (2022). Disability in influencer marketing: A complex model of disability representation. *Journal of Marketing Management, 39*(11–12), 1012–1042.

Suharto, S., Kuipers, P. and Dorsett, P. (2016). Disability terminology and the emergence of 'difability' In Indonesia. *Disability & Society, 31*(5), 693–712.

Thohari, S. (2019). Promoting "Difabel", promoting social model of disability in Indonesia, study of disability movement in Yogyakarta. *Brawijaya Journal of Social Science, 3*(1), 79–99.

Triwahyudi, W. and Setiawan, E. (2014). Disability inclusion in WASH: "What has been achieved and how can this help other practitioners?" 37th WEDC International Conference, Hanoi, Vietnam.

Tsaputra, A. (2016). Portrayals of people with disabilities in Indonesian newsprint media (a case study on three Indonesian major newspapers). *Indonesian Journal of Disability Studies*, 3(1), 1–11.

Widinarsih, D. (2017). Disability inclusion and disability awareness in Muslim society: An experience of Indonesians Muslim with disability in performing worship. In International Conference on Diversity and Disability Inclusion in Muslim Societies (ICDDIMS 2017), pp. 94–99. Atlantis Press.

Yulianto, M. J. (2011). Investigation on the influence of the disability movement in Indonesia: An advance investigation on the influence of the disability movement in Indonesia. VDM Verlag Dr. Müller.

26 Understanding Indigenous disabilities

A cultural perspective of Indigenous Pashtun community

Zafar Khan

Introduction

This chapter explores the different socio-cultural aspects of indigenous disability[1] in Pashtun society. In this study, indigenous disability refers to understanding disability in the socio-cultural and historical context of Pashtun indigenous society[2]. The colonial literature more often than not missed the cultural, social, and political aspects of disability and generalized the definition of disability as a medical or individual phenomenon (Hollinsworth, 2013; Sherry, 2007). However, indigenous disability is completely different from the mainstream definition of disability (defined by colonial forces) due to the unique cultural beliefs, practices, and history of a particular indigenous society (Ineese-Nash, 2020; Anastasiou, & Kauffman, 2013). This colonized definition of disability missed the voices of indigenous people and does not take into account the cultural and colonial aspects of disability (Nasiri, Akseer, Tasic, Rafiqzad, & Akseer, 2023; Trani, Ballard, & Peña, 2016). The mainstream disability model and definition ignore those factors that intersect the marginalization and discrimination faced by indigenous people across the world.

Hence, this study focuses on the indigenous understanding of disability in Pashtun society to understand its historical and cultural aspects. Furthermore, this study explores the role of Pashtun's indigenous culture, traditions and social institutions, language, proverbs, and indigenous knowledge in understanding disability. Pashtun indigenous disability and indigenous cultural and indigenous social workers responses are also explored at the end of this chapter to give a holistic picture of disability in Pashtun society. To understand the issue at hand, it is necessary to brief readers about the origin, history, economy, and social structure of the Pashtun indigenous community.

The history and origin of Pashtuns

Pashtuns are considered the largest tribal ethnic group that lives in Afghanistan and also in Pakistan in the province of Khyber. The origin of Pashtun is a debatable issue in the available literature and no single theory or consensus can be agreed upon regarding their origins (Shukla, 2015). They seem to be descended from one of the original 12 tribes of

---

1 Indigenous disability refers to the individual experience in the context of cultural and historical context of the disability in native or indigenous society.
2 Pashtun tribal people society fulfills the criterion of indigenous society. The Pashtun tribal society was colonized by British. They have a distinct social and economic system.

DOI: 10.4324/9781032656519-31

Israel (Khan & Ahmed, 2013). It is also believed that they belong to Arian tribes or Indian European tribes (Amin, 2023). It is mentioned in the Rig-Veda, that the word Pakht or Phakta is used for the geographical surroundings where Pashtun are living nowadays (Glatzer, 2002; Khan, 2008). Later, the word Pakhtean, used in the Rig-Veda became Pakhtun. They recently merged districts (previously called the Federal Administer Tribal Areas and the province of Baluchistan inside Pakistan.

Pashtuns have limited low land and the majority live in mountainous and difficult terrain. Pashtun's land is full of natural resources, but these in both the colonial and also in postcolonial times was exploited under the federal government of Pakistan. Therefore, Pashtuns migrated to Karachi, Lahore, and Islamabad, as well as to different countries such as the United States, Europe, the Middle East, etc. to earn the livelihood for the remaining family members who live in native towns. However, in the Middle East and also in Pakistan the majority of them do hard jobs as they are not skilled laborers. The ruling states Britain and Pakistan exploited their resources, but they did not extend formal educational institutions to their homeland (Siddique, 2014).

Even though the Pashtun region was invaded by many foreigners, the British ruled this region for decades, so their colonial administration significantly influenced the Pashtun sociocultural values and exploited their resources. Pashtun tribal society was colonized by the British, in 1849, so the British sociocultural norms, values, and colonial history significantly influenced the conceptualization, practices, and understanding of disability in Pashtun society. Therefore, Indigenous disability and impairment are embedded in the colonial history and prevailing culture of Pashtun society. In the colonial period, the British labeled them uncivilized and wild so did not extend their institutions into Pashtun's Indigenous tribal society. Pakistan also continued the same policy in this region in the postcolonial period until 2018. Hence, Pashtun social institutions take the burden of disability and their cultural values and social structure to reinforce their caring responsibility for disabled people in Pashtun society. Indigenous Pashtun people's voices should be included in the contemporary literature to understand disability in the context of their culture and history.

Initially, the British adopted the policy of noninterference in the Indigenous tribal Pashtun land, but later under the viceroyship of Lansdowne and Elgin (between 1887 and 1898), the British replaced the policy of non-interference with the 'Forward Policy (Khan, 2020).This was resisted by the local Indigenous Pashtun, which resulted in the British calling them uncivilized and wild. Then, the colonialists implemented the 'closed border' policy in Pashtun tribal areas (now known as the merged districts of Khyber Pakhtunkhwa) (Yousaf, 2019).

Under the closed border policy, the British established several tribal agencies, enclosed by a chain of posts and military garrisons for the maintenance of law and order in Pashtun society. The closed border policy called for Pashtun customs and traditions to rule the region (Riwaj). This became an excuse for the British to deny reforms and build institutions in Pashtun areas that were extended to the rest of the Indian subcontinent. They introduced inhumane and oppressive laws under the Frontier Crimes Regulations (FCR), a special set of laws applicable in the Pashtun tribal areas. Under the FCR, they denied residents legal representation, the right to present evidence, and the right to appeal. They also misinterpreted their culture from the outside world and presented them as a violent ethnic group in the colonialist literature. In the colonial and also in postcolonial administrations, they bribed the local strongmen and *Jargaees* (members of Pashtun *Jirga*).

Political Agent (PA) the administrative head of the British manipulated their *Jirga* and local customs. Under the frontier crime regulation, they adopted the policy of collective responsibility and punished the whole tribe for the crime of a single person. Pakistan also adopted the same policy when the British left the region (Kanafyeva, 2022). Recently, in 2018 international pressure led the Pakistan government to extend constitutional rights to the tribal districts of Pashtun society, but the people of merged districts are still deprived of their civil and political rights. The government of Pakistan blames their culture and tribal traditions for violence in this region.

However, violent social engineering by the British and later on Pakistan has slowed down the Pashtun cultural evolution and economic development (Johnson & Mason, 2008). They are still dependent on conventional farming and domestic animals for their livelihood. These policies of colonial and postcolonial times imposed extreme poverty and increased the ratio of migration of Pashtun from their native land. The Pashtun Indigenous disability is closely associated with the Pashtun colonial and postcolonial history and culture. Thus, the Pashtun origin and colonial history are reflected to explain and understand the political and cultural aspects of Pashtun Indigenous disability.

Understanding Pashtun indigenous disability: a cultural perspective

Pashtun Indigenous society remained a colony of the British and faced a traumatic situation in colonial times; impairments and disabilities are thus embedded in their colonial history. The Indigenous cultural disability definition is more comprehensive compared to the colonized biological definition of disability. The bio-psychological disability model defines disability as resulting from dysfunction in individual bodies (Ferguson & Nusbaum, 2012). The core meaning of 'disability' is confined to blindness, being crippled, visually impaired, autistic, and handicapped. The mainstream disability models confine disability to functions or biological and psychological fitness. However, it does not shed light on the cultural and historical aspects of disability, especially, in the context of disability in Indigenous societies.

The Pashtun Indigenous community understands and defines disability in the context of their economy and socio-cultural traditions. It is argued that cultural identity and social roles are affected differently by disability in different Indigenous societies (Goodley et al., 2021). They live in a patriarchal structure, so men have the power to make decisions and women are responsible for indoor chores. This means disability is embedded in the prevailing culture and social structure both at the micro and macro levels. The disabled identity of an individual is closely associated with the culture of the Indigenous community (Bodammer, 2021) and also culturally assigns different social roles to people with impairments. For instance, in the Pashtun Indigenous community, men and women with disabilities are affected differently, as the Pashtun patriarchal society further marginalizes women with disabilities. The cultural aspects of disability are missing in the available literature on disability in Pashtun society.

Therefore, it is important to give a brief sketch of Pashtun's major cultural values and social institutions to understand the cultural aspects of disability. Pashtun are famous for their tribal traditions, collective structure, and customs. They live in joint and extended families and have close and strong ties with other relatives and neighbors. They have a strong *beradari* (brotherhood) and in the immediate family and also at the community level (Tainter & MacGregor, 2011). This prevailing culture, economy, and social structure have a significant influence on people with disabilities in Pashtun Indigenous society as they have different cultural expectations from the people with disabilities. This has evolved in the light of their culture and history. Disability is imposed on top of the impairments. Pashtun culturally excludes certain types of people from full participation in sociocultural affairs. The social situation, expectations, and social roles in which people with impairment cannot fit make them culturally disabled. For instance, Pashtun culturally appreciate physically strong people because they do hard work and because they take part in family feuds. So, they ignore physically disabled people. In this case, Pashtun culture further intersects the marginality of people with disabilities.

Pashtun Indigenous culture imposes certain types of restrictions or a lack of ability to perform any activity in a manner within the range considered normal for a human being in other Indigenous or advanced societies. However, in colonial times the suppression and uncivilized stigmas confined the whole ethnic group to certain types of disabilities. For instance, handicap depends on valuations and expectations that put the disabled person at a disadvantage. However, this valuation depends on the cultural norms and Pashtun society, so it is evaluated differently. Pashtun Indigenous society understands and so defines and treats people with disabilities in the context of their prevailing sociocultural norms and values. For instance, the culturally defined identities of an individual in Pashtun society are affected differently by disability that affects and intersects various social categories such in terms of age, gender, class, ethnicity, and sexuality. The following lines further elaborate the different aspects of stigmatizing disability in Pashtun indigenous culture.

Stigmatizing disability in Pashtun Indigenous culture

Language is an important element of culture, yet culture cannot be transmitted without language. Indigenous Pashtuns speak the Pashtu language; however, they label and stigmatize disabilities and discourage people with disabilities. Disability is portrayed as a stigma, so the family of a disabled person hides the disability of close relatives. Pashtun Indigenous people culturally and socially stigmatize disability so people with disabilities are considered a burden on family resources. In the Pashtu language, they do not have proper and respectable words for disability, thus, they do not express themselves respectably toward the different types of disabilities. For instance, they call the physically handicapped with the term *gudh* (physically handicapped) and *londha* for the visually impaired. They usually ridicule people with disabilities in social ceremonies, tease them and speak to them rudely about food, especially, at marriage and religious rituals.

They believe it is a sin in a family if a disabled child is born. The family initially tries to hide the disability of the child. This cultural understanding of disability creates problems for the family of a disabled person and also for the person with a disability. The majority of Pashtuns do not think scientifically about disability. They sometimes consider a person with disabilities as a sign of evil for a family. The mother of the child with a disability takes the responsibility, so it becomes difficult for her. Moreover, masculine traits are appreciated in Pashtun society so culturally they stigmatize transgender people as disabled. As well, a person who does not participate in tribal or family feuds is considered disabled. For instance, this is the Pashtu proverb: "*da na nar day aw na khaza*" (that he or she is not male or female). This refers to transgender as the transgender culture is considered a disabled character in Pashtun society. They also declare a person disabled who does not participate in cultural or social gatherings. They do not respect those, who do not take part in the family feuds. Furthermore, the British and Pakistanis labeled Pashtuns as a Martial race (meaning lazy and not skilled or strong enough to fight) so a person who cannot fight is considered disabled.

Moreover, in Pashtun society, certain sociocultural capitalists facilitate or violate the rights of disabled persons. As discussed above, family, brotherhood, and kinship facilitate the disabled person, but cultural honor creates problems for disabled people. Honor is associated with women, but those who are in certain spheres of life are culturally declared disabled. In Pashtun society, women are not allowed to go outside the home; however, those with mental health issues cannot understand these Pashtun cultural restrictions. The family cannot understand the mental health issue of women and she is not allowed to go outside of the home. It is also very difficult for the families of disabled women to deal with abnormal women due to cultural restrictions.

Disabled by the colonialism: impairment injected in Pashtun Indigenous culture

As colonists, the British were a powerful state, so they defined the Pashtun culture and policy and imposed it on Pashtun's Indigenous people (Stienstra & Nyerere, 2016), which kept them underdeveloped and presented them as violent people to the outside world. The British stigmatized them as uncivilized, martial, and wild people and culturally defined them as disabled. Thus, colonial traumas brought different types of disability for the whole ethnic group as they were declared unfit for certain types of jobs so they could not work in any business organization and were not able to form a business/organization. The British declared that they were only fit to work as watchmen or to join the army to protect the interests of the British in colonial times and postcolonial times of Pakistan. They suppressed them, exploited their resources, and imposed war on the Indigenous people (Meekosha & Soldatic, 2011). This policy is reflected in understating the cultural and political aspects of disability in Pashtun society. British policies remained intact for a long time, which still haunts the Pashtun Indigenous people.

In the postcolonial time, Pakistan deliberately adopted and continued the same policy for their political interests in the region, so they also confined the Pashtun to certain types of professions and made them unfit for more modern ones. Thus, again, the Pashtun were represented as watchmen, truck drivers, or wild warriors in art and dramas. The violent social engineering of Pashtun's Indigenous society brought a new wave of violence, war, and suicide bombing into this region in the wake of the 'war on terror'. This created new kinds of impairments, disabilities, and mental health issues among the Pashtuns. The British and Pakistan policy in this region intersects disability, racism, and discrimination in the Pashtun Indigenous society.

Indigenous disability intersects Pashtun marginality

Pashtun, as a minority Indigenous ethnic group, faced discrimination and racism in both the colonial era and also in the postcolonial period. The British policies divided them into different administrative zones as well as divided this ethnic group into two different countries Pakistan and Afghanistan. Pakistan as a state doubts the loyalties of the Pashtun so they are deprived of their political rights. They say that "being Indigenous, having experienced colonization and institutionalization, racism and discrimination experiences, and living with disabilities gave rise to multiple identities that go unseen by people with or without experiences of disability" (Frederick & Shifrer, 2019; Moodley & Graham, 2015; Shaw et al., 2012).

Colonization and the institutionalization of racism and discrimination in both colonial and postcolonial periods intersect the problems of people with disabilities in the Pashtun Indigenous community. They are deprived of their political rights and neither the British nor Pakistanis deliberately extended state institutions to this region. The political aspect of disability in Pashtun Indigenous society is, therefore, not highlighted in the contemporary literature in this region. Thus, the Pashtun Indigenous people carry the burden of disability and take care of their people with disabilities without state help.

Pashtun Indigenous sociocultural values, social organizations, and disability

As mentioned above, Pashtun are famous for their strong tribal traditions and customs. Pashtun are divided into different sub-tribes and endogamous types of marriages are common among them (Pervaiz et al., 2018). Endogamy marriages are one of the causal factors of disability and impairment. The Pashtun cultural values and traditions compel women and men to marry inside a sub-tribes or family, so they are hesitant to marry outside of their sub-tribes. Socially, they prefer to marry in the immediate family. Women are culturally supposed to accept the marriage proposal of a person with a disability, if he is from their immediate family. However, if women have disabilities or impairments, then men are not bound culturally to marry them.

Pashtun Indigenous community members are culturally bonded to support the immediate family members in the joint and extended family (Khan & Shah, 2021). The family members in the joint family often support the person with a disability. Their cultural values and religious beliefs both appreciate individuals who support persons with disabilities and consider it an honor to support the member with a disability. However, due to poverty, it is difficult for them to support a person with a disability. Reciprocity is also a cultural value in Pashtun society, so they support each other in hard times. For instance, if the head of the family who earns a livelihood becomes disabled, then it is the responsibility of the immediate or extended family members to support him and provide economic and social protection to his family. However, most of the Pashtun are poor and it is difficult for them in certain cases to support the family of a disabled person. In certain cases, though, close relatives give clothes and show them to people with disabilities. Then, the rest of the family members take this burden in the absence of state institutions.

On the other hand, family feuds exist among Pashtun, but they do not target the person with a disability, and culturally it is not allowed to target a person with a disability. They also do not support a person with a disability due to family rivalry, but it is a shame for Pashtun to target a person with a disability in a family vendetta. The Pashtun Indigenous community is resilient, so they tolerate a person with a disability and dare to spend life with a disability. This is a Pashtu proverb "*Ensaan tar kanhe kalak, aw tar gul nazak dai*" *A human can be as strong as a stone and as delicate as a flower.* Pashtun Indigenous cultural values encourage and heal the person with a disability (Khan et al., 2019). People with disabilities thus become resilient to tolerate hardship due to their disability. Pashtun family members of people with disabilities face challenging situations and sometimes other family members get mental health issues due to the person with a disability because people with disabilities are dependent on family institutions.

Moreover, Pashtuns are also scared of disabilities. In Pashtun society, they are dependent on close family members, but the family also exploits and ignores disabled people in sociocultural matters. There is a Pashtu proverb in response to the indifferent attitude of the family and society "*Khpala laasa gula laasa*" the labor of one's hand is beautiful. People often give negative responses and ignore people with disabilities, so the disabled individual relies upon the local sociocultural institutions, especially, on the family in the absence of the state. Due to the fear of family members, people with disabilities cannot be compliant in public about any maltreatment (Nasiri et al., 2023). They must tolerate it because they have no other option.

It is a social humiliation for the family if a disabled family member complains about their treatment by family members. The close family members sometimes do not allow a disabled person to interact with other relatives or neighbors, and women with disabilities are strictly restricted to home. It is a dishonor for the family of a person with a disability if he or she gets help from outside their immediate family. Families sometimes exploit the disabled person's rights. They do not give them property or share the family assets. People with disabilities prefer death over disability because they know it is very difficult to depend for their whole life on other family members. If the disabled person does not have close kin, then they are compelled to beg, but sometimes the family members exploit them to earn money through begging for them.

Pashtun overall culturally gives a sympathetic response to people with disabilities. Pashtun sympathy with disabled people is reflected in the socioeconomic affairs of indigenous Pashtun. However, they culturally assign different roles to people with disabilities in terms of gender, age, and class. Gender differences can be seen in terms of understanding and one's response to disability (Cardozo et al., 2004). Women with disabilities are not treated the same as men. A sign of a good woman is if she takes care of a disabled husband and relatives, so she is culturally appreciated. Male members of the family do not care for females with disabilities and ignore them. Women are not entitled to property. Therefore, women with disabilities are more marginalized compared to men with disabilities. Pashtun Indigenous people, furthermore, do not easily accept the proposal of a disabled person. However, women cannot deny the proposal of a disabled cousin because they are culturally bound, and it is appreciated in Pashtun society to accept the proposal of a person with disabilities. Men are reluctant to propose to a girl with a disability. These patriarchal values benefit men with disabilities compared to women.

Social roles are assigned to people with disabilities in Pashtun Indigenous society in their cultural context. Disabled persons physically or visually impaired often get religious education in madrasas (Islamic schools). They believe that people with disabilities are not fit for any other profession so send them to religious schools. Pashtun Indigenous people discourage them from getting formal education (Trani et al., 2019). If the parents of disabled children send them to formal education, other parents discourage them and ask, "Why are you spending money on them." People with disabilities, who belong to poor families, are mostly involved in begging or doing low-paying jobs. Pashtun religious beliefs and cultural values, as well, influence the role assigned to people with disabilities. They think that disabled people are good, and are not involved in sin. Therefore, Pashtun give jobs to those inside the family, and they think that physically handicapped or intellectually challenged people would not harm them and that they are innocent. Therefore, Pashtun help people with disabilities and expect them to pray for them.

Pashtun do hard jobs or go abroad, especially to the Middle East for manual work. Disabled people cannot contribute to the family financially. There are no respectable social positions to engage people with disabilities, so they are socially humiliated and are not called with socially respectable names. Pashtun, therefore, ignore them, and their voices are missing in decision-making. Even a male member who is disabled is usually not part of family-related decisions. Moreover, the women who are already deprived of their rights and abilities further intersect their marginality so face a lot of problems being disabled. They suffer due to historical and intergenerational traumas, which cause mental health problems that make them more susceptible to different types of disabilities. Pashtuns also have limited access to resources, so they depend on their kinship ties. Families face these issues and without state help, it becomes difficult for them to accommodate and provide facilities for people with disabilities. They have, therefore, developed a strong cultural coping mechanism regarding disability.

Coping disability in Pashtun Indigenous society

Pashtun Indigenous people cope with disability without state help. As mentioned earlier, they live in joint or extended families. Family members are culturally bound to help and take care of their disabled member. Within the family institution, women are responsible for taking care of people with disabilities. Moreover, Pashtun people have strong kinship ties so they support other relatives reciprocally; if a family cannot support a disabled person (Trani & Bakhshi, 2013). It is a sign of prestige to support a person who is disabled. The majority of Pashtun are poor so live in poverty due to the policies of the British and Pakistanis in this region in colonial and postcolonial times (Rais, 2019). It is difficult for the family of a disabled person to support them financially. Men and children with disabilities, therefore, start begging for their livelihood. It is culturally a shame for the family of a disabled person, but they have no other way. People with disabilities accept donations or religious tax (zakat) from financially stable people. Pashtun Indigenous people respect those, who support people with disabilities, but they are not bound to support them permanently. Disabled people cannot buy new clothes and shoes, so mostly the family members give them used clothes and shoes, but they are ignored in any kind of family and culture matters. People tease the mentally retarded or disabled person, if he or she belongs to a poor family. Disabled children are also more susceptible to sexual and physical abuse.

Disabled people's accommodation in the occupational structure of Pashtun

Disabled people such as physically handicapped, impaired, visually impaired, etc. find space in the informal occupation structure at the Indigenous level. Family is the basic unit of production, so it is easy for disabled people to contribute as the family working conditions are very flexible (Holton, 2011). The family members try to accommodate those with disabilities, and they do not expect culturally what the disabled person cannot do. However, they engage them in low-paid or unpaid jobs. Sometimes they engage people with disabilities without a salary and only give food to them. Disabled people only work for a short time and then spend time with different people to find a refuge.

In Pashtun society, family members do hard jobs like farming and domesticating animals. Impairment does not disqualify people from working in substance production, domestic tasks, or even home-based handicraft production for the market. Therefore, they sometimes work with other family members to take care of the animals or go to the nearby shops to bring purchase items home. The Pashtun trust people with disabilities and do not fear them, so allow them to go inside the home to work with women. They culturally believe that people with disabilities are innocent. Women, as well, often need a male partner to attend ceremonies so may be accompanied by men with disabilities, who do not mind attending different types of ceremonies without invitation. They are happy to accompany women because they believe women treat them as well as they do other men.

Culturally inspired Indigenous social workers in Pashtun Indigenous society

Pashtun Indigenous people are culturally motivated to help and support other Indigenous people. Mostly in the name of religion or cultural beliefs, they collect donations and religious tax (zakat) from the rich and help all those people who are disabled Pashtun. Pashtun Indigenous social workers are not professional or certified, so do not have the knowledge and skills of modern social work techniques and are dependent on the traditional skills to help people with disabilities. However, with the help of their local community, they support the families who are poor who can't support a disabled member of the family level (Lang, 2000). Indigenous social workers are not culturally bound to take initiative as social workers, but they are culturally appreciated and earn the honor of the community that supports Indigenous people with disability at the local level (Gray et al., 2008). They use the Indigenous social organizations and sociocultural capital to mobilize funds and resources to help Indigenous disabled people (Weaver, 1999). The local indigenous people trust these social workers, who have the potential to help them.

Conclusion

Disability is a multifaceted phenomenon. Culture has significantly influenced the conceptualization, experiences, and understanding of disability in Indigenous societies. Pashtun Indigenous people are no different. It has strong traditions, and cultural values which shape the different aspects of disability. Pashtun historically remained a colony of the British for decades, who exploited their values and traditions and distorted their tribal traditions. The British left many blueprints on the Pashtun society which are important for understanding Pashtun Indigenous disability. In the absence of state institutions, people with disabilities are dependent upon the family, kinship, and brotherhood, who collectively support them.

The British and later Pakistan labeled the Pashtun as a disabled ethnic group so expelled them from certain professions. They also institutionalized racism and discrimination, which intersect disability and marginalized them. They have only their sociocultural institutions to take the burden of disability. Pashtun Indigenous people confined and ostracized people with disabilities. In the current scholarly work, the political and cultural aspects of Indigenous disability are not properly highlighted, so it is necessary to investigate the political and cultural aspects of Indigenous disability further for an effective policy to counter the worst effects of Indigenous disability in Pashtun society.

References

Amin, H. (2023). Pashtun neo-ethnonationalism. *The Review of Faith & International Affairs,* *21*(3), 137–150.

Anastasiou, D. and Kauffman, J. M. (2013). The social model of disability: Dichotomy between impairment and disability. *Journal of Medicine and Philosophy, 38*(4), 441–445.

Bodammer, E. (2021). Disability studies and new directions in eighteenth-century German studies. *Goethe Yearbook, 28*(1), 307–314.

Cardozo, B. L., Bilukha, O. O., Crawford, C. A. G., Shaikh, I., Wolfe, M. I., Gerber, M. L. and Anderson, M. (2004). Mental health, social functioning, and disability in postwar Afghanistan. *Jama, 292*(5), 575–584.

Ferguson, P. M. and Nusbaum, E. (2012). Disability studies: What is it and what difference does it make? *Research and Practice for Persons with Severe Disabilities, 37*(2), 70–80.

Frederick, A. and Shifrer, D. (2019). Race and disability: From analogy to intersectionality. *Sociology of Race and Ethnicity, 5*(2), 200–214.

Glatzer, B. (2002). The Pashtun tribal system. *Concept of Tribal Society, 5,* 265–282.

Goodley, D., Lawthom, R., Liddiard, K. and Runswick-Cole, K. (2021). Key concerns for critical disability studies. *International Journal of Disability and Social Justice, 1*(1), 27–49.

Gray, M., Coates, J. and Bird, M. Y. (Eds.). (2008). *Indigenous social work around the world: Towards culturally relevant education and practice.* Ashgate Publishing, Ltd.

Hollinsworth, D. (2013). Decolonizing Indigenous disability in Australia. *Disability & Society, 28*(5), 601–615.

Holton, J. W. (2011). The Pashtun behavior economy an analysis of decision making in tribal society. Doctoral dissertation, Monterey, CA. Naval Postgraduate School.

Ineese-Nash, N. (2020). Disability as a colonial construct: The missing discourse of culture in conceptualizations of disabled Indigenous children. *Canadian Journal of Disability Studies, 9*(3), 28–51.

Johnson, T. H. and Mason, M. C. (2008). No sign until the burst of fire: Understanding the Pakistan-Afghanistan frontier. *International Security, 32*(4), 41–77.

Kanafyeva, S. (2022). Historiographical aspects of the pashtun culture in pakistan. хабаршы, 117.

Khan, H. I. (2008). New wine in old bottles: An analysis of Pakistan's conflict in the Pashtun tribal areas. Doctoral dissertation, University of Kansas.

Khan, H. U. and Ahmed, N. (2013). A genealogical study of the origin of Pashtuns. In Intelligent Computing Theories: 9th International Conference, ICIC 2013, Nanning, China, July 28–31, 2013. Proceedings 9 (pp. 402–410). Springer Berlin. Heidelberg.

Khan, S., Faheem, M. and Gul, S. (2019). Understanding Pashtunwali and the Manifestation of Pashtun Nationalism in Pakistan: A conceptual analysis. *Global Social Sciences Review, 4*(1), 264–270.

Khan, Z., & Shah, Z. A. (2021). Pashtun community Indigenous resilience to changing socio-cultural and political challenges. In The Routledge International Handbook of Indigenous Resilience (pp. 121-133). Routledge.

Khan, A. (2020). The British Colonial Policies in the North West Frontier of India: 1849-1901. *FWU Journal of Social Sciences, 14*(2), 164-79.

Lang, R. (2000). The role of NGOs in the process of empowerment and social transformation of people with disabilities. *Asia Pacific Disability Rehabilitation Journal, 1*(1), 1–19.

Meekosha, H. and Soldatic, K. (2011). Human Rights and the Global South: The case of disability. *Third World Quarterly, 32*(8), 1383–1397.

Moodley, J. and Graham, L. (2015). The importance of intersectionality in disability and gender studies. *Agenda, 29*(2), 24–33.

Nasiri, K., Akseer, N., Tasic, H., Rafiqzad, H. and Akseer, T. (2023). Disability types, determinants and healthcare utilisation amongst Afghan adults: A secondary analysis of the Model Disability Survey of Afghanistan. *BMJ Open, 13*(1), e062362.

Pervaiz, R., Faisal, F. and Serakinci, N. (2018). Practice of consanguinity and attitudes towards risk in the pashtun population of khyber pakhtunkhwa, pakistan. *Journal of Biosocial Science, 50*(3), 414–420.

Rais, R. B. (2019). Geopolitics on the Pakistan–Afghanistan borderland: An overview of different historical phases. *Geopolitics, 24*(2), 284–307.

Shaw, L. R., Chan, F. and McMahon, B. T. (2012). Intersectionality and disability harassment: The interactive effects of disability, race, age, and gender. *Rehabilitation Counseling Bulletin, 55*(2), 82–91.

Sherry, M. (2007). (Post) colonising disability. *Wagadu: A Journal of Transnational Women's & Gender Studies, 4*(1), 14.

Shukla, A. (2015). The Pashtun Tribal Identity and Codes. THAAP Journal 2015: Culture, Art & Architecture of the Marginalized & the Poor (pp. 45–64).

Siddique, A. (2014). *The Pashtun question: The unresolved key to the future of Pakistan and Afghanistan.* Hurst & Company.

Stienstra, D., Nyerere, L. (2016). Race, Ethnicity and Disability: Charting Complex and Intersectional Terrains. In: Grech, S., Soldatic, K. (eds) Disability in the Global South. International Perspectives on Social Policy, Administration, and Practice. Springer, Cham. https://doi.org/10.1007/978-3-319-42488-0_16

Tainter, J. A., & MacGregor, D. G. (2011). Pashtun social structure: Cultural perceptions and segmentary lineage organization. Macgregor Bates: Cottage Grove, OR, USA.

Trani J. F. and Bakhshi, P. (2013). Vulnerability and mental health in Afghanistan: Looking beyond war exposure. *Transcultural Psychiatry, 50*(1), 108–139.

Trani, J. F., Ballard, E. and Peña, J. B. (2016). Stigma of persons with disabilities in Afghanistan: Examining the pathways from stereotyping to mental distress. *Social Science & Medicine, 153,* 258–265.

Trani, J. F., Fowler, P., Bakhshi, P. and Kumar, P. (2019). Assessment of progress in education for children and youth with disabilities in Afghanistan: A multilevel analysis of repeated cross-sectional surveys. *PloS One, 14*(6), e0217677.

Weaver, H. N. (1999). Indigenous people and the social work profession: Defining culturally competent services. *Social Work, 44*(3), 217–225.

Yousaf, F. (2019). Pakistan's colonial legacy: FCR and postcolonial governance in the Pashtun tribal frontier. *Interventions, 21*(2), 172–187.

27 Intersectionalities of Indigenous disabilities

Breaking down colonial barriers

John T. Ward

Introduction

The United Nations has helped push the public policy by focusing on the intersecting features of Indigenous cultural identity with the lived experience of disability. The current knowledge systems reflecting how Indigenous peoples live, work, learn, and thrive with disabilities are within communal perspectives and that of activists/lobbyists and academics, many of whom are Indigenous. These have allies who support their fight of bringing the debates to seats of power – the UN and WHO, both colonial institutions, can become a beacon for hope, resilience, and ultimately change. In a show of unity towards the building of international collaboration and acknowledgment of the intersectional rights of Indigenous people living with disabilities, this has contributed to a steadfast forward movement in the literature of disability from international partners (Connell, 2011; Gilroy et al., 2021; King et al., 2014; Soldatic, 2018; Ward, 2022).

However, much of the information being presented abroad is by non-Indigenous allies, who are able to provide voices to the voiceless by sharing specific content that might otherwise be excluded due to the limited coverage of this essential intersection – Indigeneity and disability. Also, a great deal of information is being published and shared on Indigenous disabilities by non-Indigenous non-allies, who focus on cultural knowledge relating to disability specialists and what type of service is provided that pertains to equipment, housing, and old age services (Gilroy et al., 2021). The historical outlook of this research is first and foremost zeroed in on the producing of challenges through impairments and how these limitations in human progress and development have benefited the socioeconomic interests of the elite – White-settler-colonial-scholarly-professionals fixated on subjugating and limiting those who do not follow their ways – Indigenous people and those of color.

Through this need, this book came to be, as much of the academic content of Indigenous disabilities published often reflects Western and Northern countries, yet the majority of Indigenous, especially, those with disabilities reside in eastern and southern regions. For this reason, an accumulation of international contributions gave such a richness by their sharing and revealing Indigenous knowledge and belief systems as they tried to illustrate how disabilities are understood, conceptualized, and brought forth within their predominantly White-settler-colonial influences. The intersectionalities of Indigenous disabilities provided the necessary steps for breaking down colonial barriers by allowing Indigenous content, enabling our voices to be heard and our written text to be read. Sharing our wisdom and lived experiences offered ways to navigate these once predominantly controlled and regulated colonial establishments and institutions.

DOI: 10.4324/9781032656519-32

The fact remains, though, that there is a limited amount of resources that emanate from an Indigenous perspective, whether it be from a personal journey, communal experience, or issues related to schooling, healthcare, or social services (Gilroy et al., 2021).

Intersectionalities and how they are used

Agosto and Roland (2018) examined how intersectionalities can be an insightful tool when researching a typical field or area that has predominantly been researched in a certain way by reassessing the circumstance and including intersectionalities to give an overall new understanding. An example that comes to mind is Critical Disability Theory (CDT) and Critical Disability Studies (CDS), which according to Bell (2006) argued that this field should be renamed 'White Disability Studies', given the act of exclusion of "individuals of color treated as second-class citizens" (p. 281). Only with the added intersectionality of Indigeneity did a new take on a new theory become a reality of Indigenous CDT and Indigenous CDS. Moradi (2017) reviewed how intersectionality as a research tool has been used in psychological research, which revealed insight related to "feminist scholars and activists [who] adopted the intersectionality perspective to address the ways in which sociopolitical systems involving multiple forms of oppression and privilege shape people's experiences" (p. 105).

McCall (2005) further revealed that intersectionality gives "the most important theoretical contribution that women's studies, in conjunction with other related fields, has made so far" (p. 1771). These two authors provided a solid outlook as to the validity of the use of intersectionality within their field. This approach can also be applied to other disciplines to obtain a similar prospect.

Creating multiple lenses can provide alternate research perimeters that might not previously have been undertaken. It is in this direction of adaptation that CDT and CDS can expand by including the intersection of 'Indigeneity', which goes beyond the original CDS and CDT perimeters. A few of these intersectionalities can be applied to fields of 'research in data collecting interviews' from a settler-colonial perspective or from an Indigenous standpoint 'knowledge gathering sessions'. These intersectionalities can become a helpful tool within other areas that have historically been limited. The only limitation is the person – researcher – knowledge seeker who limits their creativity in providing new intersections.

The coupling of Indigeneity and disability – The nexus of knowledge

The intersectionality of Indigeneity and disability, as it relates to the nexus of knowledge, can indigenize the CDT and DS. This infusion of knowledge transforms these predominantly White-settler-colonial theories to become more – as Indigenous Critical Disability Theory (ICDT) and a new way to understand DS by including an infusion of Indigenous knowledge, belief systems, and spiritual connections that are often excluded from DS. Through this process of applying Indigenization or decolonization, it metamorphosizes a theory into a belief – like that of a caterpillar to a beautiful butterfly.

The intersectionality of disability and Indigenous people has given rise to a limited source of research and of theories, which has impacted the already fraught depiction of Indigenous disability in a negative settler-colonial context that directly clashes with traditional Indigenous belief systems. Therefore, in my work, I define CDT as a way to support the transformation of society that enables disabled people to thrive within all their diversity as equal members and full participants in their communities. Whereas, a new Indigenous theory, possibly called ICDT, allows for an Indigenous perspective that has not always been reflected within CDT, which is based on a settler-colonial mind frame. These two theories allow for a synergy of ideals and concepts that can assist how disability is viewed and understood by Indigenous Elders, teachers, academics, and community members within the greater disability worldview. The very necessary CDT offers ways of understanding disability, portrayed from a settler-colonial standpoint, whereas an Indigenous Disability Theory is lacking. It leaves CDT in a negative light, which adversely effects the ability to select a theory that aligns with Indigenous disabilities as the majority of them revolve around settler-colonial research. After conducting an extensive search within the literature review, it can be seen that a new type of Indigenous theory is needed, which gives Indigenous knowledge seekers, such as myself, the ability to work with knowledge shared by the Elders, teachers, and community members. Therefore, a new Indigenous theory would address disability through an Indigenous lens, which honors the knowledge shared as they have provided the ability to analyze the information presented. CDT is used when observing and analyzing how settler-colonial information is reported, but it doesn't apply to Indigenous scholarly sources. Since most of the work within the field of disability has been conducted by utilizing CDT, however, it lacks direction from an Indigenous perspective as it was designed and modeled for the settler-colonial framework. It has limited if not excluded an Indigenous presence (Gilroy et al., 2021), so any infusion of Indigenous context begs for a new Indigenous-oriented CDT to emerge.

Senier (2020) looks at this interweaving of Indigenous disability cultures as a way of understanding how disability situates itself within traditional knowledge as well as in postcolonial thought like a blending process. Although Senier and Braker (2013) stated that actually "Disability is pervasive in literature written by Indigenous people" (p. 123), which could explain the divide of Indigenous disability knowledge – as a split between traditional and postcolonial knowledge systems. Indigenous pedagogy is rooted in the "socio-cultural perspective of education … culture, disability… identity and language" (Gibson, 2012, p. 356). Senier (2013) reveals from a conversation with an Elder that "in ancient times […] the Indian was healthy because he ate only clean, pure food and lived close to nature. Then came the new people with their strange ways and food, and dreadful diseases" (p. 222).

CDT lacks an Indigenous ability to include identification markers such as sociocultural perspectives, oral histories, and belief systems – educational value. Therefore, a need to reflect Indigenous philosophical/belief approaches should include ideas that lie beyond CDT (Newman, 2022). This provides more than just an alternative critical theory, as it is a method specifically thought out to combat racial biases. Newman (2022) states that

> Indigenous Methods and Critical Disability Theory provide a means of examining early and/or Indigenous cultures that can assist in pulling down the existing structures that oppress people based on gender, disability, and indigeneity. In so doing, they inform our understandings of embodied difference and challenge us to rethink our assumptions.
>
> (p. 20)

She goes on to say, that "Indigenous Methods (IM) speak directly to this call and dismantle oppression by looking directly at lived experiences" (p. 12). According to Newman, she further suggests that CDT and IM, when combined, become an 'Indigenous Critical Disability Perspective' without definitively naming it as such. This type of combined theory is needed to understand the information presented on Indigenous disabilities in this chapter. Therefore, it is time for the field of DS, which has primarily been under the stewardship of Western academia with few Indigenous scholars and academics, to be decolonized by including Indigenous belief systems, sociocultural theories, and perspectives. Understanding the inevitability of Indigenous sociocultural perspectives being included offers a greater insight into the challenges faced by Indigenous people within the field of DS with only CDT. Erevelles (2011) revealed that "Invisibility is costly. Recognition, on the other hand, can inspire action" (p. 131).

CDT was not designed for Indigenous people and their belief systems, which include – oral history, metaphors, language, dream knowledge, and spiritual interactions. This difference contributes to more assessments and misdiagnoses of disabilities among Indigenous peoples (Ward, 2024). Therefore, by including an Indigenous lens in a multitude of forms such as, but not limited to Indigenous counselors and psychologists, teachers, Elders, and/or Knowledge Keepers/Holders, grandmothers, or other tribal members, who have some sort of community connection who can provide an Indigenous link to the individual by offering alternative educational formats, specialized trainings, and even teachings beyond the colonial scope that measures in deficits (Ward, 2024). The implementation of an Indigenous lens onto the preexisting CDT Indigenizes it. It infuses the gaps of CDT but allows for a sociocultural perspective to be applied that takes into account the unique Indigenous ways of sharing knowledge through oral testimony from a distinctions-based approach to first-person testimony.

Indigenous learning style or a colonial learning disability – How abilities are misunderstood as disabilities

A learning style or a disability is an area of inclusive education that is often passed over with mere criticism. There is a need to separate both and to carefully look at how each is understood before surpassing a debate that needs to move beyond the current understanding. Battiste and McLean (2005) provided a methodology direction through "a variety of pedagogical approaches, or 'holistic' approaches to teaching helps to engage students who have many different learning styles" (p. 13). They go on to explain that by including a multifaceted approach such as the "integration of media literacy, visual arts, industrial arts, physical education, and music into all subjects enhances learning for students who have visual or oral learning styles" (p. 13). These recommendations would enable Indigenous people, who struggle to learn within a predominantly settler-colonial schooling to be able to adapt their learning style so that it remains as an ability, rather than a disability when instructed by non-Indigenous teachers using a curriculum that hinders the Indigenous learning process. This outlook advances an understanding of what an Indigenous learning style could encompass and provides insight into the unique cultural perspectives when it comes to learning within an educational setting. Senier (2013) suggests that "many indigenous people, at Mohegan and elsewhere, seem reluctant to embrace disability culture" (p. 227). He continues to reflect on this path that "traditionally, disability was not seen as such" (p. 213). The claim is not merely descriptive, revealing on ageless ways of gathering knowledge, which is distinctly different from that of settler-colonial society as not being developed in this compacity. This could suggest that disability from an Indigenous perspective was not on the same equal footing as that of settler-colonial standards as they taught, advised, and pushed towards supporting a deficit explanation.

Consequently, disability is complex, which makes it difficult to define, especially, among Indigenous societies, which do not have a viable presence in providing knowledge and insight into how disabilities are understood (Gilroy et al., 2021; Ward, 2023). How one views oneself can go a long way in providing a distinction between a learning style and a disability as a deterrent for quality of life.

Learning style or colonial learning disability – What or who is correct?

A disability assessment based on a White-settler-colonial deficit approach can be viewed and understood in a different context from cultures that place cognitive development differently such as from an Indigenous perspective. One such example derives from Cramblit (2014), who revealed that "many Native students have a visual learning style [so] rely on visual input to guide them in the learning process. This comes from traditional instructional techniques that rely on modeling" (para 2). He goes on to explain that

> many American Indian students have a visual learning disorder, which means dyslexia, numeric dyslexia, amblyopia (lazy eye), focusing slowness, blurred and low vision … Change the system to meet the needs of students & families, not the other way around.
>
> (paras 3–4)

What Cramblit shared gives a deeper look into the complexity of teaching Indigenous students because the majority of educational practices have not worked to the point of being inadequate, given the cultural and linguistic differences to learning. Indigenous peoples learned well before contact and had done so within their own compacity, which is slowly becoming recognized and utilized by non-Indigenous teachers as alternative learning approaches such as multisensory learning, which changed as a direct result of colonialism (Cameron, 2022; D'Souza, 2021; Obed, 2022). It is not just the learning style of Indigenous students that must change, but it is how they are conditioned for their environment, which is why Indigenous people possess superior visual-spatial learning abilities (Siegle et al., 2016).

The Alberta Education Board stated (2005) "Aboriginal learning was often a multisensory small group activity, beginning with observation and evolving into tactile, hands-on experiences" (p. 42). This also includes utilizing a total physical response (TPR) that benefits all students, especially, those identified as 'gifted' or those who struggle because English is not their first or second language. Cramblit (2014) also showed that "Western education models, by and large, are not the best options for teaching many Native learners… American Indians typically learn best by visually reinforced teaching approaches, not lecture and copy" (para 2). This approach has been implemented in various Indigenous schools; however, more research is needed to see if this is a common approach or merely done by a few varied participating Indigenous schools. Reyhner and Eder (2017) attested that Indigenous people must be able to access and "control their educational systems … [with] their own languages, in a manner appropriate to their cultural methods of teaching and learning" (p. 339). This measure would ensure a gradual response to learning based on their own ideals, beliefs, and knowledge systems, which would positively reinforce their own learning systems instead of assessing and subjecting Indigenous students to a battery of colonial tests.

Gifts or curses – Let's see what happens

The one identifying marker among Indigenous peoples is how their spirituality teaches them that those born with a disability are seen as a gift from the Creator (Lovern, 2021; Phillips, 2010; Stienstra, 2015), some others believed the disabled had a direct communication to the spirit world (Nielsen, 2012). As well, reflecting on settler-colonial 'impediment' being a negative symptom does not allow for Indigenous beliefs that it is 'a gift' and strength, but rather deems Indigenous ways of knowing as backwards (Alberta Education, 2005, p. 123). Conner (2018) acknowledged how disabilities are conceptualized as gifts from the Creator, Jesus, or God from the perspective of the individual's own spiritual connection. Conner (2018) provides insight from a communal approach towards people with disabilities and a "recognition of their gifts and value to faith communities" (p. 35). These gifts must be looked upon beyond what any person, group, or society deems as being 'disabled' or 'different', as these labels do not fit within the paradigm of the Creator, who places the soul or spirit as a perfect being. Jaimeson (1991) explains that "since our lives are primarily gifts, we cannot take credit for any of our strengths or talents. To take credit for these would be a form of plagiarism" (p. 3).

This path that Cervantes and Parham (2005) reflect on is that "Native Americans ... view life as sacred, are interrelated through the spiritual dimension, and understand human development as a spiritual journey" (p. 740). Here, one might interject as many Christian denominations have very similar beliefs that life is sacred, and we are on a spiritual journey through life and all our talents and abilities come from God. This type of understanding may also reflect many of the other world religions. This idea follows the Hopi way of living, which suggests that "a person born with a condition that inhibits mobility is not disabled, if they can still contribute to the functioning of the community" (Durst et al., 2006, p. 13). The Indigenous perspective must be taken within a distinctions-based approach as not all cultures, societies and peoples are the same as each group has their own belief system; although, there are various Indigenous beliefs on mentality that people are created by the Creator, and have a spirit (Grandbois & Sanders, 2009). Thus, their actions have consequences that can affect themselves or the community. The colonialist way stripped off all that makes Indigenous people who they are to "get rid of their way. Their religious spiritual beliefs ... putting them away in boarding schools...and forcing the white man's teachings on them" (Gone, 2007, p. 293). Their spirituality remained intact, though, which has led to their strong belief systems.

This type of dysfunction undermines an Indigenous person's natural abilities that are culturally connected to their way of life, learning, communicating, and self-expression – the outcome is the concept known as 'soul wound' (Gone, 2013, p. 4). Peters et al. (2019) suggested a need "to develop the talents of and meet the learning needs of all students, some who require 'gifted' or advanced educational interventions to have their needs met" (p. 280). Failure to do so could result in 'an ability' becoming 'a disability' as the system labels them as disabled so without the receiving the possible accommodations, they would not succeed (Gentry et al., 2014; Robinson et al., 2018).

When it comes to viewing disability as a negative aspect, there are only a few examples to consult. Lovern and Locust (2013) looked at the Yaqui belief that "Witchcraft may be effective against a person who is spiritually weak, and is usually responsible for sudden physical illness, disability, stillborn infants, emotional illness and unexpected death" (p. 113). There are oral stories that lend to this type of experience such as engaging in incest, which genetically could cause a mental and/or physical disfigurement, which could be interpreted as one's being cursed or condemned by the Creator God. The fact remains that some of these so-called disabilities were not truly disabled because they were still able to contribute to society despite a limitation or disadvantage, yet this did not matter in the grand theme of their life story.

There is one person of many who comes to mind that reflects a famous Indigenous person with a disability. Peacemaker, a Huron, had a severe speech impairment but was still able to convey his message "the Great Law of Peace to the Iroquois" with his helper, Hiawatha, as a guide, which was a form of accommodation (Nielsen, 2012, p. 1). Peace-maker's message brought a lasting peace and unity among the Iroquoian peoples with the aid of Hiawatha because Peacemaker had listened to his pain when his daughters died. This ability to connect beyond words allowed Hiawatha to share his ability to speak, which Peacemaker would use to spread his words of peace. Regardless of how someone speaks, writes, or expresses themselves, their knowledge, dedication, compassion, humil-ity, resilience, and empathy are qualities that would allow their 'dis' to become an ability, and thus their greatest contribution would be conveying their knowledge and wisdom.

By turning negative comments regarding disabilities into abilities allows for the gradual acceptance that all humans are created with 'dis' and 'abilities' and that we can change them in order to change the conversation around disability labeling so that the narrative will inspire itself. This acts as a social change, which will ultimately alter the narrative to a less oppressive one. Therefore, instead of evaluating the 'dis' and the 'abilities' of a per-son, a positive reinforcement might also align with one's distinct cultural identity, with various "intersections between disability and other categories such as Indigenous and disabled" (Kuppers, 2014, p. 7). As well, other areas could positively portray learning disabilities/learning differences or embrace dyslexia (Gibby-Leversuch et al., 2019). Re-gardless of the actions, the 'dis' can become an 'ability' to obtain much needed resources such as accommodations, and other alternatives or other methods of communicating information. If this occurs, then every human can be considered as disabled for humanity is not perfect as the Creator God has allowed for a pure spirit to use the body, knowing what challenges will lay ahead.

To be or not to be – Who is speaking for us?

Gilroy et al. (2021) declare the intersectionality of Indigenous and disability in research has a "limited international comparative exploration of the embodiment of disability by Indigenous people… led by Indigenous disability scholars. Much of what is written is in fact by non-Indigenous people with limited or no Indigenous input" (p. 2079). Thus, Indigenous perspectives on disability have historically been ignored and not stud-ied enough (Gilroy et al., 2021a). This proves once again that non-Indigenous scholars have been providing their voice, time, and dedication to speak for Indigenous disabled people and the issues they face. This action can be construed as being racist by selec-tively controlling the Indigenous voice and their fight. Moreover, the disability field has not yet fully developed in terms of the potential present and future contributions it can make to different Indigenous communities (Gilroy et al., 2018; Grech, 2015; Lovern, 2014). Gilroy and Emerson (2016) explains that research by Indigenous people is an area that needs to be developed within their confines to reflect their own belief systems and is a growing area that requires Indigenous participation. This also includes how Indigenous people can use their histories and languages in "reclaiming, reformulat-ing and reconstituting" their own cultures and identities when looking at disabilities

(Smith, 2012, p. 143). Reclaiming derogatory labels can empower those who have suffered (Cooley, 2022; Mauldin & Brown, 2021; Olsen & Pilson, 2022). This will go far to enable a new understanding of how to view and interpret how disabilities are understood from an Indigenous perspective (Kress, 2022). Understanding that people learn differently does not make learning disability an intersectionality. This could offset potential hatred and even hatred direction, which could undo what is occurring in academia and so enable a more positive outlook and commitment. There is a necessity for "teachers with an Indigenous background or of other intersecting identities to reflect the diversity of the community" (International Disability Alliance, 2015, p. 2). The more intersectionalities there are will only deeply convey a richness in perspective by including a multitude of lenses, which would offset potential discrimination based on a few intersections. A greater number of lenses can enrich the experience of the individual so that their experience will speak for themselves, not through anyone else. It is with this dedication and resilience that people must speak up, not only for the rights of those who have been labeled, classified, and limited due to who they are, what they do, or how they live their lives, but also by providing a voice, a chance and/or a platform to make their voice heard, see their hands up high, or take in their message. To be or not to be is entirely up to the labeled and those who choose to ignore them. They must all be offered a chance for dialogue and to allow them to speak for themselves.

References

Agosto, V. and Roland, E. (2018). Intersectionality and educational leadership: A critical review. *Review of Research in Education*, 42(1), 255–285.

Alberta Education (2005). *Our words, our ways: Teaching First Nations, Métis and Inuit learners*. Edmonton, AB: Alberta Learning and Teaching Resources Branch (pp. 123–149).

Battiste, M. and McLean, S. (2005). *State of first nations learning*. Saskatoon, SK: Canadian Council on Learning (CCL).

Bell, C. (2006). *Introducing white disability studies: A modest proposal*. In L. J. Davis (Ed.), *The disability studies reader* (2nd Ed), (pp. 275–282). New York, NY: Routledge.

Cameron, L. (2022). Indigenous ecological knowledge systems – Exploring sensory narratives. *Ecological Management & Restoration*, 23(S1), 27–32.

Cervantes, J. M. and Parham, T. A. (2005). Toward a meaningful spirituality for People of Color: Lessons for the counseling practitioner. *Cultural Diversity and Ethnic Minority Psychology*, 11(1), 69–81.

Connell, R. (2011). Southern bodies and disability: Rethinking concepts. *Third World Quarterly*, 32, 1369–1381.

Conner, B. T. (2018). *Disabling mission, enabling witness: Exploring missiology through the lens of disability studies*. New York, NY: InterVarsity Press.

Cooley, J. A. (2022). Mad objects and soft screw. In K. Watson & T. W. Hiles. (Eds.), *The Routledge companion to art and disability* (pp. 385–400). Hiles: Routledge.

Cramblit, A. (2014). My rules for teaching American Indian students. Indian Country Today. Doi: https://indianz.com/News/2014/08/11/andre-cramblit-my-rules-for-te.asp.

D'Souza, B. (2021). *Interactive technologies and Indigenous art: Exploring the use of immersive resources to increase audience engagement with ceramic pieces in the Andean and Amazonian Indigenous art and cultural artifacts collection*. Doctoral dissertation. The Ohio State University.

Durst, D., Gay, A., Morin, G., Rezansoff, M., Ram, K., Maurice, J., Suzuta, H., Duggleby, P. and Zimmerly, K. M. (2006). *Urban Aboriginal families of children with disabilities: Social inclusion or exclusion? Participatory research: Working together for the inclusion of Aboriginal families of children with disabilities*. Regina, SK: National Association of Friendship Centres.

Erevelles, N. (2011). The color of violence: Reflections on race, gender and disability. In K. Q. Hall (Ed.), *Feminist Disability Studies* (pp. 117–135). Bloomington, IN: Indiana University Press.

Gentry, M., Fugate, M., Wu, J. and Castellano, J. A. (2014). Gifted Native American students: Literature, lessons, and future directions. *Gifted Child Quarterly, 58*(2), 98–110.

Gibby-Leversuch, R., Hartwell, B. K. and Wright, S. (2019). Dyslexia, literacy difficulties and the self-perceptions of children and young people: A systematic review. *Current Psychology*. Doi: 10.1007/s12144-019-00444-1.

Gibson, S. (2012). Narrative accounts of university education: Socio-cultural perspectives of students with disabilities. *Disability & Society, 27*(3), 353–369.

Gilroy, J., Dew, A., Lincoln, M., Ryall, L., Jensen, H., Taylor, K., Barton, R., McRae, K. and Flood, V. (2018). Indigenous persons with disability in remote Australia: Research methodology and Indigenous community control. *Disability & Society, 33*(7), 1025–1045.

Gilroy, J., Uttjek, M., Lovern, L. and Ward, J. (2021). Indigenous people with disability: Intersectionality of identity from the experience of Indigenous people in Australia, Sweden, Canada, and USA. *Disability and the Global South, 8*(2), 2017–2093.

Gilroy, J. & Emerson, E. (2016). Australian Indigenous children with low cognitive ability: Family and cultural participation. *Research in Developmental Disabilities, 56*, 117–127.

Gone J. P. (2013). Redressing First Nations historical trauma: Theorizing mechanisms for Indigenous culture as mental health treatment. *Transcultural Psychiatry, 50*(5), 683–706.

Gone, J. P. (2007). "We never was happy living like a Whiteman": Mental health disparities and the postcolonial predicament in American Indian communities. *American Journal of Community Psychology, 40*(3–4), 290–300.

Grandbois, D. M. and Sanders, G. F. (2009). The resilience of Native American Elders. *Issues in Mental Health Nursing, 30*(9), 569–580.

Grech, S. (2015). Decolonising Eurocentric disability studies: Why colonialism matters in the disability and global south debate. *Social Identities: Journal for the Study of Race, Nation and Culture, 21*(1), 6–21.

International Disability Alliance (2015). *The right to education of persons with disabilities: The position of the international disability alliance.* New York, NY: United Nations Press.

Jaimeson, (Gawitrha), N.A.C. (1991). *Dwanoha: One earth, one mind, one path.* Six Nations of the Grand River, ON: Pine Tree Publishing Group.

King, J. A., Brough, M. and Knox, M. (2014). Negotiating disability and colonisation: The lived experience of Indigenous Australians with a disability. *Disability & Society, 29*(5), 738–750.

Kress, M. (2022). *Reclaiming disability: Of Mino-Pimatisiwin, belonging, and gentle teaching.* In T. M. Christou., R. Kruschel., I. A. Matheson., and K. Merz-Atalik (Eds), *European perspectives on inclusive education in Canada* (pp. 172–195). Routledge

Kuppers, P. (2014). *Studying disability arts and culture: An introduction.* New York, NY: Palgrave Macmillan.

Lovern, L. L. (2014). Embracing difference: Native American approaches to disability. *Tikkun, 29*(4), 37–40.

Lovern, L. L. (2021). *Global Indigenous communities: Historical and contemporary issues in Indigeneity.* Palgrave.

Lovern, L. L. and Locust, C. (2013). Chapter 5. Traditional beliefs about disabilities. In L. L. Lovern & C. Locust (Eds.), *Native American communities on health and disability: A borderland dialogue* (pp. 1–237). New York, NY: Palgrave.

Mauldin, L. and Brown, R. L. (2021). Missing pieces: Engaging sociology of disability in medical sociology. *Journal of Health and Social Behavior, 62*(4), 477–492.

McCall, L. (2005). The complexity of intersectionality. *Signs: Journal of Women in Culture and Society, 30*, 1771–1800.

Moradi, B. (2017). (Re)focusing intersectionality: From social identities back to systems of oppression and privilege. In K. A. DeBord, A. R. Fischer, K. J. Bieschke & R. M. Perez (Eds.),

Handbook of sexual orientation and gender diversity in counseling and psychotherapy (pp. 105–127). Washington, American Psychological Association.

Newman, S. (2022). Valdivia statuettes and hybridity in the Americas of 3500–2500 BCE: An Indigenous critical disability perspective. In K. Watson & T. W. Hiles (Eds.), *The Routledge companion to art and disability* (pp. 7–25). London: Routledge.

Nielsen, K. E. (2012). *A disability history of the United States*. Boston, MA: Beacon Press.

Obed, D. (2022). Chapter 11. Synergies between Indigenous ways of knowing and meditative inquiry. In A. Jumar (Ed.), *Engaging with meditative inquiry in teaching, learning, and research* (pp. 154–169). London: Routledge.

Olsen, J. and Pilson, A. (2022). Developing understandings of disability through a constructivist paradigm: Identifying, overcoming (and embedding) Crip-dissonance. *Scandinavian Journal of Disability Research*, 24(1), 15–28.

Peters, S. J., Gentry, M., Whiting, G. W. and McBee, M. T. (2019). Who gets served in gifted education? Demographic representation and a call for action. *Gifted Child Quarterly*, 63(4), 273–287.

Phillips, R. (2010). "Try to understand us": Aboriginal Elders' views on exceptionality. *Brock Education Journal*, 20(1). Doi: https://doi.org/10.26522/brocked.v20i1.146.

Reyhner, J. and Eder, J. (2017). *American Indian education: A history* (2nd Ed.). Norman, OK: University of Oklahoma Press.

Robinson, A., Adelson, J., Kidd, K. A. and Cunningham, C. M. (2018). A talent for tinkering: Developing talents in children from low-income households through engineering curriculum. *Gifted Child Quarterly*, 62(1), 130–144.

Senier, S. (2013). Traditionally, disability was not seen as such: Writing and healing in the work of Mohegan medicine people. *Journal of Literary & Cultural Disability Studies*, 7(2), 213–229.

Senier, S. (2020). *Disability in Indigenous literature*. In Alice Hall (Ed). *The Routledge companion to literature and disability* (pp. 9–20). New York, NY: Routledge.

Senier, S., & Barker, C. (2013). Introduction. *Journal of Literary & Cultural Disability Studies* 7(2), 123–140.

Siegle, D., Gubbins, E. J., O'Rourke, P., Langley, S. D., Mun, R. U., Luria, S. R., Little, C. A., McCoach, D. B., Knupp, T., Callahan, C. M. and Plucker, J. A. (2016). Barriers to underserved students' participation in gifted programs and possible solutions. *Journal for the Education of the Gifted*, 39(2), 103–131.

Smith, L. T. (2012). *Decolonizing methodologies: Research and Indigenous peoples* (2nd Ed.) New York, NY: Zed Books.

Soldatic, K. (2018). Policy mobilities of exclusion: Implications of Australian disability pension retraction for Indigenous Australians. *Social Policy and Society*, 17(1), 151–167.

Stienstra, D. (2015). For Michael Charlie: Including girls and boys with disabilities in the global South/North. *Disability and the Global South*, 2(2), 632–648.

Ward, J.T. (2022). Chapter 22. Reframing disabilities: Indigenous learners in Canadian educational systems. In Hilary Weaver (Ed). *The Routledge International Handbook on Indigenous Resilience* (pp. 335–348). New York.

Ward, J.T. (2023). *Nòswàhanà-n Wìsakedjàk of Indigenous Elders' knowledge of disabilities, learning disabilities, and dyslexia through the lens of Indigenous disability methodologies*. Ottawa, ON: University of Ottawa Press (PhD).

Part V

Interpretations, narratives, and lived experiences of grassroots teachers and social service providers

The chapters in Part V illustrate a perspective that has often been excluded within the disability studies. The authors in this final section all derive from Africa and India. As with many sources related to Indigenous disabilities, they have been excluded if not limited from this geographical area. For this reason, these perspectives reflect a common theme of poverty from social service perspectives. These authors represent Uganda, Malawi, India, Kenya, Burundi, and Rwanda. It is worth noting that these authors are all first-time publishers based on their lived experiences. Many of them have written, but for regional organizations that relate to the current objectives within this book. These perspectives make this section an ideal realistic final part to conclude this book on Indigenous Disability Studies as their insight gives a unique viewpoint into parts of the world that have historically been forgotten. These authors, their stories, and who they share are not forgotten as we are all children of Mother Earth. Through this collective approach towards understanding disabilities, we can move forward in this pursuit of knowledge so that no one suffers alone just because some look, act, and appear different. Humanity is a buffet of diversity, and these stories and insights will reflect just that and more.

The need for diversity of the unknown – The forgotten

These authors emphasize the realization that disabilities are not limited to learning differences but can be brought on through alternative approaches such as sexually transmitted diseases, anomalies, and even acts of torture. By extending the area of disability knowledge beyond the traditional viewpoint in Western thought (medical and physical differences) that can be medically treated or helped with specialized educational teaching, this alternate perspective provides additional insight into the term disability. Further to this, the extension of a cultural viewpoint of disabilities includes the teachers and social service providers, who are often on the front lines in providing help to those in great need. Many of these professions live in a dangerous world where their occupation can lead to death of themselves or the people they care for. In many of these places and indeed well beyond, other lay professionals struggle to support those who are in need, regardless of physical, mental, emotional, and/or spiritual challenges. There are great survival challenges to people in times of peace, but in times of war and uncertainty, those who struggle with disabilities are often alone or face the worst challenges.

The authors in this chapter reveal a hidden side of disabilities not just from a visual representation as depicted in the photos, a few even considered as graphic, but through

DOI: 10.4324/9781032656519-33

the experiences of those who chose to share their stories by contributing to these chapters. It is also worth reflecting that within the academic sphere of Disability Studies, information pertaining to Africa and the labels of "underdeveloped countries" or "3ʳᵈ world", there is little to no written information from these areas. Most of the disability information derives from the global north. So, with this insight, there was a significant need to share the hidden side of Mother Earth of these people. We are all connected as humans in our challenges of living and this ability to connect and share experiences will ultimately influence Disability Studies as a global response to how information is taught and how knowledge and belief systems are understood and learned.

Colonial manipulation and transformations

The information presented in Part V by the authors illustrates the impact of colonialism by Western influences, which has negatively impacted the natural development of the original inhabitants. The typical viewpoint of these Indigenous peoples has been represented through the eyes, voices, words, and actions of those who try to help in a world that might seem to be consumed by chaos. Although there are viewpoints that reveal the transformation of social and cultural perspectives due to colonialism that have bettered or impacted the use of conflict as a measure for conquest, the influence of Christian churches and organization has become the primary tool for colonization. However, it has also been their salvation beyond a spiritual connection, through a humanitarian aspect. The common practice of land acquisitions done by injuring or killing off landowners has become a common belief by victims within these stories as a way to occupy fertile farmland. Yet if the conflicts don't leave people dead, it leaves them disabled. These actions have all led to the current situation in many of these so-called developing regions as a consequence of colonial exploitation as capitalist priorities have contributed to the subjugation of peoples and their land. The relationship of tribalism to colonialism to present-day outcomes have all contributed to the current situation faced by these authors, but also much more for those they take care of.

28 Disabilities in Uganda
Understanding community challenges and barriers

Twinerugaba Barlton

Introduction

I come from the Banyankole tribe in Uganda, also known as the Ankole people, and I live in the same area I was born in. The Banyankole tribe is a Bantu ethnic group native to the southwestern part of Uganda and is part of the larger Bantu-speaking family that resides in various countries across Africa. The Banyankole are known for their distinct cultural practices, language, and social organization. They speak Runyankole, a Bantu language, which is one of the four official languages of Uganda. Banyankole people refer to people with disabilities as "Ebimuga," which literally means disabled people.

I received training about disabled people during my "Senior SIX vacation" period (one to two years), which is given to all students who complete their Uganda Advanced Certificate of Education before they join University. Thus, I was given Community-based Rehabilitation CBR Guidelines Volumes 1–7 By the World Health Organization (2010) to read when in my four-day training before we began moving around to various communities (Figure 28.1).

At the end of the training, we were also given: Community-based Rehabilitation: Supplementary booklet by the World Health Organization 2010. I worked there with the National Union of Disabled Persons of Uganda (NUDIPU). Now, I have graduated with a degree in Computer Science from Bishop Stuart University so I can better support my family. In this comprehensive discussion, I will explore the situation of people with disabilities in Uganda, covering topics such as disability rights, education, employment, healthcare, social inclusion, and the role of government and non-governmental organizations in improving the lives of individuals with disabilities.

History

Uganda, officially known as the Republic of Uganda in East Africa is bordered by South Sudan to the northwest, Kenya to the east, Tanzania to the south, Rwanda to the southwest, and the Democratic Republic of the Congo to the west. Kampala is the capital and largest city in Uganda. It serves as the political, economic, and cultural centre of the country. This paper is divided into various aspects regarding disabilities including its history, culture, economy, and current challenges.

Uganda has a complex history, shaped by a series of kingdoms and chieftaincies prior to colonial rule. Uganda gained its independence from Britain on October 9, 1962, and became a republic with a parliamentary system of government. It later experienced a series of political upheavals and instability over the decades, including under the tyrannical

DOI: 10.4324/9781032656519-34

Figure 28.1 Visiting the communities, September 2010.

Source: Photographer: Twinerugaba Barlton

rule of Idi Amin from 1971 to 1979, which was marked by human rights abuses and mass killings. Yoweri Museveni's Regime came to power in 1986 after a successful guerilla war and has remained in power for over three decades. He has been re-elected multiple times as the President. Its political stability remains a concern, and the country has faced political unrest and human rights issues in the past.

Culture and society

Uganda's culture is diverse, with over 56 distinct ethnic groups and languages spoken, which make policies or community action in unity. The Baganda, Banyankole, Basoga, Bakiga, and many others contribute to the nation's cultural richness. The majority of Ugandans are Christians, with both Catholicism and Anglicanism having a significant presence. Islam is also practiced by a notable minority. Traditional African pagan religions are followed by some communities. English is the official language and is widely spoken, especially in urban areas and for official communication. Luganda, Runyankole, and many other local languages are spoken across the country as well.

Uganda's economy is diverse, with a mix of agriculture, services, and industry. Agriculture is the backbone of Uganda's economy, employing the majority of the population. Major crops include coffee, tea, maize, bananas, and cotton. The country is often referred to as the "Pearl of Africa" due to its fertile land. Uganda's industrial sector includes manufacturing, mining, and construction. The country has mineral resources, including copper and cobalt, which are important for its economy.

Usage of traditional knowledge in understanding disabilities and learning disabilities

In Runyankole, a Bantu language spoken in southwestern Uganda, the term "disability" is referred to as "omushaija" or "omushaijja," which means "a person with a problem" or "a person with a challenge that affects their ability to function in daily life". In the Ankole culture, people with disabilities were seen as "cursed" or "possessed" by evil spirits, so were rejected, ignored, and excluded from the community. However, attitudes towards disability have started to change, so there is a growing recognition of the importance of inclusivity, respect, and support for people with disabilities and their rights and dignity. Today, people with disabilities are often referred to as "Abalwanyi," which means "people with different abilities." – with unique skills and strengths and is a more positive and inclusive view of disability. It may also be viewed as a family or community issue, rather than an individual problem so families are expected to support and care for those with disabilities.

Uganda's challenges and opportunities

Uganda faces a range of challenges, including poverty as a significant portion of the population live in poverty, with limited access to basic services and healthcare because of unfinished roadways – inadequate infrastructure. Uganda has been working to improve its roads, electricity, and telecommunications, to support economic growth. Another key challenge is the healthcare system, as there are not enough healthcare centres or professionals, particularly in rural areas.

Despite these challenges, Uganda has several opportunities for growth and development. The country has significant agricultural potential, a burgeoning services sector, and a youthful population, which, if harnessed effectively, can contribute to economic growth and development.

Disabilities – A global issue

Disabilities are a global issue that affects millions of people worldwide, and Uganda is no exception. The Republic of Uganda recognizes the rights of persons with disabilities, as outlined in the United Nations Convention on the Rights of Persons with Disabilities (CRPD). The Persons with Disabilities Act of 2020 provides a comprehensive framework for the recognition, protection, and promotion of the rights of persons with disabilities in Uganda. Under this legislation, disability is defined as a substantial functional limitation, impairment, or restriction that affects an individual's ability to perform activities within the range considered normal.

In this comprehensive exploration, I will delve into the various aspects of disabilities in Uganda, including its prevalence, and causes, which are much different from the western developed world so it has many challenges, as well as the progress made in addressing these issues. The aim is to provide a holistic understanding of the disability landscape in Uganda, shedding light on the experiences of individuals with disabilities and the efforts being made to enhance their lives and inclusivity within the Ugandan society.

Prevalence of disabilities in Uganda

The prevalence of disabilities in Uganda is significant. These can be categorized into various types, and each type has its unique set of causes. According to the Uganda Population and Housing Census of 2014, approximately 12.4% of the population reported having a disability. This figure, however, likely underestimates the true prevalence due to stigma and a lack of comprehensive disability identification mechanisms. Moreover, the World Bank estimates that 15% (Uganda National and Housing Census, 2014) of the global population has some form of disability, and Uganda is expected to have a similar prevalence. Several factors contribute to the high prevalence of disabilities in Uganda. These include:

• Disabilities in Uganda are considered as a significant health concern attributed to preventable health issues, such as maternal and neonatal conditions, malnutrition, and infectious diseases like malaria and HIV/AIDS.
• Inadequate access to healthcare as many Ugandans, especially in rural areas, lack access to proper healthcare, which results in untreated or poorly managed health conditions that can lead to disabilities.
• Road traffic accidents are a growing concern in Uganda, resulting in injuries and disabilities for many individuals. The lack of road safety measures and poor infrastructure exacerbates this problem. Unlike rural roads in the west that are paved, most rural roads in Uganda are not upkept and are very poor dirt roads with no proper drainage, rocks on the road, and unsafe drivers (often without licenses)
• Armed as in many other African countries, again unlike the West, Uganda has experienced periods of ongoing civil wars and conflict, which have led to injuries and disabilities among the population. As well, there is religious persecution where Islamic groups enter a church or village and shoot anyone close by as well as burn down houses. Uganda has faced several armed conflicts in the past, including the Lord's Resistance Army insurgency in the northern region and deadly skirmishes between tribes. These conflicts between tribes have led to uncountable disabilities, both physical and psychological.
• Neglected Tropical Diseases: Neglected tropical diseases, such as river blindness and trachoma, continue to affect many Ugandans, leading to disabilities if left untreated.

Causes of disabilities

Understanding the causes of disabilities in Uganda is vital for prevention and intervention strategies as various factors contribute to this. Some of the common causes of physical disabilities in Uganda include congenital conditions such as heart defects, birth defects, and genetic conditions such as cerebral palsy often present from birth. These can result in disabilities from an early age. Non-communicable diseases such as meningitis, diabetes, and hypertension may lead to conditions like lower limb amputations so resulting in long-term physical impairments (Figure 28.2).

As well, infectious diseases such as HIV/AIDS and malaria can both lead to long-term disabilities, especially, when not adequately treated. Also, Uganda, like many other African countries, has had outbreaks of polio in the past, resulting in physical disabilities among those affected. Another cause is malnutrition, which can lead to stunted growth and developmental delays in children, potentially resulting in lifelong disabilities.

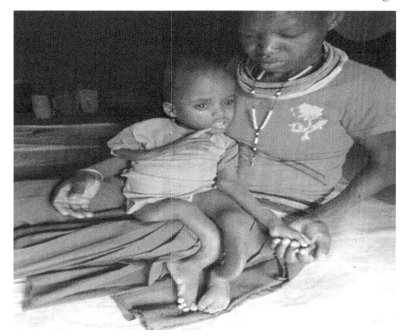

Figure 28.2 Disabled child with mother, August 2018.

Source: Photographer: Anna Summer, Uganda

This also occurs because of limited access to healthcare. Unfortunately, there are also too many disabilities from accidents, including those on roads or in the workplace, and falls, which contribute significantly to physical disabilities.

Sensory disabilities such as impairments in vision and hearing can be congenital or acquired later in life. For instance, congenital deafness may be caused by genetic factors, while acquired blindness can result from diseases like glaucoma or cataracts. Further to these, intellectual and developmental disabilities can stem from genetic factors, prenatal conditions, complications during birth, and early childhood illnesses, such as conditions like Down Syndrome and autism.

Psychosocial Disabilities often result from mental health issues and psycho-social stressors, which are frequently linked to trauma experienced during conflict, domestic violence, and other adverse life events. Then, there are also environmental factors, such as unsafe working conditions, exposure to harmful substances such as toxic chemicals in agricultural settings, and a lack of proper sanitation, which can also lead to disabilities.

Challenges faced by individuals with disabilities in Uganda
social inclusion and community support

Individuals with disabilities in Uganda face a multitude of challenges that affect their quality of life, social inclusion, and economic opportunities. Stigma and discrimination are pervasive in Ugandan society which makes it challenging for people with disabilities to fully participate in community life. This discrimination can manifest in various forms, from social exclusion to limited access to education and employment opportunities.

Some key challenges and opportunities related to social inclusion exist as it is essential for the overall well-being of individuals with disabilities. Thus, there are Community-Based Rehabilitation (CBR) Programs. These have been implemented to provide support and services to people with disabilities at the community level and aim to enhance the participation of people with disabilities in community activities.

Education for people with disabilities

Access to quality education is a fundamental right, and it is crucial for the personal development and empowerment of individuals with disabilities (Figure 28.3).

In Uganda, there are education barriers so access to quality education remains a significant challenge for children with disabilities. Therefore, there have been efforts to improve access to education for people with disabilities: Uganda has also adopted a policy of inclusive education, which aims to integrate students with disabilities into mainstream schools. While this policy is in place, there are challenges related to schools, which may lack the necessary infrastructure, special materials, and space for them as well as the availability of specialized services as well as specially trained teachers, who can accommodate the diverse needs of these students.

Challenges persist, including a shortage of qualified teachers and a lack of accessible infrastructure. Additionally, cultural beliefs and stigma can sometimes discourage families from sending their children with disabilities to school. Further efforts are needed to make education more inclusive and accessible for all.

Healthcare and rehabilitation

Access to healthcare and rehabilitation services is essential for individuals with disabilities, as it can help manage health conditions and improve their overall quality of life. However, challenges in this area are many. There is limited access to healthcare

Figure 28.3 A typical class, July 2018.

Source: Photographer: By Anna Summer

services for people with disabilities due to physical barriers, such as inaccessible healthcare facilities, as well as attitudinal barriers where healthcare providers may not be adequately trained to address the specific needs of people with disabilities. Although, efforts are being made to improve healthcare and rehabilitation services, including the training of healthcare providers to better understand and meet the needs of individuals with disabilities.

There is also a lack of specialized healthcare services, such as those for individuals with hearing or visual impairments, which are often limited and unequally distributed across the country. As well, the cost of healthcare and rehabilitation can be prohibitive for many individuals and families, particularly those living in poverty. A lack of accessible transportation can make it difficult for individuals with disabilities to access healthcare services.

Employment opportunities

People with disabilities in Uganda often face barriers, as well, to employment so are more likely to be underemployed or unemployed compared to their non-disabled peers. This leads to economic insecurity and their dependence on social support. However, the Social Services necessary for them are far from adequate. Thus, securing employment is a significant challenge for people with disabilities in Uganda, as it is in many countries. Several factors contribute to this issue:

- Stigma and Discrimination: Negative stereotypes and discrimination against people with disabilities persist and occur in the workplace.
- A lack of Accessibility: Many workplaces are not physically accessible, making it difficult for people with mobility impairments to access job opportunities.
- Limited Skills Development: People with disabilities often face challenges in accessing training and skills development programs, which are essential for employability.
- A lack of Disability-Inclusive Policies: Some workplaces lack policies that promote inclusivity and reasonable accommodations for employees with disabilities.
- Efforts to address these challenges include government initiatives to sensitize employers, improve accessibility, and encourage the inclusion of people with disabilities in the workforce. Additionally, non-governmental organizations and disability advocacy groups provide training and employment support.

Social services and support systems

Social services and support systems for individuals with disabilities are often limited in scope and reach. This includes services related to rehabilitation, getting assistive devices, and community-based programs. Further to this, there are various accessibility issues. The physical infrastructure in Uganda often lacks the necessary accessibility features for people with disabilities, which includes inaccessible transportation, and public buildings, and a lack of sidewalks, which make it difficult for individuals with disabilities to move around independently safely. While Uganda has made progress in enacting laws and policies to protect the rights of people with disabilities, their enforcement and implementation remain challenges so there are limited Legal Protections, but there is a need for more comprehensive enforced legal protections and enforcement mechanisms.

Progress in addressing disabilities in Uganda

There is great poverty and marginalization in Uganda so people with disabilities are more likely to live in poverty and face multiple forms of marginalization. Poverty exacerbates their challenges and limits their access to essential resources and services. Despite all the significant challenges faced by individuals with disabilities, there have been notable efforts to improve their well-being and inclusion. Some key areas of progress include the fact that Uganda has made significant strides in developing a legal framework to protect the rights of people with disabilities.

Disability rights and legal framework

Uganda has taken significant steps to promote and protect the rights of people with disabilities which include: The 1995 Constitution of Uganda includes provisions related to the rights and protection of persons with disabilities. The Persons with Disabilities Act, Uganda, 2020, see footnote below for additional information[1] this comprehensive piece of legislation provides for the recognition and protection of the rights of persons with disabilities. It covers various aspects, including accessibility, education, employment, and social protection. National Council for Disability (NCD): The NCD is the government agency responsible for coordinating and implementing policies and programs related to disability. While these legal frameworks are in place, there is still work to be done in terms of ensuring that these laws are fully implemented and that persons with disabilities have equal access to justice and the benefits provided by these legislations.

On the global scale

Research and Data Collection on people with disabilities and their needs are being carried out. There is a growing emphasis on collecting accurate data and conducting research on disabilities in Uganda. This helps the government and the main players to understand the scope of the issue and design evidence-based interventions. Furthermore, Uganda has developed international partnerships as it has partnered with international organizations and donors to involve them in helping to improve disability services and inclusion. For example, the Ratification of International Agreements including the CRPD, which obligates the government to uphold the rights and dignity of persons with disabilities. These partnerships bring funding and technical support to advance disability-related initiatives.

Case studies of disabilities in Uganda

To gain a deeper understanding of the challenges and progress related to disabilities in Uganda, let's examine a few illustrative case studies.

---

1 An Act to provide for the respect and promotion of the fundamental and other human rights and freedoms of persons with disabilities; to re-establish the NCD as the National Council for Persons with Disabilities; to transfer the property of the Uganda Foundation for the Blind to the National Council for Persons with Disabilities; to provide for the local government councils for persons with disabilities; to repeal the Persons with Disabilities Act, the National Council for Disability Act and the Uganda Foundation for the Blind Act, and to provide for related matters.

Catherine's story: overcoming physical disabilities

Catherine, a young woman from rural Uganda, was born with cerebral palsy, a condition that affects her motor skills and speech. In her early years, Catherine faced significant challenges accessing education. Many schools were ill-equipped to support her needs, and she often encountered discrimination from her peers. However, Catherine's life took a turn for the better, when she was introduced to a local organization that focuses on inclusive education. With their support, she was provided with assistive devices, speech therapy, and the necessary accommodations to attend school. She went on to complete her primary and secondary education and is currently pursuing a degree in social work at a local university. Her journey highlights the importance of inclusive education and the positive impact it can have on the lives of individuals with disabilities in Uganda. It also underscores the critical role played by local organizations and the need for continued advocacy and support.

Apolo's experience: disability and employment

Apolo is a young man who lost his right leg in a motorcycle accident. After the accident, he struggled to find employment to support his family. The lack of accessible transportation and workplace accommodations posed significant challenges for him. His situation began to change when he connected with a vocational training program funded by a disability-focused NGO. The program provided him with training in computer skills and job readiness. He learned to use a prosthetic leg and received support to overcome mobility challenges. With the new skills and support, he secured a job in a local office, where he is thriving both professionally and personally. Apolo's story illustrates the potential for individuals with disabilities to succeed in the workplace when provided with the necessary training, assistive devices, and supportive work environments. It also emphasizes the role of NGOs and vocational training programs in empowering people with disabilities to become self-reliant.

Sylvia's struggles: autism and stigma

Sylvia is a young girl with autism. She and her family experienced significant stigma and isolation within their community. Many people in their village did not understand autism and considered Sylvia's behaviour as strange. This led to social exclusion and a lack of access to educational and healthcare services. Sylvia's life improved when her family connected with a local autism advocacy group. This group provided information and support to Sylvia's family and advocated for greater awareness about autism in the community. They also collaborated with local schools to create a more inclusive environment for children with autism, including tailored educational programs and teacher training. Sylvia's story emphasizes the importance of raising awareness about different types of disabilities and promoting inclusion at the community level. It also highlights the positive impact of advocacy groups and community-based initiatives in challenging stigma and discrimination.

Joseph's journey: access to healthcare for the deaf

Joseph was born with hearing impairment, and throughout his life, he struggled to access healthcare services. Many healthcare facilities lacked sign language interpreters, and communication barriers often led to misdiagnoses and inadequate treatment.

Joseph's situation improved when a local hospital partnered with a disability organization to provide sign language interpretation services. This initiative aimed to make healthcare more accessible to the deaf community. With the support of sign language interpreters, Joseph and others in the deaf community were able to effectively communicate with healthcare providers and receive proper medical care. Joseph's journey underscores the importance of making healthcare services accessible to individuals with sensory disabilities. It also illustrates how partnerships between healthcare institutions and disability organizations can lead to significant improvements in the lives of people with disabilities.

Ongoing challenges and future perspectives

While there has been progress in addressing disabilities in Uganda, numerous challenges still persist, and there is still much work to be done. Some of the ongoing challenges and future perspectives rest on sustainable funding from the government. Many initiatives aimed at improving the lives of people with disabilities in Uganda rely on external funding from international organizations and donors. However, to achieve long-term sustainability, there is a need for increased domestic investment and financial support from the Ugandan government.

As well, it is essential for there to be a comprehensive Data Collection and accurate and up-to-date data on the prevalence and specific needs of people with disabilities. Efforts to strengthen data collection and research in this area should be a priority to inform policy and programming. It is also of paramount importance for there to be more Awareness and Advocacy groups. Continued awareness campaigns and advocacy efforts are needed to challenge stereotypes and discrimination against people with disabilities. Public awareness can drive social change and foster a more inclusive society. This is what is really needed.

It is crucial to push for more inclusive education as this would ensure that all children, regardless of their abilities, have access to quality education. This would include making school environments more inclusive and training teachers to work effectively on all levels with students with disabilities. Again, after children have finished their schooling, there should be greater Employment Opportunities for those with disabilities. Expanding inclusive employment opportunities and addressing workplace discrimination is essential for the economic empowerment of individuals with disabilities. As well, whether in the countryside or the city, healthcare access for people with disabilities is of prime importance. Efforts to improve access to healthcare services should continue, with a focus on physical accessibility and training healthcare professionals. The many challenges faced by people with disabilities in Uganda are exacerbated in rural and remote areas. Thus, special attention should be given to addressing the specific needs of these communities.

Government and non-governmental initiatives

Both government and non-governmental organizations play a critical role in addressing disability-related issues in Uganda. Some of the key initiatives include:

- National Council for Disability: NCD plays a central role in coordinating disability-related policies and programs. It works to ensure the inclusion and participation of persons with disabilities in various aspects of life.

- Uganda Society for Disabled Children: This organization focuses on improving the lives of children with disabilities through education, healthcare, and advocacy.
- Disability Rights Fund: The Disability Rights Fund provides grants to organizations working to promote the rights and inclusion of persons with disabilities in Uganda.
- Specialized Rehabilitation Centres: Uganda has specialized rehabilitation centres and hospitals that provide services for individuals with disabilities.

Challenges and barriers

Despite the progress made in addressing disability-related issues in Uganda, significant challenges and barriers remain. These include:

- Attitudinal Barriers: Negative attitudes and stereotypes towards people with disabilities are widespread, hindering social inclusion and employment opportunities.
- Access to Services: Disparities in access to healthcare, education, and rehabilitation services persist, particularly in rural areas.
- Economic Disparities: People with disabilities are more likely to live in poverty, which further limits their opportunities and access to services.
- Inadequate Legislation Enforcement: The implementation and enforcement of disability-related laws and policies face challenges, including limited resources and awareness.
- Accessibility: Physical infrastructure and transportation often lack the necessary accessibility features for people with mobility impairments.

Conclusion

In conclusion, disabilities in Uganda are a complex issue with a wide range of causes and challenges. Uganda is home to a diverse population with various ethnicities, tribes, languages, and cultural backgrounds. Therefore, people with disabilities in Uganda face a range of challenges, including limited access to education, employment opportunities, healthcare, and social inclusion. These people represent a significant portion of the population, and their experiences are shaped by a complex interplay of factors including cultural beliefs, socio-economic conditions, and the presence of supportive policies and programs. All of these must be taken into account when preparing programs and schools for them.

However, Uganda has made significant progress in recognizing and addressing these issues through legislative frameworks, government initiatives, and the work of non-governmental organizations. Advocacy and Awareness are being promoted so that NGOs, other organizations, and advocacy groups are actively working to raise awareness, challenge stereotypes, and promote the rights and inclusion of people with disabilities. While some progress has been made in various aspects, there is still a long way to go to ensure that individuals with disabilities can fully participate in society, access education and healthcare, and enjoy the same opportunities as their non-disabled peers. The most important issue of all, though, is strengthening Legal Protections for disabled people. While Uganda has enacted legislation to protect the rights of people with disabilities, the enforcement and implementation of these laws need to be strengthened.

To improve the lives of individuals with disabilities, it is crucial for Uganda to continue advocating for their rights, raising awareness, and implementing inclusive policies. As well, continued effort in community support is vital to promote inclusivity and to improve the lives of people with disabilities. Additionally, addressing the root causes of disability, such as malnutrition and infectious diseases, is essential. With ongoing efforts and a commitment to inclusivity, Uganda can work towards a more equitable and accessible society for all its citizens, regardless of their abilities. People with disabilities in Uganda, as in many other parts of the world, still face a range of challenges and experiences. While Uganda has made significant strides in addressing disability-related issues in recent years, there are still many hurdles to overcome.

References

Community-based Rehabilitation CBR Guidelines (2010). Volumes 1–7. The World Health Organization.

The United Nations Convention on the Rights of Persons with Disabilities (CRPD). Uganda Persons With Disabilities Act, 2020 Act 3 of 2020.

World Health Organization (2010). Community-based Rehabilitation: Supplementary Booklet, The National Union of Disabled Persons of Uganda (NUDIPU).

World Bank (2014). Uganda National Population and Housing Census and World Bank Estimates 03, 20182014 National Census Main Report 2014.

29 Disabilities in Malawi

A cultural and social perspective as influenced by colonialism

Kennedy Mapira

Introduction

I come from Chamasowa Village, Malawi, Central Africa. Being an Indigenous Malawian, I belong to the Lomwe tribe, one of the many Bantu tribes in my country. I received a Malawi School Certificate of Education, at Mountain View Secondary School in 2004. Unfortunately, I failed to pursue a university degree due to financial constraints. I am also a pastor, community development advisor, and the founder of Gateway Christian Orphan School, a charity, where I support disabled children and orphans spiritually and academically. In addition to that, I also create research strategies and implement how best my community can develop. Apart from being a volunteer teacher in the orphan school, I am also a farmer on a small scale to generate income for basic daily survival so I can support my family, the church, my community, the elderly, and the school. I support the elderly and the disabled in the church with food and clothes, and build them shelters, and provide them with education. In the community, I like to establish developments that are beneficial to it such as the school for the orphans. In the church, I preach, teach, give advice, and visit and encourage the sick or the weak. I also established a center where the elderly, the disabled, orphans, and other needy people meet to receive cooked food when possible.

Bantu translation for disabled

The disabled are generally referred to as 'Ulumali', but some examples in the Nyanja translation include 'Osaona', meaning those that cannot see; 'Osayenda', meaning those that cannot walk; or 'Osamva', meaning those that cannot hear. In general, they are termed 'Opuwala'. In the precolonial period, there were no schools for the disabled as the few schools were opened by the missionaries. People worked for free in White-owned farms, where the disabled were ill-treated and regarded as useless. General schools were in distant places, more than 10 kilometers away. Learners had to cycle, so many even failed to reach them. This gave no option to the disabled. There were no rights protecting the disabled at that time.

Colonial aspect of the British

The part of Africa now known as Malawi was colonized by the British in 1891. In 1953 Malawi, then known as Nyasaland, was a protectorate of the United Kingdom within the semi-independent Federation of Rhodesia and Nyasaland, which was dissolved in 1963.

DOI: 10.4324/9781032656519-35

In 1964, the protectorate over Nyasaland ended and it became an independent country under Queen Elizabeth II with the new name Malawi. Two years later it became a republic (https://localhistories.org/a-brief-history-of-malawi/).

Some Whites opened estates and forced Malawians to work as slaves for long hours, a term referred to as 'Thangata'. The Indigenous people were tortured more, especially the disabled (mostly crippled). Those considered unproductive and useless were beaten to death and others were buried in their houses because they could not work on the estates. After being colonized, British missionaries came and opened schools. They brought a new language – English, that was adopted as an official language and used as the medium of instruction in schools. The locals had problems adapting to it. Any disabled people were not allowed to enroll in school and were discriminated against and treated as animals, though the schools had a positive impact later.

Upon gaining independence, Malawi became a totalitarian one-party state under the presidency of Hastings Banda, until 1994. Malawi has a democratic, multiparty government headed by an elected president. Malawi is extremely poor and has a low life expectancy and high infant mortality. There is a diverse population of native peoples, Asians, and Europeans, with several languages spoken and an array of religious beliefs. Although, there was periodic regional conflict fueled in part by ethnic divisions in the past, by 2008 it had diminished considerably, and the concept of a Malawian nationality had reemerged.

Indigenous people, disability, and tribal ways

Malawi has vast ethnic groups and shares similar cultural experiences and perspectives with the Bantu, which is the original tribe of central and southern Africa. However, there are variations in the viewpoints of disabilities from one community, tribe, or country to another. I will dwell mostly on the experience of Malawian culture.

The general opinion of tribes is that they regard the disabled as inferior and counterproductive, so they are sidelined, isolated, discriminated against, and seen as unproductive citizens. Thus, they are given less attention and are not involved in decision-making and development work. These disabled people are also seen as wizards and witches, so they are scorned and mocked, and normal people mimic their behavior. The disabled are, of course, vulnerable to insults and harm, rape, bullying, and labeling. Due to other problems, these circumstances go unattended. As well, the children do not have inclusive education due to insufficient special needs schools.

Current disability conditions – postcolonial

In the past, people regarded being disabled as curse, but now people understand it as natural.

Disabilities are conditions that prevent one from actively performing or accomplishing things because of social or inborn characteristics. Different types of disabilities exist in Malawi, for example, visual impairment, hearing impairment, mental impairment, language, and communication difficulties (dyslexia), specific learning difficulties, emotional and behavioral difficulties such as autism, developmental difficulties, and gifted learners. In my orphan school, there are some disabled children, and their disabilities influence their learning process.

Learning disabilities prevent a person from learning and can be different categories of impairment. Some cannot completely learn and need caregivers or special attention, socially or spiritually. Still, others with dyslexia must struggle in school due to rooms not suitable for learning and no proper materials. Even though initiatives have been implemented throughout the country, there are still some disabled people, who have not yet received any support because they live in remote areas where access to social services is a critical challenge.

Causes of disabilities in Malawi

The main problems are to do with little or no health care and health education, so many infections are unnecessarily caused because of infection during pregnancy as a result of sexually transmitted diseases or if the mother excessively drinks alcohol during pregnancy, the baby can also develop a hearing impairment. As well, there are many accidents due to bad roads and unlicensed drivers that lead to head injury, or hereditary factors lead to hearing impairment. There is also a great deal of visual disability.

Mental Disability may be caused by diseases such as meningitis, measles, sexually transmitted diseases, and Malaria. It may also be caused by drinking alcohol or smoking during pregnancy. As well, malnutrition may cause brain damage. Children may have it, again, because of premature or postmature birth. As well, there are other types of learning difficulties, which may be caused by acquired trauma due to again maternal alcohol drinking or malnutrition. As well, it may be caused by an injury from medical instruments at birth from incompetent doctors or a head injury later. It can also be caused by high fever, or a lack of oxygen to the brain (anoxia) may have occurred at birth, by genetic and hereditary influences, or other diseases.

Problems in general – Racism

People with disabilities in Malawi, often have numerous problems getting access to services as most of them come from very poor families that cannot afford to give them a decent life and to buy them wheelchairs, crutches, or special shoes. Now, because they are isolated, it becomes difficult for those concerned to give them extra help. Worse still, these people lack proper accommodation, they live in dilapidated and leaking homes, as they cannot erect or construct proper homes for themselves and sometimes resort to staying in deserted homes.

These vulnerable people are most of the time subjected to all kinds of torture. Their tribes, communities, and schools do not allow them in decision-making processes. They are called nasty names, for example (saona ndege) *'cannot see an airplane'* – referring to the blind; 'Bubu' just repeats the same syllable words – *referring to the dumb*, etc. They are also prone to rape and bullying by other children, as they normally do not fight back.

The disabled face racism in hospitals in many forms. Racism occurs in a sense that there are Chinese hospitals, which are so expensive that Africans can't afford them so cannot get effective drugs. In most cases, there are different wards for Chinese and Malawian patients. While Malawi hospitals are substandard and usually public hospitals, so foreigners and even wealthy Africans shun them.

As well, most of the hospitals do not have proper facilities for vulnerable disabled people. There are no specialist doctors, appropriate drugs, or suitable physiotherapy facilities. Furthermore, the government mostly fails to construct these necessary special hospitals and rehabilitation centers, so there are very few. They are also often at a distance for most of the disabled. Again, there are also few specialists, as most of them leave for foreign countries, seeking for greener pastures. As well, there is racism in the cities.

People regard themselves as a higher class of people. As they have proper facilities, they treat country people badly and tease them because they are farmers and produce their own food.

Tribe-to-tribe racism is evidenced as well, but even more so, especially, during the run-up to or after elections. Tribes usually follow a nepotic approach as they are very disapproving of the disabled and use their power or influence to get good jobs or take unfair advantages of members of their own family, so they don't care about the disabled at all. Other tribes bully the tribes in their locations or regions.

A case study: how disabled people live and the problems they face

Shaban Padoko, is a Malawian disabled person, from Chamasowa village. He has been blind from birth and lost both parents at quite a tender age. He bemoans living miserably, in absolute poverty, and discriminated against. He feels he is not part and parcel of society and expresses and explains his most and explains his most difficult experiences. "As a God-fearing person, I feel painful to my inability to personally read the scriptures" laments Padoko. He further says this condition made him illiterate because of "a lack of or a distant special school for the blind." He explains that he can't move around without an escort. So, says, "I cannot answer to a call of nature myself in the absence of an escort. You can just imagine yourself at that particular moment." He adds to say that he "depends on charitable people to acquire domestic needs such as proper shelter, bedding, food, and clothes." Malawi being a very poor country does not reach out to all vulnerable people.

He adds that

> I live in fear when it comes to stormy weather as I am not able to observe the intensity of that particular storm. Also, at times I am given the least food portion and sometimes none at all. Unfortunately, the food may sometimes be snatched from me by naughty individuals.

With the crisis in Malawi, people including him are going on empty stomachs. He can't cultivate and depends on cash or food handouts.

He goes on to say, "I am a human being and sometimes need entertainment, but my state bars me from access to visual entertainment such as Television. I feel myself rejected, further to this, detective walking sticks [blind canes] are unaffordable to local Malawians." Therefore, if there is no personal assistant, the blind cannot walk around anywhere alone, as this may expose them to various dangers. He says, "Worse still I am always isolated in policy and decision-making processes and regarded as a useless citizen or community member." In conclusion, Padoko says he is praying for God to intervene in the matter, in finding solutions to the problems the blind and the disabled at large encounter face in Malawi in their day-to-day life.

Problems children with disabilities encounter in schools

The disabled meet a lot of problems in schools, especially as there is a lack of special classes and rooms, a lack of specialist teachers and caregivers among other challenges. It is a major area of concern. Some enroll in inclusive schools, where fellow learners isolate them because they fear they will have to be busy assisting them, for instance, pushing their wheelchairs. The schools too do not have assistive devices or suitable terraces for easy movement of wheelchairs. Most of the time, the disabled lack special education tools such as Snellen charts, braille for the blind, audiometers, and voice and noise makers for the deaf, one-word pictures for communication, and, of course, special teachers.

Other problems exist – due to a lack of funds and perhaps living remotely; some disabled students have problems going to school because of a lack of clothes/uniform and shoes (Figures 29.1 and 29.2).

Alt text: This image reflects the same building as previous one but from an interior perspective, which has large stones where the children sit on to learn. This straw building has big holes with one single wooden pole for supporting the already damaged straw roof.

Some have fears of being raped on the way, if going alone. They are also treated as inferiors, who cannot perform academically. This makes them lose their self-esteem. Sometimes, their food is snatched by fellow children, as they cannot pursue it. Worrisome enough, they are given nasty names, making them lose interest in schooling. They sometimes if unchecked are teased and bullied by fellow learners, which makes them decide to withdraw from school.

Figure 29.1 A typical remote orphanage (destroyed by a typhoon), October 2003.

Source: Photographer: By Kennedy Mapira

Figure 29.2 After typhoon's destruction, October 2003.

Source: Photographer: By Kennedy Mapira

Problems encountered by families, neighbors, and government

Malawi being a poor and agricultural country, many people go to the fields to cultivate them. Some of the disabled people may not be able to participate in these activities. They are thus left at home unattended, which makes life hard for them, as they can stay for hours without food and proper care. Again, they are less considered for some privileges as they seem not to participate in the family's financial contributions. This leads the disabled to mental and moral decadence.

Problems with their neighbors

Neighbors usually distance themselves from disabled people. They isolate them because they think that they cannot make any physical and mental contributions or achievements. To the neighbors, they are not part and parcel of their neighborhood. They refrain from helping them if they are in need when their family members are away. This is a very bad misconception because, although, disabled people may sometimes be physically handicapped, but they are mentally capable.

The government

Even though poverty sounds like a repetition in this article, I am not afraid to say that Malawi is one of the poorest countries in the globe. The government does, though, realize the bad situation of the disabled. Although the disabled can claim their apparent needs, like effective and suitable health care, special education needs, social welfare, and domestic needs, the government seems to take a blind eye on them. Sometimes, it is negligence evidenced by a lack on the part of the government to assess or identify the correct relevant data and reach out to all the disabled. They continue a perpetual construction of schools without facilities for the disabled, inadequate vocational schools for disabilities, and insufficient health experts for the disabled – just to mention a few. There is also a massive failure to allocate enough funds in the budget regarding disabilities. However, the government needs to acquire enough funds or involve donors to ensure the needs of the disabled are addressed.

The government, NGO's, and schools working to get disabled into education programs

The government, charitable organizations, schools, and various stakeholders are working collectively to get disabled back into school. The government has managed to build special education schools, but there are very few because of poverty. Some nongovernmental organizations and charity bodies have come forward to assist the disabled with wheelchairs, canes, special shoes, and other requirements. There are enactment of laws and declarations protecting the rights of the disabled. On top of that, government and other stakeholders provide vocational training, for example, tailoring courses for the disabled to generate income for themselves. Due to civic education, the disabled are given more respect and fairness. Religious leaders are also preaching love for the disabled.

Sensitisation campaigns have been conducted in the communities on awareness and the importance of educating the disabled. The Malawi government is also sensitizing the people, on the evils of scorning the disabled through radio and television broadcastings, and conducting sensitization seminars for local or traditional leaders, on the importance of treating the disabled equally. Thus, schools paste posters up concerning protecting the rights of the disabled. The government has also incorporated the rights of these special groups into the curriculum. Some schools are involved in inclusive learning, but special education needs are great as specialist teachers must be involved in special classrooms.

It is also encouraging to note that charitable organizations have come forward to assist the disabled by providing financial assistance, in acquiring the important learning resources and some domestic needs. This has motivated a lot of disabled in education. Some schools are also built with facilities that meet the needs of the disabled, for example, special classrooms. All these are efforts to bring back or hold the disabled in schools. Yet, the school too may not have funding to purchase the necessary teaching materials. In schools, there is a lack of special classes and rooms, lack of specialist teachers and caregivers among others.

The communities are always trying to overcome these problems in various ways. The religious leaders are always preaching love and peace. Civil societies are actively advocating for the rights of special groups, for example, freedom of association, cultural and mindset change among others. These leaders in turn deliver the awareness messages to their perspective subjects in the communities. In addition to that, the government is also enacting laws that protect the rights of disabled and giving stiffer penalties to those that violent them.

Human Rights Commission

The government did establish the Human Rights Commission (HRC) that deals with the rights of people, which mandates against discrimination. Disabled people do have the right to expression, right to life, right to basic human dignity, right to equality, right to education, right to employment, and also right to participate in social-economic activities.

Figure 29.3 Malawi government passes new disability law, November 2023.

Source: Photographer: By Kennedy Mapira (LinkedIn Account)

Anyone against these rights is brought before the courts. Disabled people should be accepted as any other human being. Now, people are starting to show their respect and to love disabled people. Thus, discriminating and labeling are declining little by little because of the religious leaders, who mostly teach people about love (Figure 29.3).

Among the various tribes in Malawi, these children struggle in school in different ways as specific learning programs are not used such as for dyslexia. Even though initiatives have been implemented throughout the country, there are still some disabled people, who have not yet received any support from the government because they live in remote areas where access to social services is critical challenge. I have noticed some schools with disabilities meet the relevant special education needs. The disabled concentrate on their education and sometimes perform better academically than normal students. Where there are sports facilities, they entertain themselves and feel they have a place in the society. However, Malawi as a poor country needs donor support to ensure that the needs of the disabled are met not only in education but in all aspects of life.

30 Society's manner towards disabilities
A perspective from India

Manisekhar Palle

Introduction

I am an Indigenous student from south India and obtained my B.Ed. from Adikavi Nannaya University. I am interested in psychological research, as well as critical and logical thinking. I am the first person in my entire family to study at university. This is why I became a Disability Community Advisor. Thus, in my spare time, I spend time with children at the Spurti disability home. In my academic career, I have participated in many programs with disabled children, and at present, I help at a school for disabled children who have physical and mental challenges. I am hoping to start teaching regular school this year.

Disability is a physical, mental, or emotional challenge viewed by society as an inability. Disability means "Unable to do anything without any other support." This is society's thinking and the way they treat people with disabilities in the surrounding society, but we do not know the facts of their own ability…! Currently, society's humanity is only shown due to others' impairments and sad situations, which is ridiculous. However, most public figures choose this way to demonstrate their pre-eminence and heroism. It is totally the wrong track for us human beings and most of the world knows this cruel fact about disabilities, but they do not change their behaviour. Why? I believe "disability" will not appear if everyone helps each other without any discrimination (the author). We need to find this real fact in our colourful society.

India and disabilities

India has 2.2 billion (2011 census) people with disabilities, who do get a lot of assistance from the state and central government. Right now, India is the world's largest populated country. The demographic data from the United Nations Population Funds (UNFDA) in the world population report states that in 2023. India's dense population has given it one of the world's most heavily occupied countries. India is the greatest financially secular country in the world with technology.

Discrimination

Here, there are different types of religious people, with their own traditions, cultures, languages, habits, and attitudes. They have their own importance in society and protect their own religious traditions. However, here Indigenous people have become real barriers to Indigenous disabilities. Why? Because everyone has learnt from childhood about things

DOI: 10.4324/9781032656519-36

or ways of life or from their parents' behaviour. Therefore, they often feel that people with disabilities should be discriminated against as they are lower or inferior to normal people. These irrational prejudices make people with disabilities victimized in society.

First, we have to know that disability is not a sin, which is how it is perceived. These people have their own individuality and play a vital role in every generation. People with disabilities have their own social relationships such as with family, friends, school, and neighbours. They have own thoughts, attitudes, and their behaviour patterns, which are vitally affected by the nature of society's behaviour towards them. That is why most of the affected disabled people's attitudes have not changed yet.

History of society's manner towards disabilities in India

According to old scriptures, India has a great cultural heritage because there were many rulers and many religions given birth there with their own cultures. Afterwards, their descendants have continued to follow them. In medieval India, Muslim rulers established hospitals, orphanage homes, and Zakat (charity) for Muslim disabled people, which gave them livelihood assistance for their entire lives so those who belonged to the Muslim religion could use those facilities. The dumb, the deaf, the blind, the physically and mentally handicapped were given those opportunities in "Akbar's" ruling as well. In the 18th century, a random change came about as the old orders were totally changed. Some people with disabilities lost these opportunities so started begging in the streets. The new ways of life made unknown and heavy demands on those with disabilities. Some committed suicide to cope as they were hungry. During the age of kings ruling, they established workshops for the vocational rehabilitation of the physically handicapped as well as other socially and economically handicapped members in the kingdom. They also provided many employment resources to those who got disabled during the War such as for husbands wounded in the war or for any other reason. They provided work for them to help society. Widows, crippled women, girls, mendicants or ascetic women, and mother prostitutes were employed to cut wool, fibre, cotton, etc.

During Gupta's period, especially "Chandragupta" and his grandson "Ashoka" established many support resources for people with disabilities. They were staunch believers in Buddhism so provided free medicines (ayurvedic) for the disabled and people crippled in war.

"Koutilya", one of the greatest politicians of his time, made it a special point for dwarfs, the hunchbacked, and other people with disabilities to work as political spies as well as secret agents in royal palaces.

Christian missionaries

At the end of the 19th century, some great efforts were made to set up hospitals and charitable homes for destitute people. A great deal was done by Christian missionaries to establish schools for blind and deaf people but nothing for the crippled. The problems about the crippled were not solved until World War II. After several years, government-subsidized organizations were established to provide some facilities for crippled people.

Mother Teresa (1910–1997), who everyone has heard of, also established a charity for the poor, HIV/AIDS, leprosy, and tuberculosis patients. She collected funding in many ways and showed her kind heart in India. (Wikipedia)

Some common attitudes of present-day society towards disabilities attitudes of the family

Families play a major role in every human being's life. Sometimes the parents feel pressure and burden if they have a child with disabilities, especially, because of a lack of living assistance, if they are from a poor background. There may be financial burdens associated with getting healthcare, special aids (walkers), special education, and social services that they need for the child. Also, families experience the burden when there is a lack of coordination surrounding them with appointments, etc. Some families, as well, do not pay any attention to the child's thoughts and their likes or dislikes. This means no one cares about them. Cousins are called nicknames based on their impairment. Children with disabilities or without disabilities have a very friendly relationship with their families without any fear. They feel very comfortable and share their thoughts and curiosity. They imitate their parents' emotions in every situation, so they start to think based on their parents' or family's behaviour. Thus, the child acquires their parents' attitude in their home environment. The basic needs of a child or adult are to feel loved, secure, and independent. Every child wants affection from their parents. The family with children with disabilities observes them from all sides not only their dreams, or their desires, but about all family matters such as their lifestyle, their studies to change their family position, and not comparing themselves with others. Sometimes people with disabilities can understand the family situation and can think as normal people. They feel normal.

Sometimes, more often than not, the disabled child creates disharmony in the family. There may be a lack of understanding regarding the child's emotions and thoughts in their needy situation. Sometimes these disabled children create outbursts as protests as their desires are not met. In some unconscious cases or off-mood stages, they cannot change their thoughts so stagnate with their words and oppose others' words. At that time, they behave like a younger 2–5-year-old child. In those situations, we have to give them extra attention, until they can explain what they want to say. Then, they will start to realize and understand others' perspectives, so we must maintain a strong bonding with them to make them feel secure.

Therefore, the attitude of the family towards them is essential. We need to accept every disabled child and adjust to their mental or physical handicap. So, the family has to always accept them and try to understand their situation.

Attitudes in school

School is a secondary learning centre in everyone's life and creates the children's attitudes towards the society. Here, children make their peer groups and experiment with their individuality among them. They also should begin and continue good relations with their teachers. However, according to a United Nations Educational, Scientific and Cultural Organisation (UNESCO) report nearly 3/4 of 5-year-olds and 1/4 of kids aged 5–19 with disabilities in India are out of school.

Disabled or not, deaf and dumb students, slow learners – all mature their relationships with each other. However, in some cases of children with disabilities, they face many obstacles, especially because of the manner of negative teachers towards them. Teachers do not understand their feelings and don't care about them in some inclusive education systems based on the normal student ratio.

According to Special Needs Schools, special needs children face many struggles in their learning process because of a lack of equipment. The students cannot express their thoughts clearly enough to make their needs understood because of only low "understanding" (not sufficiently trained) teachers working there. Most of the teachers will never allow a child with a disability to do anything new or innovative, so sometimes they are annoyed by other students based on their impairment because society is stuck on one thing that disabled/impaired people are lower than normal people. This is the main barrier for new developing generations, so they are killing the ethics and values of society because as I mentioned before that families and schools have the key role in changes happening in society.

Education law for disabled students in India

The Right to Education takes in all children/citizens including those with disabilities. "Article 29(2)" of the Constitution provides that no citizen shall be denied admission into any educational institution maintained by the state or receiving aid out of state funds on the grounds of religion, race, caste, or language. Article 45 of the Constitution (86 Amendment Act 2002) directs the state to provide free and compulsory education for all children (including the disabled) until they attain the age of 14 years. No child can be denied admission into any educational institution maintained by the state or receiving aid out-of-state funds on the ground of religion, race, caste, or language. Although this is not always the case. Further to this, as well, it imposes:

- Inclusive education or integrated education
- Special education facilities for differently abled children
- Low GST (goods service tax) on disabled products
- 40% reservation in all central and state government recruitments
- Specially trained teachers appointed for different abled children
- Right of children to free and compulsory education Act-2009 (6–14 years)
- According to the Individuals with Disabilities, Education Act (IDEA) is a law that makes available appropriate public education to eligible children with disabilities throughout the nation and ensures special education and related services to those children.

Attitudes of health centres on disabilities

India provides a great deal of medical assistance for people with disabilities, but ground-level authorities do other things with the money than what it was allotted for as they are polluted by corruption. Some health centres also discriminate against people with disabilities only because they are termed or labelled as a "disability". They perhaps haven't even met the person. And nobody questions their negative judgements. That's why service directors continue their critical mentality towards people with disabilities. Doctors and staff workers collect money for unnecessary services from the ones they victimize. In India, 80% of people come from remote villages so don't know what their rights are and also don't know about fraudulent government schemes and acts because of their innocence and lack of education.

Arrangements for people with disabilities designated by the health department

There are special arrangements made for people with disabilities, but because of remote distances that people live, it may not be the case either. They should have:

- Caregiver allowance
- Free treatment based on the central scheme of Ayushman Bharat
- Travel assistance (some discounts, reserved seats in travel vehicles)
- Financial assistance for those getting 40% or above disability
- Medicines, monthly check-up, free eligible certificate from central government provided
- Assistance for disabled people to purchase/fitting aids and appliances (ADIP scheme)
- Deendayal Disabled Rehabilitation Scheme to promote voluntary action for those with disabilities (DDRS scheme)
- National awards and national scholarships for people with disabilities, etc.
- Schemes for implementing People with Disabilities Act, 1995 (SIPDA) to provide financial assistance to understand various activities outlined in the Persons with Disabilities Act (equal opportunities, protection of rights, and full participation)
- Vikaas (Day Care)
- Samarth (Respite Care)
- Gharaunda (Group Home for Adults)
- Niramaya (Health Insurance Scheme)
- Sahyogi (Caregiver Training Scheme)
- Sambhav (Aids and Assistance Devices)

Attitudes of colleagues in the workplace

People with disabilities face many struggles concerning their physical appearance and other challenges. They feel poorly based on others' critical perceptions of them and compare themselves with others. Then, they have low self-esteem and feel inferior. They feel some colleagues try to degrade them with their words and looks – bullying, as society treats them as lower-ability people. This perception emerged from the past as mentioned earlier or from ancient heritage behaviour. So, some people with a disability think they have lower capabilities than normal people. Therefore, they are always waiting for assistance without really a true need. So, they must always be treated as normal people and encouraged to go forwards with confidence – without any assistance. These basics should be taught to children from primary school level. Peer groups and work groups play an important role in changing the perception of society. If they have a management position, disabled people can then gain a lot from them, especially, regarding self-esteem.

Attitudes of political leaders

First, I have one question why don't voters choose people with disabilities as political leaders?

In India, the caste system rules and protects the political leaders for their existence. Here, politicians play mind games with the needs of the people. Therefore, elected persons only win by their large process of money distribution. So, every day people can't do anything. Only after independence were some disabled people elected, which amounts to maybe 10 members in 76 years of the independence period. Why I'm sad and stressed; this point is because people with disabilities are also part of society. So, we need to elect them as they know what the problems are regarding disabilities in a neighbourhood. If they have authority, they would support all disabilities. All would be known, and the financial amounts needed would be allotted! However, this is still not happening... why?

The Spurthi welfare society

The Spurthi Welfare Society is a disability welfare centre near where I live that I visit often. Here, various children live and continue their academics. Director Sk. Bhanu has worked there for the past 15 years. She, thus, has a lot of experience with different types of disabled children. She knows their psychology. As well, five other teachers and non-teaching workers have worked there for the past seven years. They come from different religions but work united in their goals (Figure 30.1).

They celebrate all festivals and all the students' birthdays. The director says, "through these things, they should learn unity and diversity". Here they have lots of problems with funding, but she receives donations from higher officials in the area. In the COVID situation, they acted as front-line warriors to protect the disabled students (Figure 30.2).

Therefore, every day, doctors came to check all the students' health conditions and give medicines to them. The residents also live like cousins and give assistance to each other. It is a very nice environment for them.

Figure 30.1 The Spurthi Welfare Society, October 2023.

Source: Photographer: By Manisekhar Palle

Figure 30.2 Teachers working outside together, October 2023.

Source: Photographer: By Manisekhar Palle

My experience with special needs people (disabilities)

I felt very happy in my university days during my research as I enjoyed spending time with special needs children. They have good skills as normal people and good focusing skills. Physically, mentally, and emotionally depending on their disability, they may be lower than normal people, but they are equal as human beings. I gained lots of experience from visiting special education schools without studying any course, which was wonderfully amazing. Through research, I found some points that should be implemented concerning the implications of disabilities (Table 30.1). These are:

- Encourage inclusive education with specially trained teachers from primary level to postgraduate level education.
- Encourage vocational and skill based education for people with learning challenges.
- Bring amendments that government teachers' children must study in government schools. This would reform teachers and make them take responsibility and encourage equality.
- Take school field trips to orphanage homes, or disability homes where normal children and disabled are integrated – minimum once a month to change regular children's perception.
- Conduct seminars on those topics related to disability to build awareness. Let everyone participate without fear, so the children with learning challenges would lose their fear and improve their speaking skills.
- Give some lessons about achievers who had disabilities and yet had great success.
- Conduct parents' meetings and present reports on student's psychology and interests instead of about marks.
- Teachers should encourage parents to teach ethics and values in their homes.

Table 30.1 Image of stretch away your disability – with your self-confidence

Take Away---- Dis   Make it as --- Ability
:) dis<---♿ 🦯--->Ability (:

Source: Designed by Manisechaar Palle

- Provide skill-based education and encourage students with disabilities to learn about technology for a new era.
- Control corruption in government policies and in educational schemes.
- Implement vocational training centres for those with disabilities.
- Politically encourage those with disabilities to empower them. Make reservation for them.
- Give subsidy loans for them without any mediators.
- Conduct job Mela every year for those only with disabilities to encourage their innovations.
- Encourage disability sports and give awards to encourage them.
- Implement NGOs.
- Control corruption in government policies and in educational schemes.

Therefore, to conclude, I believe with all the amendments followed and more support given to Special Ed schools, which would be more readily available to disabled children, these children would find themselves in a better position in society and treated as equals as they should be.

31 Taking care of disability people in Kenya

Duke Makori Mogusu

Introduction

Who I am and why I am here to share my experience of disability in Kenya

We are of the Gusii tribe in Kenya, Africa. My story begins with many difficulties as my parents died when I was 16 leaving me to look after 5 brothers and sisters of varying ages. I tried to find places for us to live, but each one ended so I decided to just take them home. I could not afford to send them to school, so the police authorities would come to harass me to get the children into school, but with little money, I could do nothing. We were barely surviving. Finally, I had a break by getting a job at a hardware store, so I could put my siblings into school. Just recently, my younger brother, even after being out of school for four years, won a top primary exam in Kenya. He received 400 marks and the highest student got 435. This national event allowed him access to a better educational opportunity. However, the story of my family is very similar to that of others in Kenya and the government does very little about it, especially very little for people with disabilities.

Disability in Kenya

The word 'disability' in our Gusii culture 'means' a physical or mental condition that limits a person's movement, sense or activities, a disadvantage, or a handicap, especially one labeled or recognized by the law. Disability is any condition of the body or mind that makes it more difficult for the person to do certain activities and interact with those around them. There are many types of disability: difficulties in seeing, in hearing, in moving, in feeling in hands and feet, in speaking, using strange behaviors and difficulties in learning. Basically, we also understand disabilities as a disorder that affects the ability of one to understand or use spoken or written language properly.

Sometimes, a person with a severe learning disability may depend on someone for their seeing, hearing, speaking, and moving. They may have little speech, difficulties with social skills, and need support with daily activities. One such disability is dyslexia, which involves difficulties in reading and spelling due to problems identifying speech sounds and learning how they relate to letters and words. Also, it is called a reading disability. It is a result of a difference in areas of the brain that process language.

DOI: 10.4324/9781032656519-37

Causes of disability

There are also many causes of disabilities within our Gusii tribe. Poverty and malnutrition are one of the biggest causes of disability. Some are born with congenital problems due to the mother taking drugs or drinking alcohol while pregnant. One may have poor access to health services and information, cures for illness, medicine, and injections. Others may experience dangerous work conditions, accidents, occupational hazards, and war – in today's wars, more civilians than soldiers are killed or disabled and most of them are women and children.

Let me tell you the sad story of one young girl, Damaris Mongare, who was born in December 1999 in Nyangusu village in a local clinic named Mwamogunde Kisii county at 2:00 in the morning of the eighth. She was born in Kisii of the Kisii tribe. Her parents married in 1988. Damaris was born well in her right senses and was a brilliant girl since day one until she was five when she started developing complications of the brain and normal functioning of her body. At first, people said that it was not natural since she behaved like a mad. Others in the village said she was being attacked by witches and witchcraft. She was later taken to the Nyangusu level 4 hospital commonly known as Mwakemo where she was treated, but she didn't recover as expected.

Her parents later took her to a native doctor as they faced a stigma from the community and people around them. She was given natural herbs, but still, she didn't recover. She was later taken to a teaching and referral hospital a level 6 hospital in Kisii, where they treated her brain and the neuro system, but the parents were later told to take her to India to be examined more with therapy. Due to the poverty level in the family, they weren't able to take her to India since they required 300,000 Kenyan shillings (2006).

When she was seven years of age, she became mentally handicapped completely. If she lay down, she wasn't able to move as her spinal cord couldn't support her movement from one point to another. She thus dropped out of school at the age of 8 since she was unable to go back to school as required. She stayed that way even going to the bathroom in her clothes. Due to the devastating conditions, the parents asked for help and later took her to an Eldoret teaching and referral hospital where she was treated. Within two years, she was able to walk again but not speak. She started speaking slowly in 2013 by stammering in a way.

The parents then took her to Magena school for the mentally handicapped. Still goes there. Both parents died in a car accident on their way home during the COVID-19 pandemic after attending their late brother's funeral. Until their demise, her parents loved her so dearly and on their dying bed told a close friend to keep her under their care and to honor their plea.

Challenges disabled people encounter with their families and schools – Trapped in poverty

There are many drawbacks in life for disabled people. Sometimes, people with disabilities, especially Indigenous ones, get trapped in poverty for their entire lives for many reasons such as they were possibly born poor, and the family spent their entire fortune on the individual's health. There are also some instances where people with a disability grow up in care centers as their parents neglected them, so there is no future for them.

The first challenge faced is school as the physical environment of a school may not be accessible. It may be remote or else not suitable for a wheelchair. As well, there may be a definite lack of relevant assistive technology and accessibility to the internet. Then, in school, children with a disability are not fast learners and have poor study skills; thus, they need more attention from teachers. As well, unfortunately, there is social exclusion and barriers to their social welfare as there may also be a negative attitude of others towards disabilities – others calling them names and labeling them.

Further to this, Indigenous people with a disability in our country have problems in getting access to the services, and proper schools and accommodation with the extra help because of bad roads or a lack of services to their area.

The role of teachers

On the whole, children with disabilities are treated well by teachers. However, students with disabilities need to be given extra time to follow directions and make transitions. The teachers need to be extra helpful with them and not be judgmental or punitive. They should always use polite language and non-verbal communication. Teachers should go out of their way to explain certain tasks or concepts to them (this is when it is good for a teacher to have an assistant) if they don't understand. They should also avoid punishing them when they have gone wrong, but try to correct them gently. Teachers should also be honest if they can't understand the student.

Teachers can also help those with learning disabilities by breaking learning tasks into small steps; probing regularly to check their understanding, by providing regular quality feedback, and presenting information verbally. Also, one can use diagrams, graphics, and pictures to support the instruction and provide independent practice. Teachers must remember that they are setting up the student's confidence for life.

Lack of education

Uneducated Indigenous people, with or without a disability, do not easily find a job unless they work as manual laborers, delivery boys, etc. However, these tasks are impossible to complete, especially for people with walking disabilities, blindness, etc. The problem with education for people with a disability is that none of them chose not to be educated. Circumstances may have forced them to go their entire lives without an education simply because their parents didn't want them to go through the stigma at school or they could not comprehend what was being taught. However, many people with disabilities complete their studies and even acquire lucrative degrees that see them working nationally with recognized organizations.

Later years – Employment

Getting and keeping employment

When people with disabilities get through high school or college degrees, there may be other problems in the workplace. Poverty would hinder the individual no matter how qualified they become due to having to dress well as they attend interviews or daily in the workplace. Also, it is never definite whether they would be chosen for the post, so to avoid failure, the majority of disabled people who could work just stay at home for lack of finance to groom themselves for job opportunities. People with diverse learning styles can learn in different ways and not only meet their unique challenges but also excel in school, opening businesses, and becoming their own bosses. However, it is not always as easy as it sounds because instead some organizations would prefer to hire people without a disability and a high-school graduate rather than a person with a disability-degree holder.

Stigmatization

Working in an office job can be challenging for a person with a disability, especially if they are Indigenous (tribal conflicts and competition), so do not get along with other employees. People with a disability often face stigmatization – labeling, especially if their disability is visible such as an inability to walk. Some employees may become isolated by their peers, who fear that the disability might be transmitted. This is a higher level of ignorance since no person can contract a disability from another unless they were engaged in a fight that left the other person without a disability, having a disability.

Employer doubt

For many business owners, employing a person with a disability is a sign of poor leadership since there is considerable skepticism and misconception concerning this disabled people. Doubt emanates from the employer's inability to recognize the qualities of the person with the disability. No matter how they try many people with a disability, though, do not fit into the workplace when they get employed, so they are given meager roles, which the boss thinks is the only thing they can handle. In such instances as this, it may lead to the disabled person suffering from depression and lowered self-esteem. Doubting an individual's capabilities doesn't bode well for an employer. They might let go of the best employees they have hired because they doubted their ability; whereas, a person with a disability might carry out their objectives easily and make their employers profit after being given a chance.

Negative attitude

It has been noted that people with disabilities live very uncertain lives as their employers expect them to carry out their tasks in very unconducive environments. Jeers and bullying alternating from employees are the central champions of the depression and other issues that affect people with a disability at work. Some people are just angry at people with disabilities for no reason. They try to complicate their lives as much as possible as they do not wish to continue working with them. These people make the people with a disability feel as if they do not belong in the organization and lower their self-esteem. Negative stereotypes about people with disabilities have caused many organizations to shy away from employing them and if they do, they keep a keen eye out for them in case they mess up. The organization leaders' attitudes towards the person with disability may cause climatic results that would stigmatize them for their lifetime as it becomes internalized.

It is good to care for people with a disability and show them how to make their work as comfortable as possible. Employers and fellow employees need to understand people with disabilities and drive their strategic options do not kill their morale but boost it. This would change the dynamic of any organization.

Disparity between supply and demand

With the disparity between supply and demand, people with disabilities experience a considerable employment gap caused by their tendency to quit a job due to stigmatization and other physical challenges. The reasons for leaving are obvious. Therefore, employers are advised to make the working conditions suitable for them. Imagine having to climb stairs on crutches or locating your office chair in an office you have never been in since it is not equipped with the right amenities for people with disabilities. Paying attention to the needs of people with disabilities could reduce the rate at which disabled people commit suicide out of depression through poverty and isolation.

Transportation and accommodation facility

As noted earlier in our country, Kenya, many disabled people may live far from available work, so there needs to be a specialized and affordable bus service to take them back and forth daily. Many organizations lack proper amenities for people with disabilities. This makes it almost impossible for people with a disability to cope with work and other factors. To begin with, people using a wheelchair, for example, require room for mobility. If they work upstairs, the organization should be fully equipped with an elevator for them or an escalator to aid their movement. Although such changes will be costly to many organizations, it is a by-law that people with a disability work in an environment that is comfortable and friendly for their needs. In the example of a person using a wheelchair, if there is no space to move, how can they maneuver through the organization and even carry out simple mundane tasks?

Conclusion – Ways of overcoming difficulties of a disability

The golden rule – A solution

People with disabilities should and can help themselves by first, grieving and accepting all the five stages of grief due to their disability. They should accept their disability and giving one's best. They should remain polite and calm and avoid comparison with others and celebrate their own accomplishments. In conclusion, we should all practice the Golden Rule. We should treat everyone as we would like to be treated ourselves. One should always ask before giving assistance because they may not necessarily need or want your assistance. So, think before you speak. Avoid showing pity or patronizing. Speak directly with the person, not to any companion that they may have. Avoid making assumptions about what assistance they need. Ask how you can help them and respect their answers. As well, presume that person with disabilities is competent to handle their own medical care.

32 Conditions of disabilities in Uganda

Muganga Edison Twinemuhwezi

Introduction

I am from the Amukiga tribe in Uganda, Africa near Kampala. I am a self-employed electrician as well as a Disability Advisor working with disabled children. I teach them how they can work and live in the community depending on the disability they have. I also often talk to their families about how to handle these children. Most people become disabled because of civil war and fighting in African countries, which contributes to women's disability, so effects people of different tribes.

Challenges disabled people meet at home and in the community

Due to challenges in Uganda mostly in my community, a person with disabilities sometimes gets challenges from his family because of poverty or from people within the community. Most disabled people are also seen as shameful and are even unloved by their families. They are not treated well as no one cares. This is mainly because it is very expensive to take care of a disabled person, so they are seen as a burden. Therefore, how they are looked after is not good due to a lack of facilities because they may come from low-income families. As many families have neglected them and are even careless about how they live, so most disabled people are left behind in the community, as few people can care for them. This is due to a lack of facilities to care for them and even money to care for them. There are problems for them with feeding, as most disabled people don't have enough food or even people to feed them or help them with other needs.

Their challenges thus consist of mobility issues or trying to do things themselves when they cannot, finding a place in the community when there is no place for them, being abused in the community as they are not properly loved and cared for, being neglected at home, and being rejected and abandoned by families. All these affect people with disabilities in Uganda. They need combined assistance from parents, the community, and the government.

Again, some parents or tribes think being disabled is a curse on the community, so the disabled person ends up neglected, with no help. Witchcraft doctors give medication to witches – women, so the tribe ends up with disabled children. Also, conflicts in tribes and fighting have contributed to disabled people. Therefore, some people of the tribe don't care much for disabled children as they can't contribute to the community.

DOI: 10.4324/9781032656519-38

Types of disabilities

We have three types of disabilities in Uganda. Most of the people or children in Uganda are born with some physical disability such as with leg problems. Some are born with no legs, others have lost them due to accidents, from war, or are disabled through witchcraft. Family planning has also contributed to children born disabled.

For instance, with disabled legs, it can often also be possibly from a lack of nutrition, so they can't move from one place to another freely or walk. Thus, they have to use a wheelchair, but many families can't afford to buy one. So, they need help to get supportive tools like wheelchairs, a cane, walking stick, etc. Others have a body weakness disability, so again, they may be provided with supportive tools for movement. Due to this, some disabled children are unable to go to school and are often neglected. A lack of money and poverty in the family make the disabled person be neglected by both family members and the tribe members. There may also be even a lack of government facilities in the community, which doesn't alleviate their problems.

Other disabled people are born with no arms or hands or cannot use their hands and arms, as their parents may have taken drugs like thalidomide. This affects them in their studies, or they cannot work. Even eating or doing domestic work is hard for them. Due to this, they too are neglected. Some parents don't take care of their disabled children at all, or if they do, they have a lot of challenges with obtaining medication, education, and financial help. If the parents have neglected them, the disabled child may be taken by government facilities, and other agencies to help them.

Many may also be born unable to see – they are blind – sight disabled children, which makes them remain at home, and miss out on education and other things. Some communities don't have facilities for such disabled children, but the government has put a few facilities, not all parents can manage/afford to reach it, so they keep the person with disabilities at home, so they don't get an education (Figure 32.1).

Other children are hearing-disabled, so their speech may also be affected. Then, there are brain-disabled children, so some of them can't understand or even learn. Some have reading or spelling problems (dyslexia). They may be looked after in schools but may experience challenges from other children teasing them, abusing them, and mocking them. Physical challenges in some school facilities are going to the toilet, washing, and even talking with other children.

Educational facilities and accommodations

Many types of accommodations are needed for disabled people; however, they are often abandoned and mistreated. For blind people, we help them with a walking stick, and teach them how to understand some things and even take them to schools where they can learn. If a person doesn't have arms, we help them with supporting tools, and teach them how to use their legs to do work and take them to school.

There is also a lack of facilities for disabled people as no one can afford to help. Most disabled people, thus, have no education as it has been a big challenge to educate them. To sum up, they need education facilities, accommodation, clothing, medication, access to good food and basic care, and as mentioned, support from their families, community,

Figure 32.1 Disabled Teko, Uganda, August 2018.

Source: Photographer: By Mrs Anna Lomonyang

and government. As well, education facilities for teaching them are needed; however, there are some special education places where they are taught.

Response from families, community, and government

Care is needed, as disabled people are not loved by their families as they should be. Due to the lack of personal and government resources for families to care for their own disabled person, the person is often neglected for many reasons. In most cases, it depends on the disability.

The response from families, community, and the government is still not enough and actually very poor for disabled people. This is often because the disabled people are scattered throughout the country and maybe in remote areas without proper services, even of water. Often, other people such as outsiders, churches, and NGOs try to step up to help the families that have disabled people and care for them. Therefore, the government depends a lot on these churches and religious communities to help.

Disabled people in my community can get some support through the government. Sometimes, they receive help from friends, from NGOs that try to help, or they are taken care of by other good Samaritans, who may see a disabled person or children suffering and try to care for them. These Good Samaritans could be just individuals or people with a good heart from other countries or communities or other tribes or from churches, but it is not enough. The Red Cross, the UN, and even some rich countries may come to look

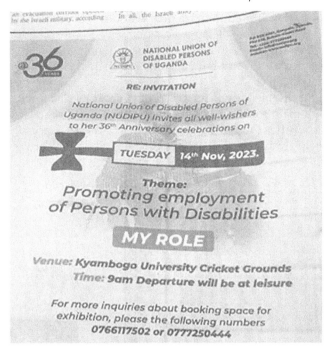

Figure 32.2 Image of promoting new initiative, 2023.
Source: Photographer: Muganga Edison Twinemuhwezi

after the people. Churches also work as good Samaritans, by helping disabled children, not only by teaching them, and praying for them, but also by providing for their needs (Figure 32.2).

A solution

These people with disabilities are all treated in different ways in the community depending on their disability. The tribal communities have started some centers where some of these disabled children or people can go. Some schools with good facilities have also been set up by the government for special people who are disabled. Some live there and others may go home. This depends on the family. If no family members support them, they must remain in the school or government facilities. Some facilities, like a government facility or an agency one, are free, and while in others, people pay.

Also, governments in Uganda are trying to help such disabled children by providing free facilities for them, and free education, medical services, and accommodation. However, it's not enough, which is why some other agencies such as churches also are doing good work helping disabled children, and they try to teach families how to handle their disabled children or people in the community. The treatment is not a good stable care, from family members, so there are many side effects from their care.

Disabled people are always trying to move forward and sometimes, if they can, they do some work, but with help from parents. In my tribe, we support them. We take them to government, and other community training schools, where they train special people and care for them, and even give them medication. Now disabled children, and poor people in my tribe can learn, and work, after training in schools. As well, parents are being trained on how to care for them. Many doctors as well are being trained on how to care for special disability people.

All in all, love for disabled people in my community is needed. I tell them to live their life as if it is God's plan, for them and we are to love one another. We must help each other and provide a better life for disabled people in Uganda, especially, in my community. With God, help always comes to a few of these disabled children or disabled people.

33 Weaving a Human-Centric tapestry

A Rwandan perspective

Diane Umuhoza Rudakenga

Introduction

My personal journey: embracing neurodiversity and community healing

My journey is deeply intertwined with the rich and complex history of my family. Born in Burundi in 1983, to Rwandan refugee parents, my life began against a backdrop of displacement and resilience. My parents, Tutsi refugees, had fled the growing anti-Tutsi violence in Rwanda, a prelude to the horrific genocide that would later engulf the country. They sought refuge in Burundi, where they met, married, and started a new chapter of their lives, marked by hope amidst adversity. Stanton's framework in 'The 10 Stages of Genocide' (Stanton, 1988) provides a comprehensive understanding of the historical context of the 1994 Rwandan Genocide against the Tutsi and its impact on intergenerational trauma. It offers a lens to view the complexities of ethnic conflict and its effects on community mental health. Understanding these stages has been crucial in my work with communities affected by trauma and in fostering resilience. Stanton's stages, from classification to extermination and denial, helped me contextualize the experiences of my family and community during the 1994 Rwandan Genocide against the Tutsi, deepening my understanding of the long-term psychological impact of such events.

Immigrating to Canada

In 1988, the rising wave of violence in Rwanda, which had begun to spill over into Burundi, compelled my parents to seek a safer future for us in Canada. We immigrated to Québec City, a move that marked the beginning of a new set of challenges and opportunities. Growing up in Québec City in the late 80s and early 90s was characterized by isolation as often I found I was the only black student in my classes, exposing me to the stark realities of racism and exclusion. I vividly remember being racially insulted by being called the N-word at the age of five, a significant moment in my journey with racial trauma. Throughout my elementary school years, I faced both overt and covert racism, including a physical attack in the third grade for being black. I frequently encountered exclusion and prejudice, sometimes even from the parents of my classmates.

Amidst these challenges, another aspect of my identity was silently shaping my life – ADHD. Despite my achievements in academics and social skills, I always felt different, yet I remained undiagnosed with ADHD as I did not seem to fit the typical profile. As a child, I devoted considerable time to practicing in front of the mirror, rehearsing speeches, mimicking behaviors, and experimenting with various accents and tones. This

DOI: 10.4324/9781032656519-39

was not only a learning tool, but it was also a means to develop my ability to adapt to social contexts. At the same time, it served as a coping mechanism for my anxiety. Unfortunately, the healthcare system's inadequate understanding of mental health issues meant that my chronic anxiety and panic attacks were overlooked.

During my teenage years, my mental health battles intensified. The shame from my struggles with anxiety, depression, suicidal thoughts, and emotional dysregulation forced me to mask these issues. I felt burdened by the privilege of being alive, yet I was unable to understand my own mental turmoil. My adeptness at masking was so effective that it led everyone – my family, friends, community, and healthcare providers – to miss the signs. This ultimately culminated in a failed suicide attempt, misinterpreted as a reaction to a virus or food poisoning. During my teenage years, I also battled silently with self-mutilation as a way to cope. My turning point came when my school principal, noticing a change in my behavior, expressed concern and guided me to the school social worker. This introduction to therapy opened new avenues for coping with my mental health issues and sparked my interest in psychology, leading me to become a confidante for friends with personal issues, earning the nickname 'psycho-Diane' in high school.

All was further complicated by hormonal changes and the traumatic impact of having witnessed the Genocide against the Tutsi in Rwanda from abroad, which claimed the lives of many of my family members. These experiences, though fraught with pain, were instrumental in shaping my resilience, instilling in me a profound sense of empathy, an understanding of the importance of community bonds, and the courage to advocate for justice. From that point on, I have continued to face episodic mental health challenges. However, supporting others in my community with similar struggles has been immensely therapeutic for me.

In Québec City, the immigrant community, comprised of refugees from various countries, became a haven for us. We formed close-knit communities to cope with the daily challenges of racism and discrimination. This experience underscored the importance of community healing, a concept deeply rooted in my Rwandan heritage. Engaging in storytelling, listening to elders, and expressing ourselves through art and music became therapeutic and empowering. Raised in an environment that valued strength and resilience, I was taught to conceal any signs of weakness. While this approach was beneficial during crises and aligned with my Rwandan heritage, it proved detrimental in dealing with my anxiety and depression, leading to further isolation. At that time, the significant lack of discourse and understanding about mental health left me struggling silently with undiagnosed ADHD, which exacerbated my mental state, and the intergenerational trauma my family and community experienced.

It was only during my later years, amidst a period of intense struggle with mental health as a mother, that these feelings began to make sense. Motherhood, while a source of immense joy, also highlighted the challenges I had been concealing. The demands of parenting made it increasingly difficult to hide my struggles, leading to burnout and depression. A friend's suggestion that I might have ADHD was a possibility I had never seriously considered. Pursuing this led finally to a formal diagnosis in September 2019, a revelation that helped me understand my differences and how I process information.

My background in disability management and understanding of accommodations proved advantageous. I began to implement strategies that worked better for my brain, guided by the principles of positive psychology. My educational and career choices in the organizational health and wellness industry further helped me develop strategies to compensate for my impairments. My social intelligence, a strength developed through experiences and learning from social successes and failures, has been instrumental in my interactions and adaptability.

In sharing my story, I aim to illustrate that being neurodivergent, while presenting daily challenges, can also be a strength with the right accommodations and an inclusive environment. My advocacy for diversity, equity, inclusion, and belonging (DEIB) stems from my personal and professional experiences as a black, cisgender woman with African Canadian heritage, a mother, and a first-generation immigrant. My narrative intersects with my professional acumen, lending authenticity to my advocacy efforts and highlighting the importance of understanding and embracing the full spectrum of human diversity.

Integrating Indigenous perspectives and non-Western views

In aligning with my Rwandan heritage, I recognize the significance of non-Western, Indigenous perspectives in understanding mental health and disability. Our approach to healing and well-being is deeply communal, interwoven with the fabric of storytelling, and anchored in the wisdom of our elders. This perspective challenges the often individualistic and pathologizing lens of Western psychology, offering a more holistic, community-centered view of mental health.

Key concepts and research references: blending storytelling with education

My life exemplifies the intersectionality of race, gender, and neurodiversity. Crenshaw (1989) framework has been pivotal in understanding the multifaceted nature of my experiences and the nuanced ways in which different aspects of identity intersect. Her work helped me navigate the complexities of being a black woman with ADHD in a predominantly white society. Her theory illuminated how overlapping systems of oppression affected my access to mental health care and societal acceptance.

Nadeau (2015) comprehensive look at ADHD in her *the 'lost girls' of ADHD* addresses the unique challenges they face. This book has been instrumental in shedding light on the often-misunderstood aspects of ADHD in females, resonating with my personal experiences. Nadeau's work highlights how ADHD in girls often manifests differently than in boys, leading to underdiagnosis and misdiagnosis. Her insights helped me understand my own journey with ADHD, where symptoms like inattentiveness and internalized hyperactivity were overlooked.

By looking at how racial trauma and mental health impacts personal development (Williams et al., 2018) exploration of racial trauma provides a critical lens through which to view my early experiences of racism. Her work underscores the profound impact of racial trauma on mental health, particularly in non-Western communities. It has been instrumental in my healing journey and in understanding the experiences of others in my community. Williams' research on the psychological effects of racism and discrimination provided a framework for understanding my own experiences of racial trauma in school and their long-term impact on my mental health.

Lai and Baron-Cohen (2015) looks at the *masking and code-switching in neurodiversity* in research on the challenges faced by adults with autism, particularly in terms of masking and social adaptation, which has been key to my understanding of the complexities of neurodiversity and the coping mechanisms employed by individuals. Their study discusses how neurodivergent individuals often develop sophisticated strategies to mask their symptoms to fit in with societal norms. This resonated with my experiences of learning to mask my ADHD symptoms, which, while helping me to adapt socially, also led to internal stress and anxiety.

Seligman (2011) approach towards *positive psychology in neurodiversity management* will work on positive psychology aligns with my approach to embracing neurodiversity. His emphasis on strengths and well-being echoes my belief in focusing on the positive aspects of our diverse identities. His principles have been a guiding force in my professional practice and personal growth. His concept of 'flourishing' – thriving in various aspects of life despite challenges has been particularly influential in my approach to managing ADHD, emphasizing the importance of recognizing and building upon my strengths rather than solely focusing on deficits.

Gone and Kirmayer (2010) analyses the *role of culture in healing and empowerment* with their emphasis on cultural and contextual factors in understanding and addressing mental health issues that aligns with my Rwandan heritage. Their work highlights the importance of community and storytelling in the healing process, offering a non-Western perspective on mental health. Their research underscores the need for culturally responsive mental health care that acknowledges and integrates the beliefs, practices, and values of diverse communities, which has been a cornerstone in my advocacy for culturally sensitive mental health practices.

Edmondson (2019) concept of *psychological safety and inclusion*, especially, psychological safety in the workplace complements my advocacy for inclusive environments. Her framework underscores the need for spaces where individuals feel valued and can express their authentic selves. It has been a foundation in my work to create inclusive and supportive spaces. Her research on team dynamics and the importance of fostering an environment where people feel safe to take risks and be vulnerable has informed my efforts to create a surrounding culture that is supportive of neurodiversity and mental health.

Stanton (1988) framework of *the ten stages of genocide* provides a comprehensive understanding of the historical context of the 1994 Rwandan Genocide against the Tutsi and its impact on intergenerational trauma. His stages from classification to extermination and denial helped me contextualize the experiences of my family and community, deepening my understanding of the long-term psychological impact of such events. He also offers a lens to view the complexities of ethnic conflict and its effects on community mental health. Understanding these stages has been crucial in my work with communities affected by trauma and in fostering resilience.

Conclusion: fostering a world of inclusivity and empathy

In narrating my journey, I invite you to embrace a world viewed through the lens of empathy, understanding, and inclusivity. Our stories, diverse and rich, are the tapestries of our lives. By acknowledging and celebrating our full selves, we pave the way for a world where diversity is not just accepted but cherished. Let's commit to creating environments where every voice is heard, every identity is honored, and every individual thrives. Together, we can build a more inclusive, compassionate, and empathetic world, where the tapestry of human experience is valued in all its complexity and beauty.

References

Crenshaw, K. (1989). Demarginalizing the intersection of race and sex: A Black feminist critique of antidiscrimination doctrine, feminist theory, and antiracist politics. *University of Chicago Legal Forum, 1989*(1), 139–167.

Edmondson, A. (2019). *The fearless organization: Creating psychological safety in the workplace for learning, innovation, and growth*. Wiley.

Gone, J. P. and Kirmayer, L. J. (2010). On the wisdom of considering culture and context in psychopathology. In T. Millon, R. F. Krueger, & E. Simonsen (Eds.), *Contemporary directions in psychopathology: Scientific foundations of the DSM-V and ICD-11* (pp. 72–96). Guilford Press.

Lai, M.-C. and Baron-Cohen, S. (2015). Identifying the lost generation of adults with autism spectrum conditions. *The Lancet Psychiatry*, 2(11), 1013–1027.

Nadeau, K. G. (2015). *Understanding girls with ADHD: How they feel and why they do what they do*. Advantage Books.

Seligman, M. E. P. (2011). *Flourish: A visionary new understanding of happiness and well- being*. Free Press.

Stanton, G. H. (1998). The ten stages of genocide. Genocide Watch.

Williams, M. T., Metzger, I. W., Leins, C. and DeLapp, R. (2018). *Racial trauma: Theory, research, and healing*. American Psychological Association.

Conclusion

In this book, there were numerous threads that arose within the content of the chapters as they relate to Indigenous disability studies. These threads highlighted the prominence of disabilities from a wide range of stories, traditional knowledge translations, through oral histories, and accounts of lived experiences with insightful viewpoints that grasped the meaning/understanding of what and how disabilities and learning disabilities are understood by Indigenous peoples. These points of reflection and values are central to these Indigenous representatives as an expression of their unique cultural perspective. These gave the reader an inside viewpoint into the daily activities and other social, cultural, legal, economic, and political challenges these authors face. By understanding these differences, we can move forward into navigating the many and varied barriers that separate us as Indigenous peoples. These authors shared insightful knowledge and the challenges that impact so many Indigenous peoples, many of whom are displaced due to wars and the negative impact of colonialism.

This is the first international gathering of Indigenous representatives from 20 countries that include areas that have often been excluded or had limited involvement, the global south and east – (South America, Africa, and Asia). These countries represent the authors' perspectives: Canada, United States, Mexico, Colombia, Venezuela, Mauritius, Nepal, Algeria, Australia, South Africa, Taiwan, Indonesia, Pakistan, Uganda, Malawi, India, Kenya, Rwanda, Burundi, and the Democratic Republic of Congo. By including all of these perspectives this book truly represents a global response to Indigenous disability studies. Many of these authors are a first-time contributor some in their early academic careers, and others who have a following in their respective circles. Through this process, it was possible to develop and expand in five areas:

- The power, wisdom, knowledge, and lived experiences of Elders
- Reframing the narrative – navigating self-representation
- Learning from within – including traditional knowledge
- Challenging colonial authority – infusing regional ideals and concepts
- Interpretations, narratives, and lived experiences of grassroots teachers and social service providers

These five parts provided the necessary framework that allowed for a greater response to disabilities as it included multiple perspectives, geopolitical areas, and knowledge systems that include grassroots/front-line workers, Elders, the keepers of community knowledge, and academics, scholars, and those who work in their professions related to this topic. By

DOI: 10.4324/9781032656519-40

including Elders and grassroots/frontline workers this book took on a diverse perspective following a distinctions-based approach of being inclusive as many of these authors might have been excluded in other domains. As Bell (2006) reflects this field of 'Disability Studies' should be renamed as 'White' as it excludes "individuals of color treated as second-class citizens" (p. 281). Reading different perspectives, from various professionals, and ways of gathering knowledge made this process of inclusion a real possibility. In the first chapter, Elder Annie shared her insight into disabilities from her own experiences, and in following her wisdom, I drew upon a conversation she told me in regard to 'what is ethics' and 'how do we as Indigenous peoples approach this colonial topic'? She went on to say, that "for us, Indigenous people, ethics is all about respect" (personal communication, July 1, 2021). Using this same approach to disabilities, we must include as many perspectives as possible to give respect to others: what they share, who they are, where they come from, and how their unique knowledge and belief systems can impact the greater narrative by reshaping who we are as Indigenous peoples of the world as we take up the colonial word of 'disability' and reclaim it through our process of Indigenization. It is this reclaiming of words such as disability, crippled, handicapped, etc. and all those other colonial labels and classifications that once limited us, and controlled who we are, what we are capable of, and how we live and survive as Indigenous peoples.

Progressing forward – Disability support for Indigenous people

The contributions of the authors within this book were accumulated to create an overall narrative of a journey in discovering ourselves or how disabilities have impacted our lives. Through this process of self-reflection, there are many threads that can be shared among each other such as these five synergies that enable a new way of viewing and understanding how disabilities and learning disabilities can influence you and me, as the reader. They may also perhaps shape our own ways of interpreting the overall thread of disabilities in such a way that we can understand, learn, and even live with the disabilities or learning differences in a better non-detrimental way.

Reframing a self-expression regarding disability as a form of identity, while remaining Indigenous as a transformative viewpoint of Indigeneity can be one of the most challenging and even dangerous results of how settler-colonial labels, classifications, and name calling (teasing, assigning nicknames) can result in hurtful, and damaging outcomes, and even lead to suicide. Renaming a person because they learn, act, or appear differently can impact their natural development to a point that contributes to psychological trauma and mental abuse. How we see or understand others is not as important as treating people with dignity and respect, regardless of how we feel about them. Respect and acknowledging people who learn differently beyond what is visible so that they do not become invisible is what it means to be human in body, mind, and spirit.

Building a human-centric and inclusive learning space, while confronting the settler-colonial mindset is challenging a cultural barrier, and allows anyone to access educational platforms and participate in them. Changing not challenging the status quo, by an act of reconciliation for educational values through human dignity enables alternative learning and supports diversity in classrooms, workplaces, and social settings.

Further to this, the infusion of Indigenous epistemologies and methodologies is a way to crossover the cultural, social, and spiritual divides that so many of us take for granted when trying to find and align with an educational, medical, clinical and/or social difference in colonial spheres of influences. Being able to keep our own ways of knowing, learning, and believing as sacred without being forced to fit the cookie-cutter mold of Western ideals and concepts of learning would be progressive.

Also, the use of alternate ways of communication beyond the settler-colonial understanding of written and oral such as through the approach of signing to transmit knowledge across people, time, and distance is a superior way of communication, which can serve beyond the d/Deaf community. This approach to a bilingual language ability would suit so many in a community and, in general. Imagine losing your voice or trying to communicate in another language, using hand and body movements and gestures would be a single-sided perspective and benefit. This loss can become most frustrating, especially, in times of distress. However, being able to communicate beyond using vocal language can serve in many ways and has been used throughout the world by many people as an effective method of communication. Finally, navigating different knowledge and belief systems, and following the words of these authors on their path towards discovery and interpretation of self, opened the ways of understanding disabilities and learning disabilities.

As this book concludes, take what was shared by the authors, and see what has been said, revealed, and taught about disabilities and learning disabilities. What have you learned? What inspired you to become a better person? Have you let these experiences and their insight change your perspectives, understanding and mindset? As you move forward, how will these insights inspire or challenge your thoughts about disabilities and, lastly, what new ways or developments can you utilize to enhance the learning experience for the people with disabilities that you will connect with.

This book has taken a progressive step forward regarding diversity and inclusion by allowing a true global response to Indigenous Disability Studies that will usher in a new age for this emerging field. It will give the next generation a place, a voice, and a chance to share their own perspectives so that they can reshape how Disability Studies will unfold. Through this global response, Routledge will become a leader in Indigenous and disability information. It has embarked on this unique approach of combining both of these intersectionalities with that of more emerging areas to provide the basis for an international response, which has been limited in past publications. This book through its contributors will reshape how readers view and understand disabilities and learning disabilities as they walk along with these authors to discover new ways of working, interpreting, understanding, and viewing disabilities from traditional knowledge to everyday interaction. How we understand a topic through multiple lenses will only widen our perspectives regarding an ever-changing field. This journey is one that will never end, as it will evolve into a way of expressing self as we become the leaders, teachers, social workers, healers, dreamers, and professionals of tomorrow, who will retake and reclaim Disability Studies by making it our own to reflect an Indigenous Disability Studies.

A global gathering on Indigenous disability studies

The intent of this book was based on a global reflection of disabilities by various Indigenous representatives and through their lived experiences, wisdom, work, teaching and social services work brought us together. The accumulation of different knowledge systems has done just that and more as revealed by the authors. Their ability to share who they are, and where they come from, shapes, and reshapes our future as we, the readers, walk in their footsteps and follow their words, which are a testimony to their resilience and struggles to show what it means to be Indigenous with disabilities – learning differences.

This section is not meant to summarize what has already been revealed, but to point to the impact of this book, which has included various authors both internationally renowned Indigenous disability scholars, as well as many grassroots people, who are new to this type of format, but who have chosen to share their unique perspective. This group effort has given us a rich and diverse global perspective as we launch this first book on Indigenous disabilities.

In keeping with this theme, there were four authors who presented at the first-ever international conference on Indigenous Disability hosted at the University of Sydney in Australia (November 2023). These were the participating conference members:

- Rodney Adams, Deaf Koori researcher from the University of Sydney (Australia)
- John Gilroy, a Yuin professor at the University of Sydney (Australia)
- Sheelah Daniels-Mayes, a Gamilaraay/Gomeroi woman from the University of Melbourne (Australia)
- Scott Avery a proud Worimi Deaf man from Western Sydney University (Australia)
- Jacky Troy from the Ngargu of the Snowy Mountains in Australia from the University of Sydney (Australia)
- Aunty Ros Sackley a proud blind Ngiyampaa/Wiradjuri woman from the University of Sydney (Australia)
- Melanie McKay Cody (Cherokee, Shawnee, Powhatan and Montaukett) from the University of Arizona (United States)
- Jennifer Cullen a descendant of the Bidjara and Wakka Wakka peoples from the Universities of James Cook and Griffith (Australia)
- Margaretha Uttjek a Sami woman from the Umea University in Sweden (Sweden)
- Michelle Dickason Darkinjung/Ngarigo from the University of Sydney (Australia)
- Jocelyn Jones a Noongar woman from Curtin University (Australia)
- Jemma Chao Koori from the University of Sydney (Australia)
- Finally, myself, John Ward (Canada)

This global gathering brought Indigenous academics, scholars, professionals, and Elders together to show their insight, challenges, and developments in the growing field of Indigenous Disabilities as an Indigenous first initiative by world-renowned Dr. John Gilroy. Through his dedication and steadfast support for the need for an Indigenous led and first approach for disability education, this conference pushed the barriers of injustices through stigmas of labels in the areas of disabilities and learning disabilities. Those who have contributed to both this book, as well as the conference, will usher in a new era of development, engagement, dialogue, and networking to build on what has been shared so that the next generation of Indigenous disability scholars will be able to further push the boundaries that have limited so many Indigenous people in this developing area referred to as Indigenous Disability Studies.

The image below encompasses the ideals and needs for this global gathering as represented with this Yuin carving that depicts a timeless message regarding disabilities, which can be best seen by a closer look at the following photo (Figure C.1).

Figure C.1 First International Indigenous Disability Conference by John and Jennifer Gilroy.

Source: Photographer: By John T. Ward, November 20, 2023

Reference

Bell, C. (2006). *Introducing white disability studies: A modest proposal.* In L. J. Davis (Ed.), *The disability studies reader* (2nd Ed.), (pp. 275–282). New York, NY: Routledge.

Index

Note: **Bold** page numbers refer to tables and *italic* page numbers refer to figures.

reconciliation and rejuvenation 41; red path 42; seers as teachers, Peacemaker and Hiawatha 48; trauma impacts learning disabilities 48–49; two-eyed-seeing approach 44–46

Moradi, B. 268

More, A. J. 188

Moriyasu Ichiro 169

Mother Teresa 300

Muiscas and Teusacá experience: cultural thing 106–107; education 107–110; Indigenous 110–111; self-navigation 105–106

Murray, J. 139

Mushi and Muhavu tribes: alteration of language and information of disabilities in pre- and post-contact 181–182; impact of colonialism on Havu and Shi 180; influence of Belgian colonialism 180; traditional knowledge influences dialogue 179–180; understanding and learning disabilities from community perspective 181

Nadeau, K. G. 319

Nagy, A. 191

Nakata, M. 135

Nakoochee, P. 29, 185

National Congress of American Indians (NCAI) 51

National Indigenous Disabled Women Association Nepal (NIDWAN) 117

Nepal, women with disabilities in 119–120

neurodiversity 96–97; importance of individuals in smaller communities 101; reflecting on future 101–102

Newman, S. 269

NIDWAN 117, 119–120, 123

Nijs, G. 150

Nixon, G. 191

North American Indian Sign Language (NAISL) 86

numeric dyslexia 271

Obsessive Compulsive Disorder (OCD) 96

Ojeda, Rodolfo Andres Jauregui 62

Okazaki, S. 11

Olkin, R. 204

oral history 8, 10, 19, 40, 56–57, 127, 133, 170, 269–270, 322

Oster, R. T. 140

Pan, P.-C. 218

Papp, T. A. 12

Parham, T. A. 272

Parrish, M. S. 188

Pashtun community: coping disability 263; culturally inspired Indigenous social workers 264; cultural perspective 258–259; disabled by colonialism 260; disabled people's accommodation in occupational structure 263–264; history and origin 256–258; Indigenous disability 260–261; sociocultural values, social organizations, and disability 261–263; stigmatizing disability 259–260

Peters, S. J. 272

Phachaka, L. 152

physical disabilities 36, 161, 180, 242

Pierite, Donna M. Madere 157

Pierite, Elisabeth M. 159

Pierite, Fannie L. Ben 157

Pierite, Jean-Luc 157

Pierite, Joseph A. 157, 158

Pierite, Michael R. 157

Pitso, T. T. 146, 149

Plains Indian Sign Language (PISL) 136, 140, 141

Plato 226

Plosz, J. 187

practice-based evidence (PBE) 206

Queen Elizabeth II 292

Rabang, N. J. 10

racial-ableism 137–139

Rae, Bob 29, 35

Raera, Balriwakes 169

Rajabi, S. 252

reading disability 307

reconciliation 8

retardo *see* mental disabilities

Reyhner, J. 271

Rhea, Z. A. 10

Rodriguez, Angela Patricia Mora 105

Roland, E. 268

Romero, Natalia 65

Romero, Sergio 64

Rourke, Nancy 85

5Rs (respect, responsibility, relationship, relevance, and reciprocity) 89

4Rs framework (respect, relevance, reciprocity, and responsibility) 90

Rushongoka, Jeanine 182, *182*

Rwandan perspective: immigrating to Canada 317–319; inclusivity and empathy 320; integrating Indigenous perspectives and non-Western views 319; storytelling with education 319–320

Sachemspeaks 190

Sackley, Ros 325

Sassi, K. 189

Sehlabo, Mamothibeli 147, *147*

Sekese, A. 146

self, concept of 243

Made in the USA
Coppell, TX
03 June 2025

50267796R00197